Models of Economic Liberalization

Business, Workers, and Compensation in Latin America, Spain, and Portugal

This book provides the first general theory, grounded in comparative historical analysis, that aims to explain the variation in the models of economic liberalization across Ibero-America (Latin America, Spain, and Portugal) in the last quarter of the twentieth century and the legacies they produced for the current organization of the political economies. Although the macroeconomics of effective market adjustment evolved in a similar way, the patterns of compensation delivered by neoliberal governments, and the type of actors in business and the working class that benefited from them, were remarkably different. Based on the policymaking styles and the compensatory measures employed to make market transitions politically viable, the book distinguishes three alternative models: Statist, Corporatist, and Market. Sebastián Etchemendy argues that the most decisive factors that shape adjustment paths are the type of regime and the economic and organizational power with which business and labor emerged from the inward-oriented model. The analysis stretches from the origins of state, business, and labor industrial actors in the 1930s and 1940s to the politics of compensation under neoliberalism across the Ibero-American world, including extensive fieldwork material on Spain, Argentina, and Chile.

Sebastián Etchemendy is Assistant Professor in the Department of Political Science and International Studies, Torcuato Di Tella University, Argentina. He holds a B.A. from the University of Buenos Aires and a Ph.D. in Political Science from the University of California, Berkeley. He has published in the journals *Comparative Politics*, *Comparative Political Studies*, *Politics and Society*, and *Desarrollo Económico*, as well as in edited volumes on Argentine and Latin American politics. He won the Fulbright Fellowship for graduate studies in the United States and the Social Science Research Council (SSRC) Dissertation Fellowship. His dissertation, on which this book is based, was nominated by the Department of Political Science at Berkeley for the Almond Prize for Best Dissertation at the American Political Science Association. In 2007, he served as Visiting Assistant Professor in the Department of Political Science at Stanford University. In 2010 and 2011, he worked as adviser to the Minister of Labor of Argentina.

Advance Praise for *Models of Economic Liberalization*

"Sebastián Etchemendy's new book, *Models of Economic Liberalization*, lays to rest conventional and overly general explanations of the ways in which market-based economic reforms are undertaken. The approach Etchemendy takes recognizes that structural economic reform is very much an act of political construction, and that the same general goals can be undertaken in very different ways, based on alternative political constituencies. In an analysis that conjointly treats the politics of state-business and state-labor relations in three distinct (and distinctive) pathways to reform – in Spain, Argentina, and Chile – he provides a masterful treatment that focuses on the 'compensations,' the packages of winners and losers created in different trajectories of reform, that were part and parcel of liberalization. The result is a study that gets the politics right but also sets the interest-group groundwork for what will take place after liberalization is complete."

– Marcus Kurtz, The Ohio State University

"*Models of Economic Liberalization* provides an original theoretical framework for understanding sectoral and cross-national variation in the political compensation of economic actors during economic liberalization. Sebastián Etchemendy shows that the mix of policies by which labor and business groups have been compensated can be explained by differences in political regimes and by variation in the political organization of economic interests during the period of import-substitution industrialization. The innovative research design that contrasts sectoral adjustment across southern Europe and Latin America allows this study to open up a new dialogue with studies of economic reform in advanced industrialized countries, such as the varieties of capitalism perspective."

– Isabela Mares, Columbia University

Models of Economic Liberalization

Business, Workers, and Compensation in Latin America, Spain, and Portugal

SEBASTIÁN ETCHEMENDY
Torcuato Di Tella University, Argentina

Shaftesbury Road, Cambridge CB2 8EA, United Kingdom

One Liberty Plaza, 20th Floor, New York, NY 10006, USA

477 Williamstown Road, Port Melbourne, VIC 3207, Australia

314–321, 3rd Floor, Plot 3, Splendor Forum, Jasola District Centre, New Delhi – 110025, India

103 Penang Road, #05–06/07, Visioncrest Commercial, Singapore 238467

Cambridge University Press is part of Cambridge University Press & Assessment, a department of the University of Cambridge.

We share the University's mission to contribute to society through the pursuit of education, learning and research at the highest international levels of excellence.

www.cambridge.org
Information on this title: www.cambridge.org/9780521763127

© Sebastián Etchemendy 2011

This publication is in copyright. Subject to statutory exception and to the provisions of relevant collective licensing agreements, no reproduction of any part may take place without the written permission of Cambridge University Press & Assessment.

First published 2011

A catalogue record for this publication is available from the British Library

Library of Congress Cataloging-in-Publication data
Etchemendy, Sebastián.
Models of economic liberalization : Business, workers, and compensation in Latin America, Spain, and Portugal / Sebastián Etchemendy.
    p. cm.
Includes bibliographical references and index.
ISBN 978-0-521-76312-7 (hardback)
1. Latin America – Economic policy. 2. Spain – Economic policy.
3. Portugal – Economic policy. 4. Neoliberalism – Latin America.
5. Neoliberalism – Spain. 6. Neoliberalism – Portugal. I. Title.
HC125.E898 2011
339–dc22   2010051111

ISBN 978-0-521-76312-7 Hardback

Cambridge University Press & Assessment has no responsibility for the persistence or accuracy of URLs for external or third-party internet websites referred to in this publication and does not guarantee that any content on such websites is, or will remain, accurate or appropriate.

To my parents, for all the books

To my cousin Raúl Adolfo, for that sunny morning

Contents

Acknowledgments	*page* ix

PART I. THE INTELLECTUAL TERRAIN

1 Overview: Models of Economic Liberalization in ISI Economies	3
2 From State to Society: Neoliberal Reform and a Theory of Compensation in ISI Economies	24

PART II. THE POLITICAL ECONOMY OF BUSINESS ADJUSTMENT

3 Compensating Business Insiders: The Origins of Statist and Corporatist Models in Spain and Argentina	53
4 Statist and Corporatist Models of Business Adjustment in Spain and Argentina: Sectoral Case Studies	88
5 Exceptions That Prove the Rule: Variation within Countries in Models of Business Adjustment	126

PART III. THE POLITICAL ECONOMY OF LABOR ADJUSTMENT

6 Compensating Labor Insiders: The Origins of Statist and Corporatist Models in Spain and Argentina	153
7 Statist and Corporatist Models of Labor Adjustment in Spain and Argentina: Sectoral Case Studies	189

PART IV. THE MARKET MODEL

8 Compensating Outsiders: Chile's Market Model in the Comparative Framework	221

PART V. COMPARATIVE PERSPECTIVES IN IBERO-AMERICA

9 Models of Economic Liberalization in Brazil, Portugal, Peru, and Mexico	257

viii *Contents*

10 Conclusions: Legacies for the Liberalized Economies and
   Varieties of Capitalism in the Developing World   300

Appendix   317
Bibliography   323
Index   351

Acknowledgments

This book was long in the making and started as a dissertation project at the Department of Political Science of the University of California, Berkeley. Therefore, I want to thank in the first place my dissertation chair, Ruth Berins Collier. Ruth simply taught me to think in comparative perspective; my intellectual debt to her is tough to measure. Both Ruth and David Collier trusted a Latin American who had never been in the United States, first to study at Berkeley and then to pursue a dissertation that was atypical because it involved two continents and two types of actors that are generally studied separately. For that support, I will always be grateful. Jonah Levy, also a member of my dissertation committee, has a type of passion for political science that reminds one of what is relevant in our research and in our profession. Finally, Peter Evans always pushed me to think ahead of the obvious and to consider the implications of the social phenomena I was studying.

Fieldwork for this project was an unforgettable experience that took me to three countries, Spain, Argentina, and Chile. With the same black leather jacket, tape recorder, and notebook, I traveled through the oil enclaves of Patagonia and Castilla–La Mancha; shipyards in Asturias; auto assembly plants in Córdoba and Barcelona; steelmills in San Nicolás, Gijón, and the Basque Country; and the business communities and policy circles of Madrid, Santiago de Chile, and Buenos Aires. This extensive field research and the book it eventually shaped could not have been possible without support from a number of individuals and institutions. The Juan March Institute in Madrid supplied me with not only institutional affiliation but also the company of a lively group of students and researchers. I want to thank, in particular, Professor Ignacio Sánchez Cuenca and the excellent librarian, Martha Peach, who made my life there a lot easier. My debt to Alvaro Espina, former Employment and Industry Secretary, is enormous. He opened for me the doors to the Spanish business and government circles. Ludolfo Paramio provided insights on the Spanish political world and contacts in the socialist union. Finally, Gabriel Saro, Robert Fishman, Sergio Santillán, Ruben Vega García, Javier Barrutia, Luis Carlos Croissier, and Mikel Navarro all offered contacts and intellectual engagement. In Chile, Javier

Couso, from Universidad Diego Portales, guided me through the political and business communities. Fabian Repetto kindly provided me with contacts among social policy analysts. Dagmar Raczynski was generous enough to discuss with me the complexities of social policy in authoritarian Chile. In Argentina, the University Torcuato Di Tella was a superb platform for field research. Pablo Gerchunoff's contacts in the business sector were essential in facilitating my interviews. Carlos Tomada kindly provided me with invaluable access to Argentine unionists. Rosalía Cortés, Marta Novick, Daniel Márquez, Antonio Jara, Agustín Salvia, and Rafael Gaviola all helped me in different ways. The fieldwork was partially funded by the Social Science Research Council IDRF grant.

I was fortunate to work in scholarly environments that made the complicated process of turning a dissertation into a book both stimulating and enjoyable. In Buenos Aires, Torcuato Di Tella University has lived up to the challenge of constructing an internationalized research university in the social sciences that is also involved in Argentine and Latin American policy and political debates. I am proud to be part of such an endeavor. In particular, Cary Smulovitz, as Chair of the Department of Political Science, friend, and "institution builder," always showed me with her example that pursuing a complex book project from this side of the world was a worthy task. I cannot forget to mention the willingness of Di Tella librarians to cope effectively with my impossible requests, always in the best mood. The semester I spent as Visiting Assistant Professor at the Department of Political Science at Stanford University was essential for polishing the general manuscript and examining secondary material from the seven countries analyzed in the book. Aside from these two institutions, I received invaluable feedback at talks and seminars I delivered at the Department of Political Science at Northwestern University; the Center for Democracy, Development and the Rule of Law of Stanford University; the Department of Political Science at the University of California at Berkeley; the Department of Political Science of Brown University; the Institute Juan March in Madrid; Universidad Alberto Hurtado in Chile; and Flacso Argentina.

I am lucky in having some friends who are great academics and were willing to read many chapters: Carlos Freytes, Grigore Pop-Eleches, Ken Dubin, and Ken Shadlen. Their suggestions made the book much better. Ben Schneider read parts of the manuscript and helped me to organize my ideas and to conduct myself within the maze of writing a book. Jorge Battaglino, Philip Kitzberger, Markus Kurtz, Jim Mahoney, Isabela Mares, Gerardo Munck, Victoria Murillo, Luis Schiumerini, and Richard Snyder also read different versions or parts of the manuscript and gave me useful comments. At Di Tella, conversations with Juan Carlos Torre, Germán Lodola, Alejandro Bonvecchi, and Carlos Gervasoni were important in clarifying my argument. The excellent reviews from Cambridge University Press and the generous guidance of Lew Bateman helped me improve and reshape central parts of the book. Andrés Schipani and Federico Fuchs offered thoughtful criticism on the labor chapters. Andrés was kind enough to provide valuable insights into the world of the unorganized workers

Acknowledgments

in Chile and to assemble data. Germán Lodola graciously shared with me his database on the BNDES credits. Mauricio Morales let me use his electoral database on Chile. Finally, I must thank all the businessmen, union leaders, state officials and, especially, base-level and local union activists who opened their doors to a stranger without hesitation. Most of them were generous enough to talk to me and expect nothing in return.

Other extra-academic and noninstitutional forms of encouragement are obviously crucial in finishing a long project like this one. Jorge Battaglino, Philip Kitzberger, Marcelo Ferrante, Germán Lodola, and Germán Conte are indispensable friends. It is difficult to conceive of my life in Buenos Aires without them and without our conversations over politics and soccer, among other important topics. Marcelo, my sister Mercedes, and my beloved nephew Joaquín helped keep me sane through all these years. Mercedes Chiappe lived with me through crucial parts of this process and was a source of love and support in the final stages of this book in a way I will simply never forget. The book is dedicated to my parents, César Enrique and María Angélica, and to my late cousin Raúl Adolfo. Since I was a child, my father encouraged me toward a life of books and politics. He supplied me with contacts among his fellow Argentine business executives, and he was always ready to listen to and mostly disagree with my political ideas. Without his help and his love, this book would have never happened. I am sure he would have remembered, as I do, when I was eighteen and he put a book by his former professor, Gino Germani, into my hands.

Buenos Aires, June 2011

PART I

THE INTELLECTUAL TERRAIN

I

Overview

Models of Economic Liberalization in ISI Economies

INTRODUCTION

The crisis of the early 1970s and its aftermath was a watershed for modern capitalism. In advanced countries, it signaled the end of the golden age of postwar development based on Keynesian demand stimulus, low unemployment, and welfare state consolidation. In the less developed Southern Europe and most of Latin America, it began to show the exhaustion of postwar strategies of economic growth predicated on domestic market expansion, state intervention, and high tariff walls, the so-called model of Import Substitution Industrialization (ISI). Indeed, the pace and scope of the market transformations that have developed since then were arguably more dramatic in these semiclosed economies than in most of the advanced countries or the East Asian Newly Industrialized Countries (NICs), which were already more open to international markets and had achieved consistent rates of export-led growth *before* the phenomenal acceleration of capital mobility and trade started to sweep the world in the early 1980s.

Market-oriented officials in the semiclosed economies of Latin America and Southern Europe, by contrast, were caught between formidable external economic pressures for reform and the hostility of entrenched domestic interests with little to win, and much to lose, from a move toward more open markets. Unlike their counterparts in Eastern Europe, where civil societies were generally weak and organized actors had not been autonomous from the state for decades, market reformers in ISI economies often faced the opposition of powerful unions, industrial associations, or domestic business groups quite independent of state control. Indeed, if democratization was often seen in Eastern Europe as positively associated with economic reform and liberalization (Pop-Eleches 2009: 166; Ekiert 2003: 113; Hellman 1998: 232) and as strengthening promarket actors (independent firms, parties, or occasionally unions), in the Iberian-American world[1] the reverse was generally true: democratization was accompanied by the activation and empowerment of popular (and often

---

[1] I use the terms "Ibero-America," "Iberian-American world," and "Iberian world" to refer to Latin America (the book analyzes Argentina, Chile, Brazil, Mexico, and Peru) plus Spain and Portugal.

business) groups long opposed to economic liberalization. For these reasons, ISI economies became the center of the debate on the "politics of economic adjustment" two decades ago.[2] In politically unstable contexts, academics and officials in multilateral institutions observed that strong executives and state autonomy from hostile economic interests, such as unions or domestic business groups, were essential for the imposition of economic liberalization.

Now, however, the "critical juncture" of economic opening and reform in formerly semiclosed countries seems to be over. The main economies in Ibero-America have liberalized substantially and have deepened economic integration into the European Union, NAFTA, and MERCOSUR, often under democratic polities. Though the international financial crisis of 2008–9 has put into question the paradigm of radical economic deregulation and has redeemed Keynesian and interventionist tools, it is doubtful that trade and financial integration will be drastically reversed. So the question now is not *whether* mixed, semiclosed economies reoriented their models of development to the market, but to explain the alternative ways in which they did, and the consequences that these alternative transitions had for the workings of the liberalized political economies.

Initially, the examples of Chile and the East Asian NICs such as Korea and Taiwan, where presumably authoritarianism and bureaucratic insulation made possible the effective outward reorientation of the models of growth, loomed large in the scholarly work on the politics of economic adjustment prevalent in the late 1980s and 1990s.[3] At the same time, international political economy–oriented approaches abundantly explored the external and macroeconomic conditions under which liberalizing reforms and trade integration were more likely.[4] More recently, however, the former scholarly emphasis on bureaucratic autonomy and international economic constraints has been replaced by a wide variety of approaches that have assessed the bargains between governments and specific constituencies in the construction of market-reform coalitions (see Schneider 2004b), particularly those most hurt by liberalization. These scholars have considered the complexities of economic reform in more open polities, emphasizing the territorial,[5] economic-sectoral,[6] and partisan[7] dimensions that underpinned negotiations between reformers and insiders or "stakeholders," be they rural interests and provinces, protected business and labor groups, or populist parties.

This most recent literature, however, has not built a framework that systematically accounts for the type of established actors that are bought

---

[2] This literature was vast; seminal volumes were Haggard and Kaufman (1992, 1995), Haggard and Web (1994), Nelson (1990), Przeworski (1991), and Acuña and Smith (1994).

[3] See, for example, Haggard and Kaufman (1995) and Bates and Krueger (1993).

[4] This literature was equally copious; examples are Stallings (1992), Haggard and Maxfield (1996), and Remmer (1998); more recently see Brooks and Kurtz (2007) and Pop-Eleches (2009).

[5] See Gibson (1997), Eaton (2004a), Snyder (2001b), Montero (2001), Kurtz (2004), Remmer and Wibbels (2000), Wibbels (2005), and Falleti (2010).

[6] See Murillo (2001, 2009), Etchemendy (2001), Shadlen (2004), and Schneider (2004a).

[7] See, for example, Eaton (2002), Corrales (2002), and Levitsky (2003).

Overview

off (or marginalized) in the domain of economic interests, and the different ways in which stakeholders are drawn into market reform coalitions. Indeed, we still lack a theory that explains the different ways in which countries achieved successful market reorientation in ISI, protected economies. This book is an attempt to fill this gap. It seeks to provide a unified framework for understanding economic liberalization in Ibero-America by focusing on the interactions between reforming governments and business and labor actors. My primary concern is not with whether general economic liberalization occurs – as has been the norm in the literature – but rather with variations in the modes or types of market transitions, and with the legacies they produced. Based on the compensatory measures employed to make reform politically viable and the policymaking strategies, this study posits three alternative types of industrial and labor adjustment in countries that have liberalized after decades of ISI, which I call Statist (Spain 1982–96 and Brazil 1990–2002), Corporatist (Argentina 1989–99 and Portugal 1985–95), and Market (Chile 1973–89 and Peru 1990–2000). The main goal of the book is to conceptualize and explain the principal causes of these three different models of economic liberalization, which are summarized in the next section. I will also contend that neoliberal Mexico (1982–94) constitutes a "Mixed" or "Hybrid" mode of adjustment in terms of my framework.

The book will argue that the most important factors that account for the alternative adjustment paths[8] in Argentina, Spain, and Chile, the main empirical cases analyzed, as well as those in the other major ISI economies, are the type of regime (whether reforming countries were democracies or not) and the nature of the prior ISI actors, namely, the economic and organizational power with which industrial business and labor emerged from the inward-oriented model. These two variables, the degree of the liberalization of the polity and the power of actors and the institutional legacies from the old order, have been crucial in the assessment of alternative paths of liberal economic reform and institutional building in the post-Communist literature.[9] Curiously enough, they have not been investigated systematically in the mixed, ISI Iberian-American economies, which had generated their own set of powerful insiders.

THREE MODELS OF ECONOMIC LIBERALIZATION: STATIST, CORPORATIST, AND MARKET

By the early 1980s it was pretty clear that constraints posed by the international economy had rendered autarchic strategies of growth in Latin America and Southern Europe scarcely viable. Not all economic groups were, however, equally

---

[8] The idea of "adjustment path" has been increasingly used in the political economy literature that analyzes alternative national responses to globalization pressures (Hall 1999: 159; Stark and Bruszt 1998: 101). In this book I use the concepts "path," "mode," and "model" to/of economic liberalization or adjustment interchangeably.

[9] See Stark and Bruszt (1998), King (2002), Eyal et al. (1998), and Ekiert (2003).

affected by these epochal changes. The working class, especially its most protected formal sector, and domestic industrial firms saw many of their past privileges jeopardized by the advent of economic opening. Import liberalization and enhanced competition, monetary and fiscal stringency, and the need for more flexible labor markets undermined domestic firms, unions, and workers that have historically benefited from protection, subsidies, and state-sanctioned monopolies. Moreover, in addition to the contractionary effects of stabilization, most of these liberalizing governments established variants of fixed exchange rates to tame inflation – such as fixed parity in Chile and Brazil, a currency board in Argentina, and integration into the European Monetary System in the cases of Spain and Portugal. Thus, in the context of financial deregulation and capital inflows, increasingly appreciated domestic currencies undermined local industrial actors even more. In sum, for domestic industrial firms, unions, and individual workers economic liberalization could simply mean bankruptcy, organizational disarticulation, and unemployment and poverty.

This study examines the relations between state and economic actors in the subset of liberalizing policies that affect established industrial firms, unions, and workers most: tariff liberalization, industrial privatization, labor deregulation and downsizing, and aspects of social policy reform. These measures will be referred to alternately throughout the book under the labels of "industrial and labor adjustment" or more simply "economic liberalization." The book studies adjustment through the lens of the compensatory policies that a reform government can bestow on the "potential losers" under neoliberal reform – that is, on formerly protected actors such as industrial firms (especially domestic), unions, and workers. Liberalizing governments often forged alliances with these actors through the administration of compensation. These alliances facilitated rather than obstructed neoliberal reform.

The paths of industrial adjustment essentially signal who got what, and how, in the domain of compensation. The "how" concerns the policymaking formula. I identify three patterns of policymaking under industrial adjustment: *unilateral state imposition*, *concertation* with the relevant interest groups, and *state dirigisme*, that is, a policymaking style in which the state formulates the major restructuring plans from above but is willing to bargain about aspects of their implementation.

The "what" refers to the menu of compensatory measures available to the neoliberal reformer. They can be broadly divided in two types. The first type of compensation policy includes various forms of *subsidies*, such as direct monetary infusions, soft credits or tax exemptions to industrial firms, and employment programs (in which the state provides temporary jobs) or unemployment subsidies in the context of labor downsizing. The second general form of compensatory measure is *market-share compensation*, which serves to protect the economic roles of established actors in more open markets. This includes the direct award of ownership to firms and their workers or unions through privatization and the partial deregulation (i.e., preserving barriers to entry or establishing tariff regimes) of different markets, such as labor, or specific industries.

Overview

This study argues that such "partial" or "protectionist liberalization," which grants market reserves to specific actors in business and labor – for example, barriers to foreign firms in particular sectors or monopoly of representation in collective bargaining – while the rest of the economy is opened and subjected to unfettered competition, constitutes an important type of side payment. Hence, the basic distinction (which is more fully developed in the theory of Chapter 2) is between policies that help business, unions, or workers to face increasing competition through subsidies and state-backed programs of technological innovation or labor training and those that allow for the concentration of future open markets by bestowing state assets or administering a biased deregulation or tariff regime.

Finally, the "who" refers to the target of compensatory policy. For analytical purposes I first broadly distinguish two general types of actors. ISI *insiders* are the formerly protected industrial firms, their workers, and the national unions. Domestic industrial firms were often part of broader "business groups," that is, the family-controlled multisectoral holdings under the same direction typical of developing economies (Leff 1978). Thus, I term "ISI business group" those large domestic holdings that originated and maintain a substantial part of their assets in manufacturing and/or oil/fuels businesses. ISI *outsiders* are the unemployed or poor workers in the informal sector who either had been employed in the distant past or had never made it to the formal sector or stable employment.

These three dimensions of policymaking style, compensatory measures, and target cohered in a way that produced the Statist, Corporatist, and Market models of liberalization. The Statist path involves subsidy compensation to certain ISI insiders and state *dirigisme* as the main policymaking strategy. The government formulates reconversion plans for selected ISI sectors from above (most often core manufacturing sectors such as steel and transport equipment) and provides monetary subsidies to firms and laid-off workers affected by enhanced competition. Although the process of formulation of these restructuring plans is heavily centralized in the executive in a *dirigiste* manner, implementation – for example, the amount and type of subsidies involved or the timing of plant closures or mergers – is usually subjected to negotiations with affected companies and unions, particularly at the local or firm level. Crucially, privatization in the Statist mode *is not* used as a massive reward for established ISI business groups. Rather, ownership is more diversified among institutional and financial investors, and the state preserves substantial leverage in selected privatized "national champions" through golden-share mechanisms and management supervision. The Statist mode is represented by the Spanish case between 1982 and 1996, most extensively analyzed in the book, and by Brazil under the Collor and Cardoso governments (1990–2002).

The Corporatist path combines market-share compensation channeled to certain ISI business and labor insiders with more negotiated, concertational policymaking. The state compensated established industrial business and national labor leaders (rather than laid-off workers) through state assets directly awarded to firms and unions amid a generally vast privatization process, and through the partial deregulation of certain markets, especially labor and specific industries. These compensatory measures were delivered through formal or informal concertation and negotiation with national unions and the selected domestic industrial groups largely rewarded through privatization. Argentina under the Menem presidency between 1989 and 1999 is the main instance of Corporatist adjustment studied in the book, but Portugal under the Cavaco Silva (1985–95) administration closely resembles the Corporatist model.

A central point is that in both the Statist and Corporatist paths the bulk of compensatory measures (albeit of different types) were bestowed on the *insiders* of the ISI model, that is, industrial firms and segments of the union-represented working class – national union leaders in the Corporatist mode and laid-off workers backed by local unions in the Statist model. Unlike the other two modes, in the Market path the government did not negotiate any major compensatory measure with ISI organized actors, and tariff liberalization and downsizing were unilaterally imposed. Industrial sectoral readjustments were largely left to the market. Yet, we find an explicit government attempt to compensate, subsidize, and eventually mobilize politically the unorganized and poor workers in the informal sector, or *outsiders*. Unmitigated commercial liberalization combined with extended means-tested social compensation renders "Market" an apt label for this mode of adjustment.[10] Chile under Pinochet (1973–89) and Fujimori's government in Perú (1990–99) are instances of this type.

Significantly, in all models a crucial component of the effort to impose market reform and industrial adjustment involved the administration of compensatory measures for some of the losers among manufacturing firms and/or the working class. Yet, the *political process*, *type of compensation*, and *target* differed among the cases (Table 1.1). In a language borrowed from Barrington Moore (1966), one finds three main roads to industrial liberalization in Ibero-America: the Statist one in which the government reconverted strategic industrial sectors from above and gave out subsidies to ailing firms and workers, the Corporatist in which the state rewarded domestic industrial groups and national unions with market share in the future order, and the Market in which policymakers excluded ISI insiders and focused compensation on the informal poor.

Of course, the identification of Statist, Corporatist, and Market as three distinct models of national industrial adjustment echoes the lineage of classic political economy works by Shonfield (1965), Zysman (1983), Berger (1981), and Hall (1986) on advanced countries. My typology has similarities with this tradition. For example, the book explains modes of industrial/sectoral reconversion that are more state led, collaborative or negotiated with peak-level actors or associations, and company led (see Zysman 1983: 94). Yet the conceptualization of Statist, Corporatist, and Market paths is adapted here to the realities of adjustment in developing, semi-closed, economies, essentially denoted by more abrupt and extensive economic liberalization, and by profound crises that made compensation crucial for political survival.

---

[10] To quote Esping-Andersen's classic work (1990: 22), means-tested poor relief "will compel all but the most desperate to participate in the market."

Overview

TABLE I.I. *The Outcome: Compensatory Policies and Models of Economic Liberalization*

Defining Features	Statist Model Spain 1982–96 Brazil 1990–2002	Corporatist Model Argentina 1989–99 Portugal 1985–95	Market Model Chile 1973–83 Peru 1990–99
Nature of Policymaking	State *Dirigisme* (centralized formulation, negotiated implementation)	Concertation	Unilateral State Imposition
Main Compensatory Measure	Subsidy	Market Share Compensation (partial deregulation and/or state assets)	Subsidy
Main Actors Compensated	ISI Insiders (domestic industrial firms/ groups and laid-off industrial workers)	ISI Insiders (domestic industrial firms/ groups and national unions)	ISI Outsiders (atomized informal poor)

It is also worth stressing that I study the dominant from of compensation. Of course, countries did a lot of things under neoliberal reform: that is, governments granted protection (e.g., an antidumping measure) to this or that subsector, while a single protected firm may have been rewarded in various cases. The question is what compensatory scheme was clearly prevalent, deliberate, and politically more relevant under neoliberalism. Statist, Corporatist, and Market configure a typology of adjustment paths around which most of the major countries of Ibero-America cluster.[11] The typology is the result of the combination of "values" or categories in these three dimensions of policymaking strategy, compensatory measure, and target. Certainly, a number of other combinations of these dimensions would be, in principle, theoretically possible in the typology property-space. For example, a policymaking style based on unilateral imposition could be combined with market-share compensation targeted to ISI insiders Or, alternatively, concertational policymaking could be in principle compatible with subsidy compensation.

Still, most of the dimensions are logically connected, and the major Iberian-American countries (except Mexico) empirically fall under each type. *Dirigiste* officials (who want to redesign industrial sectors from above) will be more ready

[11] Seawright and Collier (2004: 311) define a typology as a "coordinated set of categories or types that establishes theoretically relevant analytical distinctions." The models of liberalization constitute both a conceptual or descriptive typology (a set of types defined by different dimensions) and an explanatory typology (that is, outcomes to be explained) in the terms of Collier et al. (2012).

to give out subsidies in strained sectors and preserve leverage than simply to hand over the control of state assets or market reserves to private groups. Concertational policymaking seems to be more feasible with nationally organized actors such as ISI business groups and national unions rather than with informal workers. Likewise, the atomized informal poor could hardly be compensated with market-share deals such as the control of state assets or sectoral tariff regimes.[12]

The cases compared in more detail in this book, Spain, Argentina, and Chile, are the most complete instances of each type, in the same way that, for example, political economists often consider Sweden the model-case of a social democratic welfare state, or Germany and the United States as the embodiment of Coordinated and Liberal market capitalism, respectively (Esping-Andersen 1990, Hall and Soskice 2001). They show the most extended repertoire in their type of compensation: a series of top-down reconversion plans based on subsidies to industrial firms and dismissed workers in Spain, various forms of market-share compensation negotiated with ISI insiders in Argentina, and a wide array of informal sector-targeted antipoverty and employment programs in neoliberal Chile.[13] Other cases of extensive neoliberal reform in the Iberian-American world can be assessed in the light of the same dimensions (for example, if major ISI actors were rewarded through privatization, subsidies, or not rewarded; if a massive national program for the informal poor was implemented during adjustment or not) and located under each type.

The approach is not meant to suggest that the politics of neoliberal reform and its long-run consequences were restricted to the interaction and deals with the ISI potential losers in industry and labor – some of which became in fact political winners. Alliances with "straight winners" such as internationalized finance and multilateral institutions, transnational corporations (TNCs), or competitive agriculture were also vital in the crafting of market-oriented coalitions, and their complexity also worth studying. Indeed, the role played by some of these more internationalized actors will surface recurrently throughout the book – especially that of TNCs in the sectoral studies on business.

Yet, the analysis concentrates on how neoliberal reformers grappled with domestic industry and popular actors, for three reasons. First, dealing with industry and the working class (whether through effective marginalization/repression or via compensation) was crucial for the governability of market reform. Established unions and sheltered businesses were simply the most dangerous foes of liberalization in the domain of economic interests. Second, in most

---

[12] Besides, as the methodologists George and Bennett (2005: 235) argue, to be heuristically useful, a typological theory need not show empirical instances of all its possible property-space combinations. On the extensive use of typological theory in comparative historical analysis see also Mahoney (2004: 86) and Collier et al. (2012).

[13] I refer to Spain, Argentina, and Chile as model cases of each path rather than ideal types, given that the latter rarely can be found in practice. In Goertz's (2009: 192) terms, ideal type concepts have zero extension.

Overview   11

cases of thorough economic liberalization actors such as the International Monetary Fund (IMF), big landlords, neoliberal think tanks, TNCs, and international banks sided with reformers. By contrast, the relation with the popular sector and protected industry varied a lot more: some neoliberal governments elicited the support of, and rewarded extensively, ISI firms/groups; some did not. Some closed deals with established national unions to soften the costs of adjustment, while others directed extensive compensation to the mass of informal poor; others privileged laid-off industrial workers. Finally, the analysis of compensation is also relevant in view of the important legacies that the exclusions and deals forged during neoliberalism left for the organizational configuration of the more open economies.

ALTERNATIVE EXPLANATIONS: PARTISAN, INTERNATIONAL, FISCAL, AND IDEAS

An examination of Table 1.1 suggests that two of the most typical explanatory factors found in the literature on globalization and economic policy outcomes, the international (see Stallings 1992, Brooks and Kurtz 2007) and the partisan variables (see Boix 1998, Murillo 2009), do not offer reliable accounts of each model in terms of both the policymaking strategies and the actors targeted for compensation. The Argentine Peronist Party and the Spanish Socialist Workers' Party (PSOE) were labor-based parties (i.e., parties whose core constituency was organized labor) prior to reform. However, they pursued alternative forms of compensation to the working class – bureaucratic payoffs primarily aimed at union leaders in Argentina versus employment programs in Spain. Cavaco Silva's center-Right Social Democratic Party (PSD) government in Portugal and the populist Peronist Party in Argentina interacted with the potential losers from reform in a remarkably similar way: they negotiated partial reform of the labor law with national unions and used privatization to compensate local business groups. Indeed, the partisan explanation does not hold in within-case analysis. Collor in Brazil headed a center-Right government, and his successor, Cardoso, was from the center-Left of the political spectrum. Nevertheless, their strategies of industrial adjustment through state *dirigisme* in some sectors and compensatory subsidies administered by the National Bank for Economic and Social Development (BNDES) look quite similar. Likewise, in Spain, the right-wing Popular Party's sequential approach to industrial privatization after 1996, which helped empower national champions in gradually privatized sectors, was essentially analogous to that of its socialist predecessor.

The international explanation would focus on alternative forms of regulatory pressures emanating from the European Union (EU) and MERCOSUR in the cases of Spain, Brazil, Portugal, and Argentina. However, under a similar process of EU accession, Spain adjusted through state *dirigisme*, industrial reconversion plans, and subsidies, whereas the Portuguese government prioritized concertation and market-share compensation deals with domestic business groups. Similarly, two MERCOSUR countries, Argentina and Brazil, underwent divergent adjustment paths that involved alternative policymaking formulas and compensatory schemes. Though this international dimension will be addressed in the analysis – especially concerning the influence of the EU in the Spanish business adjustment – its explanatory power of the variation in compensatory arrangements remains limited.

Two other explanatory factors may appear plausible: the fiscal situation of the state and the role of ideas. The fiscal argument would contend that in the Statist or Market models reformers distributed monetary subsidies as the dominant form of compensation because their economies were not affected by a major budget deficit. Conversely, countries that lacked the resources to develop reconversion or employment plans based on subsidies could only rely on market share compensation. Yet Statist and subsidy-based adjustment plans unfolded in Brazil amid a complicated state financial situation during the 1990s. Indeed, Chapter 9 shows that subsidies distributed by the developmental state bank BNDES literally boomed during neoliberalism in Brazil. Market share deals (involving biased privatization and/or tariff regimes) with major ISI industrial players took place in fiscally unstable Argentina, in the more stable Mexico, and in fiscally responsible Portugal. In the wake of a stabilization and fiscal crisis, the Chilean and Peruvian governments developed or strengthened their national programs targeted at the informal poor and the unemployed, while Argentina did not. The availability of a minimum of fiscal resources is of course necessary to accomplish subsidy-based Statist adjustment, or to build large, informal-poor-oriented social programs. Nonetheless, as in Spain, those resources can be from public debt emissions or from other areas of the budget if the government is bound to that type of compensation strategy. In virtually all the countries studied, neoliberal coalitions welcomed capital market integration, which generally made resources available via debt at least in the medium term. In short, the fiscal situation does not seem to explain variation in adjustment paths, and in the patterns of compensation and groups rewarded.

Finally, the place of ideas in the explanation of economic policy outcomes has a venerable tradition in the comparative political economy literature, revitalized in recent years (e.g., Hall 1989, Sikkink 1991, Blyth 2002, Berman 2006; see also Fourcade 2009). Politicians and officials often seek legitimacy for their policy choice in economic theories or ideas that are popular in certain circles or carry a respectable pedigree. For example, Valdés (1995) and Huneeus (2000) have illuminated the origins of the extraordinary influence of the Chicago School of economics in Chile, and the way in which the orthodox free marketers positioned themselves and shaped the military economic thinking. The main traits of the Market path to adjustment – massive tariff deregulation, the trimming of social spending for organized urban actors, and the antipoverty policies targeted to the informal poor – are indeed perfectly coherent with the radical ideological version of free market economics propounded by the Chicago School. Likewise, the role played by the Bank of Spain and by BNDES in Brazil in the spread of the complex mixture of market-oriented and nationalist ideas that lurk behind Statist forms of economic liberalization is also noticeable.

Overview

The question becomes, first, whether ideology is a consistent factor that can account for the *variation* in the models of adjustment. The penetration of free market ideas and the consolidation of a neoliberal technocratic cohort educated in the United States within the state were also powerful in Mexico with the rise of Salinas, as demonstrated by the work of Centeno (1997). In Argentina, neoliberal think tanks such as the Foundation for Economic Research in Latin America (FIEL) and the Center for Macroeconomic Studies (CEMA) also bore considerable influence on the Menem economic teams, especially after 1996, when CEMA economists were put in charge of the Ministry of the Economy and the Central Bank. Yet this book shows that Chile, Argentina, and Mexico present alternative patterns of policymaking formulas and compensatory measures during adjustment.

Second, as Peter Hall (1997: 185) has observed, it is sometimes difficult to disentangle the influence of ideas from other kinds of variables in economic policymaking. For example, one can point out the importance of BNDES in Brazil, or of the Bank of Spain and the Spanish state holding INI (National Industrial Institute), in the formation of a solid public industrial bureaucracy and in the dissemination of reformist-nationalist ideas throughout the political elite that carried out Statist liberalization and empowered privatized national champions. However, is this reform worldview a sign of the relevance of a specific set of ideas, of greater prior state strength in the industrial realm, or of both? In short, while it is hard to deny the impact of the neoliberal creed as spread from multilateral institutions and think tanks (see Fourcade and Babb 2002), and the central influence of concrete traditions and ideas that permeated among policymakers in certain cases – fundamentally in Chile, but also in Spain and Brazil – the place of ideas in a systematic explanation of alternative models of adjustment is less clear.

In sum, this book by no means suggests that the explanatory factors outlined later, regime and the power of prior ISI actors, are the only variables that shaped the alternative models of adjustment in specific countries. Rather, the comparative analysis deployed argues that these two domestic variables systematically explain a good deal of the variation (or, one could say, potentially necessary conditions)[14] in the models of economic liberalization across cases. To the specification of this causal argument we now turn.

EXPLAINING MODELS OF ECONOMIC LIBERALIZATION: REGIME TYPE AND POWER OF ISI ACTORS

This study argues that the model of adjustment pursued in terms of policymaking and compensatory measures to specific actors is shaped by two main factors: the type of regime under which liberalization took place – essentially whether adjusting governments were fully democratic or not – and the power of

---

[14] On the identification of potentially necessary conditions as a minimum claim in causal assessments based on the most-similar cases comparative approach see Gerring (2001: 211); see also the section on methods later.

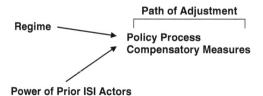

FIGURE 1.1. A Stylized Causal Assessment of Industrial and Labor Adjustment under Market Reform.

the prior ISI actors, that is, the economic and organizational strength with which business and labor emerged from the inward-oriented model (Figure 1.1). The hypotheses that follow, more fully explained in the theory laid out in Chapter 2, summarize the relations among regime, type of actors, and mode of adjustment.

> **Hypothesis 1**: *Democratic reformers prioritized compensation (of any kind) to the organized actors of the ISI model, that is, protected business and unions or union-represented workers. Authoritarian neoliberals could bypass (costly) compensation to the organized ISI actors and were left with the informal poor as the main arena to cultivate some form of mass support.*

This book seeks to restate the question of the political regime in the study of alternative economic policy strategies in the developing world. Although the relation between regime and different economic approaches was pervasive in the scholarly work in the 1970s and 1980s,[15] it started to fade away in the 1990s as most countries – fully democratic or not – had embarked on relatively similar stabilization plans and had reoriented their economies to the market. Yet, the regime variable may not be important to assess whether a country liberalizes or not, but, I argue, it is important to assess the type of economic liberalization that unfolds. Under democratic regimes, labor and business, the organized actors of the ISI model, could use alternative forms of pressure: mobilization, bankruptcy threats, and lobbying. Committed neoliberal reformers in democratic settings found it very hard to avoid compensating established organized actors. Authoritarian neoliberal regimes, by contrast, attained the coercive power needed to avoid costly compensation to ISI insiders – as targeted antipoverty policies tend to be cheaper than business subsidies or more universal, formal sector-based, welfare entitlements. Thus, authoritarian neoliberals are more likely to deprive protected industrial firms and urban workers linked to organized labor of past gains, indeed generally repressing the latter. In addition, the unorganized informal sector remained the main arena for neoliberal authoritarian regimes, which, for

---

[15] See, for example, O'Donnell (1973), Foxley (1978), Sheahan (1987), Pion-Berlin (1989), Johnson (1987).

Overview

reasons of political survival, wanted to gain popular legitimacy beyond their coercive means. Therefore, compensating the informal poor through "targeted" national programs may be important both to cushion waves of protest and to obtain support for authoritarian elites in future democratic or semidemocratic contexts. Of course, as will be shown in the following chapters, the fact that these social policies were "targeted" (i.e., directed to the informal or extreme poor) and supported by multilateral institutions did not make them less politically driven or clientelistic.[16]

> **Hypothesis 2a:** *When domestic ISI business groups/firms were economically strong vis-à-vis the state and growing in the years prior to reform, they were more likely to engage in concertational/negotiated policymaking and lobbied for market-share compensation (state assets and partial deregulation) as the main compensatory measure. Weak domestic ISI business groups/firms in relation to the state, in decline before reform, were more likely to be subjected to state plans and could only demand subsidies or were left to their fate.*

Economically strong private industrial groups, which generally developed in concentrated sectors (i.e., with a small number of players), faced fewer collective action problems, which made formal or informal concertation with state authorities more likely. Moreover, unlike foreign companies, which derived important advantages from liberalization, local industrial groups depended more crucially on those markets consolidated via state favors in transitional contexts. Thus, when certain domestic ISI business groups had been growing vis-à-vis both state and foreign companies in the run-up to liberalization, they were likely to wield the economic capacity and know-how to take over state assets or profit from politically sanctioned market reserves. Powerful local economic industrial groups reduced the uncertainty implied by economic opening by concentrating markets in the short run, a much more tangible payoff than eventual subsidy favors from fiscally strained governments. Domestic firms or business groups that have remained economically weak in relation to the state or foreign firms under ISI, generally unable to take over state assets or expand in the short run, were only left with the various types of state subsidies as the only possible form of compensation. Indeed, a weak and indebted company is more likely to claim subsidy compensation to pay off debts and clear the balance sheet than to buy state assets in a biased privatization. At the same time, a state that had engaged in massive and successful industrial production under ISI (overshadowing the private industrial *grupos*) could boast the bureaucratic capacity to make the formulation of reconversion plans from above feasible.

> **Hypothesis 2b:** *Organizationally strong national unions (monopolistic and centralized) made negotiated/concertational policymaking more*

---

[16] Hypothesis 1 does not neglect that in democratic countries, for example, Argentina and Brazil, clientelistic policies in certain districts often reached the informal sector during neoliberalism. However, this party-based local patronage should be differentiated from *national government social programs* and strategies that target the informal poor explicitly for compensation, as will be argued in Chapters 8 and 9.

likely and lobbied for market-share compensation (state assets and partial deregulation especially of the labor law). Organizationally weak, that is, plural and decentralized, unions contested adjustment and demanded subsidies for their laid-off base.

First, organizationally strong unions had something to gain (and negotiate) in the new liberal order, namely, the maintenance of traditional regulatory inducements such as monopoly of representation, centralized collective bargaining, and other corporatist prerogatives, through partial deregulation. Monopolistic and centralized national unions that did not fear competition from alternative labor organizations and could control the pressure from below from their own workers were more willing to enter into concertation with neoliberal reformers and negotiate these concessions. In addition, high affiliation provided leaders in monopoly unions with a relatively secure base (e.g., all of their member workers) for the businesses opened by market-share compensation, such as the managing of state assets, stock programs, or pension funds. Leaders of more decentralized and plural union movements had, by contrast, little to win in the new market economy. Organizationally weak union movements had built poorly bureaucratized national structures. They were less interested in market-share compensation such as the preservation of the (often anti-union) labor law or the management of stock programs or welfare and pension funds for workers. Moreover, their leaders generally experienced more pressures from below, and from other unions, which hampered national negotiations and concertation over bureaucratic payoffs, and built more incentives to seek compensation for the laid-off base.

Hypotheses 1 and 2, that is, the type of regime and the strength of prior ISI actors – whether private domestic groups or the state dominated core ISI sectors; and whether unions were decentralized and pluralistic, or centralized and monopolistic – combined to produce specific outcomes in each country (Table 1.2). It is important to stress that I refer essentially to prereform *economic power* in the case of industrial business groups (measured in the following chapters in dimensions such as prior growth, sales, and profits in relation to the state and foreign companies) and *organizational power* (measured as degree of union monopoly and centralization) in the case of labor.[17]

In the democratic cases the dominant compensatory schemes benefited ISI insiders. As I show in Chapters 3, 6, and 9, Argentina and Portugal had generated powerful industry-based family groups vis-à-vis the state, and a relatively centralized labor movement under ISI. Domestic business groups, especially in concentrated sectors, had the economic power to lobby for (and manage) state assets and market reserves in the midst of vast privatization processes. Plus, a relatively strong and centralized labor movement entered into a concertation in which

---

[17] Though not always irrelevant, industrial business associations were not a central locus of decision making in the compensatory deals around economic liberalization. They were relatively marginalized in the Statist- and Market-led models, and direct relations between the state and the economic *grupos* predominated in the Corporatist path.

Overview   17

TABLE 1.2. *Explaining Economic Liberalization Paths: Regime Type, and Power of the Prior ISI Actors*

	Regime Type	
Power of the Prior ISI Actors	Democratic	Authoritarian
Weak ISI Actors	Spain Brazil (rewards domestic industrial firms and laid-off workers with subsidies) **Statist**	Chile Peru (excludes ISI actors and rewards informal poor through targeted programs) **Market**
Strong ISI Actors	Argentina Portugal (rewards domestic industrial firms and national unions with market-share compensation) **Corporatist**	Mexico (combines market-share compensation to ISI actors with labor repression and programs targeted to the informal poor) **Mixed**

they sought to preserve the regulatory benefits and inducements obtained under the inward-oriented model.

In the Statist mode of Spain and Brazil, by contrast, there was no major pressure for market-share compensation: relatively weak private industrial groups vis-à-vis the state were unable to take over and control state assets massively. In these countries, a strong bureaucratic-industrial elite had grown sheltered in large developmental state holdings or banks, such as the INI in Spain and BNDES in Brazil. This solid industrial technocracy and the power of state companies in core ISI sectors combined to produce top-down adjustment implementation – though Spain put in place a broader series of subsidy-based reconversion plans. The existence of this public technocratic elite also eased the construction and empowerment of national champions in gradually privatized sectors. Moreover, the plural and decentralized nature of the union movement in both countries made labor concertation over adjustment policies less likely, as competing unions were ready to exploit a leader's defection. Relatively autonomous lower-level union bodies in decentralized structures were much more ready to contest adjustment from below. This militancy could only be tamed with subsidy programs targeted at local unions and dismissed base workers. In the Statist cases subsidy compensation of the base workers (more systematically developed in Spain and restricted to the conflictual cases in Brazil) evolved parallel to the adversarial relations between the government and the main national unions.

In the Market path of Chile and Peru, the state attained the coercive power that enabled neoliberal reformers to avoid compensation and unilaterally to impose adjustment on ISI organized actors, especially labor.[18] Yet the type of social actors (in particular, business) also interacted to produce the Market outcome. In effect, the local private ISI business groups (and unions) that confronted neoliberal reformers in Chile and Peru were relatively weak vis-à-vis the state, thus facilitating the unilateral imposition of adjustment. Plus, after their offensive against the organized working class, authoritarian reformers in the Market model knew that the informal sector remained the main popular constituency in which they could aspire to build a support base. The system of means-tested poverty alleviation and employment initiatives targeted to the informal sector (delivered through the State Planning Office [ODEPLAN] in Chile and the National Fund of Cooperation for Developmnet [FONCONDES] program in Peru) became, therefore, an important vehicle for the construction of a popular base for the regime and the parties associated with it, the Democratic Independent Union (UDI) in Chile and Cambio 90 in Peru.

In sum, strong ISI actors, that is, growing private industrial groups vis-à-vis the state and an organizationally powerful and centralized labor movement, fundamentally shaped the Corporatist adjustment path and its set of winners and losers. Conversely, weak prior ISI actors, that is, a domestic industrial bourgeoisie relatively subordinated to the state under the inward-oriented model and an organizationally weak and bottom-up structured union movement, established the basis for a Statist path. In the Market model the state also became the hegemonic industrial producer in the decade prior to reform, eventually weakening domestic capitalist opposition to neoliberalism. In addition, an authoritarian regime avoided costly compensation of ISI actors and was left with the informal poor workers as the main potential mass support base.

The historical trajectory that generated alternative state, business, and labor industrial actors prior to reform, as well as the dynamics of compensation under neoliberalism in each path are studied in the empirical chapters of this book. It should be noted that the power of labor under ISI generally mirrors that of the local business industrial sector. For example, organizationally weak indepenedent labor movements matched local private industrial groups relatively subordinated to the state in both Spain and Brazil. By contrast, Argentina historically developed relatively strong domestic business groups vis-à-vis the state and powerful national unions, under ISI. This "parallel development" in the structural and/or organizational strength of economic actors, frequently noted in the literature on varieties of capitalism for advanced countries, is further analyzed in Chapter 9.

Finally, neoliberal Mexico under De la Madrid (1982–88) and Salinas (1988–94) witnessed a "Mixed" strategy in terms of the framework constructed in this book. Unlike in the three models sketched, Mexican reformers from the

---

[18] Indeed, it is no accident that in both cases top labor leaders that were explicitly opposed to neoliberal labor and economic reforms, Tucapel Giménez in Chile and Pedro Huillca, secretary general of the Peruvian Worker's Confederation, were assassinated by regime death squads. When outright murder is an option, compensation to organized labor is obviously less likely to be on the table.

Overview

Revolutionary Institutional Party (PRI) did not focus a compensatory strategy more or less exclusively either on ISI insiders or on ISI outsiders. Rather, they bestowed compensation on *both* types of actors: hence the "Mixed" or "Hybrid" label for the case. Market-share deals and concertation with certain industrial business groups and unions coexisted with labor repression and the courting of the informal poor through an extended antipoverty program. The mixed case of Mexico will be explained in Chapter 9 in the light of the atypical combination of authoritarianism and the presence of some strong ISI actors. Of course, the type of authoritarian neoliberal government was qualitatively different in the cases of Chile, Peru, and Mexico. Yet, in all the cases democratic accountability and civil liberties were restricted, and authoritarianism served to take resources away from the labor and partisan interests more associated with ISI into the less organized informal sector.

METHODS AND RESEARCH DESIGN: LEVELS OF COMPARISON

This book employs the comparative-historical method to test its main hypotheses. Following standard methodological advice for qualitative studies (see King et al. 1994: 129, Collier and Mahoney 1996: 73–74, Munck 2004: 114), the research design seeks wide variation and contrasts in the explanatory and dependent variables. In other words, the cases studied in more detail in the volume, Spain, Argentina, and Chile, are broadly diverse in the forms of industrial liberalization and in the variables that help account for them. As argued earlier, they constitute the most complete empirical instances of each model. At the same time, the analysis makes extensive use of quantitative data sets as a source of insight into key economic actors and the dynamics of the sectors in which they are located.

With regard to the small-n component, the research design is based on the most similar systems design (Przeworski and Teune 1970) combined with process tracing. Outcomes and explanatory factors present alternative scores, while context or control variables are roughly similar in that (1) Spain, Argentina, and Chile were all middle-income countries that had developed mixed (i.e., private and state-owned) industrial sectors before economic liberalization;[19] (2) they have experienced a period of prolonged Import Substitution Industrialization with high tariff levels, generally above 50%; (3) the three countries have been widely considered as exemplars of neoliberal reform among emerging economies.[20] Indeed, these

---

[19] It is important to make clear that I am comparing the initial conditions before the market-oriented governments took power. In 1981, Spain, with a GDP per capita of $5,200, was a middle-income country according to the World Bank classification. The inward-oriented pattern of development in Argentina, Chile, and Spain is illustrated by the fact that, at the beginning of reform, the sum of exports and imports totaled less than one-third of the GDP. All three countries fundamentally differed from the East Asian NICs: in 1981 the ratios of exports plus imports to GDP were, for example, 75% in Korea, 105% in Malaysia, and 376% in Singapore (World Bank, *World Development Report*, various issues).

[20] In the index of "Economic Freedom" developed by Gwartney et al. (2001) for the conservative think tank the Fraser Institute, Argentina, Spain, and Chile are ranked at the top among the major

TABLE 1.3. *Assessing Economic Liberalization Paths: Levels of Comparison*

Cross-National Level of Comparison	Argentina Corporatist Model	Spain Statist Model	Chile Market Model
Dominant Pattern of Compensation	Market Share Compensation	Subsidies	Subsidies (only to informal poor)
Sectoral Case Studies: Business	Oil Steel Autos	Shipbuilding Steel	Steel Paper Pulp
Sectoral Case Studies: Labor	Oil Steel Autos	Shipbuilding Steel	Unemployed/ Informal Poor
Within-Country Level of Comparison (deviant cases in business)	Subsidies	Market Share Compensation	–
Sectoral Case Studies	Petrochemicals	Oil	–

countries, plus the other cases analyzed in the book – Brazil, Portugal, Peru, and Mexico – constitute the sort of laboratory that social scientists always crave: all share an Iberian-Catholic cultural legacy, mixed industrial sectors, and ISI trajectories sheltered by high tariff walls; and all underwent broadly similar processes of economic stabilization and liberalization in the relatively short historical span from the mid-1970s to the late 1990s.

Furthermore, the research design on the main cases of Spain, Argentina, and Chile includes a multilevel comparison (Table 1.3):[21] First, national models are compared through a general assessment of the politics of industrial and labor adjustment in each country. This general cross-national comparison is complemented with detailed case studies of industrial and labor restructuring in specific sectors that are representative of the dominant pattern in each country. Comparative case studies have considerable methodological advantage for our theoretical purpose. As McGillivray (2004: 6) states eloquently in her work on modern industrial policy, "industrial assistance and protection rarely leave a smoking gun." The protection or aid conveyed by certain (de)regulatory initiatives such as a tariff modifications, complex privatizations, antidumping measures, or a promotion program are often opaque and deliberately obscured by protagonists. Thus, the dynamics by which market share or subsidies become the salient form of compensation is more clearly untangled in case studies that

developing countries of Latin America and Southern Europe for the years 1995 and 2000 (www.freetheworld.com).

[21] I take the concept of multilevel comparison from Murillo (2001: 20). The idea of investigating sectoral or within-country variations is a frequent strategy to increase the number of observations in small-n designs. See, for example, Lijphart (1971) and more recently Snyder (2001a).

Overview 21

present a relatively detailed analysis of events, and the options that are ruled out or available to state and economic actors are closely scrutinized.

The selection of sectors for the case studies followed two criteria. First, all are ISI capital-intensive sectors in relative terms, that is, basic, intermediate industries (steel, oil, paper pulp, petrochemicals) or complex transport equipment (autos and shipbuilding). I avoided both light ISI sectors, in which labor abundant developing countries presumably tend to have more comparative advantages – and are therefore in less need of compensation – and capital goods or high-technology industries, less extended in this set of countries. Second, the sectors chosen are paradigms of the model of adjustment in each path. Thus, the book analyzes in more detail the steel and shipbuilding sectors in Spain (the largest sectors subjected to Statist reconversion in terms of manpower and resources poured), the three industries with the highest production value out of the six major sectors that were rewarded with market share compensation in Argentina (steel, oil, and autos), and the two most important cases of industrial privatization (in terms of asset value) that illustrate the general no-compensation path in Chile, steel and paper pulp. The cross-national comparison seeks to explain why countries chose different paths characterized by a "dominant" set of compensatory arrangements. It is further illustrated by the comparative assessment of the national adjustment trajectories of Brazil, Portugal, Mexico, and Peru developed in Chapter 9.

In addition to the comparison of national models, the book develops a within-country comparison in business sectors that deviate from the compensatory pattern prevalent in the Statist and Corporatist cases of Spain and Argentina. While compensatory policies for labor were relatively homogeneous in the different models, specific case studies in business reveal significant within-country contrasts in the democratic cases of Argentina and Spain. Each has an important sectoral "exception" to the national model of business adjustment. In Spain, established private firms in a single tradable sector – the oil industry – were favored with market share compensation, that is, with a combination of state asset allocation and protectionist or partial deregulation. The petrochemical industry is likewise an atypical case in Argentina. Domestic private groups only strove for subsidies, and they were eventually eliminated from the market, while the state showed great leverage in the reconfiguration of the industry.

Not surprisingly, oil proved to be the single core ISI sector in Spain in which domestic private firms (controlled by the main local banks) had managed to counter the influence of the state during ISI, developing considerable political and economic power, and consistent preferences for market-share compensation in the run-up to liberal reform. By contrast, a close analysis of the political economy of petrochemical production in Argentina shows that it was the single core ISI sector in which the state had managed to attain considerable power vis-à-vis private producers under the inward-oriented model, which made possible a sectoral reconversion largely driven from above.

LEGACIES FOR THE LIBERALIZED ECONOMIES

Finally, models of adjustment left decisive legacies for the workings of these political economies in the contemporary liberalized order. The course of liberalization in these countries can be understood as a "critical juncture," that is, "as a period of significant change, which typically occurs in distinct ways in different countries ... and which is hypothesized to produce distinct legacies" (Collier and Collier 1991: 30).

Once a particular reform path is followed and consolidated, be it sequential and "noncompensatory" privatization in Spain or unfettered labor deregulation in Chile, it is difficult to reverse: new relations of forces emerge, and subsequently the window of opportunity for further institutional change becomes increasingly narrow. The way in which actors use the reformed set of policies and institutions to deepen asymmetries of power is one of the "increasing return" mechanisms that make path-dependent phenomena difficult to reverse (Pierson 2000: 257, 262). For example, limited and negotiated labor reform in Argentina preserved the organizational power of traditional unions for the postliberal setting, while thorough (and repressive) labor deregulation largely hindered Chilean unions' role in the open economy. Market-share compensation in Argentina, Portugal, and Mexico benefited private ISI business groups in the short run. However, these politically sanctioned market reserves proved difficult to sustain as markets became increasingly open, and many compensated local business groups eventually sold their assets to major TNCs. The national champions empowered amid Statist restructuring in Spain and Brazil, by contrast, proved more effective in international competition and preserved decision making in the domestic economy to a larger extent. These and other legacies of the adjustment paths for the configuration of the liberalized political economies are analyzed in the concluding chapter.

PLAN OF THE BOOK

Chapter 2 sets the argument in the context of the debates on economic reform in developing economies in the last two decades and presents the theory just sketched on the origins of state-driven compensation under market reform. Parts II and III explore the dynamics of industrial and labor adjustment in the Statist and Corporatist models of Spain and Argentina, which primarily compensated insiders, that is, the organized ISI actors in business and labor. Chapter 3 explains the main traits of Statist and Corporatist models of business adjustment at a national level. Chapter 4 reinforces the argument through more detailed case studies that were paradigmatic of the industrial transformation in each country. Chapter 5 explores within-country variations, in which firms in core industries deviated from the dominant pattern of industrial liberalization in both Argentina and Spain. Chapter 6 explains the way in which Statist and Corporatist models of labor adjustment focused compensation on alternative segments of the formal sector and union-represented working class. Chapter 7

Overview 23

replicates the argument in more detailed case studies of labor adjustment in selected industries in Argentina and Spain.

Part IV studies the Market path to economic liberalization, which, unlike Statist and Corporatist models, focused compensation on ISI outsiders in the working class, and is most fully represented by Pinochet's Chile. Thus, Chapter 8 conceptualizes and explains the Chilean neoliberal experiment with a comparative lens. Finally, Part V situates the argument in Ibero-America. Chapter 9 extends the framework to the other major countries and neoliberal reformers in the region: Brazil, Portugal, Peru, and Mexico. The chapter describes the dominant compensatory strategy in each case. As earlier in the book, it proceeds to explain this outcome through a focus on the regime question, and through both a general historical account of the evolution of major ISI actors under the inward-oriented model and a quantitative measure of their power prior to reform. Chapter 10 concludes by hypothesizing the main institutional and structural legacies of these transition models for the liberalized political economies and by discussing them in the light of recent extensions of the "varieties of capitalism" debate to emerging markets.

2

From State to Society

Neoliberal Reform and a Theory of Compensation in ISI Economies

INTRODUCTION

The original debates on the politics of market reforms in developing countries, spawned in the late 1980s by the debt crises and the acceleration of financial internationalization, posited a fundamental contradiction between the logic of economic adjustment and democratization. Indeed, in most of the neoclassical and institutionalist accounts of marketization, which dominated the field in the 1990s, liberalization was essentially seen as a process driven from above. Societal forces, in particular domestic business and labor, were regarded as antireform actors who should be marginalized by an executive that concentrates state power. While neoclassical economists asserted the need to avoid "rent-seekers," institutionalists stressed the idea of state capacity and encapsulation as a crucial perquisite for market transformations. Two decades later, however, unfolding events and scholarly work have challenged these assumptions. First, almost every major developing country in Ibero-America and Eastern Europe has fundamentally reoriented its economy to global markets, more often than not under democratic and plural regimes. Second, a copious literature has highlighted how actors once considered "antireform," such as populist parties, state enterprise managers, labor unions, provincial bosses, or protected business groups, played a fundamental role in the construction of market-oriented governing coalitions.

This chapter argues that, although this more recent scholarly work has illuminated crucial aspects of the relationship between politics and economics in contexts of dramatic market transformations in the Iberian world, it has been less successful in providing (1) a clear general map of the alternative modes or "paths" of neoliberal adjustment and (2) a systematic theory that can account for these different paths, and for the variation in the alternative sets of actors compensated or sidelined by market reform coalitions. Indeed, in Chapter 10 I argue that these alternative modes of economic liberalization may be important to understanding the different types of market organization that eventually consolidate, and the way countries cope with post-neoliberal trends such as the return of state interventionism or popular sector activation.

From State to Society

Although many Iberian-American economies started to liberalize a decade earlier, the analytic conceptualization of divergent reform paths has been more pervasive for the post-Communist world (e.g., Stark and Bruszt 1998, King 2002, King and Szelenyi 2005, Iankova 2002, Burawoy 1996, Ekiert 2003) than for the former mixed economies. Indeed, the study of the political sociology of market reform in Eastern Europe and Russia, which emphasizes the role of organizational legacies of the old order, provides us with useful heuristic tools to assess diverse trajectories of liberalization in mixed, ISI economies systematically. Drawing in part from this literature, I propose an approach that is designed to capture the dynamics of state-society interactions in the midst of market reform and is underpinned by a general idea: economic liberalization is essentially a task of political construction, and yet, both the organization of society and the polity provide opportunities and constraints for what strategies are available to reformers for crafting a coalition. In a nutshell, the main question in the initial debates on market reform and development, particularly in the mixed economies of East Asia and Latin America, was which types of states (for example, more or less insulated) are pushing market transitions? This book complements that approach by posing a different general question: which types of societies or economic actors are reformers confronting?

The approach is based on a systematic analysis of the patterns of state-driven compensation that market reformers can bestow on formerly protected actors in business and labor. It aims to explain why and how market-oriented administrations sought to buy off alternative business and labor actors, producing in the process three patterns of industrial and labor adjustment, Statist, Corporatist, and Market. As already introduced in the Overview in Chapter 1, the book argues that the type of regime and the power of prior ISI actors that coalesced before neoliberalism – essentially whether private business groups or the state was hegemonic in industrial production and whether unions were decentralized and pluralistic or centralized and monopolistic – decisively shaped the alternative adjustment models.

The first part of the chapter reviews traditional and more recent perspectives on the politics of economic liberalization in the developing world. The second part argues that the literature on market transitions in Eastern Europe and Russia offers useful heuristic tools for our comparative endeavor in Ibero-America. The third section systematizes the menu of compensatory mechanisms available to the neoliberal reformer, which is essentially built upon the general notions of "subsidy" and "market-share compensation." It also introduces a theory based on the main factors that shaped the policy choice of neoliberal reformers, industrial business, and labor in the domain of compensation. The last part of the chapter summarizes the explanation of the variation in the concrete historical models of adjustment that is developed in the rest of the book. It takes the causal argument one step backward and argues that the power of actors in business and labor that confronted adjustment in Argentina, Spain, and Chile (and in the other cases analyzed in Chapter 9) and their preferences over compensation are rooted in the pattern of late industrialization, and in the mode

26 The Intellectual Terrain

of labor organizational development, that each country consolidated under the inward-oriented model.

THE POLITICAL ECONOMY OF MARKET REFORM IN DEVELOPING
COUNTRIES: TRADITIONAL AND CURRENT PERSPECTIVES

The Initial Debates

International political economy–oriented approaches bore an important influence on the original literature on market transitions in developing economies. Works such as Stallings (1992), Haggard (1995), and Haggard and Maxfield (1996) explored the extent to which financial flows and/or trade integration conditioned domestic policymaking in hard currency–starved economies.[1] However, the public choice and institutionalist literatures, more focused on domestic politics, came to dominate the field in the 1990s. The public choice, or neoclassical, approach rests mainly on the idea that economic liberalization is a public good, and, therefore, the dynamics of market reform are governed by a collective action problem: losers from market reform are concentrated, whereas beneficiaries are diffused. Consequently, the former deploy powerful resources to block any possibility of change (Krueger 1993; see also Bates and Krueger 1993: 457, Edwards 1995, Sturzenegger and Tommasi 1998). The central actor in this view is the "rent-seeker." Once state economic intervention develops, a powerful set of incentives that maintains the "artificial" benefits emerges and, as a result, rent-seekers devote resources to preserving protection rather than marshaling them for a productive purpose. Curbing the resistance of protected actors provokes short-term costs, "the valley of tears," until the new set of market incentives yields results. In a similar vein, authors such as Przeworski (1991: 164–65), Geddes (1994: 95), and Bates (1992: 53) consider the particular institutions or circumstances that can help solve the collective action problems inherent in economic liberalization. Overall, this approach tends to take the behavior of "rent-seekers" as given and focuses on the politicians' incentives to overcome the reactions that emanate from the old network of interests or the electorate. More recent works by Stokes (2001) and Weyland (2002) maintain this elite-centered approach. While not fully adopting a public choice framework, they focus primarily on the type of incentives (most prominently the eruption of economic crises) or microfoundations that would compel individual politicians and state officials to enact market policies in the face of presumably hostile electorates and economic interest groups.

Sparked by the turbulent path of new Latin American democracies in the late 1980s and 1990s, a corpus of studies that may be labeled "institutionalist" also came to play a leading role in the research on the politics of reform in developing countries. The implications of this analysis were straightforward: in an environment

---

[1] More recent approaches in this vein, though combining both external and domestic variables, are Remmer (1998), Brooks and Kurtz (2007), and Pop-Eleches (2009).

From State to Society 27

of deep economic crises and social dislocation, reformist executives build upon the social demand for "authority" in order to bypass, and even openly challenge, the power of representative institutions such as Congress, political parties, and interest organizations (Haggard and Kaufman 1992; Nelson 1990, 1994; Acuña and Smith 1994; Torre 1998). An elective affinity was thus posited between neoliberal economics and unilateral decision making, which often (implicitly or explicitly) ranged from forms of delegative democracy to plain authoritarianism. Significantly, the underlying political logic of economic liberalization in many of the neoclassical and institutionalist accounts is quite similar: market reforms are taken as public goods that generate collective action problems that need to be solved by a strong executive (Haggard and Kaufman 1995: 118).

Institutional and neoclassical approaches were important to understanding the political dilemmas posed by the exhaustion of inward-oriented strategies of growth. Indeed, in many episodes of radical neoliberal adjustment such as Chile 1975, Bolivia 1985, or Argentina 1990, governments recentralized authority and gained power vis-à-vis established interests after hyperinflationary crises. Yet, the definitive consolidation of market-led models of development involved wider and more complex tasks of political construction. The continuous and simultaneous unfolding of democratization and economic liberalization cast doubt on the analytical power of these approaches based on the idea of bureaucratic insulation and unilateral decision making. More than simply "sidelining and dismantling" organized ISI actors, as Joan Nelson (1994: 148) puts it, governments often compensated entrenched economic interests of the old order through a variety of policies that granted specific players subsidies or some sort of market reserves in the liberalized economy. Moreover, lurking behind most neoclassical and institutional approaches was the idea that countries follow a rather similar path of adjustment, consisting in a set of initial stabilizing measures followed by more or less uniform rounds of market enhancing policies such as tariff liberalization, privatization, pension reform, and labor deregulation. This view, which generally stressed the common content of neoliberal projects, is scarcely useful for our comparative endeavor.

A different perspective posed that the transformation of inward-oriented economies should be essentially explained by the pressure from business interests that, by way of their structural positions in the economy (for example, export-oriented financial/industrial conglomerates or holders of liquid assets), became "winners" in the new order (see Schamis 1999, 2002; also Frieden 1991). However, this type of approach based on the primacy of certain capitalist interests fails to capture the multidimensional logic of economic liberalization. Particularly in labor and business tradable sectors, important actors can lose and win at the same time. The government might undermine the rents and market reserves of some unions and firms through radical import liberalization. Yet, reform-minded officials might grant those same actors special concessions or protections in other policy areas such as the health and labor markets or privatization, strengthening their position in the newly liberalized order. Plus, in this more structural view, the economic coalition underlying neoliberal

28 *The Intellectual Terrain*

projects – led by financial interests – tends to be rather similar across countries. This book shows, by contrast, that the inclusion and cooptation strategies of neoliberal governments with respect to domestic business and popular actors varied remarkably.

Building Constituencies for Neoliberal Reform

Initial state elite–centered or essentially economic/structural approaches to the politics of market transitions would be soon replaced by others more focused on state-society interactions, and on the political construction of reform coalitions. The new emphasis was on how officials may buy off stakeholders in order to gain their acquiescence to the marketization project. For instance, Kessler (1998) and Pérez (1997) showed how general economic liberalization in Mexico and Spain involved the allocation of market reserves to the local financial sector. Murillo (2001, 2009), Teichman (2001), Corrales (1998), and Etchemendy (2001) have argued that concessions funneled to unions and/or heavily protected business groups in the form of state assets, partial labor law deregulation, or market reserves were inherent in the process of neoliberal reform in Argentina, Mexico, and Chile. Gibson (1997), Gibson and Calvo (2000), and Kurtz (2004) have underlined that the courting of overrepresented regional and peripheral constituencies, often through spending or market-inhibiting mechanisms, has helped consolidate the general neoliberal trend in these same countries.[2]

Overall, these studies have shown that governments that have undertaken extensive market liberalization in semiclosed economies engage in complicated bargains with certain established interests in order to make the reform path politically sustainable. In this quest for shaping market-reform coalitions, many traditional liberal orthodoxies are left to the side. In a Polanyian (2001 [1944]) logic of movement and countermovement, the construction of more open markets mixes liberal with illiberal measures. Tariff and financial deregulation are combined with the erection of market reserves and barriers to entry; fiscal stabilization with massive targeted spending and worrisome borrowing; privatization through competitive bidding with the direct handout of state assets; and so forth. Of course, these facts, in and of themselves, do not make these projects less "market oriented." Nor should they obscure the reality that these countries have largely abandoned inward-oriented models of growth, curbed state participation in industry, and opened their economies to international trade and financial flows. In the same way that old leftists had to confront the disappointing realities of "real socialism," many neoliberals had to confront how "real market reform" works.

That said, we still lack a systematic theory that explains variation among countries (and within countries) in terms of stating both *why* some established

---

[2] More generally, the shift from unilateral decision making to more consensus-based politics under neoliberalism in Latin America was pointed out in Torre (1998), Hagopian (1998), and Oxhorn and Ducatenzeiler (1998).

From State to Society

business and labor actors receive valuable compensation in some cases but not in others and the *different ways* (for example, through the awarding of state assets, partial or biased deregulation, or monetary subsidies) in which these actors were bought off. Building on his earlier work on Russia, Treisman (2003: 104) insightfully notes that market reformers in Argentina and Brazil essentially offered stakeholders "three co-optation currencies: money, property or rents." Yet his analysis does not elaborate on this realization. Which mechanism is more likely to be used in specific circumstances? Which actors are likely to be benefited by each compensatory measure? More recently, social scientists have analyzed alternative patterns of liberal economic reform and the type of markets that emerge in Latin America – see, for example, Murillo (2009) on public utilities, Shadlen (2009) on intellectual property, and Madrid (2003) and Brooks (2009) on pensions. Burgess and Levitsky (2003) have explored the conditions that prompted adaptation to neoliberalism by former populist parties. Yet, we still do not have a more general causal map of alternative neoliberal trajectories and the institutional arrangements that they entailed. A focus on the politics of compensation can provide such a blueprint.

Assessing Reform Paths: The Comparative Political Economy of Market Transitions in Eastern Europe

This book goes beyond established approaches to economic reform mostly applied to ISI mixed economies. The recent political sociology of marketization in Eastern Europe and post-Communist countries, however, may help us to conceptualize the course of liberalization in the Western less developed economies. In particular, the work of Stark and Bruszt (1998); King (2002); King and Szelenyi (2005); G. Eyal, I. Szelenyi, and M. Townsley (1998); Burawoy (1996); Iankova (2002); Ekiert (2003); and Ekiert and Hanson (2003), despite important differences, share an emphasis on two general points.[3] The first is that the organizational features of "insiders" under Communism – party bureaucracy, state managers, official unions – help to shape alternative liberalization paths, especially in areas such as privatization and the emerging patterns of property. For example, in Hungary and Poland, where Communists and associated interest groups remained powerful, the privatization process was carried out through a series of bargains between the state and the main parties and social groups such as managers or unions. In the Czech Republic, by contrast, where the Communists had capitulated after years of suppressing almost all institutions in civil society, reformers were freer to undertake privatization through a system of vouchers that enabled citizens to acquire stock (Stark and Bruszt 1998). The

---

[3] For an overview on the political sociology of market reform in Eastern Europe, in which the question of alternative institutional legacies from the old order figures prominently, see the fascinating debate among Burawoy, Eyal et al., and Stark and Bruszt in *American Journal of Sociology*, Review Symposium (2001). For a critique to approaches based on institutional continuity in Eastern Europe see McDermott (2004).

patterns of institutional cross-ownership and interenterprise organization in Hungary were shaped by the economic networks that emerged as a result of Communist reforms, under which managers had acquired considerable autonomy to deal with suppliers and clients (pp. 142–53). More generally, Ekiert and Hanson (2003: 28) assert that the legacy of informal networks under state socialism "has had perhaps the most important impact on post-communist institutional change."

The second general point present in this literature is that different patterns of political competition (substantially democratized or more restrictive regimes) also bear an important influence on the resulting mode of economic liberalization. Burawoy (1996) makes this case more forcefully with respect to Russia and China. In this view, unlike in Russia, in China the consolidation of the party-state has made possible the controlled decentralization of property relations to regional and local governments and the hardening of budget constraints, which have enhanced market reform. The relationship between the modes of elite political competition and regime breakdown and the alternative courses of economic reform is also studied in Stark and Bruszt (1998), King (2002), Iankova (2002), and Ekiert (2003).

These two dimensions identified in the political sociology of market reform in post-Communist countries – the preexisting organizational configurations of actors or insiders and the type of elite political competition when market reform is launched – will be crucial in the explanation of alternative adjustment paths in mixed economies offered in this book. Of course, some scholars have noted the salience of past institutional legacies to understanding economic liberalization in the Iberian world. Teichman (2001) points out how the "Iberian strain," consisting in a blend of patrimonialism, clientelism, and personalism, has affected the market reforms of Chile, Argentina, and Mexico. Murillo (2001) underscores that populist reforming parties were reluctant to dismantle corporatist legacies of labor organization. Surprisingly enough, however, prereform structural and institutional legacies have seldom been systematically explored in the search for *variation* in the modes of market transition in ISI economies. If institutional legacies of the old order matter in comparative assessments of divergent marketization paths in the former Communist world, why should they be ignored in mixed and semi-closed capitalist economies that, over decades, generated their own set of powerful economic insiders?

Alternative Views on Compensation under Neoliberal Adjustment

The idea of "compensation" is present in many of the approaches just reviewed and is obviously an important part of economic liberalization. For example, Nelson (1992: 244) and Haggard and Web (1994: 23–25) conceive of compensation under market reforms largely in terms of subsidies to the poor/unemployed. Indeed, the idea that neoliberalism could be (or should be) compatible with extending social compensation for the newly enlarged informal sector or

From State to Society 31

the poor is found in the early work of social policy analysts (Graham 1994), as well as in the scholarly work on neopopulism in both Latin America (Roberts 1995, Weyland 2001) and Eastern Europe (Greskovits 1998, Weyland 1999). In the case of Southern Europe, attenuating the costs of economic reform and integration through unemployment and welfare expenditure has been the trademark of a "social-democratic" model of adjustment (Maravall 1993). In her analysis of PSOE's welfare and unemployment policies during the 1980s and early 1990s in Spain, Hamann (2000: 1043) maintains that "policy implementation can be used to selectively *compensate* [my italics] key support groups for the potentially adverse effects of adjustment policies." Of course, the idea of subsidizing the losers (generally workers or popular sectors) from increasing economic liberalization echoes similar uses in the literature on neocorporatism and, more recently, on the transformation of state-led models of growth in Europe and Latin America (e.g., Katzenstein 1985, Levy et al. 2006, Kaufman and Segura-Ubriego 2001).

However, as suggested previously, compensation in adjustment contexts has also taken a different meaning. Paul Pierson (1994: 23, 98) introduces "compensation" as one of the strategies to minimize the costs of welfare reform in advanced countries, others being "obfuscation" and "division." The compensation strategy includes alternative measures, such as biased deregulation (e.g., "grandfather clauses" that spare current recipients from social policy cuts) or the allocation of rents through privatization, such as the direct awarding of ownership in the retrenchment of the state-run housing system in Britain. Likewise, in their analysis of economic reform in Russia, Shleifer and Treisman (2000: 9) write that "stakeholders are unlikely to relinquish their veto without *compensation*" [my emphasis]. In this case compensation refers specifically to rents created "through enacting legal and regulatory restrictions" that market reformers offer to established managers or business actors, rather than to subsidies targeted at the poor or unemployed. A similar notion of compensation to insiders, which relates more to market concentration and barriers on entry than to welfare expenditure, is also found in Corrales (1998), Greskovits (1998: 139), and Etchemendy (2001: 22). Finally, the World Bank distinguishes two types of compensation in liberalizing contexts: "severance packages," which are not geared only to the poor but may also target "bureaucrats, managers of state enterprises," and "equity incentives," that is, the distribution of shares to employees that can help to circumvent their opposition to privatization (World Bank 1997: 154).

COMPENSATION UNDER NEOLIBERAL ADJUSTMENT: A FRAMEWORK FOR ANALYSIS

Building upon these different notions of compensation found in the literature on economic liberalization, which, as I have shown, can refer to a variety of policy arrangements ranging from social relief for the poor and jobless to the awarding of stock to entrenched collective actors, this section constructs a general framework of the compensatory mechanisms available to the neoliberal reformer. As stated in the introductory chapter, the logic of these compensation policies can be divided into two groups. Subsidies are essentially incentives to cope with full competition in open markets. Firms and workers are subjected to unfettered liberalization and downsizing, yet the subsidies and programs will help soften that transition. In the case of the direct awarding of state assets and "partial" or "protectionist liberalization," which I refer to as *market-share compensation*, selected firms, workers, and unions may (or may not) be eventually subjected to open competition. However, in the run-up to full-scale liberalization they may be granted some type of market niches or property that will automatically increase (or help preserve) their market share once the sector is deregulated. Table 2.1 summarizes the compensatory measures that may be targeted at employers, unions, and union-represented workers in the formal sector – which I have called *ISI insiders* – and at the poor or unemployed in the informal sector, or *outsiders*. The following sections describe the compensatory mechanisms in more detail.

Subsidy

As noted previously, this notion refers to any form of state monetary or financial infusion designed to alleviate the situation of individual firms, unions, laid-off workers, or simply poor workers in the midst of the adjustment process. Subsidies can be directed at both business and labor. Compensatory subsidies

TABLE 2.1. *Compensatory Measures under Industrial and Labor Neoliberal Adjustment*

	Business	Working Class	
	ISI Insiders	ISI Insiders (unions and formal sector workers)	ISI Outsiders
Subsidy	• Financial Credits • Direct Monetary Infusions • Tax Exceptions	• Unemployment Compensation • Employment Programs (formal sector) • Early Retirement • Severance Payment	• Means-Tested Employment Programs • Means-Tested Subsidies/Poor Relief to Vulnerable Groups • Infrastructure/ Community Projects
Market Share	• Targeted Privatization • Special Tariff Regimes • Partial Sectoral Deregulation/ Barriers to Entry	• Targeted Privatization • Special Tariff Regimes • Partial Deregulation of the Labor Law and Other Union-Related Markets (i.e., health, pensions)	–

From State to Society

aimed at employers can take three general forms (Table 2.1). *Financial credits* include public loans issued at low interest rates, also called "soft credits," and state bailouts of business debts to public credit institutions. *Direct subsidies* comprise monetary allocations to be used for firms' capitalization or for direct investment. In contexts of sweeping liberalization, they are often accompanied by state-sponsored programs of technological updating. Finally, *tax exemptions* are typically applied to social security payments and to mergers or acquisition of industrial firms under restructuring. They may be also applied to investments, profits, or firms' capitalization processes. The varieties of subsidies to industrial business granted by the Spanish state and its National Industrial Institute (INI) and by the developmental state bank BNDES in Brazil under neoliberalism, studied in Chapters 3, 4, and 9, are central examples of this compensatory mechanism.

Subsidies to the working class may be directed to insiders – dismissed formal sector workers generally backed by unions – and/or to outsiders, that is, long-term unemployed and poor workers who have been out of the ISI system of employment and welfare entitlements. Within the first group, *unemployment compensation* is often targeted to formal sector workers who have been contributing to a state-managed unemployment fund (Table 2.1). In the formal sector *employment programs*, the dismissed worker receives an income (and generally training) while program officials seek to relocate him in an alternative job. *Early retirement* financed by the state is a measure typically targeted at older workers. Finally, *severance payment* implies a one-shot monetary allocation to the dismissed worker. All these measures are generally delivered to workers who have been contributing to social security arches while employed. Of course, they imply different degrees of compensation: in general, employment programs that preserve past wages, retrain workers, and seek alternative jobs – for example, the Employment Promotion Funds in Spain analyzed in Chapters 6 and 7 – are more generous than common unemployment subsidy or one-shot severance payments.

Means-tested and poverty alleviation programs, by contrast, are typically directed to ISI outsiders. This approach was strongly advocated by pro-neoliberal institutions such as the IMF and World Bank during the 1980s and 1990s, and by some policy analysts, most notably Carol Graham (1994). Subsidies are distributed to the unemployed or informal sector worker as a policy of poor relief, regardless of his/her past employment or contributions to unemployment funds or social security. They include state-funded employment programs generally in public works; welfare entitlements directed at vulnerable groups such as mothers, pregnant women, or children; and broader community or infrastructure projects, which frequently employ workers under the means-tested job programs. Given that they tend to provide compensation only to the extreme poor, these are often called "targeted programs." Prominent examples of this type of compensation measure are the employment and antipoverty initiatives put in place by the Pinochet dictatorship, and the National Solidarity Program (PRONASOL) and the National Fund of Cooperation for Development (FONCONDES) programs in neoliberal Mexico and Peru.

Market-Share Compensation

Market-share compensation carries the following logic: every market is politically constructed; consequently – especially in contexts in which the boundaries between state and markets are being redrawn – officials can regulate the future "share" of actors in more open markets. This can be accomplished through a privatization that involves the direct allocation of state assets and substantial market concentration, the enactment or maintenance of the monopoly of representation to a sectoral union, the permanent or temporary erection of barriers to entry (for example, to foreign firms) or a special tariff regime that preserves the market position of insiders. In short, market-share compensation seeks to preserve, via regulation or ownership, the participation and roles played by economic actors in the newly liberalized environments. While subsidies imply some form of direct or indirect cash allocation, this form of compensation stems from state regulation – though it can also entail important fiscal costs.

Privatization, which entails the purchase of state assets by private agents, is one of the main mechanisms of market-share compensation that cater to domestic business. The direct and political award of ownership through privatization, in a context in which business is increasingly affected by market liberalization, constitutes an important form of side payment. Of course, in the case of business the method of state divestment – for example, through open bidding or direct sales – and the type of control involved, that is, whether a single firm is allowed or not allowed complete control of the assets, will result in a different degree of compensation. In Chapter 5, I assess the "compensatory degree" of industrial privatization in relation to domestic business in eight industrial sectors in Argentina, Spain, and Chile.

The second general form of market-share compensation well suited to business is partial deregulation. A neoliberal government need not implement sweeping deregulation in all markets and sectors at the same time. Reforms that I call "protectionist" or "partial liberalization/deregulation" constitute important side payments. They generally grant protection to certain actors, while the rest of the economy is being relentlessly exposed to increasing competition. For example, some firms may be protected by a special tariff regime or by extensive and strongly biased antidumping measures in the run-up to liberalization – such was the case of the Argentine auto and steel sectors studied in Chapter 4. Likewise, a reforming government might grant established firms future privileges vis-à-vis foreign players in markets formerly controlled by the state, for instance, through discretionary access to infrastructure (as occurred in the Spanish oil deregulation, in which only local companies obtained access to the privatized transportation network; see Chapter 5). Hellman (1998), who originally coined the concept in the context of neoliberal transitions in Eastern Europe, argues that "partial reform" essentially unfolded as a consequence of committed but weak market-oriented officials facing unexpected stakeholder resistance and power. This book argues, however, that partial deregulation is often deliberately

From State to Society   35

designed by neoliberal reformers to appease certain constituencies. Moreover, unlike Hellman's seminal article, I contend that partial reform may often become a condition for a successful liberalization drive in other sectors.

Market-share compensation may also constitute a valuable reward to labor (Table 2.1). First, both unions and individual workers can participate in privatization and acquire firms (in the case of unions) or stocks to increase their market power. Labor can also benefit from tariff regimes that spare industrial sectors from general economic opening and downsizing. Most importantly, unions may seek the partial deregulation of the labor law, which can entail the preservation of state-sanctioned corporatist prerogatives such as monopoly of representation and other collective rights (for example, centralized frames for wage bargaining or de facto representation of nonunion members in collective contracts) that strengthen their market role in the future. Finally, unions can also lobby to maintain barriers to entry for new actors in markets in which they are already economic agents or pressure for privileged access to a new business created – such was the case in Argentina's health and pension reforms,[4] respectively, analyzed in Chapter 6.

Of course, state subsidies and the erection of market reserves are hardly policy innovations that stem from the liberalization wave in developing countries. In fact, both are well-known forms of industrial and labor policy that can be traced back to the nineteenth century or before and are exhaustively treated in the literature on late industrializers (for a more recent discussion see McGillivray 2004). The innovation of this book is, in the first place, that it applies the framework to a situation of economic liberalization in heavily protected ISI economies, combining the traditional tools of industrial and labor policy (i.e., tariffs and subsidies) with measures that are more typical of the global wave of state retrenchment in the last part of the twentieth century, such as the release of state assets or the uneven deregulation in a variety of industries and markets such as health or labor. Second, this book attempts to explain the type of economic actors that are going to choose and get alternative forms of compensation. Third, the approach here underscores that the allocation of varieties of subsidies and market share in the form of stocks, partial deregulation, or market reserves can be targeted to business *as well as* to organized labor.

Finally, this analytic framework is agnostic about the normative status of each compensatory measure. It rejects the idea that some of them result in better or more desirable market economies or are more or less prone to "bad equilibrium." Obviously, market-share compensation entails more protection and direct, politically sanctioned benefits to some key business and labor

---

[4] Danani (2003: 240) illustrates the notion of market-share compensation nicely when she asserts that the Argentine unions' strategy in the deregulation of health services was oriented "to obtain the reserve of a 'quota' in the market."

actors. However, as the recent literature on varieties of capitalism makes abundantly clear, open and overall outward-oriented economies are compatible with a wide variety of institutional arrangements and political forms of coordination.

THE THEORY OF COMPENSATION: REFORMERS, BUSINESS, THE WORKING CLASS, AND POLICY CHOICE UNDER NEOLIBERAL ADJUSTMENT

Neoliberal Reformers

What would be the most valued compensatory measure for neoliberal officials, industrial business, and labor? It seems plausible to argue that, in principle, state officials in committed neoliberal governments, such as the ones analyzed in this book, would be reluctant to grant compensation. Compensatory policies, either in the subsidy or market-share form, entail a cost for the reformer. Subsidies are financially burdensome in adjustment contexts where hard currency is badly needed. Multilateral financial institutions or foreign powers, whose support devoted neoliberals almost always seek, dislike political payoffs such as the direct award of assets during privatization or biased deregulation, particularly as those measures generally discriminate against foreign capital. Thus, in authoritarian settings the unswerving reformer has more leeway to pursue his "natural" preference for no compensation, especially regarding protected business and unions, which neoliberals see as main foes of economic liberalism. Coercion affects labor most directly. It hinders union capacity to protest and strike. However, authoritarianism also reduces the number of avenues of dissent for protected business, closing opportunities for lobbying at Congress, at subnational elected governments, or even in independent courts, in which employers can denounce, for example, the end of promotional regimes or the threat to "acquired rights."

Avoiding compensation to entrenched ISI actors is a luxury that neoliberal reformers in democratic settings cannot afford. Under democratic regimes, when the market shift is under way and the preservation of the status quo seems to be no longer an option, labor and protected business groups will seek compensation and will use their political and economic resources to pressure the government. Thus, it is plausible to expect that democratic neoliberal reformers will privilege organized ISI actors in the compensatory deals. As Shadlen (2004) has argued, democratization often benefits the lobbying of large established actors in liberalizing political economies and hinders the capacity for interest representation of weaker and poorly organized groups. It is hard to hypothesize, though, the type of compensation to insiders that democratic reformers will pursue. A financially complicated situation, for example, may make the extensive use of subsidies less likely. Some firms may seek subsidies to pay off debts while others desire protection in their own markets as a platform for an export drive.

From State to Society

Later I argue that the type of compensation in democracies is heavily dependent on the characteristics of the alternative economic actors that reformers confront.

Authoritarian neoliberal governments, however, may find at some point that coercion and marginalization of the organized ISI actors are not enough to secure stability, particularly if the social costs of reforms seem exceedingly high. Indeed, neoliberal reforms in the last quarter of the twentieth century paralleled the third wave democratization. Even staunch authoritarian leaders could think that some democratic opening would be inevitable in the short or long run. Hence, the need to court a consensus base beyond the original finance-based coalition may become more apparent. In this case, authoritarian neoliberals, who are undermining unions and formal labor, are arguably more likely to court the atomized informal sector as a particular constituency. The support of this increasing mass of impoverished and unorganized individuals may be important both to cushion waves of protest and to preserve authoritarian elites' political standing in an eventual democratic setting. As Chapters 8 and 9 show, the fact that neoliberal social policy was "targeted" and generally backed by the multilateral institutions did not make it less politically driven and clientelistic. It may well serve the political and sometimes electoral goals of neoliberal authoritarian reformers.

Compensating the poor in the informal sector through national, means-tested programs carries two important advantages for the authoritarian neoliberal reformer. First, it involves fewer concessions that affect the neoliberal policy paradigm than those targeted at organized labor and protected business – indeed, attending to the needs of the extreme poor while the rest of the population seeks social provision through the market is perfectly coherent with the neoliberal creed. Second, means-tested unemployment subsidies and antipoverty programs, that is, "targeted social policies," tend to be financially less costly than firm subsidies and than the more universal welfare entitlements associated with ISI. Yet in adjustment contexts, the formidable redistribution of resources within popular sectors that extended neoliberal means-tested social policies imply – that is, away from ISI unions and parties and to the informal poor – is more likely to occur under authoritarian politics. The affinity between authoritarianism and the massive expansion of targeted and informal sector–oriented poverty relief to enhance market transition is even noted by Carol Graham, a well-known proponent of "safety nets" under neoliberalism. She asserts that "it may be easier for an authoritarian government to target the poorest groups because it is less vulnerable to pressure from organized interest groups (as in the case of the Pinochet regime in Chile) than a democratic regime would be" (1994: 3). Thus, Hypothesis 1, already presented in the Overview chapter, summarizes the expected policy choice of neoliberal officials regarding compensation.

> **Hypothesis 1:** *Democratic reformers prioritized compensation (of any kind) to the organized actors of the ISI model, that is, protected business and unions or union-represented workers. Authoritarian neoliberals could bypass (costly) compensation to the organized ISI actors and were left with the informal poor as the main arena to cultivate some form of mass support.*

Business

What is the type of compensation most valued by industrial firms in semiclosed economies that are confronted with far-reaching market liberalization? The question of employers' policy preferences has recently gained renewed attention in the study of the political economy of both advanced countries (Mares 2003; Hall and Soskice 2001; Thelen 2004) and developing countries (Schneider 2004a; Schrank and Kurtz 2005; Schrank 2005; Chibber 2004; Kohli 2004). My hypothesis on firms' main preferences in situations of widespread liberalization takes some elements from this literature, such as the question of the firm size and diversification (Mares 2003; Haggard, Schneider, and Maxfield 1997). Of course, not all ISI firms will oppose liberalization. Firms heavily based on competitive advantages such as locally abundant natural resources may favor a change in the status quo. Generally speaking, one could think that firms that will seek compensation (of any kind) most intensively are those that are outside the agro or food industry and do not belong to business groups extremely diversified outside industry, that is, especially in the financial sector. Plus, I argue that market-share compensation will be most valued by companies that (1) are owned by domestic capitalists and (2) are "strong," that is, are large and have been efficient under ISI, competing successfully with state and/or foreign firms in the years prior to reform.

Domestic large family-owned firms that have been relatively efficient and growing in sheltered markets under ISI face an ambiguous situation in the wake of comprehensive liberalization. On the one hand, they depend on a wide range of subsidies, promotional regimes, and protections that are going to be lifted at any moment and that had been indispensable in achieving their past growth. On the other hand, they are likely to be endowed with the economies of scale, business skills, and know-how on the local market that make plausible the preservation or increase of market share even in increasingly liberalized environments, especially if they win some state favor to soften the transition. Of course, the notion that large firms, especially in capital-intensive and basic industries, will seek and consolidate oligopolies is well backed by industrial organization theory and economic history, most notably in the classic work by Alfred Chandler (1990). The question here is that in situations of abrupt market opening in ISI economies, powerful local capitalists depend even more crucially on concentrated markets and the support of state regulation in an environment of uncertainty. Unlike small or large inefficient firms under ISI, domestic efficient players have the platform, the *means* (such as size, capital, and domestic market know-how), to turn political connections and lobbying into rapid economic gain despite the enhanced competition brought about by neoliberal reform. Moreover, as large and economically strong ISI firms tend to develop within large family-owned business groups, and in concentrated sectors such as steel, chemicals, cement, and oil, they will face fewer collective action problems to pressure the state and negotiate biased deregulation or "targeted" privatization. Finally, if sidelined, they can use their economic strength to disrupt the liberalization project, be it through capital flight, massive lobbying, or litigation.

From State to Society 39

In short, large and financially strong private domestic firms under ISI subjected to abrupt adjustment will value market-share compensation, that is, the takeover of state assets and biased liberalization, most. Obviously, in purely theoretical terms, one could argue that a certain amount of subsidy could always match the money value of market-share compensation. Yet that choice is hardly probable in a real adjustment situation.[5] Especially assuming bounded rationality, that is, that in crisis contexts actors tend to be more risk averse and have limited process information capability (see Korpi 2006: 174), it is reasonable to expect that a strong protected company will consider the granting of market share by the state as a much more plausible and concrete payoff than subsidies. Market-share deals reduce the uncertainty of competition enhancement in the short run and are less contingent on the generally strained fiscal situation of neoliberal states.

The situation of foreign firms differs in important respects. Foreign firms had generally landed in ISI economies to profit from tariff walls and expanding domestic markets. However, unlike domestic firms, they have much to win from general liberalization: they benefit from more access to imported inputs and technological transfers from mother companies. Plus, the repeal of exchange controls facilitates remittances to their headquarters in advanced countries. Therefore, market liberalization for a company like Shell or Renault entails less of a challenge than to local companies, which must face unfettered competition after decades of protection. Hence, I hypothesize that they will show only lukewarm support for the pursuit of compensatory measures.

Finally, small or large but economically weak domestic firms will be less likely to prioritize market-share compensation. Profiting from a politically granted market reserve or taking over state assets in increasingly competitive markets (and in the midst of the uncertainty brought about by liberalization) entails certain economies of scale and know-how with which small or weak firms under ISI are less likely to be endowed. Not just any company, for example, can take over a large state firm or monopoly built under ISI – no matter how biased in its favor the privatization is. Those "white elephants" (for example, a large steel mill, shipyard, or oil refinery) carry logistics and financial costs that only firms with certain structural features can bear. Likewise, a transitional tariff regime or partial reform may delay liberalization and bestow benefits to insiders, yet, as the case studies to follow indicate (for example, the Argentine oil and auto industries analyzed in Chapter 4 or the Spanish oil deregulation examined in Chapter 5), this type of payoff does *not* imply a simple preservation of the status quo. The market almost always becomes gradually more competitive. By contrast, firms that are not powerful enough to be compensated through state-granted assets or market reserves will welcome subsidies but will have to comply

---

[5] As McGillivray argues (2004: 6), for scholars it is very difficult to compare the size of subsidies that is equivalent to the dollar amount of tariffs won by a specific economic sector. Of course, for real actors it is even harder.

with unfettered deregulation. Indeed, firms that are in bad shape or burdened by financial obligations in the short run will be obviously eager to receive subsidies and direct cash transfers to pay off debts and clear the balance sheet.

Finally, I contend that state firms do not have preferences on their own, since they tend to be subjected to the authority of the government, which in these cases is assumed to be a liberalizing, pro-market government. Therefore, in principle state companies have much less autonomy to exert pressure for compensation on governments that have already converted to neoliberalism and are indirectly running those firms. To sum up, it is quite obvious that any firm, foreign or domestic, large or small, will welcome any state favor, so in that sense all companies are all for compensation. The issue is *which* firms have incentives to lobby for compensation harder, and for *which type* of compensation, once adjustment seems unavoidable. On the basis of the logic just presented, Hypothesis 2a summarizes the factors that conditioned policy choice for the relevant business actors.

> **Hypothesis 2a:** *When domestic ISI business groups/firms were economically strong vis-à-vis the state and growing in the years prior to reform, they were more likely to engage in concertational/negotiated policy-making and lobbied for market-share compensation (state assets and partial deregulation) as the main compensatory measure. Weak domestic ISI business groups/firms in relation to the state, in decline before reform, were more likely to be subjected to state plans and could only demand subsidies or were left to their fate.*

The Working Class

Important studies on labor under market reform and workforce adjustment (Golden 1997, Murillo 2001, Burgess 2004) ask a fundamental question: in a context hostile to the working class, under what conditions are union leaders willing to enter the typical political exchange, that is, moderation for organizational power or stability? The analytical focus of these studies on the incentives and strategies of national and sectoral union leaders is understandable, since union leaders are the critical gatekeepers to mobilization. Yet, in the context of neoliberalism and an increasingly disarticulated working class, compensatory politics is hardly ever an exclusive matter of negotiations with national union leaders. My goal here is to assess the survival strategies of neoliberal governments in relation to the working class in general, in addition to the crucial question of unions' reaction to adjustment.

What drives the policy preferences of the different working class segments over compensatory policies? In his classic article Pizzorno (1978: 292) posited that union organizations that present more "dispersion of power" are less likely to give leeway to political exchanges. Coherent with this idea, unlike business (for whom preferences over compensatory policies, or so I argued, are essentially a function of the economic structure of firms), I contend, union leaders' strategy over compensation is shaped by labor law and institutions, which constitute the

From State to Society

most prominent determinant of the "dispersion of power" within trade unions alluded to by Pizzorno. The horizontal axis of union organization, which denotes whether one or many unions are able to organize workers (i.e., the degree of monopoly pluralism), plus the vertical axis of organization, which signals the statutory powers of plant-level union bodies vis-à-vis national/ sectoral organizations, reflect the degree of power dispersion within unions and, therefore, of organizational strength. Centralized and monopoly unions tend to be *organizationally strong*, since they have more members and resources due to their status as single representatives of workers in collective bargaining, and often in the provision of social welfare.[6] The concentration of power in the national or sectoral leadership vis-à-vis lower union bodies and the rank and file also tends to favor organizational coherence and strength. Conversely unions in plural and decentralized settings (i.e., where more than one union can organize workers, and local/firm-level unions have statutory powers to collect dues, call strikes, or bargain) tend to be, in comparison, *organizationally weak*; they tend to have fewer members and to manage fewer resources nationally.

One can make the reasonable assumption that, in situations of sweeping adjustment, union leaders in organizationally strong labor movements will value market-share deals most. Indeed, organizationally strong unions have, from the outset, something to negotiate in the new liberal order, namely, the preservation of monopoly of representation and other corporatist prerogatives and the partial deregulation of markets in which strong unions often participate, such as health or popular housing. Plus, high affiliation provides leaders in strong unions with a relatively secure base (e.g., all of their affiliated workers) for the businesses opened by market-share compensation, such as the managing of stock programs, or pension and welfare funds.

Union leaders by definition have more concerns for organizational survival, especially in contexts of massive adjustment (sometimes around 70% of the sector's workforce; see Chapter 7), when it is often the very existence of the union that is at stake.[7] Crucially, the two main challenges that a national/ sectoral union leader seeking organizational survival can face in situations of adjustment, the "external" from other unions, and the challenge "from below," that is, from his own rank and file, tend to be low in contexts in which unions are

---

[6] As Golden et al. show (1999: 215), in advanced countries monopoly and centralization generally go together, for example, in the Nordic countries and Austria, and relative union decentralization and pluralism also tend to coincide, as in the cases of France and Italy. The same can be said of Ibero-America; see Chapter 9.

[7] In a classic work on bureaucratization and democracy in trade unions Lipset (1960: 224, 231) argued that the insecurity of the leadership, the need to strengthen the union against employers, the differential high status and skills that union leaders possess vis-à-vis ordinary workers, coupled with the low possibility that a union leader has to achieve a similar "status" in society outside his union job, are all factors that induce higher levels of bureaucratization and entrenchment of oligarchies in labor movements than in other organizations. Of course, Lipset had in mind the typical centralized (boss-oriented) U.S. union more than the plural and more decentralized (and ideological) unions that historically developed in countries such as France, Italy, or Spain.

monopolistic and centralized. Hence, a direct negotiation with the government, that is, concertational policymaking, around organizational or "bureaucratic" payoffs becomes more likely.[8] In short, leaders of organizationally strong unions are relatively unhindered to negotiate market-share compensation.[9]

In organizationally weak unions – that is, plural and decentralized – the leaders' position is more complicated. National leaders may also value organizational payoffs, such as the management of stock programs or social services. Yet, relying exclusively on bureaucratic payoffs in times of adjustment may be problematic in plural and decentralized unions, where both challenges, the external from other unions and the challenge from below, tend to be more intense. Competing unions will be ready to exploit a leader's defection in favor of market-share compensation, rallying the support of threatened workers. Lower-level union bodies, which may wield important powers (for example, to collect dues and to call strikes), will be ready to question the leader's authority to bargain with neoliberal officials and will be more likely to mobilize strongly to protect the laid-off rank and file. Moreover, in an environment of low affiliation and union competition, individual workers' future cooperation in the possible ventures opened by market-share compensation, such as the managing of stock options or pension funds, becomes more uncertain for each national or sectoral labor leader. In short, I hypothesize that, in the case of organizationally weak unions, leaders will have few options but to contest adjustment measures and will generally favor subsidy compensation targeted at the laid-off base.

Base or ordinary formal sector workers subjected to the strains of adjustment, who depend less on and are less related to the union bureaucracy for individual survival, will naturally favor more diverse forms of subsidy over market-share compensation. As argued earlier they will likely choose generous unemployment subsidies or state-funded employment programs over one-shot severance payments. The long-term unemployed worker or the unorganized worker who survives by himself in the informal sector will only find relief in means-tested employment programs, that is, those subsidies that do not depend on previous contributions while in his formal job. Yet, the preferences of the informal poor and unemployed are less relevant as "demand makers" in the politics of economic adjustment. As Huber and Stephens (2001: 18) argue in their work on the welfare state, despite being targets of welfare, the long-term unemployed without connection to the process of production "lacks organization

---

[8] In the case of business, market-share compensation is fundamentally oriented to increase or preserve profits. In the case of organized labor, though future monetary profits may be part of the deal, in general market-share compensation is primarily geared to strengthen the union as an organization. So throughout the book I also call this type of compensation labor "organizational" or "bureaucratic" payoffs.

[9] Of course, not just any market-share compensation would go against the short-term interests of the worker. In particular, tariff regimes that eschew competition and boost sector performance may help sustain employment levels.

From State to Society

and power" and thus is generally acted upon rather than being an actor in shaping policy.[10]

In sum, as in the case of firms, union activists in every context would naturally welcome any form of compensation for both the union bureaucracy and the mass of workers, whether employment programs or stock options. However, in a context of sweeping adjustment in which actors know that resources are scarce, the question is what will be the form of compensation most valued by each working class segment. Hypothesis 2b summarizes the policy choice for the most relevant working-class actors in environments of massive adjustment.

> **Hypothesis 2b**: *Organizationally strong national unions (monopolistic and centralized) made negotiated/concertational policymaking more likely and lobbied for market-share compensation (state assets and partial deregulation, especially of the labor law). Organizationally weak, that is, plural and decentralized unions, contested adjustment and demanded subsidies for the laid-off base.*

ALTERNATIVE MODELS OF ADJUSTMENT AND POLITICAL DYNAMICS: SPAIN, ARGENTINA, AND CHILE

The preceding sections have outlined a series of state compensatory mechanisms available under market adjustment and a set of hypotheses on the factors that shaped compensation policy choice for neoliberal reformers, industrial firms, and working-class segments. Of course, in the event of adjustment in particular countries, not all types of compensatory measures were put in practice; nor were all actors in business and labor likely to be rewarded. However, in every case of neoliberal reform analyzed in this book we find at least *some* initiative for compensating potential losers within business and the working class.

This study identifies the prevalent type of compensation and the actors targeted in each country. As stated in the introductory chapter, the compensation awarded, plus the actor targeted and the policymaking style, constitute the locus of the definition of alternative models of adjustment, Statist, Corporatist, and Market. The book offers an explanation on the origins of these concrete alternative historical outcomes based on the theory and hypotheses laid out earlier.[11] Spain, Argentina, and Chile, three countries that underwent a dramatic period of market reforms between the 1970s and 1990s, constitute model cases of each outcome. The explanatory account on these countries is summarized in the rest of this chapter. Chapter 9 will show that other cases of broad economic

---

[10] Of course, the unemployed and poor would become more organized as liberalization and adjustment spread in Latin America.

[11] Recent methodological perspectives, under banners such as "systematic process analysis" (Hall 2003) and "theory guided process-tracing" (Falleti 2006), have advocated greater integration of detailed historical narratives in general theoretical frameworks.

liberalization, such as Brazil, Portugal, Peru, and Mexico, show a variation in compensatory policies that can also be understood in the light of this typology.

In Spain, the Socialist Worker's Party (PSOE) developed a Statist model of industrial and labor adjustment between 1983 and 1996: a series of top-down restructuring plans put in place a wide system of monetary subsidies to placate established industrial firms, and unions and laid-off workers at the local level. The series of industrial reconversion plans carried out under the liberalizing government of Felipe González in Spain was the most extensive in the Iberian world. Yet, as I analyze in Chapters 6 and 7, this Statist reform from above also witnessed arguably the most violent industrial conflict in any transitional economy, in which unions managed to extract substantial subsidy compensation for laid-off industrial workers.

In Argentina's Corporatist path during the Menem presidency (1989–99), important industrial and union groups were awarded different forms of market-share compensation – the second general form of compensatory measure – in more or less formal concertation rounds. Certain domestic, industry-based business groups had a privileged access to a vast privatization process through which they diversified into other sectors and, most importantly, substantially concentrated or preserved (at least in the short run) the markets in which they operated under ISI. Mainstream labor negotiated in formal tables the partial deregulation of the labor law and of the health system in which they were main providers, and many sectoral unions obtained handsome state assets in privatization. Finally, in Chile's Market path (1973–88), the neoliberal government showed a determined reluctance to compensate any of the traditional ISI actors or insiders, leaving industrial and sectoral readjustments largely in hands of market forces. At the same time, the Chilean government directed compensatory subsidies to the unemployed and the atomized and informal poor through means-tested programs in a manner unrivaled by the Statist and Corporatist models.

Hypothesis 1 stated that the political dynamics of compensation policy starts with the regime question. Major compensation to organized ISI actors is found in the democratic cases in which firms, unions, and workers in the formal sector can deploy their lobbying and/or mobilization resources. Put simply, the democratic Corporatist and Statist paths of Argentina and Spain concentrated compensation (albeit of different types) on ISI insiders. In authoritarian Chile, by contrast, established industrial firms and unions were initially sidelined or repressed. Neoliberals, however, courted the only group in which a repressive and radical neoliberal government could cultivate some form of mass support: the unemployed or informal poor workers. As analyzed in Chapter 8, authoritarianism enabled a formidable shift of resources out of the formal sector and traditional welfare entitlements into the informal poor. This pattern of "targeted" social compensation that was intimately linked to the buildup of a patronage machine in urban areas and the construction of the *Pinochetista* political party, the Independent Democratic Union (UDI).

In addition, Hypotheses 2a and 2b argued that the type of prior ISI actor – essentially whether domestic private industrial groups were dominant, and

From State to Society

whether unions were monopolistic and centralized or plural and decentralized – conditioned the political process and the type of compensation awarded. In Argentina's Corporatist model, strong ISI business groups, that is, the top echelons of a domestic industrial bourgeoisie that had been growing and displacing the state and foreign companies in the years prior to reform, gained enormous leverage over the privatization process and were also able to extract concessions in the form of partial deregulation and tariff regimes. An organizationally powerful labor movement (monopolistic and with weak shop-floor bodies) welcomed bureaucratic payoffs (such as stock programs or the partial reform of the labor law and the health system) in exchange for demobilization.

By contrast, Spain had developed weak ISI insiders prior to reform. An already declining industrial bourgeoisie was subjected to state dirigisme once reform was launched, compensatory subsidies notwithstanding. Weak local ISI business groups simply lacked the economic and financial means to make the option of market-share compensation credible. At the same time, a powerful state that had heavily expanded in the industrial realm under ISI had developed the capacity to elaborate reconversion plans from above. Moreover, a demo-cratic neoliberal regime could not let entire industrial sectors fall, which rein-forced the willingness of state planners to combine thorough, top-down liberalization with subsidy compensation. Finally, a weakly bureaucratized and factory-based union movement did not find organizational side payments attractive. Rather, it mobilized aggressively for employment programs targeted at shop-floor laid-off workers.

The Market path of adjustment in Chile was also cleared by the presence of weak ISI organized actors. The state had, as in Spain, displaced and debilitated the main capitalist foe of economic liberalization – domestic private manufac-turing – in the years prior to reform. Thus, the initial and more radical neoliberal team in Chile found more leeway to sideline established industrial groups and consolidated its main alliance with the financial sector. The explanation of the national models of adjustment in the following chapters involves, in the first place, a sequential assessment of the interaction between state officials and different types of private actors in labor and business during neoliberal reform, looking at both the industrial sector nationally and specific sectors. In addition, the book takes the causal assessment one step backward and delves into an analysis of the *formation* of ISI actors before the period of economic liberaliza-tion began.

THE HISTORICAL ORIGINS OF BUSINESS AND LABOR PREFERENCES DURING ADJUSTMENT

A complete causal assessment of the variations in liberalization models should lead us to investigate the historical origins of the different types of economic actors that helped drive alternative outcomes. The configuration of specific types of business and labor actors under the inward-oriented model is fundamental to

46 *The Intellectual Terrain*

understanding the definition of their interests once neoliberal reform was launched. How did Spain generate a decentralized and pluralist union movement that contested adjustment? Why did the ISI model in Argentina spur the growth of strong, domestically owned private business groups in core sectors, while in Spain and Chile the state emerged as the dominant industrial actor? Table 2.2 summarizes the sequence in the causal model for the three main cases analyzed in this study, given by the preform trajectory, the regime type and the power of ISI actors during adjustment, and the compensation outcome.

The *pattern of late industrialization* and the *mode of labor's organizational development* under the inward-oriented model are decisive to understanding the

TABLE 2.2. *Models of Economic Liberalization: Historical Trajectories and Explanatory Factors*

Models of Adjustment	Statist Spain (1982–96)	Corporatist Argentina (1989–99)	Market Chile (1973–89)
Antecedent Conditions under ISI			
• Mode of Late Industrialization	• State-Led	• Business Groups–Led	• State-Led
• Mode of Labor Organizational Development	• State-Controlled	• Labor-Based-Populism	• Electoral/ Partisan Leftist Radicalization
Explanatory Factors			
Power of Prior ISI Actors			
• Business	• Weak: Subordinated Industrial Bourgeoisie	• Strong: Dominant Industrial Bourgeoisie	• Weak: Subordinated Industrial Bourgeoisie
• Labor Movement	• Weak: Plural/ Decentralized	• Strong: Corporatist/ Centralized	• Weak: Plural/ Decentralized
Type of Regime	Democratic	Democratic	Authoritarian
Outcome	Rewards domestic industrial firms and laid-off workers with reconversion plans and subsidies	Rewards domestic industrial firms and national unions with market-share compensation	Excludes/ represses ISI actors and rewards informal poor through targeted programs

From State to Society 47

variation in type of firms and unions that emerged at the outset of adjustment and their consequent policy choice regarding compensation. The former dimension essentially asks whether private business groups or the state became the main engine of industrial development, in particular in the deepening into the production of basic and intermediate goods and transport equipment after the easy stage of ISI (simple consumer goods). In the *state-led* pattern of ISI development in Spain and Chile, preform industrial growth was decisively shaped by a powerful state holding created on the eve of World War II. CORFO (Corporation for Development) was established in Chile only two years before the Spanish INI (National Industrial Institute), in 1939. Interestingly, state groups and coalitions that were on opposite sides of the political spectrum sponsored both institutions. The INI was born out of the initiative of a nationalist military faction within a regime with fascist features – Francoism in the early 1940s. CORFO, by contrast, emerged out of the interventionist desires of the Popular Front in Chile, a typical interwar coalition among communists, socialists, and middle-class parties. Yet, both initiatives echoed the climate that prevailed in the aftermath of the 1930 depression, which dictated state planning and intervention. Indeed, in both Spain and Chile, the state performed as the main agent of industrial growth during the postwar period, and, moreover, its role in the production realm (particularly in secondary ISI sectors such as chemicals, steel, paper pulp, and transport equipment) increased markedly as liberalization approached. The weakness of ISI local business groups and their failure to lobby for (or their scarce interest in) market-share compensation during adjustment should be understood in the light of this prior antecedent trajectory, namely, a state-led mode of late industrialization.

The industrial trajectory of postwar Argentina, by contrast, can be labeled as *business groups–led*. It witnessed the slow rise to a hegemonic position of a group of local, industry-based, and family-owned private conglomerates independent of both the financial sector and the state. Populism in Argentina initially supported labor-intensive light and food industries in the 1940s but inhibited a sustained expansion of the state in basic industries of the type that one finds in the state-led models of Chile and Spain. Once industrial deepening began, state industrial policy generally supported local private production to a much greater extent than it did state companies – particularly after the 1966 military coup. Therefore, postwar industrial development generated local private groups based in core ISI sectors of intermediate and durable goods, such as autos, steel, aluminum, cement, and oil, whose power relative to the state and foreign companies at the outset of neoliberal reform was unmatched, not only in Spain and Chile, but arguably in other countries studied in this book such as Brazil and Peru. These large and domestically owned private companies, as argued earlier, would develop strong preferences and lobbying for market-share compensation: they wanted politically induced market concentration to reduce the uncertainties of enhanced competition. The only major exceptions to this pattern of state-led and business groups–led development in the core ISI sectors of Spain and Argentina are analyzed in Chapter 5.

Labor's organizational development was heavily influenced (though not totally determined) by what Collier and Collier (1991: 783) define as labor incorporation, that is, "the first sustained and at least partially successful attempt to legitimate and shape an institutionalized labor movement." It is also crucial to understand the type of union consolidated under the ISI model. The organizational dimension essentially assesses whether national unions (1) allied to a governing labor-based party, (2) were granted inducements in terms of the collective labor law (especially representation and bargaining monopoly) and finance (i.e., the control of social services), and (3) became centralized vis-à-vis the power of shop-floor union bodies.

Spain can be labeled as a case of *state-controlled* union organizational development prior to neoliberalism. After the civil war, the Francoist state aimed to depoliticize and control hierarchically the labor movement from above. The regime eschewed major union mobilization and institutional empowerment. It set up the so-called Vertical Syndicates, the official union movement, to promote loyalty and to channel working-class demands formally in a "harmonic" fashion. As analyzed in Chapter 6, in practice the Vertical Syndicates were little more than a vehicle for affiliation to the official party, lacking any bureaucratic power, welfare function, or real influence in the Francoist coalition. In the context of the regime's partial liberalization after 1959, the government allowed for some degree of plant-level collective bargaining and the election of works councils or "worker's commissions" at the factories. Left-wing opposition groups used those works councils elections to infiltrate the official union movement from below. Thus, the reemergence of independent (i.e., nonofficial) unionism from below in the authoritarian context of the 1960s and 1970s sowed the seeds for a strongly plant-oriented union movement with powerful works councils and plural and financially weak national bureaucratic structures. Union leaders' option in Spain for subsidy compensation targeted at the base over bureaucratic payoffs can only be fully understood in the light of this prior development.

In Chile, state-authoritarian labor incorporation (one that aimed to depoliticize labor and granted very few inducements) during the late 1920s and early 1930 (Collier and Collier 1991) was followed by labor's partisan-electoral radicalization in the mid- to late 1960s. Though unions were part of the leftist Unidad Popular (1970–73), in the context of instability and polarization the coalition was never able to consolidate major institutional or financial inducements for labor. Plus, in Chile the repressive character of the adjusting regime vis-à-vis labor renders its prior trajectory less relevant for the outcome of no compensation.

In Argentina, effective labor incorporation was carried out by Peronism in the 1940s. Labor-based populism shaped a union movement organized around monopoly unions that was strong in terms of both labor law inducements (monopoly and centralized bargaining) and the control of social provisions and economic resources. Plus, as Chapter 6 analyzes, the Argentine labor movement witnessed an organizational development in the three decades prior to reform through which sectoral/national union structures systematically gained authority over shop-floor bodies. The legacy of labor-based populism was a monopoly and financially powerful union movement with a thoroughly centralized leadership

From State to Society

and weak plant-union bodies. Again, the preferences of the Argentine labor movement for market-share compensation primarily targeted at the union leaders and insiders and, crucially, the capacity of the union leadership to curb base reactions from below during neoliberalism can be fully understood only in the light of this antecedent trajectory.

CONCLUSIONS

This study builds upon two bodies of literature. First, I engage the mounting scholarship that, since the late 1990s, has highlighted the multidimensional logic of market liberalization in the developing world, attending to the fact that general deregulation and fiscal adjustment in some policy areas were often combined with the preservation of pockets of protection, subsidies, and a variety of deals with stakeholders in other areas. Yet, this scholarly work has not produced a general theory that explains which established interests are brought into the reform coalition, and under what circumstances, in the domain of industrial and labor actors. To address this limitation, I draw upon a second strand of research on market transitions in Eastern Europe that place prereform organizational legacies – the various sets of actors and institutions generated within the different types of command economies – at the forefront of the accounts of alternative liberalization paths.

In order to assess the reform paths in former ISI economies, I have developed an explanatory model based upon the politics of compensation. The menu of compensatory measures provides a framework through which I scrutinize the different deals and policies that reformers crafted with (or targeted at) a group of "potential losers" from market enhancement. This analytical strategy avoids both a perspective that dwells primarily on state elites (like the standard institutionalist and neoclassical approaches to economic liberalization prevalent in the 1990s) and a structural view exclusively based on class and financial interests as the primary force behind neoliberal adjustment. Rather, this approach is centrally concerned with state-society interactions and intends to illuminate the institutions and the types of actors (analyzed in terms of both their strength and their historical configuration) that conditioned the coalitional strategies available in the context of dramatic economic liberalization. In particular, I have argued that the type of regime and the alternative patterns of labor and business actors combined in specific ways to produce three defined adjustment paths, Statist, Corporatist, and Market, embodied in the model cases of Spain, Argentina, and Chile. Finally, I have sketched how the type of actors that coalesced before reform – whether hegemonic or weak ISI business groups, or organizationally strong or weak unions – and their consequent policy preferences regarding compensation are rooted in the alternative modes of late industrialization and labor organizational development under the inward-oriented model.

PART II

THE POLITICAL ECONOMY OF BUSINESS ADJUSTMENT

3

Compensating Business Insiders

The Origins of Statist and Corporatist Models in Spain and Argentina

INTRODUCTION

Beginning in the early 1980s and 1990s, respectively, Spain and Argentina underwent bold projects of market transformation. In addition to the policies aimed at stabilizing the currency and curbing inflation, liberalization programs involved trade reform and integration into regional markets, industrial privatization, and attempts to deregulate the labor market in the two countries. In contexts of fixed exchange rates and increasing currency overvaluation, these policy reforms resulted in the widespread disappearance of local firms, massive layoffs, and a pronounced rise in unemployment. In neither Spain nor Argentina, however, were the sectoral realignments triggered by these seismic transformations simply left to the operation of market forces. Rather, the government shaped market outcomes by providing some kind of policy compensation to particular groups of industrial firms and formal sector workers that were potential losers from reform. Chapters 3 to 5 explain business-state relations during trade reform, sectoral deregulation, and industrial privatization, all of which were key components of industrial adjustment. This chapter concentrates on the national patterns, that is, the origins of the dominant compensatory strategies for industrial business in Argentina and Spain. Chapter 4 studies particular industries compensated in order to give a closer assessment of the causal factors at work. Chapter 5 will analyze core ISI sectors that deviate from the pattern of adjustment prevalent in Argentina and Spain in a way that is, or so I argue, coherent with the explanatory framework presented in the book.

Even though both countries had undertaken attempts at liberalization before the 1980s, it was under the administrations of Menem in Argentina (1989–99) and González in Spain (1982–96) that the model of development became fundamentally reoriented toward the market. The governments, however, pursued radically different paths of industrial adjustment in terms of (1) a dominant pattern of policymaking (*state dirigisme* in Spain vs. formal or informal *concertation* with particular business groups in Argentina) and (2) a defined set of compensatory measures geared toward particular industrial firms (subsidy allocation in Spain vs. market-share compensation in Argentina). The main

53

54 *The Political Economy of Business Adjustment*

TABLE 3.1. *The Outcome: Models of Business Adjustment in Argentina and Spain*

Features	Statist Spain 1983–96	Corporatist Argentina 1989–99
Nature of Policymaking	*Dirigisme*: Centralized Formulation/ Decentralized Implementation	Selective Concertation
Compensatory Measures	Subsidy Allocation	Market-Share Compensation (state assets/partial deregulation)
Consequences	Retrenchment of Prereform Industrial Bourgeoisie	Initial Expansion of Prereform Industrial Bourgeoisie in Compensated Sectors

consequences of these alternative types of industrial adjustment were the initial consolidation of the compensated segments of the Argentine industrial bourgeoisie and the disappearance of traditional firms and industrial groups that had constituted the core of the Spanish industrial class (Table 3.1).

What explains the models of adjustment in terms of both their policymaking styles and compensatory strategies? As stated in Part I, two main variables orient the causal assessment, the type of regime and the power of the prior ISI business actors. Democracy is a common factor behind models of adjustment that concentrate compensation on the ISI insiders. Therefore, the main source of variation in the models of industrial liberalization in Argentina and Spain stems from the alternative constellation of business and state actors that emerged from the inward-oriented model. Here I restate the two hypotheses already introduced in Chapters 1 and 2, with respect to business adjustment.

> Hypothesis 1: *Argentina and Spain were democratic countries during adjustment, and therefore neoliberal governments prioritized compensation to the business insiders of the ISI model, namely, domestic industrial firms and groups.*

Unlike other extensive market reformers under more authoritarian or repressive regimes such as Chile and Peru, in Argentina and Spain liberalization took place within highly competitive democratic regimes, and with very low levels of state repression. Even thoroughly market-oriented officials could not simply sideline established industrial producers and ignore *all* business pressures and the political consequences of massive bankruptcies or business lockouts. When governing elites are committed to neoliberal reform, protected domestic industrial firms and groups have, ceteris paribus, more opportunities to lobby for compensation in democratic than in authoritarian regimes.

> Hypothesis 2a: *In Argentina, economically strong ISI business groups vis-à-vis the state, which were gowning in the years prior to reform, were more likely to engage in concertational/negotiated policymaking and lobbied for market-share compensation (state assets and partial deregulation) as the main compensatory measure. In Spain, weak ISI*

Compensating Business Insiders

> *business groups vis-à-vis the state, already in decline before reform, were subjected to government plans and could only demand subsidies.*

The strength of the main ISI business groups[1] in relation to the state varied sharply between the democratic cases of Argentina and Spain. In Argentina, the salient economic power and concentration of *some* key domestic industrial groups at the outset of adjustment, vis-à-vis both the state and foreign industrial players – what I term *strong* ISI business actors – resulted in their privileged access to policymaking and in the negotiation of deregulatory measures. Conversely, Spain is a case of *weak* ISI business actors. The core local private firms and groups in the industrial sector were already in retreat in the years prior to reform. Their economic power was fading, and their sectoral associations were relatively new and feeble. At the same time, the formidable expansion of the industrial public sector under ISI, led by a solid caste of technocrats who had gathered important expertise on a variety of sectors, helped to set the stage for a state-led pattern of adjustment.

The economic strength with which actors emerge from the inward-oriented model strongly conditions the *type* of compensatory measures implemented. In Argentina, powerful domestic capitalists chose to concentrate markets via privatization, tariff regimes, and biased deregulation. Strong family industrial groups found the market reserves brought about by privatization and negotiated liberalization a much more tangible payoff than eventual subsidies from a state in retreat. By contrast, in Spain private industrial groups were powerless to lobby for privatization or protectionist deregulation as their economic performance under the ISI model had been poor. In this case, industrial businessmen were economically too weak to opt credibly for market share and were left with few options but to take a form of subsidy. Indeed, in the Spanish Statist mode, a strong and democratic state – which could not let uncompetitive sectors simply fall apart – reorganized most revamped industrial sectors under new public economic groups. Some of them were later sold to international investors; others – for example, in natural gas, oil, electricity, information technology, and paper pulp industries – were empowered as state companies. These national champions were later subjected to a "sequential" disinvestment in which the government prevented foreign takeovers and preserved substantial leverage over the privatized company.

The economic power of prior compensated and noncompensated ISI firms will be measured at the national level in three dimensions at the outset of reform: (1) share of total sales among top industrial firms, (2) share of total profits, and (3) production value in relation to concentration. The more specific and sectoral comparisons of Chapters 4 and 5 will include a fourth measure of the economic power: the evolution of local, foreign, and state firms' domestic market share prior to neoliberal reform. In short, all measures, whether at the national or

---

[1] In Chapter 1, I classified as "ISI business groups" those large, generally family-controlled domestic holdings that originated and maintain a substantial part of their assets in manufacturing and/or oil/fuels businesses.

56   *The Political Economy of Business Adjustment*

sectoral level, yield roughly the same result: in these democratic settings, market-share compensation was only bestowed on strong private industrial players generated under the inward-oriented model, that is, those that prior to neoliberalism shared the highest percentage of sales and profits among top firms, those that showed a comparative high ratio of production value in relation to concentration, and those that had been winning market share vis-à-vis the state and foreign players in the run-up to reform.

The first part of the chapter introduces a brief description of the political and economic context of adjustment in both countries and provides a description of a common antecedent condition: the relative low specialization of domestic industrial production. Next, the chapter delves into the conceptualization of each national mode of restructuring. The final part analyzes the causal origins of each mode. This is done in two steps. First, I analyze the alternative trajectories of state and private industrial groups under ISI. Subsequently, I lay out an explanation of the liberalization period based on interviews of key actors and on descriptive statistics that assess the economic power of domestic, foreign, and state industrial players at the outset of reform.

SPAIN IN THE 1980S AND ARGENTINA IN THE 1990S: MACROECONOMIC AND STRUCTURAL REFORMS

The Spanish Socialist Workers' Party (PSOE) took power in 1982 in the midst of a serious economic crisis. The second oil shock had hit the country hard, inflation was on the rise, and the political weakness of the center-Right government had postponed indispensable adjustment. In spite of the timid liberalization policies carried out by the Franco regime, the country's economy was still quite closed, and the state companies played an important role in the sectors of public utilities, banking, and industry, boosting an increasingly worrisome fiscal deficit. In 1980 Spain had the lowest rate of trade as a percentage of gross domestic product (GDP) in all of Western Europe. In a dramatic change in the traditional positions of the party, the PSOE chose what many labeled a neoliberal program. As a result of monetary and fiscal adjustment policies, inflation fell as wages decreased in real terms, the current account deficit was curbed, and business confidence was reflected in increasing levels of investment (Lieberman 1995: 278). Furthermore, the country began to reduce tariff barriers with the aim of joining the European Union (at the time the European Community) in 1986. Likewise, the goal of full integration into the EU implied that the real exchange rate could not diverge extremely vis-à-vis other European currencies and, ultimately, drove Spain to join the European Monetary System in 1989. The PSOE fundamentally stuck to a policy of monetary restraint and a pro-market orientation until it lost power in 1996 (Recio and Roca 1998: 141, Bermeo 1994).

The policy shift carried out by the Argentine Peronist or Justicialista Party (PJ), the archetype of a populist party in Latin America, was no less surprising than the Spanish Socialists' U-turn. Menem took office in 1989 in the midst of a hyperinflationary spiral and therefore did not have much room for maneuver. In an initial

Compensating Business Insiders

context of macroeconomic instability, the government did not hesitate to deepen liberalization by lifting capital and exchange controls. In March 1991, the recently appointed economy minister, Domingo Cavallo, launched the "Convertibility Plan." Congress fixed the exchange rate at one to one relative to the dollar. The convertibility law also required the monetary base to match the amount of foreign reserves in the Central Bank. This feature of the scheme, that is, the government's self-imposed constraints on economic policy, was geared toward creating business confidence (Gerchunoff and Torre 1996, Palermo and Novaro 1996: 288). The process of economic integration with Brazil, Uruguay, and Paraguay in the context of MERCOSUR, formalized in the Ouro Preto Agreement of 1994, further deepened the liberalization trend. As in the Spanish case, after successful stabilization the country experienced a period of sustained growth: GDP grew at an average rate of 7.6% between 1991 and 1994. After the Mexican crisis of 1995, the country resumed growth, albeit at a slower pace, during 1996 and 1997, only to succumb to recession in the last two years of the Menem presidency. By 1999, however, most structural market reforms had been accomplished, and the vast majority of Argentine public enterprises had been transferred to private hands.

THE INDUSTRIAL SECTOR: LOW SPECIALIZATION AND THE LIBERALIZATION CHALLENGE

It is worth noting that by the late 1970s, before neoliberalism, the Spanish manufacturing sector[2] was structurally closer to that of the major Latin American countries than to that of the East Asian Newly Industrialized Countries (NICs). In the first place, as argued in the Overview, it had not reached a stage of sustained Export Oriented Industrialization (EOI). Second, as the major Latin American countries had, Spain had integrated into the world economic system through the inflow of massive amounts of Foreign Direct Investment (FDI) and through the establishment of Trans National Corporations (TNCs) seeking protected markets. The East Asian NICs, by contrast, had integrated into the world economy through direct U.S. aid and extended domestic export promotion.[3] Third, as Argentina did at the outset of liberalization, Spain concentrated its manufacturing production in primary and secondary ISI sectors of low and medium technology.[4]

---

[2] Unless otherwise stated, I use the terms "manufacturing," "manufacturing industry," and "industry" interchangeably, to refer to the economic activities included in the manufacturing section of the International Standard Industrial Classification of All Economic Activities (ISIC), Third Revision, plus petroleum production (which, unlike petroleum refining, the ISIC lists under "mining").

[3] See Ellison and Gereffi (1990: 372); for comparisons between industrialization trajectories of East Asia and Latin America see Evans (1987) and Haggard (1990).

[4] Both prereform Argentina (1990) and Spain (1980) concentrated around 60% of their value added in industrial production in what the United Nations Industrial Development Organization (UNIDO) considers low-technology industries such as the food industry, industrial commodities such as steel and oil, and textiles, and produced almost the same share of value added (22% and 23%, respectively) in medium-technology industries such as chemicals, petrochemicals, and transport equipment, against 26% in Brazil by 1990 (data from UNIDO 1997).

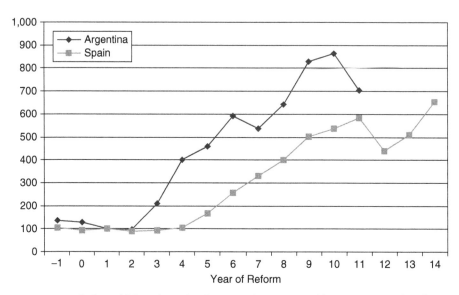

GRAPH 3.1. Index of Manufacturing Imports (in current US$); First Year of Reform Government = 100 (Year 1: Spain 1982, Argentina 1989). *Source*: Elaborated from World Development Indicators Database, World Bank.

The rise of manufacturing imports during the restructuring period was impressive in both countries (Graph 3.1). In Argentina, industrial imports in dollar terms increased by almost 900% during the Menem administration, boosted by both the increasingly overvalued exchange rate set by the currency board and general tariff deregulation. In Spain, the fifth year of the Socialist government in the graph, 1986, shows an increase that signals Spain's integration into the European Community. Integration into the EU and the initial overvaluation of the peseta, sustained in order to join the European Monetary System in 1989, resulted in an increase in imports of almost 700% during the Socialist administration.

STATIST AND CORPORATIST MODELS OF INDUSTRIAL ADJUSTMENT

Industrial sectors with low specialization and sheltered from international competition were strongly challenged by the imperatives of economic liberalization, tariff deregulation, and exchange rate appreciation in both Argentina and Spain. How would these democratically elected governments cope with the dire consequences of this phenomenal increase in foreign competition for established industrial firms? Their adjustment paths differed fundamentally in two respects: the nature of the policymaking process and the patterns of compensation targeted at industrial firms.

Spain's Statist Business Restructuring: *Dirigisme* from Above and Subsidy Compensation

In Spain the government designed a series of sectoral and subsectoral reconversion plans over which the private business sector had relatively little leverage. In this Statist path, moreover, the government resorted to alternative types of subsidies aimed at updating the firm and/or funding mergers and plant closures and financing layoffs as its principal compensatory policy.

The Nature of the Policymaking Process: Dirigisme *and Decentralized Bargaining*

In 1984 the PSOE passed the law Reconversion and Reindustrialization, which empowered the government to administer a variety of financial and monetary subsidies to industrial firms and to sponsor labor relocation programs for laid-off workers. Two mechanisms put forward by this law are crucial for understanding the dynamics of industrial business restructuring in Spain. First, the Ministry of Industry designed a series of reconversion plans in sectors considered "strategic" and submitted them for approval to the Cabinet Commission for Economic Affairs (Comisión Delegada de Gobierno para Asuntos Económicos) composed of representatives of the Ministries of Finance, Commerce, Industry, and Labor. The commission analyzed the plan and, if it was accepted, declared the sector "under reconversion." Second, the law created two types of institutions that governed the implementation of the sectoral plans, the Gerencias and the Reconversion Societies (Sociedades de Reconversión). The Gerencia (Management Office) was a state agency created for the specific industrial sector declared to be under reconversion. Its main goals were to administer subsidies to firms and monitor the way firms used those resources. In the case of the Reconversion Societies, the government promoted joint ventures between private enterprises (or between private companies and the state) in order to increase efficiency, set the basis for future mergers, and administer the subsidies received from the government.

After 1984 the Socialist government decisively pushed forward restructuring in the sectors of steel (in the three subsectors of integrated steel, common steel, and special steel), shipbuilding, home appliances, and chemicals (fertilizers). These sectors constituted what the foremost analyst of industrial reconversion in Spain, Mikel Navarro (1990: 118), has called the "core" of industrial restructuring in terms of both productive capacity and employment.[5] The administration issued a decree that governed restructuring in each sector declared "under reconversion." Even though most of the Spanish auto sector was internationalized and profitable by 1983 – and, therefore, was not included under a "reconversion plan" – the state-owned auto company, SEAT, the largest automaker in

---

[5] Good overviews of Spanish industrial performance and restructuring since the early 1980s are F. Maravall and Fanjul (1987), Segura and Gonzáles Romero (1993), Castañer (1998), and Smith (1998).

Spain, had its own reconversion plan. In practice, capacity cuts and state-induced workforce adjustment rounds in sectors such as shipbuilding, autos, and steel continued until the end of the Socialist period in 1996.

The participation of private social actors in the *formulation* of the sectoral reconversion plans was limited.[6] In fact, the plans were designed by state officials in the Ministry of Industry in the case of the smaller sectors, and through the Gerencias[7] and Reconversion Societies in the larger ones. As Navarro (1990: 128) puts it, this strategy of "non-concertation" often intensified the opposition of social actors. The participation of business and union organizations in the *implementation* of the plans was, however, formally instituted by Law 27/84 in the Control Commission of the Sectoral Plans. This commission was to receive periodic reports from the Gerencias and Reconversion Societies. Yet, the law mandated that, in order to join a Control Commission, unions and business organizations had to consent previously to the sectoral plan designed by state officials.[8] At a lower (i.e., decentralized) or firm level, participation of social actors took place through day-to-day negotiations between the technical organs of implementation and business and labor groups. In the case of business, even if there was no major push to nationalization or formal ownership control, the state was, in practice, in charge of the management of most of the firms and sectors under reconversion plans.

Moreover, unlike in Argentina, privatization – which would only take off after the end of the Socialist period in 1996 – was not geared to boost certain domestic industrial conglomerates in the context of market restructuring and international economic integration. Rather, the government sought to empower the most efficient state companies, especially in the energy sector (oil, natural gas, and electricity). It then developed a strategy of sequential privatization, through which the government floated stock gradually that would be generally acquired by domestic banks and institutional investors. Sequential privatization, in addition to the golden share mechanism, would largely preserve decision making in the local economy despite state disinvestment and would be completed by the Popular Party (PP) center-right government after 1996 (see Etchemendy 2004a).

---

[6] Though the Reconversion Law formally authorized the government to consult unions and businesses involved, in practice it did not require the consent of social actors to declare a sector under reconversion and formulate an adjustment plan (see Navarro 1990: 130). With respect to the peak national business confederation CEOE, Minister of Industry Luis Carlos Croissier (1984–88) stated: "The CEOE followed reconversion from behind.... It was not that they were opposed, but they were not enthusiastic either. They would not push to make the reconversion." Author's interview, Madrid, October 10, 2001.

[7] "The Gerencia monitored the way funds were used; it carried out technical controls over the firms and elaborated constant sectoral reports ... it was our 'armed' division in the reconversion process." Author's interview with Fernando Sánchez Junco, former general director of industry at the Ministry of Industry (1984–89), Madrid, October 15, 2001.

[8] "The Control Commission was a sort of small parliament; everyone talked there, but the major decisions were taken at the Ministry of Industry." Author's interview with Sánchez Junco, ibid.

Compensating Business Insiders

In sum, the Socialist strategy for industrial liberalization was twofold. First, the government plans would generally result (through successive mergers and state takeovers) in the creation of big public groups in each sector. By the early 1990s the state groups CSI-Aceralia (integrated steel), SIDENOR (special steels), IZAR (shipbuilding), INESPAL (aluminum), INDRA (information technology), Tabacalera and ENDIASA (agro industry and food), ENCE (pulp and paper), Repsol (oil), ENDESA (electricity), ENFERSA (fertilizers), and CASA (aviation and defense electronics) consolidated and encompassed most or all firms in their sectors. Second, the Ministry of Industry and the INI decided to sell those revamped companies or groups in which they saw no potential for international competition to foreign TNCs – such was the case of steel, aluminum, autos, and home appliances. In other cases – oil and natural gas, electricity, electronics, pulp and paper – officials would follow the strategy of sequential privatization through stock offers that largely preserved, as noted previously, government leverage and domestic decision making.

The case studies in the next chapter will show how the established private industrial class was finally displaced in the pivotal sectors of steel and shipbuilding. Local firms also faded away in other important ISI sectors subjected to restructuring, including chemicals, home appliances, and electronics. In the case of home appliances, under successive restructuring plans the production of eighteen local firms (about 80% of the sector) was concentrated in three Reconversion Societies: Balay-Safel, the Glibsa group based in Catalonia, and Gruvesa, which incorporated the main Basque firms in the sector. The first two were finally sold to the multinationals Bosch-Siemens and Electrolux, respectively, in the midst of the restructuring process. Those takeovers were induced by the government, which held a prominent role in the negotiations (Navarro 1990: 221). The largest Spanish private ISI groups, AHV and Explosivos Río Tinto (ERT), based on steel and chemicals and petrochemicals, respectively, were dismembered and their units sold, mostly to multinationals (De Quinto 1994: 74, Guillén 2001: 88).

The Compensatory Policies

The crucial tool of state intervention in the reconversion process was the system of subsidies put in place by Law 27/84. The Spanish government implemented the three types of subsidies mentioned in the typology of compensation constructed in Chapter 2: financial, direct cash transfers, and tax exemptions.

1. Financial subsidies: Loans at below-market interest rates were channeled by the state bank BCI (Bank for Industrial Credit). In some cases the state also bailed out private debts with public credit institutions.
2. Direct cash transfers: These were subsidies that flowed from the state budget. They were used for the firm's capitalization, for direct investments, and for financing workers' compensation and severance payments. Capital infusions by the National Industrial Institute (INI), the national holding of state-owned industrial companies, to its own firms was an important form of direct subsidy.

62   *The Political Economy of Business Adjustment*

3. Tax exemptions: These were applied both to social security payments and in the case of mergers or acquisition of industrial firms. Tax exemptions were also provided for investment or for firms' capitalization processes and applied to both the firms under reconversion and new investments located in the so-called Areas of Urgent Re-Industrialization.

The quantification of business compensation in Spain is not an easy task. The first reason for this is that the data from the Ministry of Industry do not establish what part of public aid went to the company or to labor compensation. Nor do the data include a quantification of the compensation through tax exemptions. Plus, the Ministry of Industry ceased to publish data on direct subsidies and public credits in the annual *Informe Sobre la Industria Española* (Report on Spanish Industry) after Spain's integration into the EU in 1987. The ministry, however, published data on investment in the firms undergoing reconversion. The fact that almost all of the investment by firms under restructuring was from public aid[9] provides a good way to check the portion of subsidies that were channeled to the firms but *not* used for labor compensation. If we consider the period 1982–91, total investment reached 793,870 million pesetas (around $7.6 billion).[10]

Argentina's Corporatist Business Restructuring: Selective Concertation and Market-Share Compensation

Unlike in the Statist path, in the Argentine Corporatist model, no encompassing plan for restructuring was designed concurrently with trade reform and general deregulation in the industrial sector. Yet certain groups of firms did get to the bargaining table and managed to wield substantial leverage over the policies governing liberalization in their respective sectors. The government was willing to compensate certain industrial groups through two principal means: protectionist/partial deregulation and the awarding of state assets.

The Nature of the Policymaking Process: Selective Concertation

I use the label *Corporatist* to characterize the Argentine industrial adjustment pattern, because it conveys two ideas frequently associated with the concept. First, the term reminds us that access to the locus of public policy is unequal, and that only some actors in the sphere of production are represented. Second, Corporatism has often been associated with a strong degree of participation by private interests in policy formulation (see Collier 1995, Schmitter 1982). In Argentina, the design of deregulatory policies for certain industrial sectors was crafted with private interests (both labor and business) at the bargaining table,

---

[9] This fact was confirmed in my interviews with public officials and businessmen. These numbers, however, do not include the business rationalization processes carried out outside formal reconversion plans.

[10] Ministry of Industry, *Informe Sobre la Industria Española* (1987, 1990, and 1991).

Compensating Business Insiders

indicating a pattern of policymaking that entailed either informal or formal concertation with economic actors.

Soon after taking office in 1989, the Menem government passed legislation that brought an end to the system of sectoral subsidies and promotional regimes that had constituted the core of Argentine protected capitalism (Gerchunoff and Torre 1996: 736; see also Acuña 1994) and plunged ahead with major commercial liberalization. At the same time, the State Reform Law set the basis for a vast privatization process. In this "disarticulated restructuring" (Kosacoff 1995), firms in seven major tradable sectors clearly benefited from compensatory measures: petroleum, steel, autos, aluminum, cement, petrochemicals, and pharmaceuticals. Except for the petrochemical sector (which will be studied in Chapter 5), all main groups and firms in these sectors were rewarded with market-share compensation.

Liberalization in these industries was negotiated with business. Of course, the Spanish Statist case also involves negotiation to some extent – in both the Statist and Corporatist models the government deals with, and compensates, business insiders. Yet in Argentina, (1) there was no prior general state industrial strategy of reconversion, (2) the private economic firms and groups in the compensated sectors enjoyed comparatively more leverage over the formulation of the deregulatory frames, and (3) generally the compensatory measures emerged as a pressure from below rather than as a previous policy initiative.

Autos and petroleum were the most eloquent cases of economic deregulation policies crafted in tripartite tables formed by state, business, and labor. The auto sector was favored by a special tariff/reconversion regime that was formally bargained with the business association and the sectoral union in a committee created by decree after the main firms and labor united to lobby the government. In the case of the oil sector, the two series of measures that overhauled the industry, the deregulation decrees of late 1989 and the reconversion of the established private companies' service contracts of oil extraction into new concessions, were drafted in negotiation with affected business and union leaders.[11] In the case of steel, aluminum, cement, and pharmaceuticals the pattern of negotiation was more bilateral (between state and business), ongoing, and informal. The steel-based domestic group Techint was involved in the design of the privatization of the main Argentina steel mill from its early stages. The dynamics of deregulation and compensation to business insiders in autos, steel, and oil will be more closely studied in Chapter 4 as paradigmatic cases of Corporatist adjustment.

The cement-based local groups obtained nontariff barriers that severely limited the opening of the industry in June 1991. According to one journalistic

---

[11] For example, Alberto Fiandesio, adviser to the secretary of energy and government representative in the committee that bargained with private oil contractors, stated, "We worked in conjunction with firms and the union, and all members of the commission agreed that the old contracts had to be revamped." Author's interview, Buenos Aires, November 13, 2000. These negotiations and the compensatory arrangements involved will be more closely analyzed in Chapter 4.

account, Loma Negra, the main domestic producer in the sector, "participated directly in the creation of the norm."[12] Aluar (owned by the Madanes family group), the single aluminum producer in the country, was particularly threatened by the eventual privatization of the Futaleufú dam, which had historically provided its major plant in Patagonia with energy at subsidized prices – electricity is by far the main component of the cost equation in the manufacturing of aluminum. With the advent of general deregulation and privatization Aluar's contract for cheap energy supply was put into question. Haroldo Grisanti, at the time the chair of Agua y Energía, the state company that owned Futaleufú, stated that "if Aluar had to pay electricity at market prices it would be straight out of the market."[13] One observer of the industry considered that "with the energy subsidy terminated by privatization, the future of the company is black."[14] Accordingly, business executives from Aluar openly manifested their interest in Futaleufú. Since 1992, the company had deployed extensive lobbying and was finally awarded the control of the dam.[15] Despite the fact that two other companies presented bids, it was clear to observers in the industry that the privatization was targeted to the domestic group Madanes.

Market reform also threatened the three main pillars of the domestic pharmaceutical industry under ISI. First, in 1990–91 the government liberalized imports of pharmaceutical products, and international competition eventually heightened with the launching of MERCOSUR in 1994 (Burachik and Katz 1997: 107–08). Second, the Ministry of Health simplified and deregulated the procedures for administrative approval of new pharmaceutical products – a long and cherished demand of multinational pharmaceutical companies in Argentina. Third, and most importantly, in the context of the neoliberal policy U-turn and the international alliance with the United States, Cavallo's economic team pledged to comply with the international obligations of the WTO regarding intellectual property, the Trade Related Aspects of Intellectual Property Rights (TRIPS). In Argentina the absence of a patent regime for pharmaceutical products had traditionally benefited the local industry, which could freely produce and import versions of new drugs patented in the advanced world. Indeed, a report from the conservative think tank FIEL stated in 1990 that the granting of patent protection to pharmaceutical products in Argentina was "expected to generate an increase in the market share of foreign companies in detriment to local industry" (FIEL 1990: 80).[16]

In 1993 the government submitted to Congress a patent bill that contemplated the main requisites of TRIPS. After complicated negotiations, however,

---

[12] *Página 12*, June 15, 1991.

[13] *La Nación*, March 15, 1993.

[14] *La Nación*, March 15, 1993. Likewise, the economic newspaper *El Cronista Comercial* asked: "What would happen with Aluar if it loses Futaleufú?" (October 27, 1992).

[15] See *El Economista*, March 27, 1992; *Página, 12* September 18, 1992; *Ámbito Financiero*, August 6, 1993.

[16] In other words, local companies would be limited to the manufacturing and marketing of products for which no patent exists, or for which the patent had already expired (FIEL 1990: 75).

Compensating Business Insiders

and in view of the extensive lobbying deployed by CILFA (the chamber of local pharmaceutical producers), a watered-down version of the intellectual property regime was finally passed by Congress in 1996.[17] The implementation of intellectual property reform in Argentina constituted a clear case of partial deregulation benefiting business insiders: the practical beginning of the new regime was delayed until 2001 (10 years after the initial commitment, and later than in any other Latin American country), the law established broad transition periods for new patent enforcements, local firms were allowed to develop generic versions of drugs prior to patent expiry, and domestic generic producers could obtain administrative approval without costly clinical trials (Shadlen 2006: 30). In the words of Ken Shadlen (2006: 29), "Argentina implemented its TRIPS obligations in such a way to give the local pharmaceutical sector time to adjust and legal space to thrive."[18]

The Compensatory Policies

Except for the petrochemical sector analyzed in Chapter 5, the government compensated domestic industrial groups with market-share compensation, that is, the direct awarding of state assets and partial deregulation (Table 3.2). First, the local private groups dominant in these industries – especially in oil, autos, cement, and steel – obtained participation in the privatization of services, mostly telecoms and utilities. In these cases domestic groups did not get operating control and would eventually sell their stakes to foreign groups on advantageous terms.

Most importantly, privatization in certain industrial sectors in which domestic business holdings were based or in industries that were vital suppliers to the local economic groups consisted in a more or less direct awarding of controlling stakes. Open bids were rare and, when implemented, generally biased in favor of domestic producers. Domestic oil companies were favored with central production areas and oil refining facilities. The main private steel group obtained the country's largest state mill. In the case of aluminum, as noted, the domestic hegemonic producer, the Aluar group, was granted the control of the dam, and of the electricity transportation network, that supplied its vital energy input. Finally, Loma Negra – the cement group – won without competition Ferrosur Pampeano, the cargo railway of the southern part of the province of Buenos Aires and northern Patagonia, which enabled the company to significantly

---

[17] Admittedly, in the case of pharmaceuticals the government was more divided than in the compensation bargains with other industries: Minister of Economy Cavallo was aligned with the U.S. and TNC demands for strong intellectual property enforcement. The Justicialista or Peronist Party (PJ) legislative group, by contrast, echoed the position of local producers, who actually fought in diverse arenas. President Menem initially pushed for a patent law along with Cavallo but later acceded to the final passage of a diluted version of the reform. One analyst of the pharmaceutical industry argued that "one can conclude that the strategy of President Menem, despite his declared alliance with the US, was to forestall real change" (Irigoyen 2006: 430).

[18] The United States actually objected to the new legislation before the World Trade Organization (WTO) and retaliated by curtailing trade privileges of Argentine products; see Irigoyen (2006: 395).

66   *The Political Economy of Business Adjustment*

TABLE 3.2. *Market-Share Compensation in Argentina: Sectors and Main Firms/Groups*

Sectors and Main Business Groups Compensated	Market-Share Compensation	
	State Assets (most important)	Partial Deregulation
Steel Techint and Acindar Groups	• Minority Stake in Telefónica (telecom, Techint) • Control of State Mill SOMISA (Techint)	• Strong Antidumping Measures
Autos Macri and Ciadea Groups	• Road Tolls and Maintenance, Natural Gas Distribution (Macri)	• Special Tariff Regime for Auto Sector
Oil Pérez Companc, Astra, and Bridas Groups	• Minority Stake in Telecom (telecom, P. Companc) • Minority Stake in Edenor (electricity, Astra) • Minority Stake in Edesur and half of Transener (electricity high-tension network P. Companc) • San Lorenzo Refinery (Pérez Companc) • Central and Periphery Oil Fields	• Partial Deregulation of Service Contracts of Oil Extraction
Aluminum Aluar-Madanes Group	• Electricity Dam Futaleufú • Transpa Electricity Distribution Network (joint control)	
Pharmaceuticals Bago and Roemmers Groups		• Partial/Delayed Deregulation of Intellectual Property Law
Cement Fortabat Group	• Control of Ferrosur Pampeano (cargo railway in southern Buenos Aires and Patagonia)	• Nontariff Barriers to imports

improve interconnectedness among its plants and between them and lucrative ports.

Second, protectionist deregulation took different modalities: the establishment of a differential tariff regime (autos, cement), the partial deregulation of the service contracts of oil extraction with the state (oil), and the enactment of antidumping measures that consistently attenuated the opening of the sector (steel). The local pharmaceutical industry benefited from the partial and diluted reform of the intellectual property law. All of these measures are forms of partial deregulation systematized in Chapter 2 and were underpinned by the same goal: to secure market reserves to traditional producers in the newly open economy.

Compensating Business Insiders

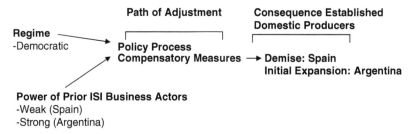

FIGURE 3.1. A Stylized Causal Assessment of Industrial Restructuring in Argentina and Spain.

EXPLAINING THE OUTCOME: REGIME AND POWER OF PRIOR ISI BUSINESS ACTORS

This study argues that the two most important factors that explain the variation in business adjustment models in the Iberian-American world, in terms of both the policymaking strategies and the actors compensated, are the type of regime and the nature and power of business and state actors that surged after decades of Import Substitution Industrialization (Figure 3.1). The next sections spell out the logic of this argument for the cases of Argentina and Spain.

Democracy and Compensation to Business ISI Insiders

The *regime question*, or whether a government was democratic and the level of state repression, was a central concern in explanations of alternative economic and development strategies in developing countries in the 1970s and 1980s. In general, authoritarian regimes were associated with orthodox policy recipes in Latin America (O'Donnell 1973, Sheahan 1987, Pion-Berlin 1989) and with the effective performance of state-led models of growth in East Asia (Johnson 1987, Haggard 1990). Yet, toward the mid-1990s, the regime question slowly disappeared from the debate on the political determinants of economic policy in the developing world as most countries, whether fully democratic or not, substantially liberalized the economy and converged in certain areas of macroeconomic policy. Indeed, the regime may be irrelevant to assess whether or not a country reoriented its economy outward. This book argues, however, that it is decisive to understanding the type of adjustment path that eventually unfolds.

Two points should be stressed regarding business adjustment and the regime question. First, democracy obviously alters the time horizons of politicians, broadens the repertoires of action of formerly protected business, and delimits which adjustment measures are plausible: massive layoffs are a sensitive issue for any democratic government, a fact that may favor certain business lobbying for state aid to prevent bankruptcies. Though subordinated to state plans, many steelmakers, electronics producers, or shipbuilders in Spain knew that an elected government could not simply let their sectors fall in a context of massive

68   *The Political Economy of Business Adjustment*

unemployment and separatist turbulence in the regions subjected to industrial restructuring.[19] Likewise, the capacity of certain industrial firms to modify initial projects of deregulation in Argentina was undoubtedly facilitated by the democratic context. For example, as will be analyzed in Chapter 4, Argentine oil contractors lobbied successfully in different state arenas to preserve their old (prereform) service contracts in the liberalized market. When asked why a government pressed for financial resources would not revoke the contracts and call for new auctions for those oil fields, a top official of the Argentine secretary of energy at the time replied:

And do you believe that Pérez Companc [the main domestic producer affected] would have stayed with its arms folded? They would have sued the government; they would have talked to the union to promote an upheaval. This was not only a technical issue, it was political and you had to know how to deal with that.[20]

Whatever the actual results of the business pressure through the legislature, the regional governments, or the courts in Argentina and Spain, it is quite evident that, ceteris paribus, such avenues will be more "available" under a democracy. The massive and successful lobbying that the Argentine pharmaceutical industry deployed in the advent of the patent regime reform initially sponsored by the neoliberal government and multinational companies, which had Congress as its main battleground, would certainly be more difficult to stage in an authoritarian regime.

The second point to be underlined is that when one studies economic liberalization through the lens of compensatory policies, the regime question is decisive for assessing *which* actors are *more* compensated by the adjusting government. A democratic regime increases the political potential of those losers from market reform who have more resources to organize and pressure the state. Even though protected industrial groups are perhaps not leading members of the new market reform coalition, they will use their power to lobby for compensatory measures. In short, the policymaking process that defines Corporatist and Statist industrial liberalization, which includes the participation of affected business (whether as central lobbyists and policy designers, as in Argentina, or mainly restricted to negotiating modalities of implementation, as in Spain), is much more likely to emerge under democratic rule. In these cases some industrial firms and certain segments of the organized working class received the lion's share of compensatory policies. Small business and the atomized mass of unemployed or informal sector workers were relatively much less favored under democratic

---

[19] The view of the former minister of industry and of economy Carlos Solchaga (1983–93) is illustrative of the way in which democracy conditions industrial restructuring even in the context of a strongly top-down and Statist reform such as the Spanish: "We did not accomplish what a rational and economic analysis would have indicated. In the end you could get where you could get. For example, I would have closed down more shipyards that were in the Basque Country, but I could not because there the [Basque] nationalists were governing, or in Andalucía, but there the problem was that our own party was in power." Author's interview, Madrid, October 8, 2001.

[20] Author's interview, Buenos Aires, December 17, 2000.

Compensating Business Insiders

neoliberalism. Still, while democracy opens the door to compensation for business insiders, *the specific groups of firms targeted* and *the type of compensation* will be severely conditioned by the organizational and economic condition of these companies and economic groups as they emerge from the old order.

Power of ISI Business Actors and Patterns of Industrial Adjustment

Antecedent Conditions: The Making of Strong and Weak ISI Business Actors in Argentina and Spain

As argued previously, the industrial structures of Argentina and Spain shared many similarities at the outset of reform. Moreover, the instruments of industrial protection and promotion developed after World War II in both countries did not differ greatly: tariffs, tax exemptions and rebates, administrative procedures declaring sectors of "national interest," and so forth. This section will show, however, that the inward-oriented model gave birth to very different constellations of industrial interests in both countries.

SPAIN: THE SUBORDINATION OF THE INDUSTRIAL BOURGEOISIE UNDER ISI. The remaking of the Spanish business class in the postwar period cannot be understood without considering the Franco victory of 1939. The emerging business class would combine the traditional financial sector and scattered industrialists with a new powerful actor, the National Industrial Institute (INI), the military-led holding for industrial production. The Franco regime set up the INI in the aftermath of the civil war. The importance of the INI in the postwar industrial trajectory of Spain cannot be overstated. It was more than a Gerschenkronian instrument of late industrialization and would survive comfortably the regime's initial autarchic and fascist stage. Its first president (1941–63) and mentor, Juan Carlos Suanzes, a military engineer, was a longtime friend of Franco and very close to the dictator. Until 1968 the INI reported directly to the presidency and not to any ministry, a fact that helped enhance the power of its very centralized bureaucratic structure.[21] In an economy in which the size of the public sector lagged well behind that of the rest of Europe, the INI's extensive penetration in the industrial sector was striking. INI went so far as developing everything from food products, textiles, and paper to trucks, ships, steel, energy (oil and electricity), aviation, and even tourism companies.

Two crucial features of the development of the INI in prereform Spain should be emphasized for the purpose of this study. First, from the outset the INI acted as an effective counterbalance to the power of the private sector in the industrial realm. Both the ambition of the influential Spanish banking sector to extend its participation into industrial production and the development of more autonomous industrial private interests were hampered by the INI bureaucracy and its military leadership. The creation of SEAT, the state-run automaker that would come to dominate the production of commercial vehicles in Spain, is an

---

[21] On the origins and evolution of the INI two crucial sources are Martín Aceña and Comín (1991) and San Román (1999).

eloquent example in this respect. Twice in the aftermath of the war, the traditional bank Urquijo attempted to form a joint venture with the Italian Fiat in order to launch a big plant that would upgrade the meager local car production. However, both of these attempts were blocked by the INI, which in the end formed the joint venture with Fiat by itself (San Román 1999: 236–46). This dynamic of conflict and accommodation between the INI and bank-controlled and industrial private companies would likewise arise in other industrial sectors such as fertilizers, steel, and oil.[22] In brief, as Moya (1994) suggests, only the military through their new bureaucratic organization were able to challenge the capitalist class coalition upon which the 1939 victory against the republic was based.

The second important feature of the INI is that its influence in Spanish industrial production lasted until the beginning of full-scale liberalization in the 1980s. Although the "autarchic" stage of Spanish industrialization (1939–59) was the golden age of the INI, its role in the production realm did not wane with the incipient liberalization of the 1960s. In 1959, the dictatorship implemented a stabilization plan, unified exchange rates, declared the convertibility of the peseta, and joined the IMF and the World Bank. However, there is wide agreement among analysts (Anderson 1970: 236–38; González 1979: 320–30; Martín Aceña and Comín 1991: 318–28) that trade liberalization policies were rolled back by the mid-1960s, and that interventionism and industrial protection resumed (and even increased) hand in hand with a renewed role for the INI. In effect, during the 1960s the government launched a series of development plans modeled on the French Indicative Plans, the goal of which was boosting production in some heavy industries such as shipbuilding, steel, and chemicals. The participation of INI-affiliated firms in the sectoral plans, called "concerted actions" (acciones concertadas), was decisive (Martín Aceña and Comín 1991: 328).

Parallel to the development plans, major TNCs landed on Spanish soil as a result of liberalization policies, particularly in the auto and chemical sectors. The pressures stemming from state production and renewed external competition, combined with the oil crises of the 1970s – which severely affected an oil-dependent country such as Spain – constituted a final blow for the local private industrial sector. In the context of the crisis, domestic banks began cautiously to pull out of the major industrial companies, whose CEOs were left alone, struggling with faltering results.[23] By the beginning of the reform period in the 1980s, the INI was the largest Spanish nonfinancial business group in terms of sales,

---

[22] The conflicts between the INI and private banking and industrial interests are well documented in the literature, yet their implications for the configuration of the Spanish industrial class in comparative perspective are not quite developed. See, for example, Martín Aceña and Comín (1991), San Román (1999), Cabrera and Del Rey (2002), and the early study of Tamames (1966).

[23] As a percentage of deposits, industrial financial holdings went from 33% in 1975 to 14% in 1984 (Blanch 1991: 228).

Compensating Business Insiders

including both domestic and foreign companies (García Hermoso 1990: 202).[24] In short, neither listed domestic corporations (essentially controlled by management as a result of atomized ownership) nor family business – that is, the two forms of a modern bourgeoisie – could take hold as powerful actors in the Spanish postwar industrial landscape. The state and the foreign TNCs became the dominant industrial players.

ARGENTINA: THE CONSOLIDATION OF THE INDUSTRIAL BOURGEOISIE UNDER ISI. The industrial trajectory of postwar Argentina, by contrast, witnessed the slow rise to a hegemonic position of a group of local, industry-based conglomerates, independent in their ownership structures of both the financial sector and the state. Unlike the Spanish case, however, foreign companies, not the state, were the main protagonists of the initial industrial deepening to consumer durables and capital and intermediate goods. From 1958 to 1962, President Frondizi's developmentalist policies attracted major world TNCs. Postwar state participation in industrial production was rather limited from the outset and would focus mainly on the oil business through the state monopoly YPF, and on the steel and petrochemical sectors through the military-run companies. Indeed, unlike the more state-led (and less redistributive) development models of Spain and Chile, Peronist populism – which governed between 1946 and 1955 – focused on the more labor-inclusive ISI industries such as textiles, food, or simple metals and did not undertake a massive expansion of the state in basic industries.[25]

This trend toward the predominance of foreign production in the more value-added ISI sectors of intermediate goods and consumer durables would be, nonetheless, reversed after the early 1970s. The relative eclipse of foreign industrial production and the concurrent rise of a group of domestic-owned industrial holdings had multiple origins. First, the more nationalistic industrial policies of the military dictatorship of 1966–73 began to displace foreign companies in certain sectors, particularly after 1969.[26] Less liberal than their peers who had ousted Perón in 1955, the 1960s generals launched a National Development Plan, which supported intermediate sectors such as chemicals, oil, and steel. The plan included multiple forms of protection as well as a preeminent and renewed role of domestic private business in capital formation.

The second of the major forces behind the rise of the main local industrial groups were the policies of the 1976–83 dictatorship. The so-called Industrial

---

[24] Guillén (2001) insightfully points out the absence of Latin American–style business groups in Spain. My argument, however, stresses the sectoral dimension. Economic groups with stakes in various firms did flourish in prereform Spain but were concentrated in the financial and energy sectors. Moreover, the weakness of local capital in industry cannot be understood without considering the role of the state in the industrial realm.

[25] The slow progress of state steel production in Argentina is a good example of this trend. The construction of the first large plant was initiated in 1947 and finished 14 years later; see Schwarzer (1996: 207–10).

[26] This shift is well described in Chapter 6 of Schwarzer's (1996) book.

Promotion Regime sanctioned in late 1973 but largely implemented after 1977 formalized state support for some core ISI sectors and, more importantly, prioritized the role of domestic capital vis-à-vis foreign production. The regime provided tariff-free imports of inputs and capital goods and a variety of tax exemptions and restrictions against competing imports. In theory, the promotional regime enacted in 1977 would be in place for up to ten years but, in practice, was extended until the liberalization period began in the 1990s.[27] The promotional regime, together with generous service contracts granted by the state (especially in the areas of petroleum and construction), helped consolidate the position of a relatively small number of large domestic groups in heavy industrial sectors. Moreover, the policies of tariff and financial liberalization pushed forward by the dictatorship provoked the decline of FDI inflows to the industrial sector and underpinned the expansion of local big business in industry (Azpiazu and Kosacoff 1989: 167–69). Finally, political instability and leftist radicalization oddly helped to consolidate the position of the major Argentine business groups. In effect, some TNCs left the country in the context of guerrilla warfare and the expansion of workers' base-level movements during the 1973–76 Peronist government.[28] In stark contrast to the Spanish case, foreign TNCs' participation in manufacturing did not increase during the preadjustment years (Azpiazu and Kosacoff 1989: 207).

In sum, despite exchange rate and liberalization policies during the dictatorship (reversed in the early 1980s), by the mid-1980s, this handful of local business groups had become hegemonic players in many industries.[29] Most of them based their production on intermediate goods and consumer durables: Techint and Acindar (steel); Astra, Bridas, and Pérez Companc (oil); Garovaglio and Richards (petrochemicals); Fortabat (cement); Madanes (aluminum); SOCMA and CIADEA (autos). Although some had traded a percentage of shares in the Stock Exchange, their ownership structure remained essentially closed. Furthermore, the groups underwent an important diversification during the late 1970s and 1980s, entering new businesses in addition to their core sectors. However, they remained for the most part industry-based, that is, did not develop a core business in the banking sector or commercial services beyond construction engineering.

---

[27] Daniel Azpiazu's (1989) study reveals that the bulk of this subsidized investment was undertaken in the domain of intermediate goods: petrochemicals, chemicals, steel, pulp, aluminum, and cement. See also Schvarzer 1978, and, especially, 1993.

[28] A paradigmatic example of this trend was Fiat Argentina. Its CEO, Oberdan Sallustro, was kidnapped and killed by leftist guerrillas. Thereafter, Fiat moved to Brazil and sold its license to make cars to the Macri local business group.

[29] For the consolidation of the big private groups in the late 1970s and 1980s see Azpiazu, Basualdo, and Khavisse (1986); Bisang (1998a); and Ostiguy (1990). Castellani (2006) provides abundant evidence to show how the Argentine industry-based domestic conglomerates continued to displace both state companies and TNCs during the "lost decade" of the 1980s.

Compensating Business Insiders

Business Power and National Models of Adjustment in the 1980s and 1990s: Qualitative Assessment

SPAIN. Earlier I described the alternative trajectories of state and private industrial actors under ISI in Spain and Argentina. These contrasting routes cannot be detached from the models of neoliberal adjustment that eventually unfolded in each country. Not only had Spain generated very weak private industrial groups in relation to the state, but, by the early 1980s, the whole industrial sector was strained by the reverberations of the second oil crisis, which hit nonproducer countries particularly hard. By 1982 the economic leadership of the PSOE was aware that the Union of the Democratic Center (UCD) government (1978–82), besieged by union mobilization and the imperatives of the democratic transition, had only postponed badly needed industrial adjustment. Reforms were even more urgent within the horizon of European Community accession in 1986.

Thus, the future minister of industry Carlos Solchaga formed a team in charge of the matter, whose technical staff was not directly linked to the PSOE and was generally already working in the state industrial bureaucracy. This group designed a general restructuring plan, formalized in the so-called *White Book on Re-Industrialization* (Ministry of Industry and Energy, 1983).[30] The project was presented to the party leadership in the area of economics in a summit that took place in Segovia, a touristic village near Madrid, shortly before the PSOE took office in December 1982.[31] The *White Book* became the blueprint for the Law of Reconversion and Re-Industrialization passed in 1984. In short, though the successive rounds of implementation would be bargained with business and especially with segments of the union movement, the cradle of the initiative was in the group of technical cadres (most of them already working in the state industrial bureaucracy) and close political collaborators that Solchaga assembled prior to taking office.

The question becomes why the PSOE was able finally to impose in a *dirigiste* manner a plan initially drafted almost in isolation by the team of Solchaga, and why subsidies rather than market share and privatization were the main compensation targeted to the local industrial groups and firms. First, it is evident that the wide expansion of the state in industrial planning during ISI facilitated the *dirigiste* type of policymaking and the launching of an ambitious program of reconversion from above. The Ministry of Industry, which was already managing around 20% of the Spanish manufacturing GDP, and the largest industrial holding in the country – the INI – provided solid bureaucrats with experience in industrial affairs. As Smith (1998: 115) argues, "The government [industrial]

---

[30] The group was formed by Fernando Sanchez Junco – who worked in the engineer corps of the state – and Pedro Ortuni, Eduardo Santos, and Fernando Maravall, all technical cadres from the public and private sectors. "The White book was in fact written by Pedro Ortuni and me as technical staff, but the work was inspired and led by Carlos Solchaga [future minister of industry] and his team." Interview with Fernando Sánchez Junco, general director of industry, 1984–89, Madrid, October 15, 2001.

[31] Idem.

policies of Franco's final two decades had fostered the emergence of a technocratic elite whose members prized rationality, efficiency and planning." In addition, the state enterprises already operating in those markets – regardless of their (generally bad) financial situation – provided the sectoral Gerencias and the newly formed economic public groups with crucial technical inputs for the elaboration of the adjustment plans for the sectors in which they produced. It was easier for the Ministry of Industry to control the state managers under its command than to negotiate every single adjustment measure with private businessmen.[32]

Second, the main domestic ISI private players in Spain were economically too weak to engage in global competition, even if aided by special tariff regimes or state assets that would allow for market concentration in their own sectors, or would favor their expansion to alternative industries – a path more commonly followed by their peers in Argentina, Portugal, and Mexico. Their scarce economic clout, generally reflected in their low political leverage (see later discussion), precluded any major lobbying that would essentially counter the state-driven plans. The economic dimension of this power will be measured in the next section (and in the case studies in Chapter 4); the view of some protagonists is illustrative of the poor condition of Spanish private industry at the outset of adjustment. Alvaro Espina, the former Socialist secretary of industry (1991–93), stated:

There was no business pressure at all; it was nonexistent! Their business had no value. I don't know any businessman that would participate actively in the reconversion process. In fact, that is why they passed their firms to public control. Those businessmen just gave us the keys of their firms; they had ceased to be businessmen a long time ago. In the home appliances sector, for example, [after the state-led reconversion process] we sold everything to whoever we could, to Electrolux [a multinational firm] for one peseta [Spanish currency prior to the euro].[33]

Indeed the parallel strategy of empowering INI state firms in certain sectors, initially avoiding massive privatization, was explicitly presented as a means to prevent foreign takeovers in the absence of strong private local industrial groups. A top official of the INI reported:

If public industrial enterprises disappear ... large industrial groups would be in hands of foreign interests. If this country had several large, private industrial groups, I would not be speaking of public or private firms, *but such private groups do not exist*, so it is necessary to maintain a strong public group.[34] [my emphasis]

---

[32] A former head of the Gerencia for the steel sector, Fernando Pallete, stated: "It was obviously easier to control the state companies' compliance with the reconversion plans. The private companies were more difficult to inspect; people don't like when you get into their companies." Author's interview, Madrid, October 19, 2001.

[33] Author's interview, Madrid, September 14, 2001.

[34] Cited by Smith (1998: 118), who depicts the situation of private industrial capital at the outset of reform as one of "continued weakness."

Compensating Business Insiders 75

The ulterior decision of whether to sell the revamped companies to TNCs or empower them as national champions was in the hands of state technocrats and could not be influenced by any major industrial group in those sectors. Indeed the private partners of state technocrats in the sequential privatization that maintained local control – for example, the major electrical and oil groups ENDESA and Repsol – were the main private domestic banks. Local bankers sought financial participation and dividends but did not directly challenge the established state management of the firms.[35]

In fact, there is wide agreement among the state leadership and technical cadres that carried out the industrial reconversion and liberalization in Spain in the 1980s and first half of the 1990s that the main political pressures during the process were, in the first place, from the unions, and, second, from the regional governments in which the restructuring took place, *not* from a private business sector already in retreat.[36] In other words, when the government had to modify or negotiate the timing and schedules for capacity cuts, mergers and investment in renewed technology, it was due to the strong union mobilization rather than the consequence of any type of business lobbying. Indeed, Chapters 6 and 7 will show that, despite (or rather because of) its organizational weakness, labor mobilization strongly conditioned the implementation of the adjustment plans from below and favored sizable compensation to the base of laid-off workers in certain sectors.

ARGENTINA. While in Spain most private industrial groups were in retreat, undermined by the energy crisis and by a state hungry to engage in industrial production in the decades prior to neoliberalism, in Argentina by the late 1980s the largest private conglomerates possessed "industrial plants of recent launching, which standards positively qualified in the international context and constituted the most competitive segment of the local manufacturing activity . . . they controlled the few dynamic and profitable markets of the 1980s" (Bisang 1998b: 162).

It is not surprise, therefore, that when Menem announced the neoliberal policy U-turn in July 1989 he picked for the Ministry of the Economy a former CEO of the largest Argentine economic group, Bunge & Born. Menem was seeking credibility in the business world, and the appointments of Miguel Roig and his successor Néstor Rapanelli were part of a general alliance with the traditional holding based on the launching of a broad market reform project. However, Bunge & Born was a large and internationalized business group

---

[35] Likewise in the service sectors of telecoms and banking the state fostered, via subsidized mergers and protections, the consolidation of the domestic groups Telefonica, BBVA, and Santander; see Pérez (1997) and Etchemendy (2004a).

[36] For example, Claudio Aranzadi, former director of industry, INI president, and minister of industry (1982–93), reported: "The major demands came from labor in the regions with more industrial concentration. There was more labor pressure than business pressure; I have no doubt about that." Author's interview, Madrid, September 26, 2001. The former minister of industry and the economy Solchaga stated, "Pressure came not so much from business but from unions and regional governments." Author's interview, Madrid, October 8, 2001.

mainly based on food and grain trading, industries in which Argentina had comparative advantages and was scarcely challenged by the economic opening (Acuña 1994: 355). Its former CEOs were, therefore, in a good position to advance a first economic package that combined classical stabilization measures (devaluation, fiscal adjustment, and increase in the price of public services) with the two macrolaws already mentioned, which altered the Argentine industrial landscape: the Economic Emergency Law, which eliminated the various subsidies and industrial promotion regimes, and the State Reform Law, which would launch privatizations and end lucrative contracts of state suppliers.

The economic groups based in the less competitive basic and transport material industries manifested a dual attitude in this initial period. Though they formally backed the neoliberal turn and the pro-capital stance of the Menem government, they criticized the recessive consequences of the plan for the domestic market and distrusted an economic team whom they saw as too close to the interests of the rural and food exporters (W. Smith 1992: 44; Viguera 2000: 102). Indeed, the departure of the Bunge & Born team in December 1989 and the inability of the government to stabilize the economy until early 1991 could be read, at least in part, as the result of the noncooperative behavior of the large conglomerates more associated with ISI and state subsidies, which routinely violated the price agreements sought by the government and engaged in massive currency speculation.[37]

Most, though not all, of the compensatory deals with the main local holdings took place after 1990, when Minister Cavallo launched the successful stabilization plan. The government anchored the peso to the dollar in March 1991, consolidated the state fiscal situation and dollar reserves, and deepened tariff liberalization more radically. The exchange rate began to appreciate progressively, and speculative price behavior was severely limited by monetary restraint and a virulent tariff liberalization. In this context, the expansion through privatization or through some form of biased deregulation that would ensure market reserves in the future order became the only alternative for the major domestic groups in an environment of uncertainty. A handful of economic groups with internationally competitive plants, which had been gaining market share in the years prior to reform, did not seek cash to pay debts. Nor did they expect reconversion programs from a state that lacked industrial capacity and technical cadres. The largest domestic industrial players found market concentration in liberalized industries in which they had expertise, a viable alternative to cope with uncertainty. The view of the former CEO of Pérez Companc, one of the top Argentine business groups, is eloquent on this point:

---

[37] See Viguera (2000: 112). W. Smith (1992: 43), referring to this period, writes that "Menemstroika still faced a major political obstacle – the dismantling of the distributional coalition of business and labor interests tied to the postwar model of state-led industrialization in a semi-closed economy."

Compensating Business Insiders

It was 1989 and we had a great cash-flow. We had 500 million dollars and not a single peso of debt. And deregulation came in businesses that we knew. We had expertise in natural gas so we entered the distribution network. Because of our construction company we knew about electricity, so we went into the [electricity transportation network] Transener. We thought that we had to focus the company in energy: hydrocarbons, electricity and gas. In an open economy you have to be good in one area.[38]

Moreover, these were economically powerful industrial actors with well-oiled political connections and had the most potential to disrupt the consolidation of the neoliberal reformist trend, which, as noted previously, they partially did prior to the 1991 stabilization. The local groups dominant in these industries, particularly in steel, cement, and aluminum, suffered important losses in the first Menem years as a consequence of recession and the repeal of protections and subsidies (Bisang 1998b: 165). Yet, as Chapter 4 shows in more detail, they subsequently benefited from the domestic market gains entailed by compensation.

ADJUSTMENT PATHS AND THE POLITICAL ORGANIZATION OF BUSINESS. Finally, it should be noted that neither in Argentina nor in Spain were business organizations a central locus in the decision about, or distribution of, compensatory policies. When ISI-based economic holdings were powerful, as in the Argentine case, direct relations and negotiations between the state and the involved *grupos* were the rule. In the case of Spain, both individual firms and associations were subordinated to state plans in the sectors under reconversion. This is not to say, however, that business associations were absolutely irrelevant. Indeed, organizational developments often mirrored ISI economic-structural trends described earlier. In Argentina the compensated sectors had developed quasi-monopolistic business associations that grouped all the major firms in the sector. ADEFA (the automaker's association), CILFA (the chamber of local laboratories), and the CEPA (Association of Argentine Domestic Oil Producers) had been traditional players in the Argentine political economy for years. The CIS (Center for Local Steel Industrialists) was the most powerful single sectoral association within the Argentine Industrial Union (UIA).[39] The big domestic groups in Argentina succeeded in appointing José Blanco Villegas, from SOCMA – one of the main compensated local players in autos analyzed in Chapter 4 – as president of the UIA for the period 1993–97, representing essentially the coalition of big firms in intermediate and durable goods. Thus,

---

[38] Author's interview with Oscar Vicente, CEO of Pérez Companc, January 23, 2001. Of course, compensation to the *grupos* also took the form of stakes in other sectors less related to their core business.

[39] Questions of endogeneity arise concerning these structural and political variables. These firms and their sectoral associations' political power and lobbying capacity were largely due to structural endowments: they were in "strategic" sectors, they were very concentrated (i.e., they had fewer players in the sector), and they were the most powerful in economic terms. At the same time, that *political* predominance reinforced their position in the market. In any case, both the structural and political levels of power were mutually reinforcing and crucial to eventually influencing the liberalization path.

the fact that compensated companies, particularly in the steel and auto sectors, held dominant positions in the UIA helped to moderate the position of the most important industrial association vis-à-vis the government. In brief, UIA was not an institutional locus for the lobbying or implementation of compensatory policies in Argentina. Yet officials knew that buying off the big local industrial groups meant minimal support from the UIA and from the most important sectoral associations.

In Spain sectors benefited by compensation, such as textiles, did not even have a sectoral association when market reform was about to start. More crucially, the importance of public firms in Spanish industrial production allowed for a significant state role in some of the "private" business associations. For instance, during the reconversion process the Spanish Ministry of Industry exerted ample leverage over the private association of steelmakers, Union of Steel Enterprises (UNESID), in which the state firm Ensidesa held an important position due to its production volume. Ironically, private steelmakers sought to include Ensidesa within UNESID in the late 1960s in the hope of controlling the state company more closely (Tamames 1978). During the reconversion process, however, Ensidesa became a sort of fifth column of the state *within* the private association of steelmakers.[40]

The Power of Business and State Actors and Adjustment Paths: Descriptive Statistics

MEASURING ECONOMIC POWER PRIOR TO REFORM. An initial measure of the economic power of the local industrial bourgeoisie is the volume of sales of the major domestic companies relative to both state and foreign producers. The volume of sales essentially measures the "size" of a company and signals the money that it pours into the economy. Table 3.3 shows the top 30 industrial companies in terms of sales in Argentina and Spain, sorted by *type of producer*, at the outset of the reform period.

In Spain the state appeared as the single most powerful industrial producer at the beginning of reform, with eleven firms accounting for 55% of the total sales of the top 30 companies, almost twice the percentage shared by Argentine state companies in the industrial sector. Among them were the biggest INI companies, such as Enpetrol (oil),[41] AESA (shipbuilding), SEAT (autos), and Ensidesa (steel). In Argentina, by contrast, the local private sector surpassed both the state and the TNCs, accounting for 39% of total top 30 sales, almost twice as much as its Spanish counterpart. In Spain, on the other hand, TNCs were the second most

---

[40] Indeed the increasing dominance of the state in UNESID triggered a split of the common steel private producers who formed their own association in order to counter the influence of the state officials in the peak sectoral association. Author's interview with Javier Penacho, technical director of UNESID, Madrid, February 12, 2002.

[41] By 1984 Enpetrol was under the aegis of the National Institute of Hydrocarbons (INH), an entity created out of the oil division of the INI. Yet, it had long been one of the flagship companies of the INI.

Compensating Business Insiders

TABLE 3.3. *Share of Total Sales by Top 30 Industrial Firms by Type of Producer at the Beginning of Reform*

Type	Sector	Argentina 1988 Percentage of Top 30 Sales	Spain 1984 Percentage of Top 30 Sales
State	Total	28% (2 firms)	55% (11 firms)
	Oil	23% (1 firm)	40% (4 firms)
	Manufacturing	5% (1 firm)	15% (7 firms)
Foreign	Total	33% (11 firms)	25% (13 firms)
	Oil	13% (3 firms)	0%
	Manufacturing	20% (8 firms)	25% (13 firms)
Private	Total	39% (17 firms)	20% (6 firms)
Domestic	Oil	3% (2 firms)	14% (3 firms)
	Manufacturing	36% (15 firms)	6% (3 firms)
	Total	100% (30 firms)	100% (30 firms)

Source: Argentina, *Mercado Review* (August 1989); Spain, *Anuario El País* (1985).

important industrial player after the state. Given the economic importance of the petroleum sector in any economy, I have divided the industrial sector between manufacturing and oil refining/production. The table suggests that, outside the oil sector, the role of the Argentine state in large industrial production was negligible. Likewise, if we consider only manufacturing, the weakness of the Spanish private sector is clear (only 6% of total top 30 sales). In other words, the data indicate that within Spanish industry, the most powerful local private players were to be found in the oil sector. As I show in Chapter 5, this was the single industrial sector privileged with market-share compensation in Spain.

WHICH ISI FIRMS WERE COMPENSATED? THE CONFIGURATION OF BUSINESS INTERESTS AND THE DYNAMICS OF INDUSTRIAL ADJUSTMENT. However, not all the domestic industrial firms and groups in Argentina would obtain compensatory measures amid liberalization. The state granted concessions to private local groups based in the heavy industries of oil, autos, steel, petrochemicals, pharmaceuticals, cement, and aluminum. Why those sectors and not others? The answer lies in the fact that these producers of intermediate and durable goods were the dominant groups *within* the ascending local industrial bourgeoisie. At the same time, these sectors based in heavy industries were much more challenged by liberalization than others such as the food industry, in which Argentina was endowed with greater comparative advantage. The economic power of the companies, compensated or not, can be assessed on three levels: volumes of sales (the measure used in the previous section for the general comparison of largest ISI companies in each country), volumes of profits, and what I call "structural power," or the value that industrial sectors generate in relation to their degree of concentration.

80 *The Political Economy of Business Adjustment*

TABLE 3.4. *Top Nonfinancial Firms by Sales and Profits at the Outset of Reform (Argentina 1988, Spain 1982): Share of Top 30 Total Sales and Top 20 Total Profits, Compensated and Noncompensated Firms*

Top 30 Nonfinancial Firms	Argentina 1988		Spain 1982	
	Percentage of Top 30 Sales	Percentage of Top 20 Profits	Percentage of Top 30 Sales	Percentage of Top 20 Profits
Compensated Private Firms[a]	24% (10 firms)	63% (11 firms)	4% (2 firms)	0% (0 firm)
Foreign, Noncompensated	22% (8 firms)	22% (6 firms)	10% (5 firms)	26% (5 firms)
Local, Noncompensated	10% (4 firms)	7% (1 firm)	25% (8 firms)	41% (10 firms)
State	44% (8 firms)	8% (2 firms)[b]	61% (15 firms)	33% (5 firms)
Total	100% (30 firms)	100% (20 firms)	100% (30 firms)	100% (20 firms)

[a] In the case of Spain "compensated firms" refers to the firm's inclusion in the state-designed restructuring plans based on subsidies.
[b] Due to unreliability of data, state utility firms in Argentina with high volatility in their annual reports are excluded from the assessment of profits. Almost all utilities, however, were working at a loss in Argentina at the time.
Source of Rankings: Argentina, *Revista Mercado* (August 31, 1989); Spain, *Anuario el País* (1984).

Table 3.4 shows that the compensated firms in Argentina – among them Pérez Companc, Bridas, and Astra (oil); Sevel and Autolatina (autos); Techint and Acindar (steel); and Aluar (aluminum) – were the most powerful nonfinancial private companies in terms of sales and profits. They shared the highest levels of sales in the top 30 companies after the state-run firms (mostly public services) and supplied no less than 63% of the total profits among the top 20 most profitable companies in the country at time zero of neoliberal reform.[42] Thus, Table 3.4 suggests that business economic power would affect the ulterior compensatory policies in Argentina's Corporatist industrial adjustment. This does not seem to be the case, however, regarding Spain's Statist model. Only two companies later included in the compensatory plans – the steelmaker AHV and the chemical-based ERT – ranked in the top 30 list of firms in terms of sales at the outset of adjustment, and *no* firm included in any of the reconversion plans ranked among the most profitable companies at the beginning of neoliberal reform.

The level of concentration relative to economic power provides a third indicator of structural power. Not only sectors that generate more value, but also those that are more concentrated – that is, involve fewer players – would in

[42] Data were unavailable to complete the top 30 ranked companies in terms of profits.

Compensating Business Insiders

principle have more lobbying capacity vis-à-vis the state. Classical theories of collective action would predict that the fewer players in a sector, the more likely organized business pressure would arise. An estimate of the level of concentration across industrial sectors can be measured through the number of "productive establishments," or economic census units given by the last Industrial Census before neoliberal reform.[43]

Thus, an "Index of Structural Power" can be derived from the ratio between the value generated by the sector and its level of concentration (Table 3.5). The table excludes the food industry, where arguably top Argentine firms enjoy comparative advantage, and concentrates on the quintessential "potential losers," sectors where Argentina has, in principle, less comparative advantage. If we were to predict lobbying capacity as a function of the level of concentration and the resources generated (i.e., the most powerful are those sectors that generate more production value with fewer firms), the auto, oil, and steel sectors in Argentina, the three sectors most favored with market-share compensation, were by far the best endowed, and all the sectors compensated except one are in the top 10 of the index.

While economic power is a crucial element in any causal explanation of compensatory policies delivered to business in Argentina's Corporatist adjustment, that is not the case regarding the dominant pattern of compensation in Spain's Statist model – as already suggested by Table 3.4. The Index of Structural Power at the outset of reform in Spain, shown in Table 3.6, yields evidence in the same direction. The table sorts each industrial sector, first, by the *type* and *degree* of compensation, and, second, by the Index of Structural Power constructed in the same way as in the previous table on Argentina, that is, as a ratio of the sector's Gross Production Value to concentration measured in industrial establishments.[44]

---

[43] This number is not a perfect measure as it refers to the number of plants (and not firms) by sector. However, my interviews with state officials in the statistics offices in both countries and with businessmen suggest that it is a good proxy for the level of concentration of each sector: more concentrated sectors (i.e., with lower numbers of firms) tend to have overall fewer plants or "productive establishments." The International Standard Industrial Classification (ISIC), upon which the Argentine 1985 Economic Census is based, defines the productive establishment as "the economic unit that dedicates, under the same owner or control, to a single or predominant form of economic activity in a unique physical location, or in very proximate ones" (ISIC, Second Revision, UN, 1974). Therefore, the Argentine motor vehicle industry had, by 1985, 6 firms and 11 productive establishments, whereas the textile industry, with many firms, had 1,610 productive establishments. A better measure for the level of concentration for each sector, is, of course, the Hirschman-Herfindahl Index, typically used in the industrial organization literature. However, it would be almost impossible to get the data on the exact number of firms for the 83 industrial subsectors given by the ISIC four digits. Tables 3.5 and 3.6 show the first 20 subsectors in the ranking out of the 83 industrial products/subsectors given by the ISIC four digits.

[44] The CNAE (National Classification of Economic Activities) used by Spanish statistical authorities is very close to the ISIC Second Revision in its classification of industrial subsectors and products. Furthermore, it defines the census unit or "productive industrial establishment" as "the productive situated in the same physical location, with its main dependent and satellite units situated in proximity, and in which one or more persons work for the same firm" (*Encuesta Industrial*, INE, 1984: xvii).

TABLE 3.5. *Argentina: Index of Structural Power (1985) and Compensated Sectors 1989–99 Leading 20 Industrial Sectors*

ISIC[a]	Industrial Sectors	Gross Production Value (pesos 1985)[b]	Concentration (establishments)	Compensation 1989–99	Structural Power Index	Gross Production Value/ Concentration
3,530	Petroleum Industry	527,331,376	12	Market Share	1	43,944,281
3,8431	Autos (Assembly Plants)	162,431,037	11	Market Share	2	14,766,458
3,710	Steel and Iron	160,418,504	270	Market Share	3	594,143
3,140	Tobacco Products	60,770,657	127		4	478,509
3,411	Pulp and Paper	69,493,118	155		5	448,343
3,511–13	Basic Chemicals	183,219,181	589	Subsidy	6	311,068
3,842	Railway Material	12,696,410	45		7	282,142
3,821	Manufacturers of Engines	21,836,892	83		8	263,095
3,522	Drugs and Medicines	102,255,010	485	Market Share	9	210,835
3,692	Cement and Lime	29,233,479	145	Market Share	10	201,610
3,512	Fertilizers	14,803,717	83		11	178,358
3,720	Nonferrous Metals	47,422,523	266	Market Share	12	178,280
3,551	Tires	33,445,950	200		13	167,230
3,211	Finished Textiles	228,621,776	1,610		14	142,001
3,832	Radio, TV, and Communication	45,111,010	372		15	121,266
3,540	Misc. Petroleum	16,662,603	140		16	119,019
3,523	Soap, Cosmetics, etc.	61,773,613	522		17	115,106
3,214	Carpets and Rugs	5,591,827	49		18	114,119
3,825	Office Machinery	67,365,440	85		19	113,141
3,521	Paints, etc.	29,224,307	308		20	94,884

[a] International Standard Industrial Classification of Economic Activities (ISIC), Second Revision. New York: UN, 1974. Excludes Food Industry (ISIC 3111–34).
[b] Gross Production Value expressed in thousands of Argentine pesos (*pesos argentinos*).
Source: Instituto Nacional de Estadísticas (INE) (1990).

TABLE 3.6. *Spain: Index of Structural Power (1982) and Compensated Sectors (1982–95), Leading 20 Industrial Sectors (excluding food industry), plus Rest of Compensated Sectors*

National Classification of Industrial Activities (CNAE)	Industrial Sectors	Gross Production Value (millions of pesetas)	Concentration (establishments)	Compensation 1989–99		Structural Power Index Gross Production Value/Concentration
130	Petroleum Industry	1,229,425	10	Market Share	1	122,942.50
361	Autos (Assembly Plants)	645,706	21	Subsidy[b]	2	30,747.90
382	Aircraft Manufacturing	31,001	5		3	6,200.20
429	Tobacco Industry	122,280	40		4	3,057.00
370	Shipbuilding	247,802	102	Subsidy: 4.1%	5	2,429.43
221–23	Iron and Steel	634,731	332	Subsidy: 41.5%	6	1,911.84
251	Basic Chemicals	443,056	271		7	1,634.89
224	Nonferrous Metals	290,947	180		8	1,616.37
330	Office Machinery	36,250	28		9	1,294.64
343	Batteries and Accessories	25,543	20		10	1,277.15
381	Railway Material	57,360	46		11	1,246.96
471–72	Pulp and Paper	189,650	178		12	1,065.45
345	Home Appliances	115,403	121	Subsidy: 4.9%	13	953.74
252	Fertilizers	124,815	162	Subsidy: 5.5%	14	770.46
355	Radio, TV, and Communication	68,530	100		15	685.30

TABLE 3.6. (*cont.*)

National Classification of Industrial Activities (CNAE)	Industrial Sectors	Gross Production Value (millions of pesetas)	Concentration (establishments)	Compensation 1989–99	Structural Power Index Gross Production Value/Concentration
341	Wire and Cable	58,717	91	16	645.24
254	Drugs and Medicines	229,088	362	17	632.84
242	Cement and Lime	180,483	352	18	512.74
351	Telecom Equipment	97,280	222	19	438.20
383	Bicycles and Motorcycles	25,518	81	20	315.04
363	**Components (Autos)**	139,861	618	Subsidy: 1.6%	25	226.31
312	**Metal Forging**	88,342	712	Subsidy: 0.2%	39	124.08
431–36	**Textiles**	440,360	3,809	Subsidy: 23.7%	40	115.61

Note: "Subsidy" refers to the investment subsidized by Reconversion Plans in the period 1982–91. Total does not equal 100 because of the exclusion of Reconversion Plans targeted at industrial holdings. Subsidies to SEAT were not formally included in a Reconversion Plan.
Source: Instituto de Estadísticas de España (INE) (1990). Percentage of subsidized investment taken from total investment in all Reconversion Plans, Ministry of Industry and Energy, *Informe Sobre la Industria Española* (1987, 1990, and 1991).

Compensating Business Insiders

The "degree of compensation" is measured as a percentage of the total subsidized investments included in *all* reconversion plans implemented under the umbrella of the Law of Reconversion and Re-Industrialization. In other words, here I measure the *business* target of compensation in Spain, that is, the resources allocated for the purpose of business investment and *not* for labor compensation. Firms in the steel sector, which ranks sixth in the index, took around 40% of the state money allocated for investment. Yet, the textile sector, which ranks fortieth in the same index as a result of its dispersion in many firms, is the second largest recipient of investment subsidies, with 24% of the total. On the other hand, businessmen in the home appliances sector, much more powerful than the textile according to the index, took only 5% of total subsidized investment. The shipbuilding sector, fifth in the index and heavily concentrated, only took a small part of the investment money. There is a clear relationship, however, between the ranking of the petroleum sector and the market-share compensation funneled to its main firms, which will be analyzed in Chapter 5.

To conclude, these data suggest that, in contrast to Argentina, in Spain Statist compensatory policies were *not* driven by business economic power. Rather, the main factor that explains business compensation under the Statist mode of restructuring is the *administrative decision* of the state and its willingness to declare a sector under reconversion. Officials based that decision on a number of factors including the number of workers and their degree of union militancy, the regional location of the industry, and the technical assessment by state officials of its viability. However, no factor seems to have been totally decisive by itself. Some reconversion plans, such as those developed for the ERT chemical group and the electronics sector, were not particularly targeted at firms in the politically influential provinces of the Basque Country or Catalonia. The administration allocated sizable investment subsidies in traditionally strong-union sectors such as steel and shipbuilding as well as in weakly unionized sectors such as textiles.

CONCLUSION

Some of the most violent diatribes directed at the Spanish bourgeoisie in the early postwar period were not from any underground Communist publication, but rather from Juan Carlos Suanzes, the founder of the INI and Franco's minister of industry. In 1942, in the wake of the creation of the INI, Suanzes wrote:

> It is not possible to think that the economic revolution that this country needs will take place as a result of the will of the same elements which, spoilt in their action and mentality for many years, had proved powerless to initiate any transformation. That is the reason why we need the forceful [*decidida*] action of the State.[45]

Sixty years later, another former Spanish minister of industry, Luis Croissier, characterized Spanish private companies' reaction to the industrial restructuring of the 1980s and early 1990s in the following terms:

---

[45] Quoted in Martín Aceña and Comín (1991: 82).

Private businessmen had basically "thrown in the towel." Sometimes there was not even a businessman with whom to bargain; they had just left the firms in hands of the management, and there were no shareholders. We discovered that bankrupt firms without owners could work just with their cash-flow, without paying any credit or social-security debt. These firms could work endlessly if someone did not kill them.[46]

The two excerpts are part of the same tale. In the early postwar period, Suanzes saw Spanish private industry, those "spoilt elements," as powerless to bring about sustained industrialization in Spain. Consequently, backed by the military bureaucracy – the only social group that could oppose Franco's class allies – he became the architect of a program of state-driven industrialization. The industrial role of the state would soon erode the power of domestic capitalist interests in sectors such as shipbuilding, steel, aluminum, and autos, which had been the core of the national manufacturing class. Consequently, during the 1980s and 1990s a project of industrial restructuring directed from above became feasible in the context of a strong state industrial bureaucracy and a domestic manufacturing bourgeoisie that was in retreat. Indeed, in Spain state industrial interventionism *increased* markedly with the advent of economic liberalization. The combination of top-down reconversion projects based on subsidies with unfettered liberalization was also a way to "kill," using former Minister Croissier's peculiar term, private companies that the government saw as a drag on the economy without causing major social dislocation.

It should be noted, however, that the Spanish government *did* use market-share compensation (i.e., biased deregulation and targeted privatization) to reward economic actors outside the industrial sector, that is, the banking and energy industries, contesting the rules of the European Commission (see Pérez 1997, Etchemendy 2004a). Indeed, most of the state interventions that shaped adjustment in Spain were implemented against the pressure of the European Commission (EC) and the EU. The EC, for example, continuously pressured the government to curtail industrial subsidies. In other words, defining traits of the Spanish market reform were unrelated to, or sometimes at odds with, the deregulatory pressures stemming from Brussels. EU accession certainly made economic and industrial liberalization inevitable, but it did not determine the model of liberalization pursued.

In Argentina, despite the postwar nationalistic rhetoric, no major project of state-driven industrialization was launched. State industrial policy supported private production to a much greater extent than it did state companies. Indeed, the main protagonist of the initial ISI deepening was foreign capital. Thereafter, policies of industrial promotion helped to forge a relatively small group of powerful local conglomerates whose power *relative to the state and foreign companies* at the outset of reform was unmatched, not only in Spain, but arguably in other countries such as Brazil or Chile. These economic groups were endowed with the size, know-how, and capital to make market

---

[46] Author's interview, Madrid, October 10, 2001.

Compensating Business Insiders

concentration via privatization and biased deregulation a feasible alternative once neoliberal reform was launched. In sum, the prior ISI trajectory shaped both the politics – the emergence of a solid public industrial technocracy or concentrated private groups with strong organizations and lobbying over the state – and the policy of compensation: only groups that emerged strong from the ISI period had the economic power to lobby for, and profit from, market-share compensation.

Of course, my explanation does not rely only on the configuration of business interests as they emerged from the ISI period. The *democratic* factor is also crucial for understanding models of industrial restructuring based on compensatory policies to ISI insiders. The idea that "something needed to be done" and that important actors under the old model could not simply be sidelined in a democratic environment was evident in almost every interview with officials in charge of economic (and labor) policies in these countries. Yet, the fact that the government had to be responsive did not mean that all would be appeased, nor that they would be appeased in the same way.

Finally, compensation did not ensure firms' success in the liberalized economy. In Spain, technocrats would pick those sectors in which state-empowered national champions could compete and those in which the revamped domestic firms or holdings had to be sold to international investors. The major private players of the core ISI sectors succumbed to the pressure of adjustment from above, compensation notwithstanding. It could be argued that the disappearance of AHV (steel; see Chapter 4) and ERT (chemicals), the largest industry-based business groups in prereform Spain, signaled the final demise of the core elements of the traditional ISI manufacturing private class. In Argentina, as will be analyzed in more detail in Chapters 4 and 10, many of the rewarded business groups would prove incapable of sustained global competition and would sell their firms in advantageous conditions – that is, after their asset value had been shored up by compensation – by the late 1990s.

4

Statist and Corporatist Models of Business Adjustment in Spain and Argentina

Sectoral Case Studies

INTRODUCTION

The sectoral case studies presented in this chapter explain in more detail the policymaking process and the administration of compensation involved in the Statist and Corporatist models of business adjustment. The chosen sectors share two principal characteristics. First, they were *potential losers*, that is, produced intermediate or durable goods that enjoyed widespread protection, and, unlike other branches of industry with more comparative advantages – such as the food industry in both countries – were seriously threatened by economic liberalization and integration into regional and global markets. Second, these sectors were paradigms of the dominant pattern of restructuring in each country. Steel and shipbuilding will be more extensively analyzed in the Spanish case. There is wide agreement among Spanish specialists (Navarrro 1990: 118; Castaner 1998: 86) that they constituted the two core sectors in the restructuring project, considering manpower and funds involved. The largest firms in the sectors selected in Argentina, steel, oil, and autos, were, as noted in Chapter 3, the main beneficiaries of market-share compensation in terms of both volume of assets acquired in privatization and important episodes of partial deregulation. Hence, this chapter focuses on crucial "positive" cases of business adjustment in each liberalization model. Chapter 5 studies "negative cases," that is, important ISI sectors that were not compensated according to the model prevalent in each country.

The analysis of the national liberalization models in Chapter 3 advanced two major hypotheses. First, it argued that nonrepressive democratic regimes in which business has more avenues for lobbying, such as those in Argentina and Spain during the neoliberal period, make compensation to ISI business insiders more likely. Second, I posited that the model of industrial restructuring was to a great extent conditioned by the type of ISI business actors that evolved under the inward-oriented model. A trajectory in which domestic private ISI business groups have been losing ground vis-à-vis the state and are economically weak

88

Statist and Corporatist Models of Business Adjustment 89

prior to reform turns state *dirigisme* from above and (especially in a democratic environment) subsidy compensation more feasible. Conversely, a configuration in which domestic business groups have become hegemonic under ISI (displacing both the state and/or foreign TNCs) and are economically strong is more favorable to the pressure of business insiders from below, and to the negotiation of market-share compensation.

As noted in Chapter 1, case studies have considerable methodological advantage for the analysis of the politics of compensation under neoliberalism. The dynamics by which market share or subsidies become the salient form of business compensation is more clearly untangled in comparative case studies in which the options available to state and economic actors are closely assessed. Given that democracy is a common factor to all the sectoral studies, the chapter concentrates on the variation of compensation deals and on the alternative types of actors that helped produce them.

The analysis of steel and shipbuilding in Spain, once the cradle of the domestic private manufacturing class, will show that top-down plans and state *dirigisme* in the 1980s and early 1990s were eased by the slow erosion of the private groups' economic and political weight in the sector, and the parallel empowerment of state industry, in the two decades previous to neoliberal reform. A variety of subsidy mechanisms became the appropriate compensation tool for state technocrats who had clear ideas about how to reorganize these sectors and were reluctant to cede economic control to the established private industrial class. Firms under restructuring would be revamped and generally grouped into public holdings by sector or subsector and, depending on the possibilities for international competition, thereafter sold to international investors or empowered as national champions.

Conversely, the case studies of the steel, oil, and auto industries in Argentina's Corporatist model illustrate that, in the absence of any major plan or strategy of industrial restructuring, market-share compensation emerged out of the business pressure and lobbying of the state. Domestic economic firms and groups that had gathered considerable know-how in their industries under ISI, had disposable economic resources, and had been winning markets vis-à-vis the state and foreign players prior to reform sought to concentrate markets as a way to cope with the vagaries of international competition. In the first part of the chapter I explain the restructuring in the steel and shipbuilding sectors in Spain. Next, I examine the liberalization of the oil, auto, and steel industries in Argentina. Subsequently, I develop a brief analysis of other important sectors that followed the dominant adjustment pattern in each country, such as pharmaceuticals in Argentina and aluminum in Spain. In all the case studies I proceed in the same way: I analyze the compensatory policies and deals during neoliberal reform and show how the alternative patterns of state and business power that resulted from distinct ISI trajectories shaped the modes of sectoral adjustment.

90   *The Political Economy of Business Adjustment*

LIBERALIZATION AND RESTRUCTURING IN SPAIN: STATISM
AND THE DEMISE OF TRADITIONAL ISI PRODUCERS

The Restructuring of the Spanish Steel Industry

State Dirigisme *and Reconversion from Above*

This section analyzes the politics of restructuring in the three subsectors of steel production: *integrated* steel (traditional steelworks with blast furnaces that produce mainly flat products such as sheets and coils), *common* steel (smaller firms based on the production of long steel products, such as tubes and bars, through electric furnaces), and the *special* steel subsector (producers of more sophisticated goods such as stainless steel and forgings).

The three players in the integrated subsector were AHV (Altos Hornos de Vizcaya), a private steel mill in the Basque Country, and the public companies Ensidesa and Altos Hornos del Mediterraneo (AHM). Ensidesa, located in Asturias, was one of the flagship companies of the National Industrial Institute (INI), the state holding of industrial companies that promoted industrialization under Franco. AHM was located in Sagunto (Valencia) and specialized in the production of cold-rolled sheets. At the outset of reform, Ensidesa and AHM delivered around half of the production of raw steel (the main input for every steel product) in the country, with the other 50% produced by the private sector (AHV and common and special steel makers).

The integrated subsector was in dire need of restructuring: its firms were working at a loss, and the EU would demand major capacity cuts for entering a saturated market in 1989. At the same time, a chronic problem affected the Spanish steel industry: its insufficient production of hot-rolled steel, a crucial input for more valued-added steel products such as the cold-rolled sheets used in the auto industry (Navarro 1989: 85). Soon after taking power, the Socialists began to craft a restructuring plan for the integrated steel sector under the umbrella of the law of "Reconversion and Re-industrialization" analyzed in Chapter 3. The whole viability of AHM depended on the construction of a hot-rolling mill, since without the new facility, the plant would become obsolete in an integrated European market (Navarro 1989: 85; Rand Smith 1998: 175). However, the Cabinet Commission for Economic Policy declared the sector "under reconversion" and decided, through decrees 1853/1983 and 8/1983, to channel a series of subsidies oriented to modernize the existing hot-rolling mills in AHV and Ensidesa while condemning AHM to closure.

Meanwhile, in the AHM plant of Sagunto, the unions called for a series of strikes and demonstrations. Still, in the midst of serious labor strife (which will be discussed in Chapter 7) the government shut down the AHM blast furnace in March 1984. The association of steelmakers, UNESID, denounced the "short-run" vision of the government and stressed the fact that, after Spain's integration into the EU, a new hot-rolling mill could never be built with public resources (Saro 2000: 245). However, evincing a policymaking

Statist and Corporatist Models of Business Adjustment

style typical of Statist adjustment, the Ministry of Industry was reluctant to modify the general lines of the reconversion initiative but called social actors to negotiate its implementation within the "Control Commission" of the sectoral plan.

By 1986, the authorities initiated a second wave of adjustment. The government set up a Gerencia, which centralized the management of the subsectoral plans for the steel sector. In 1988 the Gerencia, which controlled the public mill Ensidesa, appointed a new CEO for AHV (the main private player). In view of the considerable subsidies already funneled to the company, it claimed a majority on the board.[1] The management of the Basque private company was in no position to resist the governmental offensive: their shareholders were in retreat and the Gerencia intervention in the board was a precondition for badly needed state aid. Although some sectors represented on the board attempted to mobilize Basque public opinion against government intervention (Navarro 1989: 148), AHV had few options but to submit to state pressure. The view of Fernando Capelástegui, executive director of Altos Hornos de Vizcaya (1983–90), is illustrative of the nature of policymaking in the Spanish restructuring process and of the degree to which leading CEOs of the AHV group were orphans of owners:

I believe that the "great families" on the board [of the company] did see the Socialist policy as too interventionist. When the Socialists came to the board of Altos Hornos, after that, it was no longer a private company! I was not in the bargain with the owners. All I know is that one day they called both the president and me. It was Sánchez Junco [general director of industry at the Ministry of Industry]. He told us: "From now on, we will be in charge and will appoint the president."[2]

In practice, the Gerencia, a small state organ with fewer than a dozen employees, had put the integrated Spanish steel industry under common management. In the context of a new sectoral crisis spawned by the overvaluation of the peseta and the European recession of 1991, the administration merged the traditional Basque steelmaker with Ensidesa and formed a new state company, Corporation for Integrated Steel (CSI), in 1992.[3] In the end, the formerly private AHV was the clear loser in the merger, for the productive capacity of the plant in the Basque Country was reduced to a much greater extent than that of the Ensidesa plant. The blast furnace on the left bank of the river Nervion, cradle of the Spanish industrialization process in the late nineteenth century, was finally closed in 1996. One of the most traditional Spanish industrial holdings and flagship of the Basque bourgeoisie was disappearing.

---

[1] Author's interview with José Ignacio Bartolomé, head of the Gerencia for the steel sector for the period 1987–90, Madrid, September 18, 2001. See also Barrutia (1988).

[2] Author's interview, Bilbao, February 20, 2002.

[3] See Sierra Frenández (2000). CSI put in practice a plan oriented to solve the problems that, despite previous reconversion rounds, still affected both public and private steelworks: low productivity, dispersion of units, and technological and commercialization deficits.

92 *The Political Economy of Business Adjustment*

Restructuring in the electric furnace, or "common steel," subsector gained momentum in the second half of the 1980s. Production was dominated by private family businesses that in 1982 generated around 40% of Spanish raw steel.[4] Capacity cuts were also needed in a subsector that, since the mid-1970s, had received massive export subsidies in response to depression in the Spanish market. Therefore, the Gerencia implemented successive plans relying on public aid and setting the basis for a series of mergers and acquisitions, after which only a handful of companies would remain.[5] In effect, by the mid-1990s, only the domestic groups Aristrain, CELSA, UCIN, and Sidegasa had survived from the group of around three dozen companies in 1984. The acquisition by this group of firms of the rest of the restructuring companies was decided in the offices of the ministry and was induced by its authorities.[6]

However, the surviving private firms in the common steel sector found themselves in a difficult position, facing stiff competition from both EU firms and the recently formed powerful local player CSI (later renamed Aceralia) in the integrated sector, which had boosted its production of long products through electric furnaces – particularly after a modern minimill was set up in the former AHV. Indeed the market of common steel would also end up being dominated by CSI-Aceralia after the new company took over most remaining firms. CELSA, based in Barcelona, was the only prereform private group that would survive as an important player in the subsector (see Table A.1 in the Appendix).

Finally, most of the private special steel companies (makers of sophisticated long products such as hot-rolled bars, billets, and stainless steel) were grouped in a Reconversion Society under the auspices of the Ministry of Industry. In the Reconversion Societies (unlike in the Gerencias) the state initially acquired stock in exchange for the infusion of public funds and appointed a majority of the board and the CEO. The joint venture administered a series of adjustment plans approved by the Ministry of Industry, which included employment and capacity cuts and investment in new lines of production. In 1988 the new company ACENOR was finally constituted out of the merger of the most profitable firms of the Reconversion Society, now under complete state control after the massive injection of public funds.[7] In 1994, the merger of ACENOR and FOARSA – the remaining state firm in the subsector – gave birth to SIDENOR, which the government was ready to privatize. In brief, out of fifteen special steel companies in 1980, three companies controlled the subsector by 2000: SIDENOR (created out of the reconversion plans); the smaller private GSB; and ACERINOX-ROLDAN, based on stainless steel.

---

[4] UNESID database, Madrid 2001.

[5] "We had to check that those firms in a bad situation would close or merge, and that the others would invest." Author's interview with José Ignacio Bartolomé, head of the Gerencia for the steel sector for the period 1987–90, Madrid, September 18, 2001.

[6] Author's interview with a top staff official of the steelmakers' association UNESID, Madrid, February 12, 2002.

[7] Navarro (1989: 336–45).

Statist and Corporatist Models of Business Adjustment 93

To sum up, after thirteen years of Socialist government and reconversion plans, the steel sector had been completely revamped. By 1995 *two newly created state groups*, CSI-Aceralia in integrated and common (electric) steel and SIDENOR in special steels, dominated what had been myriad private and public producers in the early 1980s – three integrated firms, around thirty-five common steel companies, and fifteen manufacturers of special steels. SIDENOR was by 2006 the second European producer of special steels.[8] CSI-Aceralia would become part of the largest steel holding in the world, Arcelor-Mittal, after its privatization and merger with the French firm Usinor in 2001, and with the Indian Mittal in 2006. Prereform private players – AHV and almost all common steel and special steel traditional Spanish families – were the main losers of the steel reconversion managed from above.

Explaining Statist Adjustment in the Steel Sector: ISI and the Slow Demise of the Domestic Bourgeoisie

This outcome, the consolidation by the mid-1990s of two increasingly internationalized state players out of reconversion plans that came to dominate the whole sector, would have been difficult to predict by any observer of the politics of Spanish steel production in the late 1960s and early 1970s. In fact, the political influence of AHV in Spanish policy circles can be traced back to the early twentieth century.[9] The common interpretation of Spanish analysts was that the private steel sector had unmatched political influence prior to reform.[10] Moreover, by the early 1970s, AHV was one of the two largest private industrial holdings in Spain, having diversified in the chemical and mining sectors. How, then, do we explain its demise in the adjustment period and the capacity of the government to subordinate its managers and close down its facilities in 1996?

The answer is to be found in the economic decline of the steel private sector in general and the AHV group in particular by the early 1980s. In Chapter 3 I used two main measures to assess the economic strength of a firm prior to reform: sales (which denote firm volume and scale economies) and profits (which denote market efficiency and cash resources). Sectoral studies allow us to consider a third measure: evolution of domestic market share in production under ISI, which points to the relative economic efficiency and presumably political influence with which domestic firms performed. A firm will be ready to eschew Statist subordination and lobby for market reserves and privatization when it is relatively big vis-à-vis state competitors (or at least not too small), when it has more disposable cash and financial resources, and when it has been winning market share prior to reform.

---

[8] *El Correo*, November 21, 2006.
[9] Gonzáles Portilla (1994: 123) writes that "AHV was the flagship of the Spanish industrialization, no Spanish firm gained so much influence in the economy and in the national politics as AHV, whose board members were constantly involved in political activities."
[10] See Fraile (1992) and Navarro (1988).

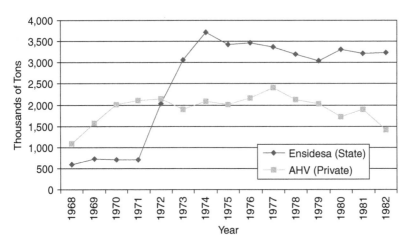

GRAPH 4.1. Spain: Production of Hot-Rolled Steel by Ensidesa and AHV in the Prereform Period (in thousands of tons). *Source*: Ensidesa and AHV Annual Reports 1968–82.

None of these applies to the largest Spanish private groups in the sector, which emerged out of the inward-oriented model as a case of what this book calls a *weak* ISI business actor. The failure of the private sector to compete efficiently with the public mills especially after 1970 was blatant. Although local capitalists in the steel sector were very influential, they were originally unable to block the offensive of the INI's military bureaucracy led by Suanzes, which led to the creation of Ensidesa in 1950. By the mid-1970s, the public steelworks managed to outperform private producers in the most important subsegments of the market. Graph 4.1 shows how Ensidesa began significantly to displace the traditional private mill in the output of hot-rolled steel (the main product of integrated companies). The crucial turning point was the early 1970s, when Ensidesa launched new installations and took over bankrupt private firms such as UNINSA. Graph A.1 in the Appendix shows similar trends in the production of raw steel.

Graph 4.2 indicates that until the crises of the mid-1970s the public mill was not only outperforming AHV in production, but consistently showed a better rate of profits. One of the reasons behind the slow fading of AHV is bad management during the 1970s. The leadership of the private steel mill bet on an ambitious program of expansion and set up a new integrated plant in Sagunto when the market was about to contract as a result of the 1973 world crises. In any case, the underperformance of AHV relative to the state company under ISI provides crucial background for understanding why politically influential managers and capitalists from the traditional Basque firm could not lobby for market-share compensation under market reform. State bureaucrats who had proved relatively efficient in development of steel under ISI (in terms of both increasing production and making profits) were more prepared to formulate

Statist and Corporatist Models of Business Adjustment

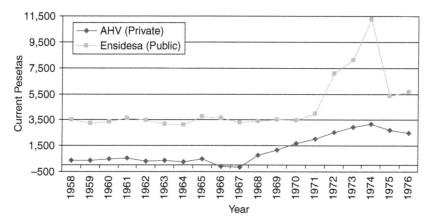

GRAPH 4.2. Profits (net profits plus amortizations) of State and Private Companies in the Integrated Steel Subsector (in millions of pesetas). *Source*: Statistical Appendix, Xavier Tafunell, *Los Beneficios Empressariales en España (1880–1981): Elaboración de una serie anual*. Madrid: Fundación Empressa Pública, WP 9601.

reconversion plans after 1983, once the international context had changed and EU accession made adjustment unavoidable. True, in the early 1980s Ensidesa was also working at a loss (like most European steel mills), though its performance was still superior to that of the private company (Table 4.1). The main point is, however, that the state had a corps of efficient bureaucrats with experience of successful management in the sector, and that the productive and financial situation of AHV (the largest private group) precluded any attempt to lobby for privatization as a means of softening the liberalization storm.

In addition, the smaller producers in the electric furnace subsector had neither the capital nor the know-how or experience to manage a big state integrated company like Ensidesa. My interviews with businessmen from the steel industry in Spain reveal some attempts by the few relatively powerful local steelmakers in the electric or common sector to participate in the privatization of CSI in 1996–97 – before it ended in the hands of the international giant Arcelor-Mittal. Yet the bid failed as not only were private local companies generally weak in relation to the state, but the revamped public steel groups were now competitive and therefore more expensive.[11] Likewise GSB, a special steel group formed by traditional Basque businessmen who had not joined the Reconversion Society, was powerless to bid for SIDENOR, the state-reconstituted group in special steel

---

[11] "There were projects to sell CSI to Spanish capital, especially to the CELSA group. But they lacked sufficient money because CSI was now a healthy [*saneada*] company and had become efficient and attractive, with domestic market dominance and export capacity." Interview with Luis Iniesta del Bricio, technical director of UNESID, Madrid, February 12, 2002. As Sierra Fernández (2000: 333) describes, "The [local] partners were appalled as the value of CSI-Aceralia assets went from 240,000 to 369,320 millions of pesetas."

TABLE 4.1. *Spain: Economic Indicators of Main Private (AHV) and Public (Ensidesa) Steel Groups (Average 1979–82)*

	AHV	Ensidesa
Sales (in millions of pesetas)	57,883.3	143,004.5
Profits/Sales (percentage)	−17.3	−13.0
Investment (in millions of pesetas)	1,300.5	7,017.8
Productivity (production/employment)	144.0	192.3

Source: Firm balances in Navarro (1989: 16, 128).

in 1995 (Navarro 2004: 179). Tellingly, it was GSB itself that would be later taken over by SIDENOR, which meant the concentration of almost all Spanish production of specialty steel (except for stainless steel) in one state company. SIDENOR was sold to a consortium formed by the Italian steelmaker Roda in 1995 and eventually acquired by the Brazilian major steel group Gerdau in 2005. In short, the only alternative for most local private producers was to take the subsidies included in the reconversion plans and sell their assets to the newly created state giants CSI-Aceralia and SIDENOR or to foreign players. The few efficient producers that did not enter reconversion plans were left in isolation and later purchased by the big steel groups that resulted from state-managed adjustment.

The Restructuring of the Spanish Shipbuilding Industry

Reconversion from Above and Massive Adjustment in the 1980s and 1990s
Shipbuilding was one of the engines of the country's rapid industrial growth during the 1960s and early 1970s, when Spain grew to be one of the five largest shipbuilders in the world (Cerezo and Sánchez 1996: 169). Yet, shipbuilding became one of the archetypical industries affected by globalization and worldwide competition, especially from Korea (Strath 1987: 1–7). In the early 1980s, the Spanish shipbuilding sector was divided into two main groups: big shipyards, all of them publicly owned (AESA, Astano, and Bazan, the latter based on military construction), and medium and small shipyards, where private capital was dominant. Big shipyards concentrated in large construction such as oil tankers, bulk carriers, and other merchant carriers, whereas small and medium firms specialized in passenger ferries, smaller merchant carriers, and fishing vessels.

When the Socialists came to power, the shipbuilding industry was burdened by overcapacity and excess employment. As in the steel sector (if earlier in the process) the government set up a Gerencia to direct the restructuring process. This small technical agency, with a dozen employees, shared some attributes with the Gerencia of the steel sector: though formally dependent on the Ministry of Industry, in practice, it was quite autonomous, and it enjoyed the freedom to subcontract any service.[12]

---

[12] Author's interview with José Luiz Cerezo, head of the Gerencia for the shipbuilding sector 1984–2001, Madrid, October 23, 2001.

Statist and Corporatist Models of Business Adjustment 97

In 1984 the administration issued decree 1271, which laid out the first reconversion plan for the sector. The policymaking style was not different from the Statist pattern of adjustment in steel: the leverage of the private business sector in the overall design of the plan remained limited.[13] The initial restructuring plan had two general components. First, it mandated a reduction of the workforce by closing six shipyards and changing the operation of two big public yards from construction to repairs. The Gerencia undertook a massive downsizing of the large public shipyards. By the end of the decade, new ships were built only in the yards of Sestao (Basque Country), Sevilla, and Puerto Real (Andalucía). The closure of AESA's facility at Eskaulduna, one of the most traditional yards in Spain on the banks of the Nervión River in the Basque city of Bilbao, was particularly traumatic. The government encountered fierce labor resistance, which will be analyzed in Chapter 7. Astano in Galicia and other minor installations were maintained only for ship repairs.

In addition, the administration created a Reconversion Society that grouped most of the small and medium shipyards. By 1989, the society, named PYMAR, included three public medium-sized shipyards and twenty-one private (all but three). PYMAR worked under the umbrella of the Gerencia. Its main task was to plan sectoral investments and to distribute the subsidies funneled by the government among its members. Furthermore, the Gerencia pushed a series of mergers in the subsector. After the integration into the EU in 1987 a new plan was issued, yet this time the sectoral project was negotiated in the European Commission, in the context of the Directives for Shipbuilding Aids (Archanco Fernández 1994). Overall, production capacity dropped by almost 60% between 1984 and 1990. In spite of successive adjustments, in 1992 AESA was still the largest state-owned shipbuilding conglomerate in Europe (*Seatrade Review* 1992: 85). By 2000, AESA and BAZAN were merged in the new firm IZAR, which became the single public group in large shipbuilding. In 2006 IZAR disinvested or closed down all the facilities for nonmilitary construction.

The subsector of small and medium yards recovered considerably after fifteen years of reconversion plans. However, very few prereform players could reap the benefits. As Table 4.2 shows, in the segment of medium and small shipyards the share in production of the private sector shrank from 60% to 50–55% percent. Indeed, only *one* prereform private player was able to thrive in the liberalized market, the shipyard Unión Naval del Levante, which specialized in passenger ferries. During liberalization state-owned yards increased production and gained market share in the subsector of medium shipyards traditionally dominated by private players.

---

[13] In the words of Ramon Lopez Eady, technical director of the shipbuilders' association UNINAVE, which encompasses the private small and medium yards, "The private sector influence in the design of the overall policy of reconversion was very low. We knew about the plans being crafted but without any direct participation." Author's interview, Madrid, December 16, 2001.

TABLE 4.2. *Evolution of Spanish Shipbuilding Industry before and after Reform: Small and Medium Shipyards: Ships Delivered in Gross Tonnage*

Shipyards	Before Reform 1985	Percentage 1985	After Reform 1989	Percentage 1989	After Reform 1995	Percentage 1995	After Reform 2000	Percentage 2000
State								
H. J. BARRERAS[a]	6,483	7%	6,545	8%	19,614	22%	26,175	17%
JULIANA	32,671	33%	14,896	19%	24,225	27%	42,456	28%
ASTANDER[b]	0	0%	1,752	2%	0[d]	0%	0	0%
Total State	**39,154**	**40%**	**23,193**	**30%**	**43,839**	**48%**	**68,631**	**46%**
Private								
ARDEAG	416	0%	576	1%	Shut		Shut	
CADAGUA	15,898	16%	Shut		Shut		Shut	
ARMON	1,615	2%	4,647	6%	1,711	2%	2,051	1%
ATLANTICO	2,000	2%	1,050	1%	Shut		Shut	
CANT&RIER	1,180	1%	Shut		Shut		Shut	
GONDAN	2,183	2%	2,258	3%	0	0%	7,486	5%
HUELVA	1,400	1%	5,229	7%	8,851	10%	1,640	1%
JOSE VALIÑA	0	0%	789	1%	542	1%	0	0%
LUZURIAGA	0	0%	447	1%	Shut		Shut	
MALLORCA	4,943	5%	0	0%	217	0%	0	0%
MURUETA	8,126	8%	1,794	2%	0	0%	6,617	4%
ANICETO	310	0%	0	0%	Shut		Shut	
CELAYA	1,350	1%	Shut		Shut		Shut	
TARRAGONA	131	0%	234	0%	Shut		Shut	
ZAMACONA	0	0%	1,142	1%	2,592	3%	4,694	3%

NERVION	0	0%	2,095	3%			Shut	
BALENCIAGA	335	0%	2,883	4%	1,059	1%	728	0%
P. FREIRE	1,584	2%	5,964	8%	812	1%	10,712	7%
S. DOMINGO	4,008	4%	2,443	3%	974	1%	0	0%
LORENZO Y CIA	1,765	2%	3,711	5%	Shut		Shut	
N. MARIN	6,483	7%	802	1%	759	1%	1,535	1%
NAVAL GIJON	0	0%	2,682	3%	0	0%	12,136	8%
U. N. LEVANTE	5,450	6%	15,336	20%	29,251	32%	22,273	15%
FERROLANOS	0	0%	1,059	1%	209	0%	638	0%
F. VULCANO	0	0%	0	0%	0	0%	9,082	6%
PASAIA[c]							1,482	1%
Total Private	59,177	60%	55,141	70%	46,977	52%	81,074	54%
TOTAL	98,331	100%	78,334	100%	90,816	100%	149,705	100%

[a] Privatized in 1997.
[b] Privatized in 1999.
[c] New.
[d] A 0 level of production means that, although the yard is operating, no ship was delivered that year.
Source: Gerencia del Sector Naval, Ministry of Science and Technology, Madrid.

Explaining Adjustment in the Shipbuilding Sector: The State Plays Alone

In the case of shipbuilding, the market retreat of the domestic bourgeoisie in the years prior to adjustment was even more evident than in the steel sector. Shipbuilding was host to some of the most traditional elements of the Spanish private manufacturing class. By the mid-1960s, the big private players Euskalduna, Sociedad Española de Construcción Naval, and Astano, together with the small and medium shipyards (all of them private), shared 60% of production. The withdrawal of the private sector began when Euskalduna and Sociedad Española merged with the public Astilleros de Cádiz and formed Astilleros Españoles (AESA) in 1969, with the goal of increasing economies of scale. This merger meant that almost 75% of production in the sector passed to state hands. The new firm would become dominant in the sector, particularly in the construction of large ships such as bulk carriers and oil tankers. In 1972, as a result of its financial troubles, the INI took over another important private yard, Astano. Therefore, when reform was about to take off, the private players were found only in the segment of medium and small yards (Cáceres Ruiz 1997). The dominance of the state in this industry would be unmatched in Western Europe.

Graph 4.3 shows that the private sector was economically defeated when reform was about to start. The private yards lacked both the capital (they were too small to buy the big yards) and the know-how (they specialized in smaller ships) to be able to pressure for industrial privatization.[14] As two experts in the industry argued, at the onset of the reconversion process "the technological level of private shipyards was on average inferior to the public yards" (Cerezo and Sánchez Jáuregui 1996: 172). The trajectory of the state yard Barreras is telling in this respect. The yard was privatized in 1997 and acquired by a consortium formed by the sea trade company Odiel and the tuna manufacturer Albacora, rather than by any of the established players in the sector. The newly private yard would become the second largest producer in the subsector. Likewise, the shipyard Astander – by 1999 specializing only in ship repairs and conversion – was purchased by the sea trade Greek group Lavinia.[15] In spite of the subsidy-based compensatory policies, preform private producers were unable to expand in the new order. In sum, in view of the dominance of the state in the sector in the run-up to reform in terms of both market share in production and technology, the Statist strategy of adjustment is not surprising. Moreover, given the general decline of the industry in the West as a result of East Asian competition, only large, efficient, and

---

[14] In the words of Ramon Eady, technical director of the Spanish shipbuilding association UNINAVE, "Private capital could not 'jump' from the medium to the big yards; they just feared managing such big companies." Author's interview, Madrid, December 16, 2001.

[15] As noted previously, the public yard IZAR was fragmented and its more profitable facilities Sestao, Sevilla, and Gijón sold to Spanish medium-size yards in 2006. However, this sell-off, 25 years after adjustment and international integration in the sector, hardly constitutes a compensation payoff.

Statist and Corporatist Models of Business Adjustment

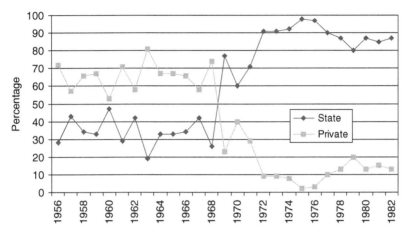

GRAPH 4.3. Spain: Ships Delivered (in gross tons) by State and Private Companies in Prereform Period (1965–82). *Source*: Statistical Appendix in Martín Aceña and Comín (1991).

dominant private players would have been able to expand via market concentration. This type of actor did not exist in the Spanish shipbuilding industry.

By 2005 the sector was a caricature of what it had been for the Spanish economy. Compared to 1983, when the reconversion plans started, employment had been reduced by an impressive 83% (Cerezo 2005; see Chapter 7), production capacity had been diminished, and all yards were in private hands. However, it should be stressed that through Statist adjustment and subsidies Spain did manage to preserve a shipbuilding industry in an environment of phenomenal below-cost competition from Korea and, increasingly, China. In 2003 Spain was the third largest producer in Europe after Germany and Italy, ahead of France and the United Kingdom.[16] While only 18% of production was exported in 1988, 52% was sold outside Spain in 2008. Moreover, after 2008 the Spanish shipbuilding industry could profit from the phenomenal expansion in sea transportation triggered by the global commodity boom (especially food, natural gas, and oil) and from the world revival of the industry despite the financial crisis. In 2007 the Spanish shipbuilding industry was progressively specializing in ships of higher technology, was still home to around 10,000 workers, and boasted sales of 1,400 million euros.[17]

---

[16] The productivity gains were striking: measured in CGT (compensated gross tonnage) production per individual worker, the public yards went from 28.1 in 1991 to 50.5 in 2002, and the private yards from 34.7 to 90.1 in the same period (all data in Cerezo 2005).

[17] *Deia*, April 18, 2008. Javier López de la Calle, general secretary of the Basque Association of Sea Industries, declared in 2007: "We need to specialize in ships of high value added and technology. We cannot compete with normal ships." *Gara*, January 14, 2007.

102 The Political Economy of Business Adjustment

LIBERALIZATION AND RESTRUCTURING IN ARGENTINA: CORPORATIST ADJUSTMENT AND THE EXPANSION OF TRADITIONAL ISI BUSINESS GROUPS

Restructuring in the Argentine Steel Industry

Negotiating Adjustment: "Informal" Concertation and Market-Share Compensation

At the outset of the neoliberal period, the state companies SOMISA and the much smaller Altos Hornos Zapla were the only firms in the integrated blast-furnace sector. The private national holdings Acindar and Techint (through its controlled firm Siderca) were the only companies producing raw steel through electric furnaces. Downward in the production chain, SOMISA controlled the production of hot-rolled flat products with about 95% of the market; Acindar traditionally concentrated in the market of long products, such as wires and steel bars; and Siderca specialized in seamless tubes, that is, steel pipes generally used in the oil industry. Techint, through a second subsidiary – Propulsora Siderúrgica – competed with SOMISA in the production of cold-rolled sheets, a crucial input for the auto industry. As in Spain, the production of raw steel was more or less evenly distributed among private and public firms. The steel industry was severely hit by the successive rounds of liberalization after 1989: prices went down, overall production shrank in the first three years of adjustment, and the sector showed a pronounced trade deficit (Bisang and Chidiak 1995: 53).

Yet, any assessment of the restructuring of the Argentine steel industry should take into account the privatization of SOMISA. The government sold the public steelworks in 1992 to a consortium led by Techint, with the minor participation of Acindar,[18] the only group that participated in the bidding. SOMISA was renamed Siderar and merged with Techint's own Propulsora Siderúrgica. SOMISA's privatization was a crucial bid for Techint. Although it would have not affected the business of Siderca (the maker of tubes), if excluded from SOMISA's privatization, the holding would have been left with few options but to sell Propulsora (Techint's mill of cold-rolled steel, which depended on SOMISA's inputs of hot-rolled coils) to the new owner.[19] With the acquisition of SOMISA, however, Propulsora would be able to achieve backward integration and form a full-cycle steel mill, from blast furnace to the cold-rolling stage.[20]

---

[18] The Techint economic group was founded in the postwar period by the engineer Agostino Rocca, an Italian immigrant. Though the family retained assets in Italy, Rocca obtained Argentine citizenship and developed most of the group in (and from) Argentina.

[19] Author's interview with Carlos Frank, finance director of the Techint conglomerate, Buenos Aires, March 1, 2001.

[20] Marcelo Bacigalupo, head of commercial and financial planning of Siderar, stated that "SOMISA's privatization was much more important for the group than the other privatizations where we participated. We can think in terms of diversification in related business, and we have

Statist and Corporatist Models of Business Adjustment

There are few doubts that the group enjoyed privileged access to the privatization process. In fact, the path to privatization was eased when, at the beginning of the Menem period, the government displaced DGFM, the military-run industrial holding, from its control of SOMISA and directly appointed successive *interventores* (supervising auditors) as head of the company. The *interventores* undertook substantial workforce reductions and capacity cuts. The displacement of DGFM – the traditional competitor of the national private sector – from SOMISA's control arguably favored the position of domestic private capital in the privatization process.[21] In short, privileged access and informal concertation and contacts with established private firms, two traits of policymaking in the Corporatist type of industrial adjustment, can be fully applied to SOMISA's privatization.[22]

In addition to compensatory policies in the form of state assets, the Argentine steel sector benefited from the mechanism of protectionist or partial liberalization. By 1994 the steel tariff had been reduced to 10% (average), and all non-tariff and administrative import barriers had been lifted. However, as the economists Gerchunoff, Bozzala, and Sanguinetti (1994: 10) argue, "Two significant trends unfolded after privatization. First the state started to accept antidumping demands that were issued before privatization. Second, new antidumping measures against steel imports were enacted, which provoked in a certain way the closure of the sector to external competition." Table 4.3 shows the number of favorable resolutions by the Ministry of Economy to antidumping demands for the period 1995–99.[23] Among the sixty-one positive resolutions issued, about a third benefited the whole spectrum of steel products. As it is doubtful that world dumping is disproportionately affecting local steel – as opposed to other industrial goods – this fact probably reflects the privileged access of Argentine private steelmakers to decision making in the context of

---

done it, especially in construction engineering. But we know about steel and engineering; we are engineers that make steel." Author's interview, Buenos Aires, October 31, 2000.

[21] Author's interview with Alfredo de Keravenant, former head of the steel division in DGFM, Buenos Aires, October 15, 2000.

[22] Ricardo Zinn (a former intellectual apologist of the 1976–83 dictatorship) was appointed head of the government committee organizing the privatization process by Supervising Auditor María Julia Alsogaray. He worked in close contact with the main bidder, Techint. As a case study of the IAE business school on Techint's takeover of the mill reports, "The privatization team [of Techint] worked very hard; Mr. Zinn tried to eliminate the obstacles and clarified the terms of the bidding form" (IAE 1997: 16).

[23] I reviewed a list provided by the secretary of industry of every resolution related to trade demands for the period 1995–98, although as Gerchunoff et al. (1994) argue, the enactment of antidumping measures that would limit liberalization of the steel market began in the early 1990s. In Argentina, when a firm or group of firms presents an antidumping case, the ministry can issue four kinds of resolutions: it can open an investigation, sanction "provisional" antidumping measures, sanction "definitive" antidumping measures (usually with a term limit), or reject the case. For Table 4.3 I counted the provisional and definitive antidumping measures as "positive resolutions" – regardless of whether they sometimes refer to the same case/product – because I was more interested in the frequency of effective access to decision making rather than in the number of products protected.

104   *The Political Economy of Business Adjustment*

TABLE 4.3. *Positive Resolutions of Antidumping Demands Passed by the Ministry of Economy (1995–99)*

Product	Number of Favorable Resolutions
Steel (semifinished and finished products)	19
Electrical Equipment (includes home appliances)	9
Machine Tools	5
Engines	4
Transport Material	4
Paper	3
Wood and Wood Products	3
Ceramics	3
Cards	2
Lockers	2
Fireworks	2
Tires	1
Textiles	1
Copper Manufacturing	1
Cement	1
Petrochemicals	1
Total	61

Source: Secretary of Industry, Ministry of Economy, Argentina.

Corporatist adjustment.[24] Partial market liberalization and privatization notably strengthened the position of the traditional private producers of steel in the domestic market (Table 4.4). By 1998 each of the traditional firms had become absolutely dominant in a segment of the market for finished and semifinished products – Acindar in long steel products (after privatized Siderar discontinued its production in the subsector), Techint in flat products (both in hot-rolled products and in cold-rolled steel through its newly formed Siderar) – and, through its control of Siderca, in seamless industrial tubes.

Explaining the Outcome: The ISI Origins of Techint's Internationalized Steel Empire

The trajectory of the Argentine steel sector under the inward-oriented model is the mirror image of the Spanish steel industry's postwar development. If, in Spain, an originally powerful and traditional private sector was weakened by the expansion of the state in the years prior to adjustment, in Argentina private companies would

---

[24] On Techint's strategy of using antidumping measures to limit market liberalization and its privileged access to state regulators see *Página 12*, January 2, 2000.

Statist and Corporatist Models of Business Adjustment

TABLE 4.4. *Argentina: Raw Steel Production before and after Liberalization (thousands of tons per year operating capacity)*

| | Before Reform | | After Reform | | | |
	1988		1994		1998	
State	2,692	56.3%		0.0%		0.0%
• SOMISA	2,500	52.3%				
• A. Zapla	192	4.0%				
Private	2,088	43.7%	3,903	100.0%	4.498	100.0%
• Total Techint	540	11.3%	2,460	63.0%	2.950	65.6%
Siderca	*540*		*810*		*950*	
Siderar	*–*		*1,650*		*2.000*	
• Acindar	1,338	28.0%	1,192	30.5%	1.258	28.0%
• A. Bragado	210	4.4%	90	2.3%	130	2.9%
• A. Zapla	–	–	161	4.1%	160	3.6%
Total	4,780	100%	3,903	100%	4.498	100%

Source: CIS (1996) and *Tendencias Económicas* (1989, 1999).

slowly undermine an initially dominant state actor. The prereform history of the Argentine steel sector can be divided into two periods.[25] Until the early 1970s, the state mills SOMISA and the much smaller Altos Hornos Zapla were the dominant actors in production. SOMISA was built in 1960 as the first and only Argentine integrated producer (i.e., producing steel out of iron ore processed through blast furnaces). The plant was placed under the authority of the defense holding Fabricaciones Militares and supplied inputs of semifinished steel to the main private firms in the downstream. As noted, Acindar and Siderca (from the Techint group) depended on SOMISA's raw steel for the production of nonflat and tubular products (wires, bars, pipes, etc.), and Propulsora (also from Techint) obtained hot-rolled coils from the public company for its cold-rolling mill.

This situation of state dominance, however, began to change decisively after the mid-1970s. In effect, the two main local producers used the Promotion Regime fostered by the military dictatorship analyzed in Chapter 3 to incorporate technology that would facilitate their backward integration. Acindar (in 1978) and Siderca (in 1976) set up new facilities for direct reduction of iron and modern minimills based on electric furnace technology, which bolstered their production of raw steel (Bisang 1989: 137–42). Consequently, SOMISA largely lost its main buyers of semifinished goods. In sum, the complementary relation between public and private firms during the 1960s turned into one of open competition by the late 1970s.

---

[25] For the history of steel production in Argentina see Bisang (1989) and Azpiazu and Basualdo (1994).

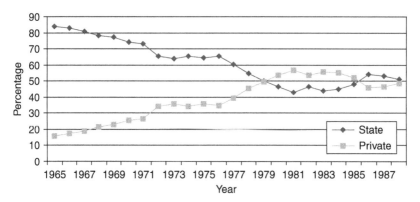

GRAPH 4.4. Argentina: Share of Production of Crude Steel (in tons) by State (SOMISA and A. Zapla) and Private Firms (Siderca, Acindar, and Acer. Brag), Prereform Period (1965–88). *Source*: CIS (1996)

Graph 4.4 shows how the private sector continually eroded state production of crude steel in the decades prior to reform. The breaking point occurred in the mid- to late 1970s, when Siderca and Acindar expanded capacity with the help of the Argentine government. Although state production would recover slightly during the 1980s, when reform was about to begin, the economic strength of the private sector, measured in production capacity, clearly matched that of the state company. Since SOMISA did not compete in the segments of nonflat products and tubes, where the private sector was traditionally dominant, a second measure of comparison of state and private sector performance would be the rate of growth in their main products, rolled steel in the case of SOMISA and seamless tubes in the case of Siderca. Graph 4.5 shows that the private sector clearly outgrew the state in the years prior to reform. The breaking point is, again, evident after 1976. Paradoxically, the orthodox economic policies of the 1976–83 military dictatorship were compatible with the growth of a heavily protected steel private group. Indeed, while state plans for expansion of public mills in the same period foundered,[26] the minimills that Siderca and Acindar had built in 1976–78 were in the forefront of international technology in steelmaking.[27]

The important point is that private groups, which by 1965 were producing only 15% of Argentine raw steel and were completely dependent on inputs from the state company, had developed both the economies of scale and the know-how to

---

[26] The projects for the installation of a second state-run integrated plant (SIDINSA) and the expansion of SOMISA were blocked or severely delayed during the same period. This fact, and Acindar's subsidized expansion, were no accident, given that Martínez de Hoz, the initial orthodox economics minister of the dictatorship, had been president of Acindar's board before taking office.

[27] Bisang (1989: 137) argues that the systems of direct reduction of iron ore and the modern electric furnaces were among the first facilities of that type to be installed in nondeveloped countries.

Statist and Corporatist Models of Business Adjustment

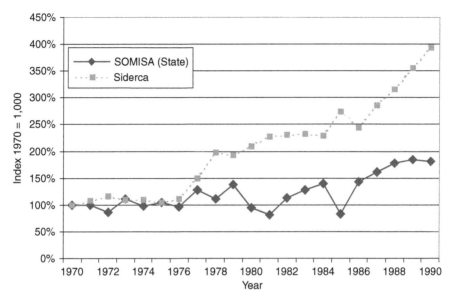

GRAPH 4.5. Argentina: Index of Production (in tons) of Hot-Rolled Sheets (Somisa-State) and Seamless Tubes, Prereform Period. *Source*: CIS (1996).

buy SOMISA by the time market reform was launched in the 1990s. Techint had become a top producer of oil pipes and was surpassing the state in the production of cold-rolled sheets for the auto industry. Acindar, likewise, was completely dominant in the market of nonflat steel after taking over smaller rivals, such as Gurmendi and Tamet.

Before 1992 some other privatization schemes were considered. For instance, one alternative foresaw that the state would hold 40% of the shares and would negotiate with the new owner future plans for the company, trying to prevent any further reduction of firm activities. Nonetheless, the government finally decided to sell the firm in one block to one major company, precluding any diffusion of property. In addition, the administration ruled that it would accept government bonds as part of the installment, a financial mechanism that directly benefited domestic holders of internal debt such as Techint. Arguing that the conditions under which the privatization was carried out were not very clear, the Italian firm Iritecnia and the German group Thyssen withdrew from the bidding, denouncing a bias in favor of domestic producers (Lozano 1992: 11; Domímguez 1993: 55). Techint's rise as a major domestic producer (and, increasingly, as an internationalized actor) in the steel market – in terms of the book's framework a strong ISI business actor – is essential background to understanding this successful lobbying. Argentine policymakers knew that "targeted privatization" benefiting Techint – even if it meant sidelining big international players such as Thyssen or Iritecnia – would not mean less revenue (in view of the financial resources of the conglomerate) nor hinder the viability of the company (given the group's solid standing in modern steel technology). Moreover, it would serve to appease a powerful and potentially destabilizing domestic economic conglomerate already affected by the end of the "national purchase regime" and of massive protection.

But the economic strength of the main local producer was not only important for the acquisition of SOMISA. The complex interplay between political and economic power in the origins of the "partial deregulation" of the steel market via antidumping measures is evident in the following statement from a top executive of the Techint conglomerate. When asked why Techint was so privileged by the state-enacted antidumping measures, which, as noted previously, significantly restricted the liberalization of the sector in the mid- to late 1990s, the finance director replied:

The answer is easy. These days, to get a favorable antidumping measure in Argentina, you need economic and financial strength and a well-organized team. It took three years before we could get a favorable resolution on hot-rolled sheets. We had to dedicate three people exclusively to that. It is a matter of power. A small business does not have the time, nor the resources to do that.[28]

As the top executive from Techint makes clear, the group benefited from antidumping measures simply because, as the most powerful Argentine industrial conglomerate, it had an internal division dedicated to studying the issue, preparing reports, and lobbying the state – regardless of eventual connections with state regulators. Other potential losers from liberalization in Argentina could hardly devote a company division exclusively to the dumping question. In other words, a political or regulatory issue such as the state enactment of an antidumping measure is also related to the economic resources of the given firm.

Techint would use the control of the domestic market – through both the purchase of SOMISA and the limited opening to imports – as its platform to build a flat steel empire in Latin America with the acquisition of the Venezuelan company Sidor (1997) and the Mexican Hysalmex (2005). These two firms plus Siderar, grouped in the Ternium consortium, were added to its traditionally powerful division of tubes.[29] By 2008 the Techint group, boosted by its more recent Latin American expansion in flat steel, showed revenues of $25,962 million.[30]

Restructuring in the Argentine Oil Industry

Concertation and Market-Share Compensation to Business Insiders
Since the first oil reserves were discovered in Argentina at the beginning of the twentieth century, the petroleum industry had been dominated by the state

---

[28] Author's interview, Buenos Aires, March 1, 2009.

[29] Between 2001 and 2005 Techint organized its steel division worldwide in two major groups. Tenaris included all the makers of tubes: Siderca and Siat (Argentina), Confab (Brazil), Tamsa (Mexico), Algoma (Canada), Dálmine (Italy), Silcotub (Romania), and NKK (Japan). Ternium became the major producer of the subsector in Latin America, but Sidor was nationalized by Hugo Chavez with compensation in 2009.

[30] http://www.techintgroup.com/group/en/highlights/default.aspx.

Statist and Corporatist Models of Business Adjustment   109

enterprise Yacimientos Petrolíferos Fiscales (YPF). Liberalization of the Argentine oil industry was the first major opening of the sector in any developing country and was often taken by business observers as a model case of liberal policy reform.[31] Yet, this case study will show how the "sweeping" deregulation of the oil industry was biased in favor of the interests of established domestic producers through what I have called market-share compensation.

The Argentine state had traditionally regulated the three major segments of petroleum activity: extraction/production, refining, and distribution.[32] Most private capital was integrated in the production subsector through service contracts with the state for oil extraction, which were signed in different periods since the 1950s. The main YPF contractors were the national companies Pérez Companc, Astra, and Bridas and the U.S.-based Amoco and Cities Services/Occidental. Prior to the 1990s, private contractors (*contratistas*) did not own the oil but had to deliver it to YPF for a fixed price. In the refining subsector, YPF would process part of the crude extracted by contractors and by itself and sell the rest to subsidiaries of Shell and Exxon, the two other refiners established in the country. YPF controlled both the volume of domestic crude funneled to private refiners (which were not allowed to import crude freely) and the price of gas and other oil products in the retail market. Finally, the distribution and retail segment was dominated by YPF and two TNCs, Shell and Exxon, which together held approximately 35% of the gas market.

Overall, the deregulation of the petroleum industry evolved in three stages:

1. Removal of state intervention in price setting, tariffs, levels of production, distribution for refining, and imports and exports. Limitations on the construction of new refineries and gas stations were also lifted.
2. Privatization of oil fields. The government followed three main strategies for the privatization of oil fields: (a) It organized an international bidding process for the so-called marginal areas, oil fields with lower productivity. (b) It promoted the privatization of low-risk, high-return reserves, also called "central areas." (c) A third policy strategy in this process of privatization was the renegotiation of old extraction service contracts with private producers.
3. Privatization of YPF itself. In June 1993, through a public auction of shares for domestic and international investors, YPF, the biggest Argentine company ($3.9 billion of net sales during 1992), passed into private hands. In 1999 the company was bought by the Spanish Repsol, giving birth to Repsol-YPF, the eighth largest private oil producer in the world by 2001.[33]

Deregulation posed severe threats to private producers upstream: their old extraction contracts became increasingly uncertain amid general restructuring

---

[31] See, for example, Vass and Valiente-Noailles (1992).
[32] In the oil industry's jargon exploration and production (or extraction) are called "upstream" activities, whereas refining and distribution are often referred as "downstream."
[33] *El Pais Economic Suplement*, November 25, 2001.

of the sector. Before 1989, contractors received a fixed rent from YPF for the crude they were producing, which entailed no exploration risks and protection from the vagaries of price fluctuations in international markets. In fact, before deregulation the state company often paid contractors prices that were higher than the operative costs of YPF for similar areas, and also higher than what YPF itself was charging to private refiners (Kozulj and Bravo 1993: 37, Pistonesi et al. 1990: 93; Gadano and Sturzenegger 1998: 80). The fundamental bases of deregulation – essentially stages (1) and (2) – were established by decrees 1,055, 1,212, and 1,589 issued between October and December 1989 under the umbrella of the State Reform Law. The decrees were written jointly with the lawyers of the main individual firms and later discussed in the ambit of the sectoral chambers of both international and national oil producers.[34]

The privatization of low-return areas was undertaken in mid-1990 and 1991 in two rounds of bidding formally open to any national or foreign producer. The four largest high-return or central areas were privatized between March and July 1991.[35] In an attempt to attract big world players and enhanced foreign expertise in the local market of oil extraction, the government had ruled in the first months of 1990 that domestic companies would not be able to bid for them. In response, the national companies lobbied both the government and the congressional committee that had to approve the final conditions for the bidding.[36] Ultimately, the legislation governing the awarding of the central areas was changed so as to allow domestic producers to participate if they formed a joint venture with a foreign company. In fact, domestic producers ended up operating the awarded areas and using foreign companies only as financial partners.[37] This "pressure from below" was in the end successful: of the four central areas, three were awarded to national companies, Astra, Pérez Companc, and Tec-Petrol; the fourth was granted to the French company Total. A simple clue that suggests that these were not exceedingly competitive bids is that in many high- and low-return areas the winners were already operating an oil field adjacent to the one awarded.[38] On the one hand, companies already operating in the area had,

[34] "I consulted with all the businessmen in the sector; the lawyer of [national private company] Astra worked with me night and day." Author's interview with a top official of the Department of Energy at the time, Buenos Aires, December 17, 2000. All the oil businessmen interviewed acknowledged the participation of the main companies in the drafting of the decrees. Juan Aranguren, vice president of Shell Argentina, asserted that "the three decrees were developed by the industry." Author's interview, Buenos Aires, February 15, 2001.

[35] These high-return areas represented 18% of total oil production and were four of the five more productive oil fields in Argentina (Kozulj and Bravo 1993: 148).

[36] "They wanted us out, but in the end the presidents of the companies talked with Menem and Cavallo, and it did not happen." Author's interview with Eduardo Zapata, main lawyer of Astra, second national producer, Buenos Aires, October 13, 2000. On this lobbying see also Gadano and Sturzenegger (1998: 85).

[37] Author's interview, ibid.; see also Kozulj and Bravo (1993: 142).

[38] For example, Astra was already operating a field adjacent to the central area Vizcacheras in the province of Mendoza, which was awarded to the company. On this question see the excellent empirical analysis in Kozulj and Bravo (1993: 126–40).

Statist and Corporatist Models of Business Adjustment

ceteris paribus, more incentives to make a higher offer for the adjacent field and therefore reduce costs in the future. However, interviews with officials and businessmen involved in the bidding process suggest that the oil fields were simply targeted at companies already operating nearby.

Finally, in the process of renegotiating the old contracts of extraction there was no competition at all. The transformation of the prereform service contracts of oil extraction in Argentina thus constitutes a model case of "protectionist deregulation" or "partial reform" as a compensatory policy described in Chapter 2. The majority of private contractors had to return their oil fields to the state within a few years. In fact, during the second half of 1989 the Argentine subsidiary of Shell consistently pressured the government to revoke the old contracts of oil extraction (relying on legal emergency powers, as it had with other state contracts at the time) and to call for new bids over those areas.[39] Shell was not integrated into the upstream in Argentina: that is, it did not own oil fields. Complete deregulation could, therefore, open attractive opportunities for domestic sources of crude. Yet, the administration chose to transform the old service contracts into concessions, making the (mostly national) private producers free owners of the oil for the next twenty-five years, with an option for ten more. For Oscar Vicente, CEO of the Argentine main oil producer Pérez Companc at the time, the proposal for the deregulation of the old service contracts of extraction was "outrageous" and would have meant "a nationalization, a socialization."[40] Quite paradoxically, a policy sponsored by Royal Dutch Shell was attacked by local producers as a policy of expropriation. Finally, decree 1,212 in late 1989 ruled the conversion of the old service contracts into concessions in which old contractors would become free owners of the oil, and in 1990 the government created a tripartite commission formed by the sectoral union Union of Oil Workers (SUPE) and representatives of the secretary of energy and the companies involved, that would decide the terms of the renegotiation of each contract.[41]

In sum, both sets of rules that reshaped the sector – the deregulation and privatization decrees and the transformation of old contracts of extraction into concessions for established producers during 1990 and 1991 – were drafted jointly with business. In the end, both pieces of legislation left all businessmen in the sector happy: Shell obtained the liberalization of crude imports and the

---

[39] Author's interview with an adviser to the secretary of energy at the time, Buenos Aires, November 13, 2000.

[40] Author's interview, Buenos Aires, January 22, 2001.

[41] Author's interview with Alberto Fiandesio, government representative to the committee that negotiated the transformation of extraction contracts, Buenos Aires, November 13, 2000. See also Gadano and Sturzenegger (1998: 90). The general rule followed was that if the price of the contract was higher than the projected market price, the oil field would be handed to the contractor. If the projected price was lower, YPF would remain associated in the exploitation of the field. Considerations such as expected production and the lag between the (generally proximate) expiration of contracts and the concession period were left out, benefiting established producers.

The Political Economy of Business Adjustment

deregulation of prices and retail sale downstream, which was its main area of activity in Argentina. Domestic contractors in the upstream succeeded in transforming the old contracts of extraction into concessions that provided them with outright ownership of the oil. The view of the then-vice president of Shell Argentina evokes the character of the agreement:

> We wanted the repealing of the old contracts of oil extraction. But when you cannot win 7–0, it is OK to win 6–4. What was more important, to establish the basis for a deregulated market or to achieve the "perfect deregulation"? There was a bargain, as always. And the "perfect" is sometimes enemy of the "good." We preferred the good. Once the process was launched, everything went forward, and each of us in the sector bet for the business that he knew more about.[42]

The imperfect deregulation, as the former vice president of Shell puts it, involved significant compensation to domestic producers. Domestic contractors would eventually have to face the uncertainty of the market, but with the invaluable help of their market share consolidated in the run-up to liberalization.[43] Table 4.5 reflects the power of the old private domestic producers to preserve their positions in the new market structure.

Another way to assess the degree to which traditional actors protected their market share is to check the oil extraction by legal regime, that is, the type of normative framework (prereform contract or new concession) under which the private agent extracts the oil (Table 4.6). The greater the share of petroleum extracted under regimes instituted (without any competitive bidding) before the reform period, the less diversified has been supply since deregulation, and the smaller the threat to traditional producers. The main legal regimes instituted before neoliberal reform include YPF's own areas and the extraction contracts signed under Frondizi and the military regimes in the period 1958–83 – which, as stated previously, were transformed into concessions after 1989. After reform, a series of new legal regimes was instituted, under which privatization was carried out. Overall, the table shows that in 1996, seven years after deregulation, 70.8% of the petroleum produced in Argentina was extracted under regimes established *before* deregulation, and only 29.8% was the result of areas awarded after the 1989 liberalization, that is, under the new regimes of extraction.

Toward the mid-1990s, Pérez Companc, a national company and a former private contractor in the industry, had almost doubled its market share and displaced the American producer Amoco as the largest private producer of petroleum in Argentina after YPF (Table 4.4). In brief, in times of economic internationalization, it was paradoxically the national bourgeoisie traditionally protected by the state who increased its market share in the subsector most, initially displacing international capital.

---

[42] Author's interview with Juan Jose Aranguren, vice president of Shell Argentina, Buenos Aires, February 15, 2001.

[43] Analyzing only 4 of the 25 contracts, Gadano and Sturzenegger (1998: 97) estimate that the transformation of contracts in concessions cost the state $120 million.

TABLE 4.5. *Argentina: Total Oil Production by Company before and after Reform (thousands of cubic meters)*

	Before Reform				After Reform			
	1987		1988		1993		1994	
YPF (State till 1993)	15,967	64.2%	17,036	65.2%	13,270	38.4%	16,502	42.6%
Domestic Private								
PÉREZ COMPANC S.A.[a]	2,218	8.9%	2,094	8.0%	5,404	15.6%	5,279	13.6%
P. SAN JORGE S.A.	129	0.5%	124	0.5%	1,290	3.7%	2,251	5.8%
ASTRA CAPSA	456	1.8%	745	2.9%	1,647	4.8%	2,026	5.2%
BRIDAS P.I.C.S.R.L.	686	2.8%	804	3.1%	1,717	5.0%	1,659	4.3%
PLUSPETROL	412	1.7%	444	1.7%	1,084	3.1%	1,096	2.8%
TECPETROL S.A.	0	0.0%	0	0.0%	1,089	3.2%	1,047	2.7%
Foreign								
AMOCO ARGENTINA OIL CO.	2,486	10.0%	2,341	9.0%	2,656	7.7%	2,721	7.0%
CITIES SERVICE S.A/OXY	1,544	6.2%	1,435	5.5%	0	0.0%	0	0.0%
TOTAL AUSTRAL S.A.	0	0.0%	0	0.0%	2,249	6.5%	2,325	6.0%
Rest (50 companies)	968	3.9%	1,099	4.2%	4,161	12.0%	3,861	10.0%
TOTAL	**24,867**	100.0%	**26,123**	100.0%	**34,569**	100.0%	**38,767**	100.0%

[a] Includes Pérez Companc S.A. and Petrolera Pérez Companc S.A.
Source: Instituto Argentino del Petróleo y Gas, Buenos Aires. Previously published in my "Constructing Reform Coalitions: The Politics of Compensation in the Argentine Path to Economic Liberalization," *Latin American Politics and Society*, vol. 43, no. 3 (Fall 2001), and in the book *Market, State, and Society in Contemporary Latin America*, ed. William C. Smith and Laura Gómez-Mera (Boston: Wiley, 2010).

TABLE 4.6. *Total Petroleum Production by Legal Regime (thousands of cubic meters)*

		Before Reform		After Reform		
		1987	1988	1992	1994	1996
Regimes Instituted before Reform	TOTAL	100.0%	100.0%	100.0%	100.0%	100.0%
	Houston Plan	0.0%	0.0%	0.1%	0.0%	0.1%
	Reconverted Contracts	**33.3%**	**32.5%**	**28.7%**	**28.1%**	**26.3%**
	Without Reconversion	0.1%	0.1%	0.1%	0.1%	0.1%
	Old Concessions	2.3%	2.2%	1.7%	1.2%	1.2%
	YPF Administration	**64.2%**	**65.2%**	40.8%	42.6%	43.1%
	Total before Reform	100.0%	100.0%	71.4%	72.0%	70.8%
Regimes Instituted after Reform	Central Area	0.0%	0.0%	16.3%	13.2%	11.3%
	Marginal Area	0.0%	0.0%	4.7%	4.0%	4.0%
	Provincial Area	0.0%	0.0%	0.0%	0.2%	0.2%
	Risk Contracts	0.0%	0.0%	5.5%	3.2%	2.7%
	New Association	0.0%	0.0%	2.1%	7.4%	10.9%
	Argentine Plan	0.0%	0.0%	0.0%	0.0%	0.2%
	Total after Reform	0.0%	0.0%	28.6%	28.0%	29.2%

Source: Instituto Argentino del Petróleo y Gas, Buenos Aires. Previously published in my "Constructing Reform Coalitions: The Politics of Compensation in the Argentine Path to Economic Liberalization," *Latin American Politics and Society*, vol. 43, no. 3 (Fall 2001), and in the book *Market, State, and Society in Contemporary Latin America*, ed. William C. Smith and Laura Gómez-Mera (Boston: Wiley, 2010).

Explaining the Outcome: The Rise of a Strong ISI Business Actor in the Oil Industry

As noted, in two crucial instances during the sweeping liberalization of the oil industry in Argentina – the privatization of central areas and the revamping of the service contracts with the state – domestic producers were about to be displaced. Actually a counterfactual in which local companies were deprived of their old extraction contracts as a result of the regulatory overhaul and were also marginalized in their bid for the most important oil areas would have not been difficult to envision in 1989–91. However, after a laborious "reaction from below," by the mid-1990s the main domestic companies emerged as winners from the oil industry restructuring. What accounts for their successful lobbying?

Statist and Corporatist Models of Business Adjustment

This study argues that the emergence under ISI of a domestic private sector that could compete locally in market power and technical capacity with the state, and especially with international producers in the oil industry, and that had developed massive financial resources is essential to understanding the outcome.

The history of the oil sector in Argentina witnessed the rise of a group of private domestic firms that would become powerful economic actors before liberalization gained momentum in the 1990s.[44] Unlike the steel sector, where foreign firms never made inroads, domestic oil producers had to compete with both the state and international players. Private company share in domestic production under the ISI model rose from around 25% (24.5) in 1967 to almost 40% (37.8) in 1989, when liberalization was about to take off.[45] Earlier, however, I showed that the winners in the deregulation of oil production were the main *local* companies Pérez Companc, Bridas, Astra, and Petrolera San Jorge. Graph 4.6 reveals that *within* a private sector that was growing before liberalization, local producers were consistently taking market share from their foreign rivals in the years prior to reform.

It is clear which types of governments favored local companies in the production contracts instituted under the inward-oriented model. The two spikes in the share of production of domestic firms before 1989 occurred during Ongania's military dictatorship (1967–70) and the Junta military regime (1978–81). In addition, the graph shows that the share of the compensated local firms soared during the liberalization period of 1989–92. Evidently, a local firm does not have the same ability to bid for a large oil field when it is managing 2% of local production versus 25% of foreign competitors as when both types of companies share similar production levels. Prereform growth of local producers meant that they had built relatively efficient management teams and had developed both considerable know-how and political contacts in the local market.[46] As the vice president of Shell Argentina, one of the losers of the upstream liberalization in Argentina, asserts:

> The local contractors had access to exploratory information that was of utmost importance. The contractors knew which tracks were attractive and which were not, and they were in a better situation than us to evaluate the utility of a field.[47]

Local producers had developed geological knowledge of the quality of tracks and oil fields in the Argentine market, which was an enormous advantage in the

---

[44] For the postwar history of the oil sector in Argentina, Kozulj and Bravo (1993) is an indispensable source.

[45] Production database, Instituto Argentino de Petróleo y Gas Privado, Buenos Aires, 2001.

[46] A common practice of domestic contractors was to hire engineers from YPF and former state officials in general. Many of the top CEOs of local private producers (for example, Oscar Vicente from Pérez Companc) started their careers in YPF. As a top executive of Amoco Argentina commented: "If you staff your company with former generals and YPF managers, you are going to have better contacts with the government." Author's interview, Buenos Aires, January 12, 2001.

[47] Author's interview, Buenos Aires, February 15, 2001.

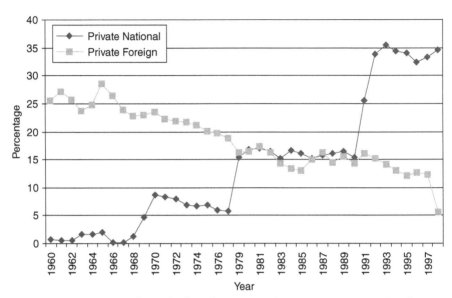

GRAPH 4.6. Argentina: Share of Oil Production (in cubic meters), Private National (Pérez C., Brida, Astral, Tecpetrol, San Jorge, Pluspetrol) and Foreign Producers (Amoco, Cities Service, Shell). *Source*: Instituto Argentino de Petróleo y Gas, Buenos Aires.

bidding process. It should be noted that the existence of private oil producers was unique to the Argentine petroleum industry among the major countries in Latin America under the inward-oriented model. In effect, PDVESA in Venezuela, Petrobras in Brazil, and PEMEX in Mexico maintained a complete monopoly in oil production during this period.[48] As the oil industry analysts Gadano and Sturzenegger (1998: 111) assert, "The presence of significant local private producers differentiates the Argentine reform process from what could occur in countries like Brazil or Mexico where this group does not exist." This difference in the type of actor set the basis for the Corporatist pattern of adjustment specific to the Argentine oil industry in Latin America.

In addition to their know-how and expansion in the domestic oil market in the run-up to reform, some of the oil local companies had massive disposable financial resources to compete with international producers. The trajectory of the major Argentine oil-based group Pérez Companc under the inward-oriented model is a paradigm of what I have called a strong ISI business actor. From a contractor that performed logistic services but did not extract oil in the mid-1960s, it progressed to controlling 8% of domestic oil production in 1988, second only to Amoco among private players. During the 1980s the Pérez Companc group grew steadily in terms of both sales and profits while the Argentine economy was plunging into

---

[48] Kozulj (1991: 136).

Statist and Corporatist Models of Business Adjustment

recession.[49] It had also diversified considerably. Though it was still largely an oil-based group – petroleum and natural gas accounted for 60% of its profits and 48% of its assets in 1988[50] – it had developed companies in cement, information technology (IT), and the agro industry, which helped enhance the cash flow available when economic liberalization began. In sum, in contrast with the main private industrial groups in Spain burdened by debt and declining market share, according to the three main indicators of economic power used in this book – volume of sales, profits, and market-share growth prior to reform – Pérez Companc was a formidable contender for the liberalizing economic team. Policymakers knew that Pérez Companc had disruptive power to hamper the liberalization process.[51] By the mid- to late 1990s Pérez Companc had become the largest private energy group in Latin America. However, as will be shown in Chapter 10, it would not experience unharmed the big economic and financial crises of 2001–02.

Restructuring in the Argentine Auto Industry

Formal Concertation and Partial Deregulation in the 1990s

Reform and restructuring of the auto industry in Argentina constitute a perfect case of market-share compensation through protectionist or partial liberalization. At the outset of deregulation, the market for family vehicles was divided between Autolatina (the merger of the TNCs Ford and Volkswagen in Argentina); the French firm Renault, which had floated 30% of capital in the Buenos Aires Stock Exchange and in 1992 sold its entire Argentine subsidiary to the Argentine group CIADEA; and Sevel, owned by the local SOCMA group (Macri family), which was the largest producer and held the licenses for Fiat and Peugeot. Three companies produced trucks and commercial vehicles: the national company Iveco (in which Fiat had a minority stake) and the foreign firms Mercedez Benz and Scania.

The "Motor Vehicle Regime" was implemented through decree 2,667 issued in December 1991. Its main features were (1) a wage agreement between firms and unions and a reduction of the prices of vehicles; (2) a tariff barrier of 30% – the average tariff for the whole economy after trade reform was around 10% at the time – combined with the possibility for the terminal industry to import units with a tariff of only 2%; and (3) import quotas, at a rate of 10% of the local

---

[49] Pérez Companc's net profits in the recession years are impressive: $81 million in 1988 and $108 million in 1989. Pérez Companc, *Memoria y Balance General 1991*, p. 8.

[50] Pérez Companc, *Memoria y Balance General 1988*, pp. 20 and 54.

[51] "They could not just develop the market over the 'dead bodies' of local producers; we would have initiated a wave of trials and no foreign company would have come in such an environment." Author's interview with Oscar Vicente, CEO of Pérez Companc, Buenos Aires, January 22, 2001. On the possibility of outright deregulation of the old service contracts, the undersecretary of fuels at the time stated that "it would have provoked big political problems, an unending series of trials. The lobby they had was impressive." Author's interview, Buenos Aires, December 17, 2000.

production per year. Furthermore, companies had to match each vehicle imported at a preferential tariff with an exported one.[52]

The regime was negotiated under the aegis of the Concertation Committee for the Reconversion of the Auto Industry, created by the Menem administration in 1990. The committee was formed by representatives from the Ministry of the Economy, the six firms mentioned previously, the autoworkers' union SMATA, and the metalworkers' union UOM, which had minority representation in the sector. In 1991 the Concertation Committee reached an agreement on the future plan for the sector, named the "Agreement for the Transformation for the Auto Sector," which the government eventually crystallized into decree 2,669. In practice, the sectoral business organization, ADEFA, acted as the unitary voice of business. Businessmen and unionists worked hand in hand in submitting the proposal for industrial policy for the sector through their peak national organizations. The plan was born out of pressure from below: that is, it was a joint project crafted by the main firms and SMATA, which was subsequently negotiated with the economic authorities.[53]

The Motor Vehicle Regime, coupled with the consumption boom spawned by economic stabilization and by an increasingly overvalued exchange rate, allowed the domestic-oriented motor vehicle industry to thrive during the adjustment years in Argentina. Industrial GDP (year-on-year variation rate) for the auto industry increased almost 50% during the period 1991–95, 20% above the second-best industrial performer (IDI 1997; see also UADE 1997).

Even if the share of automobiles produced in Argentina as part of the total national consumption shrank by almost 30 points between 1991 and 1997 (ADEFA 1992, 1997), in 1994 the market share of the main domestic producer Sevel decreased by only 3 points (Table 4.7). The same pattern can be observed for Ciadea and Autolatina, although for them loss in market share was greater. This outcome was undoubtedly associated with the specific features of the Motor Vehicle Regime. The fact that, in addition to their market reserve through tariffs and quotas, the assembly plants could import at a 2% tariff enabled them to profit from the increase in domestic consumption by importing cars. In sum, a specific and negotiated pattern of deregulation meant that the old private producers – half of them controlled by domestic business – were to a great extent spared from the costs of adjustment and deregulation.[54]

---

[52] The Ouro Preto agreements that formalized the common market Mercosur in 1994 accepted the Argentine Motor Vehicle Regime until the year 2000, when the special regime was renegotiated with Brazil and the other Mercosur partners.

[53] Author's interview with Horacio Losoviz, president of the automakers' association ADEFA 1992–98, Buenos Aires, January 29, 2001, and with Manuel Pardo, adjunct secretary of the autoworkers' union SMATA, Buenos Aires, October 19, 2000. Enrique Federico, head of institutional relations of Mereceds Benz Argentina, stated that "the government made the decree, but we gave them the philosophy, the ideas." Author's interview, March 27, 2001.

[54] Finchelstein (2004) argues that SOCMA witnessed a 181% percentage growth in sales between 1991 and 1994; 54% of that growth is explained by the auto company Sevel, signaling the importance of market-share compensation within its main sector for the Macri group.

Statist and Corporatist Models of Business Adjustment 119

TABLE 4.7. *Argentina: Domestic Market Share (Sales) in the Auto Industry in Units, Including Local Production and Imported – Familiar Vehicles (Category A)*

	Before Reform		After Reform	
Year	1988		1994	
Sevel[a]	62,289	40.4%	166,307	37.5%
Autolatina[b]	45,831	29.8%	96,517	21.8%
Ciadea/Renault Arg.	45,886	29.8%	96,695	21.8%
G. Motors			3,661	0.8%
Imported by Others			79,850	18.0%
Total	154,006	100.0%	443,030	100.0%

[a] Sold its license back to Peugeot by 1996.
[b] Sold its license back to Renault by 1996.
Source: ADEFA (various years).

Explaining the Outcome: A Strong ISI Coalition Survives the Market

The auto sector appears as a third core ISI sector in which Argentine capitalists emerged as powerful actors under ISI, for several reasons. First, unlike in the Spanish case, state companies never became strong players in the local auto industry: the Peronist government in the 1950s failed to launch a domestically based automaker, and later the Frondizi developmentalist administration bet on international TNCs. Second, as mentioned in Chapter 3, important foreign companies pulled out of the country as a result of the odd combination of political radicalization and the liberalization policies implemented by the 1976–83 dictatorship. Chrysler, Citroen, General Motors, and Fiat withdrew from Argentina between 1975 and 1980.[55] Renault would progressively sell its stakes in the Argentine subsidiary during the late 1980s and early 1990s.

Consequently, while private Argentine capital was producing less than 7% of total vehicles in 1976,[56] at the beginning of the reform period the companies Sevel (SOCMA group), Ciadea, and Iveco, which held brand licenses from (departed) foreign companies but were locally owned, held around 70% of the market share in passenger vehicles and owned three of the six assembly plants in the country. Again, the power of Argentine domestic capitalists in a core ISI sector such as autos was unmatched not only in Spain, but also in Mexico and Brazil, the other large car manufacturing countries in Latin America. As had Techint and Pérez Companc in the steel and oil industries, the main producer SOCMA had become a quintessential strong ISI business actor. Though largely built around the car company by the early 1990s (44% of total group sales),[57] the conglomerate had diversified into electronics, food, and garbage collection.

[55] For the institutional and economic history of the Argentine auto sector before liberalization, see Jenkins (1984) and Nofal (1989).
[56] Kronish (1984: 77).
[57] Finchelstein (2004: 34).

120   *The Political Economy of Business Adjustment*

Thus, local ownership by powerful actors considerably increased the pressure for a Corporatist bargain over market-share compensation. These companies did not expect a reconversion plan or subsidies from a state that had long abandoned any involvement in the auto industry and lacked any technical expertise on the matter. Domestic companies owned by healthy groups that did not need immediate cash and were much more challenged by full-scale liberalization than their foreign counterparts pursued market reserves in the future order as the obvious choice. Although foreign players such as Autolatina (Ford and Volkswagen) and Mercedez Benz also benefited from the implementation of the Motor Vehicle Regime, the main lobbyists were the local companies Sevel and Ciadea and the autoworkers' union SMATA, whose fundamental role in this coalition for compensation will be analyzed in Chapter 7.[58] Finally the concentration of the sector in only six major companies lowered collective action dilemmas and eased this phenomenal lobbying of the state.[59]

The auto sector underwent an impressive change during the Menem decade. Three TNCs were producing cars in Argentina in 1988 – Ford, Volkswagen, and Mercedes Benz. By 2000, eleven TNCs, largely lured by the special tariff regime, accounted for total production. This transformation included the establishment or return to the country of world majors such as Fiat, Renault, Toyota, General Motors, PSA-Peugeot, General Motors, and Chrysler. Meanwhile, all domestic producers had sold their licenses in a business dominated by foreign TNCs worldwide. After the financial crash of 2001–02 the Argentine auto industry recovered, underpinned by the competitive exchange rate and domestic growth, reaching a production record of around 600,000 vehicles in 2008.

FURTHER ILLUSTRATIVE CASES OF CORPORATIST AND STATIST
ADJUSTMENT IN ARGENTINA AND SPAIN: PHARMACEUTICALS
AND ALUMINUM

As pointed out in Chapter 3, the Argentine local pharmaceutical industry was rewarded with market-share compensation via partial reform during neoliberalism. In the early 1990s domestic firms were severely threatened by import liberalization and by the deregulation of the state administrative approval for new drugs. In addition, in the context of its new alliance with the United States, the Menem

---

[58] "In the early 1990s, Sevel [the major local producer from the SOCMA group] dominated ADEFA." Author's interview with Mario Dasso, executive director of ADEFA, Buenos Aires, March 7, 2001. The role played by the union SMATA, hand in hand with ADEFA in the lobbying of the regime, was acknowledged by every businessman interviewed.

[59] Horacio Losoviz, former CEO of Iveco (one of the national compensated auto firms) and president of ADEFA (automakers' association), 1992–98, puts it this way: "The auto sector had advantages over the other sectors. One was that there were few people, few actors. When the motor-vehicle regime was drafted, we were six actors, Ciadea, Sevel, Scania, Iveco, Autolatina, and M. Benz. That was a big advantage; six people can get to an agreement very easily." Author's interview, Buenos Aires, January 29, 2001.

Statist and Corporatist Models of Business Adjustment

government initially committed to comply with TRIPS (Trade Related Aspects of Intellectual Property Rights), which meant the sanction of a law that would recognize patent protection in the pharmaceutical industry – one of the largest users of patents and trademarks in the world. Such legislation would seriously affect local companies, which had traditionally imported and produced freely new drugs and components patented or developed in the advanced world. However, in view of the extensive pressure of domestic producers on both the Executive and Congress, the final intellectual property reform was delayed longer than in any country in the region (Shadlen 2006: 30), and watered down, benefiting local industrial insiders. Why was the local pharmaceutical sector, unlike so many others save the ones rewarded by Corporatist adjustment, able to exert such effective lobbying?

The pharmaceutical industry in Argentina represents another case in which national companies rose to dominance, displacing both the state and foreign TNCs, under the inward-oriented model. Pharmaceuticals was a typical ISI sector: that is, it produced largely for the domestic market sheltered by high tariffs. Domestic players' privileged access to government approvals for new drugs, their capacity to import technology and active components from non-patented sources, and their strong activism in the launching and marketing of new products contributed to the strong growth of local companies, particularly from the 1960s.[60] By the early 1970s domestic private pharmaceutical companies showed performance rates superior to those of foreign TNCs in many aspects: product diversification in different submarkets, product differentiation, and resources poured into research and development locally.[61] On the basis of his sample of seventy-six foreign and domestic firms, Chudnovsky (1979: 53) estimates that the rate of profits of local firms was on average 50% higher than those of foreign subsidiaries. Already in 1972 the first, fourth, and fifth companies in market share of domestic sales were of national capital – Bagó, Química Argentina, and Roemmers.[62] The growth of domestic companies vis-à-vis TNCs under the inward-oriented model, buttressed by protection and by the retrenchment of foreign capital in an environment of political and economic instability, only increased in the run-up to reform, as Graph 4.7 attests.

In brief, the local companies dominated around 60% of the market by the late 1980s, thereby becoming, in the words of Ken Shadlen (2006: 28), "formidable fighters" when liberalization took off. The largest domestic laboratories were strong ISI business players according to the three main indicators used in this analysis, sales, profits, and market-share performance in relation to the state or

---

[60] See Burachik and Katz (1997: 96) and FIEL (1990).

[61] Within his sample of firms, Chudnovsky (1979) finds that the average participation in different submarkets (59 therapeutic classes) was higher for local firms, that local companies produced more drugs per firm, and that they devoted more resources for R&D in relation to sales.

[62] Indeed, Chudnovsky (1979: 46) points out "the strength of the domestic sector in the industry." Another analyst of the industry asserts that the Argentine pharmaceutical industry "has possessed since its origins an astute and intelligent leadership that has enabled the formation of sizable laboratories that became true protagonists of the industry" (Irigoyen 2006: 351).

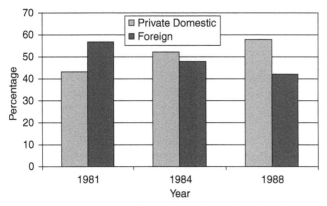

GRAPH 4.7. Argentina: Share (in total sales) in the Pharmaceutical Industry, Private Domestic and Foreign Firms, Prereform Period. *Source*: FIEL (1990: 79).

TNCs in the run-up to reform – by 1988 three of the top four pharmaceutical companies in terms of sales were of national capital (FIEL 1990: 78). Therefore, not only did they possess large resources to back their lobbying for market reserves after 1989, but they could appear vis-à-vis politicians both as powerful actors with political leverage and as credible economic players in a more liberalized market. By 2004, after this protectionist or partial liberalization that benefited insiders, two laboratories of Argentine capital, Roemmers ($152 million) and Bagó ($98 million), led the ranking of sales in the industry (Irigoyen 2006: 191).[63]

Aluminum in Spain is another clear case of a basic ISI sector subjected to Statist transformation from above in neoliberal times. Because it was not so affected by overcapacity and excess employment, aluminum was excluded from the reconversion plans formulated under the Law of Reconversion and Re-Industrialization analyzed in Chapter 3. As a first step in its revamping of the sector, in 1983 the state bought minority stakes of the Canadian Alcan in Aluminio Español, the flagship company of the state aluminum holding ENDASA. It also promoted and subsidized the merger between the two main companies in the sector, ENDASA (State) and Alugasa (from the French group Pechiney), which gave birth two years later to the public holding INESPAL (Aceña and Comín 1991: 510–11). In practice, the government had grouped all the aluminum facilities in Spain under state control. This strategy was consistent with the Statist mode of industrial adjustment, that is, the formation of public groups, especially in those industrial sectors where local private capital

---

[63] In Brazil the government also elicited the support of local companies in "health enhancing" reforms that relaxed TRIPS obligations in the first years of this century, but this was after the original patent reform supported by the transnational sector was passed in the context of neoliberal reforms; see Shadlen (2009).

Statist and Corporatist Models of Business Adjustment

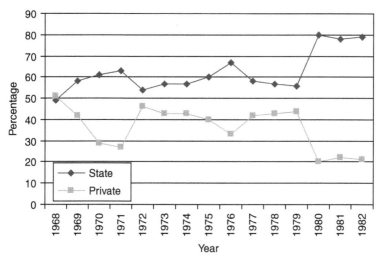

GRAPH 4.8. Spain: Share of Aluminum Production, State and Private Sector, Prereform Period. *Source*: Statistical Appendix in Martín Aceña and Comín (1991).

was relatively weak, such as CSI (steel), SIDENOR (special steels), and IZAR (shipbuilding) in the cases just analyzed. In the early 1990s the state leadership of INESPAL acquired the remaining private shares in the group and carried out further rounds of reconversion and employment adjustment in the context of declining international prices. The company was made profitable and competitive and, as in the cases of steel, autos, and electronics – in which the state technocrats envisioned no possibilities of competition vis-à-vis TNCs dominant worldwide – privatized in 1998.

This reorganization from above was evidently facilitated by the fact that the state was almost absolutely dominant in the sector by the early 1980s, and local private capital was weak or nonexistent (Graph 4.8). No major local private group would press for market concentration in the context of liberalization – as the Aluar-Madanes aluminum-based group did in Argentina (see Chapter 3). When reform was launched the state was the hegemonic producer in the sector; it dealt with multinationals with only partial interest in Spain at the time (such as Pechiney and Alcan) and thereby had ample leeway and expertise to reorganize the sector. It finally sold the revamped group to the other major world player (Alcoa) in 1998.

CONCLUSIONS

This chapter has studied the dynamics of Statist and Corporatist models of industrial liberalization in seven sectors in Argentina and Spain. In all these industries tariffs dwindled as countries integrated into regional and global markets, and all state firms were privatized. Yet neither in the Statist nor in the

Corporatist model were these transformations entirely left to the operation of market forces. Political payoffs and compensation were at stake. In Spain, state industrial interventionism increased as liberalization unfolded in the three sectors studied. The government designed a series of reconversion plans and promoted and subsidized the formation of public groups that included all of the largest firms in each sector: CSI-Aceralia (integrated steel), SIDENOR (special steels), IZAR (shipbuilding), and INESPAL (aluminum). Once capacity cuts, employment downsizing, and competitiveness had been achieved, these companies were generally sold to the major TNCs that dominated the industry[64] – unlike in other sectors, such as energy, pulp and paper and IT, in which state technocrats foresaw local potential for international competition. Two parallel (and mutually reinforcing) developments under the inward-oriented model shaped this outcome. On the one hand, the state had become the hegemonic player in these industries when liberalization was about to take off and thereby possessed the technocratic expertise to design the reconversion plans. On the other hand, the local private sector was weak and in retreat and could only accept subsidies to pay off debts. No major domestic private group based in steel, aluminum, or shipbuilding was in a condition to expand under neoliberalism.

In Argentina's Corporatist model, in all the sectors studied the government initially laid out plans for comprehensive liberalization and industrial privatization thoroughly open to international players. Yet all of them witnessed a reaction of established domestic private business "from below." These companies successfully lobbied different forms of market-share compensation: special tariff regimes or partial sectoral deregulation (autos, steel, pharmaceuticals) and "targeted" privatization (steel, oil, autos). These sectors, plus cement and aluminum (also compensated but not studied in the chapter), shared an essential trait: local private companies or economic groups had emerged as major actors under ISI, displacing both the state and/or foreign companies in the run-up to reform. Indeed, all were home to a major domestic company or group that was singularly powerful in terms of sales, profits, and prior market-share trends: Techint (steel), Macri (autos), Pérez Companc (oil), Bagó (pharmaceuticals), Fortabat (cement), and Aluar-Madanes (aluminum). Macri, Pérez Companc, and Techint had thoroughly diversified into large economic groups prior to reform, though around 50% of their total sales still stemmed from their core industries. Prior diversification increased the cash flow available for market-share compensation, and reformers knew that these major economic groups had potential to disrupt the liberalization process. In sum, these family industrial groups had built the expertise and economic power to expand in more open markets, at least *initially*, and craved political and regulatory payoffs to that end.

However, my argument is that dominant companies in the sectors studied in Argentina were powerful enough to obtain market concentration via state regulation in the short run, not that they could sustain competition in

---

[64] Shipbuilding – an industry not dominated by TNCs but by large East Asian companies that have very low costs – is an exception.

internationalized markets. As shown previously, among the six major sectors compensated, only in three – steel, aluminum, and pharmaceuticals – were the Argentine rewarded groups still active and dominant by the late 2000s. The reasons for the survival or demise of formerly protected business actors in globalized markets in each model will be hypothesized in Chapter 10. The point is, however, that while in the Statist model the technocrats decide in which sectors the revamped national industrial groups will survive or not, such strategic design did not exist in Argentina. The Corporatist model is agnostic about the future fate of the companies politically empowered during neoliberalism.

5

Exceptions That Prove the Rule

Variation within Countries in Models of Business Adjustment

INTRODUCTION

Chapters 3 and 4 explained the Statist and Corporatist models of business adjustment in Argentina and Spain through both national and sectoral evidence. In the Statist mode, the government organized top-down reconversion plans based on the allocation of subsidies that benefited companies in important sectors such as steel, shipbuilding, home appliances, and aluminum. However, the main established private firms in the sectors subjected to restructuring were eventually wiped out of the market. In Argentina's Corporatist model, by contrast, the state funneled market-share compensation (i.e., state assets and partial deregulation) to local private companies in the heavy industrial sectors of autos, oil, steel, aluminum, cement, and pharmaceuticals. Building upon these market reserves, formerly protected actors initially thrived in the liberalized economy.

This chapter aims to illuminate a second form of variation in the modes of business adjustment. In terms of the book's general research design, at a national level, each alternative reform model obviously constitutes a "negative" case of the others.[1] In addition, the case studies that follow indicate variation within countries, that is, core ISI sectors that were not compensated according to the prevalent national model of business adjustment.[2] Correspondingly, these "negative" cases should display a parallel variation in the main explanatory variable within democratic cases – the power of state and private business as they emerged from the ISI model. Unlike in the case of labor – in which adjustment models were more homogeneous nationally – two important basic ISI sectors, petrochemicals and oil, deviated from the general pattern of compensation in Argentina and Spain (Table 5.1).

---

[1] Whether as essential or as one among other useful methodological strategies, the question of including ample variation in explanatory and outcome variables in qualitative research designs is discussed in King et al. (1994: 129), Munck (2004: 114), and Collier and Mahoney (1996: 73–74); see also Mahoney (2007: 128–30).

[2] The classic formulation on increasing the number of observations in small-n research designs is Lijphart (1971); for the search for variation at the subnational and sectoral levels see Snyder (2001a).

126

Exceptions That Prove the Rule

TABLE 5.1. *National Models of Industrial Restructuring and Deviant Cases*

	Spain 1983–95 Statist Core Cases: Steel, Autos, Shipbuilding, Home Appliances	Argentina 1989–99 Corporatist Core Cases: Steel, Oil, Autos, Aluminum
General Pattern of Industrial Restructuring		
Nature of Policymaking	State *Dirigisme*	Concertation
Compensatory Measures	Subsidy Allocation	Market-Share Compensation
Consequences	Retrenchment of Prereform Established Firms	Initial Expansion of Prereform Established Firms
Deviant Case	Oil	Petrochemicals
Nature of Policymaking	Concertation	State *Dirigisme*
Compensatory Measures	Market-Share Compensation	Subsidy Allocation
Consequences	Initial Expansion of Prereform Established Firms	Retrenchment of Prereform Established Firms

In the wake of deregulation and integration into the EU, the government favored the main Spanish oil firms with market-share compensation in a pattern much like the Argentine Corporatist approach. The Spanish oil sector was not included in any of the reconversion plans crafted by the administration. Domestic firms were systematically protected in the run-up to full-scale liberalization of the oil industry and were privileged in the privatization of the main state monopoly in the sector. In Argentina, unlike in the cases of autos, steel, oil and others, the government pushed forward a radical deregulation of the petrochemical sector and excluded local players from the privatization of the main state-run industrial complexes. Domestic companies could only get subsidies in the form of state bailouts of domestic debt. Thus, industrial reform in the Argentine petrochemical sector was not very different from the *Statist* pattern observed at the national level in Spain: the state subsidized private domestic groups, nationalized one of them, and eventually sold the main assets in the sector to foreign TNCs, bringing about the demise of traditional local players.

The chapter argues that in the context of a weak industrial bourgeoisie under ISI, the oil sector in Spain was distinguished by relatively powerful local private firms. These companies (owned by the major local banks) had developed the financial power, economies of scale, and the political organization to press for market-share compensation once the deregulation process had been launched. Conversely, the petrochemical sector in Argentina, for reasons that I explain later, constituted an island of state industrial power under the inward-oriented model: public firms had been relentlessly taking market share from domestic (and foreign) private companies in some crucial subsectors prior to reform. Domestic companies, historically hindered by state dominance, lacked the resources to claim any form of market-share compensation once reform was launched and, eventually, demanded only some form of subsidy to pay off debts and accept an honorable retreat. In short, the divergent fate of local companies during neoliberal reform was rooted in the way in which domestic, state, and foreign actors coalesced in the given sector under ISI.

The first and second parts of the chapter explain alternative patterns of restructuring in the deviant cases of petrochemicals in Argentina and oil in Spain. The last part of the chapter deepens the intersectoral comparison across countries by analyzing the logic of industrial privatization in eight sectors in Argentina, Spain, and Chile. Following the framework of compensatory policies constructed in Chapter 2, I measure the "compensatory degree" of each industrial privatization. I argue that the growth of domestic companies vis-à-vis the state and occasionally foreign producers before neoliberalism is strongly associated with the direct and uncompetitive allocation of state assets to formerly protected actors – the quintessential form of market-share compensation. Thus, the chapter develops a sectoral argument that transcends national patterns: market-share compensation is bestowed only on domestic actors that have become economically powerful under the inward-oriented model, vis-à-vis both foreign companies *and* the state. Ultimately, each "national" model of business adjustment amounts to the aggregation of the sectoral dynamics that are prevalent in the basic and complex consumer durables industries.

ASSESSING VARIATIONS WITHIN COUNTRIES

Argentine Petrochemicals: From Nationalism to Dow Chemical's Revenge

State Subsidies and the Defeat of the Domestic Bourgeoisie in the 1990s
Petrochemicals are essential for the manufacturing of a wide range of goods including plastics, synthetic rubber and fibers, paints, fertilizers, explosives, and many others. The main petrochemical inputs are naphtha (a type of refined oil) and natural gas. Production is largely divided into two types: *olefins* and *aromatics*. Olefins, among which the most important is ethylene, are produced out of both natural gas and naphtha and constitute the main raw material for the production of plastics, rubber, and other products. Aromatics (such as benzene, toluene, and xylene) are cracked out of naphtha and supply raw materials for the production of explosives such as TDI and TNT, fertilizers, nylon, and other products. Since inputs are a big part of the cost equation in any petrochemical industry (in particular in the production of olefins, which are gaseous and therefore difficult to transport) the industry is often organized around poles or complexes in which a "mother company" or "cracker" produces aromatics or ethylene and supplies this feedstock to a set of second-generation companies down in the chain of production. Ethylene and the variety of plastics manufactured out of it (polyethylene, polypropylene, polystyrene, and polyvinylchloride [PVC]) are the single most important petrochemical products, accounting for around 50% of total world production by the mid-1980s (Fayad and Motamen

Exceptions That Prove the Rule

1986: 21). By the late 1980s, Argentina was the third largest producer of petrochemicals in Latin America after Brazil and Mexico.

The state and a handful of domestic and foreign groups produced petrochemicals at the outset of reform (Figure 5.1). The most important foreign producers were Imperial Chemical Industries (ICI)/Duperial, Monsanto, Ducilo – owned by Dupont – and PASA, a joint venture controlled by the Anglo American Uniroyal and other foreign producers. Some Argentine private groups had

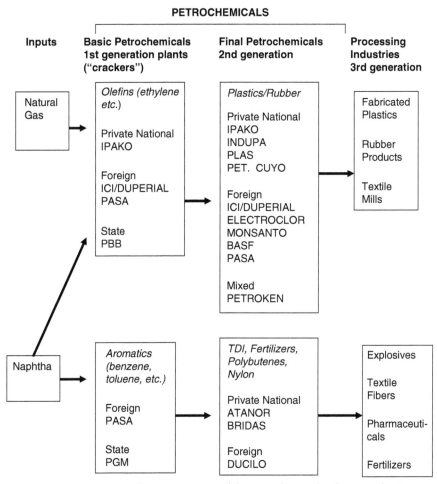

FIGURE 5.1. Argentina: The Organization of the Petrochemical Industry at the Outset of Reform (1989). Company names are in capital letters. Petroken was controlled by SHELL and IPAKO 50% each. Ownership refers to control of 51% of equity or more, except for Electroclor, in which ICI/Duperial held 30% but is coded as foreign because ICI/Duperial was the dominant shareholder. Only main companies and products in the Argentine market are mentioned. Petrochemical intermediate products were not included for the sake of clarity.

gained important positions in the petrochemicals market: INDUPA, IPAKO, Atanor, and the petroleum-based groups Bridas and Pérez Companc – the latter owned a minority stake in PASA and controlled Petroquímica Cuyo.[3] IPAKO and INDUPA were the leaders in the industry and the only petrochemical-based Argentine groups, accounting for almost 90% of production capacity in plastics.

State-owned firms were the third crucial actor in the industry, concentrated in the subsector of basic petrochemicals (see Figure 5.1). The most important petrochemical poles were that of Bahía Blanca, in which the state-owned PBB (Petroquímica Bahía Blanca) supplied ethylene to the second-generation plants controlled by INDUPA and IPAKO,[4] and the complex organized around PGM (Petroquímica General Mosconi), a state company that, together with the foreign-owned PASA, were the main producers of aromatics in the country.

As in all heavy/basic industries analyzed in this study, liberalization and economic opening threatened the foundations of petrochemical production in Argentina. The Menem government's initial blitzkrieg to neoliberal reform tore down almost all of the protections to the industry. Duties were lowered from 40% to an average of 10% in less than three years. In addition, restructured and privatized national oil and natural gas companies suspended old feedstock contracts that benefited local petrochemical producers. For example, as a result of deregulation, the price of natural gas for petrochemical use virtually doubled between 1989 and 1993 (M&S Consulting 1994: 240). On the other hand, imports of final petrochemicals, which totaled 196,200 tons in 1990, soared to 1,542,700 tons in 1997 – that is, an almost eightfold increase.[5]

Domestic firms were thus strongly affected by deregulation.[6] The main battle, however, was waged in the privatizations of PGM and PBB, the two largest state companies in the sector, which produced most basic petrochemicals that were crucial inputs to expand domestic production.[7] The government showed a great deal of independence from national groups in the organization of the bidding for both PGM and PBB. PGM, the main producer of aromatics, was scheduled for privatization in late 1992. The powerful oil-based domestic group Pérez Companc, which had recently increased its equity share and gained control of PASA – the other main producer of aromatics – and Shell bought PGM tender

---

[3] INDUPA was controlled by the Richards family, IPAKO by the Garovaglio and Zorraquín group, and Atanor by the Bunge & Born group.

[4] IPAKO's subsidiary, Polisur, had two polyethylene plants in the pole. The INDUPA group controlled three firms in the pole, Petropol (polyethylene), INDUPA (PVC), and Induclor (chlorine and caustic soda), and was the main shareholder (45%) in a third, Monómeros Vinílicos.

[5] Data from the Instituto Petroquímico Argentino (IPA) (1999a).

[6] In the words of Ignacio Noel, CEO of the domestic producer INDUPA between 1992 and 1994: "We had carried out investments and the state had approved our projects and had granted our import of equipment in the context of internal prices set by high tariffs. And, then, those tariffs were violently lowered from one day to the next. They destroyed our financial equation." Author's interview, Buenos Aires, March 20, 2001.

[7] In a first round of privatization that took place in 1990, the Argentine groups IPAKO and INDUPA acquired the state minority stakes in their companies at the Bahía Blanca pole.

Exceptions That Prove the Rule 131

documentation. Both were eager to expand their aromatics production (Chemical Week 1992: 14). Yet, the government finally decided to merge PGM with the state oil giant YPF, which was the main supplier of naphtha to PGM through one of its refineries. In other words, established domestic and foreign players were left out of the deal, and, in fact, PGM was *not* privatized but integrated into YPF – which would in turn be privatized a year later.

The second big privatization of the sector, PBB, would take place in 1995 after a series of bargains between the state and potential bidders. IPAKO, clearly the most powerful domestic group in plastics – owner of two second-generation plants surrounding the state-owned cracker – was unable to participate successfully in the auction for PBB.[8] In what was one of the most competitive biddings in the Argentine process of industrial privatization,[9] the company was finally awarded to a consortium teaming the American Dow Chemical and YPF, with the latter acting only as a financial associate. Dow-YPF outbid the consortium formed by Pérez Companc and Odebrecht – which had dropped IPAKO as a partner – by offering $385 million. After PBB's privatization, the local group IPAKO would depend on Dow – its main foreign competitor – for its central input, ethylene, and, as a result, its situation in the market became unsustainable (López 1997: 124). IPAKO finally sold all its assets to Dow Chemical and disappeared from the market. Dow Chemical, by contrast, established the PBB pole in Argentina as its doorway for supplying polyethylene, a crucial input for plastic materials, to MERCOSUR (Chemical Week 1996: 13).

Not only did the state demonstrate remarkable independence from national groups in the organization of the privatization of both PBB and PGM, but it ended up nationalizing the second largest group in the sector. In effect, by 1994, INDUPA, the main producer of PVC in Argentina, was burdened by a high level of debt (around $510 million, $350 million of that residing with the state). Facing INDUPA's bankruptcy, the state took over the company, restructured its obligations with private banks, and later privatized the company free of debt. This mechanism of swapping debt for equity was primarily aimed at keeping the company alive, albeit under new owners. However, it also implied a concealed subsidy to the original owners.[10] In other words, the state employed one of the

---

[8] Initially, IPAKO tried to assemble a consortium with YPF and the Canadian Novacor. Yet negotiations ended in a stalemate because IPAKO would not accept the limits imposed by the much larger YPF and Novacor in the future operational control of the privatized company. A second attempt to form a consortium with the national group Pérez Companc and the Brazilian group Odebrecht in order to bid for PBB equally failed in 1995. Author's interview with Alejandro Achával, former CEO of IPAKO, Buenos Aires, February 6, 2001.

[9] This assessment is the result of my interviews with state officials and the CEOs of the main companies involved. Unlike for SOMISA or most of the oil-field privatizations, the outcome was uncertain until the end.

[10] In the words of a top executive of the petrochemical division of the oil firm YPF: "Richards [family who owned INDUPA] had a company whose value was zero and would have lost the company after the bankruptcy procedure. After the state's takeover, by contrast, at least he became a passive shareholder." Author's interview, Ensenada, October 20, 2000.

132   *The Political Economy of Business Adjustment*

mechanisms identified in the typology of compensatory measures constructed in Chapter 2, namely, the bailout of private firms indebted to the state. At the moment of the state's takeover, INDUPA's debt was estimated at $510 million.[11] The company was later sold to the Belgian firm Solvay for only $91 million. Thus, it could be argued that the Argentine state had injected at least $419 million in order to preserve the petrochemical industry. The economist A. López (1997: 137) summarizes well the Statist pattern of transformation of the petrochemical industry when he argues that in spite of broad liberalization, the government had prevented the "disappearance" of the industry through a "favorable treatment of tax bankruptcies [i.e., a form of subsidy] and even the surprising temporary nationalization of a private firm with financial problems."

Table 5.2 identifies the winners and losers of the deregulation of the petrochemical industry in Argentina by showing data on the production share of the main final petrochemicals manufactured in the country – the subsector where private capital had expanded most. The reform process swept away the main established players, the domestic groups IPAKO and INDUPA. The growth of the only domestic winner in the sector, Pérez Companc – which was not a petrochemical-based group – is explained more by its acquisition of majority ownership in its joint venture PASA from a group of foreign firms than by its gains in privatization. In fact, Pérez Companc was sidelined in the two major privatizations in the sector, those of PGM and PBB, as much as were the local groups INDUPA and IPAKO. In short, in petrochemicals, the domestic bourgeoisie was the main loser of deregulation in the 1990s.

Explaining the Outcome: An Island of State Power and Dow Chemical's Revenge

By the late 1980s the local Zorraquín group, owner of IPAKO, was among the most influential industrial holdings in the country. Indeed, a May 1994 report on the petrochemical industry by a renowned consulting firm in Buenos Aires asserted that "it is probable that the concentration of the sector in local groups will deepen, and that the foreign firms that do not take part in the oil business will have to leave the petrochemical industry" (M&S Consulting, 1994: 28). The international Chemical Week (1992: 14) expected INDUPA and IPAKO to be "the leading contenders" in the privatization of PBB. Yet, as shown earlier, the expansion of national groups in the sector did not occur. This section explains why.

In the late 1950s major world players in the sector, such as Monsanto, ICIDuperial, Petrochemical Industries Koppers, PASA (a joint venture of Cities Services, Amoco, and others), Pechiney, and Dupont, all set up or expanded plants in Argentina. All of these plants were smaller than their counterparts in the developed world and principally oriented toward sheltered domestic markets (IPA 1999b). After 1970, however, the industry would witness the "national turn" described in Chapter 3 that affected many industrial sectors, in particular producers of intermediate goods. As a result of industrial promotion mechanisms

---

[11] *Clarín*, June 11, 1998.

Exceptions That Prove the Rule

TABLE 5.2. *Argentina: Final Petrochemicals (Plastics, Rubber, TDI, Nylon, Polyisobutene) Production Capacity (in tons/year) before and after Liberalization*

Firm	Before Reform (1989)	Percentage	After Reform (1999)	Percentage
Foreign				
PASA (Rubber)	55,000	8.33%	0	0.00%
Monsanto (Polystyrene)	38,000	5.76%	0	0.00%
Electroclor (PVC)	30,000	4.55%	0	0.00%
Ducilo-Dupont (Nylon 66)	20,500	3.11%	31,700	3.45%
ICI/Duperial (Polyethylene)	20,000	3.03%	19,500	2.12%
Basf (Polystyrene)	6,600	1.00%	12,000	1.31%
Dow Chemical (Polyethylene)	0	0.00%	272,000	29.60%
Solvay (PVC)	0	0.00%	79,000	8.60%
Petroken (Polypropyline)	0	0.00%	170,000	18.50%
YPF (Polyisobutene)[a]	0	0.00%	34,000	3.70%
Total Foreign	**170,100**	**25.77%**	**618,200**	**67.28%**
National				
IPAKO (Polyethylene)	225,000	34.09%	0	0.00%
INDUPA (PVC, Polyethylene)	152,500	23.11%	0	0.00%
Other National (Polystyrene)	41,400	6.27%	20,200	2.20%
Pérez Companc-PASA[b]	40,000	6.06%	201,000	21.87%
Atanor/Piero[c] (TDI)	17,500	2.65%	26,000	2.83%
Bridas (Polyisobutene)	9,000	1.36%	0	0.00%
Sniafa (Nylon 6)	4,500	0.68%	4,500	0.49%
Imextrade (PVC)	0	0.00%	49,000	5.33%
Total National	**489,900**	**74.23%**	**300,700**	**32.72%**
TOTAL	660,000	100.00%	918,900	100.00%

[a] YPF was controlled by the Spanish Repsol since 1999 and has a participation of 50% in Petroken and 30% in Polisur, the polyethylene factory controlled by Dow. It also has 26% of Petroquímica Bahía Blanca.
[b] Before the liberalization period Petroquímica Companc had a minority holding in PASA (33%), and it controlled Petroquímica Cuyo, which produced polypropylene. After it bought PASA it began to control its production of rubber and started to produce polystyrene, which are added in the table to its polypropylene production.
[c] In 1996 the Bunge & Born group sold the TDI producer Petroquímica Rio Tercero (controlled by its firm Atanor) to the firm Piero.
Source: Elaborated from *Tendencias Económicas* (1989) and IPA (1999a).

that consistently privileged national groups in the sector (López 1997: 88–89) and the political radicalization of the early 1970s – which scared foreign capital – domestic groups replaced foreign firms as the main producers in the petrochemical industry. Koppers sold its assets to the local group Garovaglio and Zorraquín (which would form the new IPAKO), and Richards acquired majority ownership in INDUPA. This trend toward the dominance of national groups became especially strong in final petrochemicals and gathered additional momentum in the years prior to reform. Significantly, this protection of national companies was maintained during the dictatorship that put the "liberal" Chicago Boys in charge of the economy (1976–83).[12]

Toward the late 1960s, and as a result of economic growth, Argentina's industrial market was demanding a major push in the production of petrochemicals that previously had to be imported, especially basic petrochemicals, such as ethylene and aromatics. After the military coup of 1966, Dow Chemical submitted to the government a major project to construct a pole at Bahía Blanca, where it stood to profit from both easy access to natural gas supplies and the city's important commercial port. However, Dow was ultimately blocked from pursing the project. The nationalistic wing of the military, through the holding Dirección General de Fabricaciones Militares (General Command of Military Industries) (DGFM), took over the initiative and decided to carry out the first stages of the Bahía Blanca pole without the participation of private capital. At the same time (1971), DGFM also launched the construction of a second aromatics pole, the future Petroquímica General Mosconi around YPF's refinery in Ensenada, again without private partners. PGM was built on schedule and came onstream in 1974. The PBB construction took more time because it involved setting up facilities for processing natural gas and a number of second-generation plants. In 1977, the military decided to include the national groups INDUPA and IPAKO as partners in the pole: private national capital would hold minority stakes in the mother plant and would own a majority in the second-generation plants. PBB's central cracking unit came onstream in 1981, but the second-generation plants would be ready only in 1985.

Thus, after blocking Dow's entrance into the Argentine market, the military held a tight grip on petrochemical production and acted as an effective restraint on the expansion of private capital in basic chemicals. Decree 593/73, issued in 1973, formalized that control. The norm granted the state the control of the supply of the main petrochemical products and mandated that the state would hold majority ownership in every first- or second-generation facility (see Figure 5.1). Although that requirement was later relaxed with the inclusion of domestic capital in the joint ventures around PBB, the dominant role of DGFM in basic petrochemicals

---

[12] A top executive of Dow Chemical Argentina asserted: "We went to talk to Martínez de Hoz [the minister of the economy of the dictatorship] and told him that we wanted to be in charge of the Bahía Blanca project and finish it correctly and on time. But they did not accept; Fabricaciones Militares [the military-industrial holding in charge of petrochemicals] had a lot of power and they would not break their compromise with national groups." Author's interview, Buenos Aires, February 15, 2001.

Exceptions That Prove the Rule

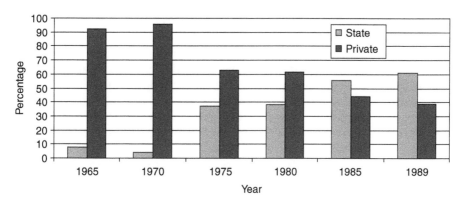

GRAPH 5.1. Basic Petrochemicals (Benzene, Toluene, Xylenes, Methanol, Ethylene, Butadiene, Ammonia, Carbon Sulfide). Evolution of State and Private Sector Share of Production Capacity (in tons/year), Prereform Period (1965–89). *Source: Tendencias Económicas*, Buenos Aires (selected years) and Instituto Petroquímico Argentino (IPA) (1999a).

was never curtailed. Graph 5.1 shows the trend in the production of basic petrochemicals in the run-up to neoliberal reform. The two increases in state production in 1975 and 1985 signal the inauguration of PGM and PBB, respectively.

In short, unlike the Argentine steel and oil sectors studied in Chapter 4, in which the state promoted domestic private companies from a relatively early stage, in the case of petrochemicals, the state never gave up its role as main producer. When liberalization was launched, the state had become the hegemonic actor in the production of *basic* chemicals (ethylene and aromatics), the main input for petrochemical production. Indeed, PBB and PGM had developed a bureaucratic capacity atypical in other state-owned enterprises in Argentina. Businessmen interviewed in the petrochemical sector praised the state managers and the efficiency of PGM and PBB at the operational level.[13] Second, and most importantly, both PBB and PGM were very profitable companies, largely because they received feedstock supplies at subsidized prices from the national oil and natural gas monopolies, and their contracts with second-generation private plants secured them profitability.[14] Put simply, the private sector under ISI could not extract extraordinary rents from the price of its main input – in this

---

[13] For example, Roberto Craig, former vice president of the foreign producer PASA and a leading consultant in Argentine petrochemicals, asserted, "Both PBB and PGM had an excellent staff of engineers and an optimal capacity of plant management." Author's interview, Buenos Aires, February 8, 2001.
[14] Gorenstein (1993: 587) shows that, although PBB did not sell its ethylene at international market prices, it enjoyed large rents: the price of its ethylene was set well above its cost of production, which was based in cheap ethane provided by the state natural gas company. As the former CEO of IPAKO puts it: "PBB was a formidable milk cow." Author's interview with Alejandro Achával, CEO of IPAKO until 1995, Buenos Aires, February 6, 2001.

136   *The Political Economy of Business Adjustment*

case, ethylene. On the contrary, PBB, the main state company in the sector, was the main actor that benefited in the ISI chain of petrochemical production.

The origins of state power in Argentine petrochemicals are varied. First, the military's tight control over the industry was unmatched in other heavy industries. Second, the main spurt to massive petrochemical production took place *relatively late* when compared to the other heavy industrial sectors, at a time when Statist nationalistic tendencies were on the rise as a result of the ascendancy of both the military right wing and, after 1970, the Peronist Left. Finally, petrochemicals was (and is) a very capital-intensive industry, with relatively few workers, who had formed comparatively weak unions to counter state power.

Yet, whatever the reasons for the historical state power in the sector, it provides a crucial background against which one should confront the dynamics of state-guided liberalization in the 1990s. The argument that national private groups were marginalized by privatization of the main petrochemical complexes in 1992 and 1995 just because they were smaller players in relation to TNCs in world markets is only partially correct – and ultimately simplistic. The important question is *what was the main source* of that economic weakness, one that did not affect, as noted in Chapter 4, other domestic companies in heavy industries that were also potentially competing against world giants such as Thyssen (steel) or Shell and Amoco (oil). The weakness was ultimately rooted in the lack of integration of domestic petrochemical private companies in the chain of production under the inward-oriented model, and the impossibility of achieving full control of their inputs of basic chemicals given the military dominance of the sector.[15]

Indeed, their former dependence on the state and the lack of alternative sources for its main ethylene input meant that, once the government awarded PBB to Dow Chemical, IPAKO's fate was sealed. The view of a top businessman from the petroleum-based group Pérez Companc (who got important payoffs in the oil deregulation) is eloquent on the weakness of the domestic petrochemical firms and of its origins:

The problem of INDUPA and IPAKO was that they were not integrated. We have the oil and put it in a port at Bahía Blanca. Then we send the ship to San Lorenzo, where I pass it through the refinery and then we have a pipeline to PASA [the petrochemical firm]. So now I have the complete chain: the oil, the refinery, and the petrochemicals. And this cost a lot of money and time; you don't get up one morning and say "I am integrated." As long as the state managed the sector, they [the local petrochemical groups] were great, but when the state died . . . well, they should have thought of it before – in our case, even under the wing of the state we started to reconvert.[16]

---

[15] Oscar Vignart, president and CEO of Dow Chemical Argentina, stated it bluntly: "Integration [in the chain of production from basic to final petrochemicals] for national companies was unthinkable before the 1990s. In petrochemicals, you had to take the state out of the way and in Argentina that was impossible." Author's interview, Buenos Aires, February 15, 2001.

[16] Author's interview, January 22, 2001. The opinion of a top official of the Defense Ministry involved in the privatization points in the same direction. "They [domestic petrochemical groups] were very dependent on the state. When you don't have a steady flow of finance from your mother

Exceptions That Prove the Rule 137

As shown in Chapter 4, in contrast to local petrochemical groups, the main comparable domestic and would-be compensated groups Techint (with its backward integration through electrical furnaces in 1977–80) and Pérez Companc (through its direct access to oil reserves) had achieved vital control of their main input – raw steel and crude oil – under ISI, which enhanced their economic power and their status as credible contenders for market reserves once liberalization took off. In other words, while state ownership was certainly present in the three sectors, only in steel and oil were private groups able to grow consistently and undermine the state control of the main input in the sector under ISI.

One question, though, remains unsettled. If domestic petrochemical companies were weak vis-à-vis state power, why were they subsidized during reform and the 1995 privatization? The answer lies in their political connections with the state, and in the importance of petrochemicals as a producer of industrial inputs, which meant that the main firms could not simply be left to die. A former CEO of INDUPA described this "residual power." Asked what would have been the reaction of the company if it had been left to the whims of the market and likely bankruptcy, the executive replied:

We had a lot of contracts with the state [subsidized inputs, promotional regimes, etc.], and the rules of the game had been changed. Our reaction would have been to sue the state and start a litigation that would have lasted for 20 years. However, I put myself on the side of the government and, well, in the end the government managed to get Dow into the business; it brought Solvay [the Belgian company]; there are new investments; the state is collecting tax revenue. The government decision [to help INDUPA] was the best.[17]

In other words, INDUPA, as a result of its established legal connections with the state and its important role in the Bahía Blanca pole, could threaten to paralyze the entire privatization process, for no foreign investor would bid under the threat of litigation and persistent debt.[18] The same could be argued, of course, with respect to IPAKO and the concealed subsidies it received.[19] In brief, domestic groups were economically too weak to obtain market-share compensation, but politically powerful enough to get subsidies and negotiate their retreat.

To conclude, petrochemicals in Argentina provide a nice example of the limits of political lobbying and even corruption in the explanation of market-share compensation, which I have illustrated in the case of the decimated Spanish steelmakers (Chapter 4). Private petrochemical groups in Argentina, very much

---

company [he refers to TNCs] or you are too dependent on the state, then you are not very solid as a company." Author's interview, March 23, 2001.

[17] Author's interview, Buenos Aires, March 20, 2001.

[18] A top official of the Department of Energy put it more bluntly: "INDUPA and IPAKO negotiated their retreat for a few million dollars." Author's interview, Buenos Aires, December 17, 2000.

[19] IPAKO had long-standing litigation with PBB over the feedstock price of ethylene and also had some tax debts with the state, albeit less burdensome than INDUPA's. Most of the businessmen I interviewed in the sector acknowledged that the state was generous in settling these disputes in order to ease the privatization of PBB, in which IPAKO had a minority stake. For a similar view see López (1997: 137).

138   *The Political Economy of Business Adjustment*

like their steel-based counterparts in Spain, were among the most politically influential capitalists in the country. Federico Zorraquin (owner of IPAKO) was a prominent member and recent president of the CEA (Argentine Businessmen's Council), the most selective business organization in the country. However, the relative economic weakness of IPAKO vis-à-vis state companies under the inward-oriented model hampered any lobbying for market concentration in the liberalized order, political connections notwithstanding. On the other hand, Dow Chemical, which had first planned the Bahía Blanca petrochemical pole in 1968 – but was blocked from pursuing it at the time – took it over in 1995. Quite paradoxically, state power in petrochemicals, which had hindered the expansion of the powerful American company in the 1960s, facilitated Dow Chemical's revenge almost thirty years later.

Spain's Oil Industry: The ISI Origins of the Market-Share Compensation

The Oil Industry in the 1980s and 1990s: Concertation and Market-Share Compensation

In the case of the oil sector in Spain, formerly protected firms, or "insiders," exerted a strong influence over the formulation of deregulatory initiatives and were quite successful in obtaining market-share compensation in the run-up to full liberalization. Between 1982 and 1996, a wide restructuring of the Spanish oil industry took place. Local private companies had developed in the segment of *refining* and not in exploration or extraction/production of oil since Spain traditionally imported most of its oil.

Among the most important private firms at the outset of reform were CEPSA, PETROMED, and PETRONOR. These companies sold gasoline and other refined products to the distribution monopoly CAMPSA, a state-owned company in which private capital (the major Spanish banks plus individual stockholders) had a significant minority stake. CAMPSA held a monopoly on (1) the import and export of oil products within the Spanish market, (2) the transportation of gasoline and other refined products via trucks and pipelines within Spain, and (3) retail sale in gasoline stations (Figure 5.2).

When the Socialists took power, many options for oil policy reform were on the table. By 1982 nationalization of the oil industry was still an alternative envisaged by sectors of the Left (Correljé 1994: 84). On the other hand, the prospect of joining the EU would imply the opening of the oil sector to European firms. Needless to say, both options seriously threatened the interests of domestic producers. Liberalization, for example, meant that private and public refiners would lose the fixed price that CAMPSA paid for refined products, which assured the companies handsome profit margins. In addition, the possible entrance of new players into the refining and retail markets or the potential increase of imports of refined products would endanger their local market share.

However, the government pursued neither nationalization nor full-scale liberalization, but rather a combination of protectionist or partial deregulation and "targeted privatization." After successive bargaining rounds with the established

Exceptions That Prove the Rule

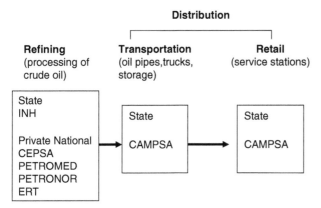

FIGURE 5.2. The Organization of the Spanish Oil Sector at the Outset of Reform (1982). Company names are in capital letters. Private capital (banks plus individual shareholders) held 40% of CAMPSA by 1982. In the retail sector CAMPSA managed service stations directly and through concessionaires.

producers, in 1984 the PSOE passed the Ley Reordenamiento del Sector Petrolero (Oil Sector Restructuring Law). This law crystallized an agreement reached in 1983 among the main private refiners, the heads of the newly created public holding in charge of state firms in the refining sector – the National Institute of Hydrocarbons (INH) – and the government. The INH (which would later become the state company Repsol) took over CAMPSA and bought the part formerly held by private banks and other smaller shareholders. It would subsequently keep 51% of the stock share of the distribution network and divide the remaining capital among the local private refiners.[20]

The important point is that the government could have pursued alternative liberalization paths. For example, it could have called for open public bidding for the stock share of the distribution monopoly CAMPSA. Such an auction could have included foreign and domestic firms and would have divided the ownership of the network among future players in the Spanish market. As it turned out, the government chose the *least* liberal approach: it maintained the monopolistic firm in the distribution of gasoline and other products, and it integrated the traditional producers into its ownership structure without any competitive bidding. The plan for CAMPSA to continue as the only distribution company, albeit owned by the Spanish refineries, originated in the private sector, specifically within CEPSA itself.[21]

---

[20] On this topic see Santamaría (1988: 113–23) and Correljé's (1994: esp. 80–96) excellent study.
[21] Author's interview with the former CEO of CEPSA Eugenio Marín, Madrid, October 22, 2001. See also Correljé (1994: 84).

140 *The Political Economy of Business Adjustment*

Imports of refined products were eased after Spain's entrance into the EU in 1986. Yet, the "new CAMPSA," with its equity in the hands of traditional refiners, was allowed to preserve its monopoly in the distribution of gasoline and oil products in Spain until 1993. This transition period between 1983 and 1993 resulted in crucial advantages for traditional actors. First, it meant CAMPSA would obviously privilege its owners in the operation of the distribution network and that foreign companies in the retail market would depend on CAMPSA for the transportation of their refined products (gasoline, lubricants, etc.) through the Spanish market.[22] The view of the former president and CEO of Shell Spain explains the dilemmas that this pattern of protectionist deregulation entailed for foreign players:

When they finally let you buy gasoline stations you had a problem with the logistics [lack of control of oil pipes, storage, etc., largely owned by CAMPSA]. But if you do not have gasoline stations, why would you invest in distribution infrastructure? It was a problem. Our only option was to get into the shareholding of CAMPSA in order to have an influence on the national transportation network. Before that, we had a lot of problems getting access to CAMPSA.[23]

Second, this pattern of protectionist deregulation permitted the expansion of traditional refiners into the downstream, that is, the retail market. Before the distribution monopoly ended, CAMPSA distributed its gasoline stations among its new owners, and, of course, no other domestic or foreign company was allowed to participate in the purchase of these outlets. In other words, privatization of service stations was clearly targeted at insiders. As a top executive of the Spanish producer PETROMED reported:

We sat around the table, the president of CAMPSA and the CEOs of the companies, with the map of the service stations. Repsol [the state firm created out of the INH] took the first fifteen, then CEPSA took part of its quota, then we chose a number of stations, and in this way, we did a number of rounds until all the service stations in the country were distributed.[24]

The result of this distribution of assets among established producers, so eloquently described by the PETROMED businessman – and that can hardly be labeled as a market allocation mechanism – can be seen in Table 5.3.

By 1999, almost 80% of the service stations in the country were controlled by Repsol (the new state firm created out of all public assets in the sector) and by private Spanish-based refiners. The European Commission opened an infraction

---

[22] Naturally, even after formal liberalization, CAMPSA privileged its owners in the purchase of gasoline and refined products. International operators such as Dineff, Conoco, and Tamoil complained that CAMPSA (later renamed CLH) charged discriminatory prices to nonowners and denied access to independent operators. See Contín et al. (1998: 8) and *El País*, May 31, 1993.

[23] Author's interview with Korstiaan Van Wyngaarden, president and CEO of Shell Spain between 1990 and 1995, Madrid, November 12, 2001. Shell obtained 5% of CAMPSA's shares in 1993, after years of persistent lobbying.

[24] Author's interview, Madrid, September 24, 2001.

Exceptions That Prove the Rule

TABLE 5.3. *The Gasoline Retail Market in Spain: Before and after Reform*

Company	Number of Gasoline Stations					
	Before Reform		After Reform		After Reform	
	1980	Percentage	1994	Percentage	1999	Percentage
CAMPSA	3,476	100%	–	–	–	–
Repsol (INH)	0	0%	3,225	58.56%	3,464	47.65%
CEPSA	0	0%	1,300	23.61%	1,800	24.76%
PETROMED-BP	0	0%	367	6.66%	527	7.25%
Shell	0	0%	113	2.05%	295	4.06%
Petrogal	0	0%	105	1.91%	175	2.41%
Continental Oil	0	0%	2	0.04%	135	1.86%
Disa	0	0%	0	0.00%	134	1.84%
Total France	0	0%	100	1.82%	133	1.83%
Meroil	0	0%	0	0.00%	125	1.72%
Agip	0	0%	65	1.18%	114	1.57%
Petrocat	0	0%	41	0.74%	67	0.92%
Dyneff	0	0%	36	0.65%	0	0.00%
Avanti	0	0%	35	0.64%	66	0.91%
Mobil Oil	0	0%	30	0.54%	0	0.00%
Others (Texaco, Ersegui, etc.)	0	0%	88	1.60%	234	3.22%
Total	3,476	100%	5,507	100.00%	7,269	100.00%

Note: **Local companies in bold letters.**
Source: 1980 data, *Enciclopedia Nacional del Petróleo, Petroquímica y Gas* (1984 and 1994); 1999 data, *Revista Oilgas: Petróleo, Petroquímica y Gas* (1994: 66; 1999: 379).

case against Spain's policy in the oil sector in July 1987 (*El País*, May 31, 1993).[25] Many multinationals and the Dutch government – which had Shell's lobbying behind it – complained bitterly about the slow pace of oil liberalization in Spain.[26] Yet, by 1994, any international oil company could freely commercialize hydrocarbon products or build oil infrastructure in Spain. The number of companies operating freely in Spain had more than doubled (Oil and Gas

[25] Asked how the government could pass this rather protectionist regulation scheme in the Commission in view of Spain's future integration into Europe, Carlos Solchaga, minister of economy during this period, replied, "Well, you know how this works: sometimes they just pretend they don't see, and later, in some other situation, you just pretend you don't see." Author's interview, Madrid, October 8, 2001.
[26] Author's interview with Korstiaan Van Wyngaarden, former CEO of Shell Spain, Madrid, November 12, 2001; see also Correljé (1994: 101).

142 — *The Political Economy of Business Adjustment*

Journal 1994). During the crucial transition period of 1983–93, however, the government funneled market-share compensation – the privatization of CAMPSA and retail centers awarded to insider producers and gradual deregulation of distribution from 1983 to 1993 – that clearly benefited established refining companies.

Explaining the Outcome: The Financial Bourgeoisie Counters the Expansion of the State Holding INI

Chapter 3 explained how the state-run National Industrial Institute (INI), founded in the civil war aftermath, emerged as the dominant industrial player in postwar Spain. In the context of the sheltered Spanish economy, it effectively countered the expansion of domestic private capital in core industries such as steel, autos, shipbuilding, aviation, electronics, and aluminum. As we have seen, the central role that the state played in the industrial sector, probably unmatched in any ISI economy in Ibero-America, paved the way for a Statist mode of industrial adjustment in the 1980s and 1990s. The oil sector, however, would constitute an exception in the INI's quest for dominance in the realm of heavy industry. Indeed, the economic and political power that local private firms developed under the inward-oriented economy would set the stage for their expansion through market-share compensation once liberalization had been launched.

In the aftermath of the civil war the oil sector was dominated by the semi-public firm CAMPSA, which, as mentioned previously, had a monopoly in the distribution of gasoline and oil products, and by CEPSA, a Spanish company in which the private Banco Central[27] had a controlling stake and that owned the single refinery on Spanish territory. CAMPSA would distribute and commercialize oil products supplied by CEPSA and imported from international markets. Its shareholding was divided between the Ministry of Finance (30% of shares at the time) and the most important Spanish banks. Thus, from the outset, INI's aim to expand in the petroleum sector would confront powerful financial/private players. Nonetheless, the initial institutional strength of INI should not be underestimated. As stated in Chapter 3, the new industrial and military-educated technocrats appeared as the single group that could contest the influence of Franco's class allies. Moreover, after the war, INI expanded considerably in the domain of hydrocarbons and built new refineries.[28]

However, burgeoning Spanish industry, boosted by the Development Plans of the 1960s, demanded still more oil products. A crucial battle was waged over the construction of a fourth refinery in the North of Spain, a dispute that would result in the counterattack of the Spanish financial bourgeoisie. In effect, in

---

[27] The Banco Central was a regular private bank. In Spain the traditional role of a central bank in modern economies was performed by the Bank of Spain.

[28] In 1949, INI established Repesa, a refining company with a capacity matching that of CEPSA. ENCASO, an INI subsidiary, set up facilities for the development of solid fuels that would become the second INI-controlled refining company in 1965.

Exceptions That Prove the Rule　　　　　　　　　　　　　　　　　143

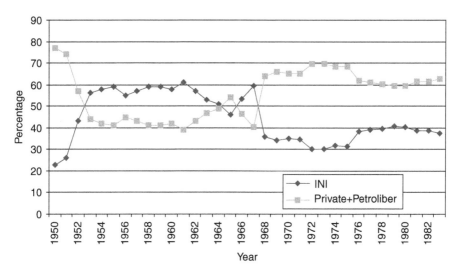

GRAPH 5.2. Spain: Share of Total Oil Refined (in tons) by National Industrial Institute (INI) and Private Refiners plus PETROLIBER, 1950–83. *Source*: 1950–65, Statistical Appendix in Martín Aceña and Comín (1991); 1966–83, *Enciclopedia Nacional del Petróleo, Petroquímica y Gas* (1970, 1974, 1979, and 1984).

1961, the Franco regime decided to award the construction of this refinery to PETROLIBER, a consortium of the Spanish private group Fierro and the Ministry of Finance, rather than to the INI, which had also lobbied to take over the project (Ballestero 1989: 32). Thereafter, private refineries would compete on an equal footing with INI for the building of refineries to supply the sheltered Spanish oil market. The INI launched a new refinery in Tarragona in 1974, whereas the private companies CEPSA, PETRONOR (controlled by CAMPSA and the Basque banks), and PETROMED (60% controlled by Banesto Bank), in partnership with foreign companies, set up refining facilities in the period between 1966 and 1971.

Graph 5.2 depicts the share of refined oil in the Spanish market in the postwar period.[29] Unlike in the rest of the industrial sector analyzed in Chapter 4, the local private sector's role in the oil business expanded in the run-up to liberalization, especially after 1966, when a number of private refineries came onstream. What is more, the resurgence of private capital against INI's influence after the mid-1960s would soon be accompanied by a massive retreat of foreign companies from the consortia that had built these refineries. This withdrawal reinforced the presence of the local private sector in the domestic market: its equity share increased as the

---

[29] The fact that the Ministry of Finance sided with the banking sector against the INI because of their common interests in CAMPSA led me to put PETROLIBER (52% owned by the Ministry of Finance until the early 1980s) on the side of the private sector.

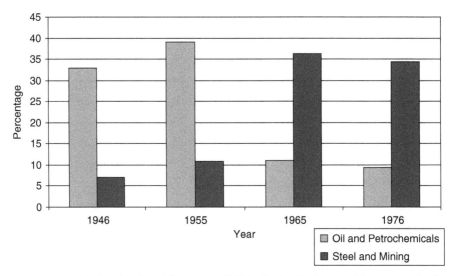

GRAPH 5.3. National Industrial Institute (INI) in Spain: Evolution of Investment in the Oil and Steel Sectors as Percentage of Total INI Investment. *Source*: Martín Aceña and Comín (1991: 152, 373), sectoral investment tables.

foreign "majors" left. Hence, contrary to the rest of Spanish industry, in which FDI actually *increased* in the years prior to reform (see Chapter 3), the oil sector witnessed the consolidation of domestic private firms.

The powerful resistance that INI encountered to its expansion in the oil business can be assessed by analyzing the prereform trajectory of the sector's share of INI's total investment (Graph 5.3). We see that the share of oil as a percentage of the total state holding's investment dwindles in the years prior to reform, while the reverse trend can be observed in the steel sector. The resultant alternative patterns of adjustment – state imposition in the steel sector and concertation with private interests in the oil sector – were no accident.

The reasons for INI's unsuccessful quest for dominance in the oil sector are not difficult to grasp. First, in petroleum, INI struggled with companies directly controlled by the single most powerful capitalist group in Spain, the financial bourgeoisie. Indeed, as noted in Chapter 3, the main Spanish banks increasingly released their industry holdings with the advent of the 1973 oil crises. But they preserved assets in the energy sector. Second, unlike local firms in other sectors, domestic oil companies could count on a powerful ally *within* the administration, namely, the Ministry of Finance, traditionally much more "liberal" and pro-business than the military-influenced INI and close to the Spanish banks (and therefore to the oil companies). The board of the oil distribution monopoly CAMPSA was a central institutional locus of the alliance between the Ministry of Finance and the major financial/oil groups (Tortella 1990: 82; Correljé 1994: 20). Additionally, the Ministry of Finance, in association with local

Exceptions That Prove the Rule

banking interests, controlled PETROLIBER. This partnership between the Ministry of Finance and the major private oil companies would remain in place until liberalization began in the early 1980s (see Ballestero 1989: 280–95).[30]

In sum, it is not surprising that, instead of being imposed from above, the formulation of the oil deregulatory framework was delivered through a sectoral bargain that resembles Corporatist adjustment in Argentina. The Ministry of Industry faced much more powerful actors, whose goal was not to obtain subsidies to pay off debts, but initially to expand market share. These actors had developed the scale economies, financial power, management capacity, and political connections to participate in the distribution network and in the retail sector.

However, isolated refiners could hardly sustain competition in an integrated Europe in the long run. During the 1990s PETRONOR and PETROMED sold their assets to Repsol and British Petroleum, respectively. CEPSA, owned by the powerful Santander bank and other minority investors, entered into an alliance with the French ELF (later merged with Total France), which acquired 40% of its shares. Unlike its former Spanish ISI partners in refining, though, the CEPSA group maintained its autonomous structure and thrived in the 2000s: it diversified into natural gas and petrochemicals and controlled assets in ten countries. Yet the 2009 crises provoked the definitive withdrawal of domestic capital from the first Spanish oil company founded in 1929 as the Santander bank sold its 36% participation in CEPSA to the Arabian state operator IPIC (International Petroleum Investment Company). The 2,900 million euros that the bank obtained for its stake in the company in large part originated in the accommodations through market-share compensation as liberalization unfolded in the 1980s and 1990s.[31]

THE COMPENSATORY DEGREE OF INDUSTRIAL PRIVATIZATION: AN INTERCOUNTRY AND INTERSECTORAL ANALYSIS

Heavy industrial sectors such as those analyzed in this book were fundamentally challenged by liberalization. In general, the major local firms in those sectors did not build upon any of the country's particular comparative advantages and had survived for years sheltered from international markets dominated by TNCs based in the developed world. Industrial privatization, however, opened a window of opportunity. Domestic companies in economies already more connected with world markets were relatively less threatened by tariff and deregulatory reform. Command/socialist economies did not generate sizable private actors. Private firms in mixed economies, by contrast, could take over state assets as a way to consolidate domestic market share and face global competition in better shape. This compensatory dimension has received little attention in the literature on privatization. Of course, the general idea of using privatization as a political tactic to buy off certain

---

[30] As one former executive of CEPSA revealed, "The lobby of the oil sector traditionally operated through the banks." Author's interview, Madrid, February 13, 2002.

[31] See *El País*, April 1, 2009.

146 *The Political Economy of Business Adjustment*

constituencies is present in the literature on the subject.[32] Nonetheless, the question of why and when governments hand out state assets to firms already operating in tradable industrial sectors subjected to deregulation has received less systematic attention.

Building upon the typology of compensation constructed in Chapter 2, this section measures compensatory degree of industrial privatization by carefully analyzing the process through which state assets are divested. Three analytically different dimensions appear to be most relevant. The *method* of privatization – whether the asset is allocated through a direct awarding or a competitive bidding – seems to be the most important. In addition, the *type of control* of assets, that is, whether a single private established actor is allowed to control the majority of the equity, and the *role of the state* in the future privatized company also seem to be relevant for assessing the degree to which local firms are benefited.

Ideally, privatization will be most compensatory when (1) state assets are *directly* allocated to an "insider," that is, an established firm already operating in the market; (2) when the given established firm is awarded total equity ownership; and (3) when the state equity holding in the privatized firm remains small or nonexistent. Therefore, an index that measures the "compensatory degree" can be constructed, scoring the process of industrial privatization along these three different dimensions weighted on a 0–100 scale (Table 5.4).

Table 5.5 scores all of the cases of industrial privatization already analyzed in Argentina, Spain, as well as the cases of privatization in the paper pulp and steel sectors in Chile, which will be analyzed in Chapter 8. It also provides data on the economic strength of local firms measured in terms of the growth in their share of production in domestic markets in the twenty years prior to reform. The privatization of SOMISA analyzed in Chapter 4, the largest state-owned steel mill in Argentina, appears as the most "compensatory." SOMISA was directly awarded by the government to a consortium that involved the two main local producers. One of them (Techint) acquired the majority of the equity, and the state did not retain any stake in the new company.

The privatizations of the four high-return oil fields – the so-called central areas – in Argentina were also heavily biased in favor of domestic companies. Established players received majority (but not total) ownership in what seem to have been quite uncompetitive bids.[33] However, the new owners were compelled to associate with a foreign company in order to increase the know-how in the domestic market, and the state initially preserved a minority holding in the consortium that would manage the areas. The privatization of CAMPSA, the distribution network of oil products in Spain, analyzed earlier, was somewhat less compensatory than the other cases, because the state privatized less then 50% of the shares and maintained the majority of the equity. Yet, assets were

---

[32] See, for example, Suleiman and Waterbury (1990: 15). More recent works that emphasize this tactical dimension of privatization are Feigenbaum et al. (1998), Manzetti (1999), Shleifer and Treisman (2000), Treisman (2003), and Murillo (2009).

[33] This assessment is based on my own interviews and on the secondary literature; see Chapter 4.

Exceptions That Prove the Rule

TABLE 5.4. *The Compensatory Degree Index: Dimensions and Scoring*

Dimension	Score
Method of Privatization (50)[a]	
Direct Awarding to Established Firm	50
Uncompetitive Bidding (and Awarding to Established Firm)	40
Competitive Bidding	10
Direct Awarding to Others	0
Type of Control by Established Firm (25)[b]	
Total	25
More than 50%	20
Less than 50%	0
State Equity Holdings after Awarding to Established Firm (25)	
No state ownership	25
Less than 50%	20
More than 50%	0
Maximum Score	100

[a] Privatization through open public offerings in the stock exchange may be considered a form of competitive bidding in which the compensatory degree depends heavily on (1) whether insiders are allowed to buy shares or not and (2) the percentage of stockholding to be privatized. However, the majority of the stockholding is never privatized through open POs in any of the cases analyzed, although minority shares might be eventually floated.

[b] Sometimes less than 50% of ownership can of course mean a controlling stake, depending on the pattern and context of corporate governance, i.e., high capitalization, thoroughly fragmented ownership, etc. It was not the case in any of the firms analyzed.

directly awarded to established players. In the main privatization of petrochemicals in Argentina, that of PBB and that of the paper pulp companies Celulosa Arauco and Celulosa Constitución in Chile (to be analyzed in Chapter 8), all that established national players obtained was the possibility of participating in competitive bidding in which they eventually lost. In the cases of steel and shipbuilding in Spain, established firms were totally excluded from the privatization process, and assets were awarded directly to other companies. Finally, in the case of the Chilean steel company CAP, as I will show in Chapter 8, private players in the sector had been almost wiped out before reform, facilitating the noncompetitive privatization biased in favor of regime associates and officials.

Of course, no method of privatization – even one in which bids are relatively open, competitive, and "technical" – is neutral. All are in a sense "political," that is, imply a policy choice that will benefit some economic actors and harm others. The Compensatory Index essentially measures a *type* of politicization of industrial privatization. Table 5.5 suggests a strong relation between the politicization of the process of state divestiture – understood as the ability of established players to bias the process in their favor – and the economic strength of national

TABLE 5.5. *The Compensatory Degree of Industrial Privatization: A Cross-Sectoral Comparison*

Privatization	Compensatory Degree Index 0–100	Growth in Market Share National Private Sector (last 20 years before beginning of liberalization)
Argentina Steel (SOMISA)	95	+125% (1970–89)[a]
Argentina Oil (Central Areas)	80	+93% (1970–89)[b]
Spain Oil (CAMPSA)	50	+33% (1963–1983)[c]
Argentina Petrochemicals (PBB)	10	−59% (1970–1989)[d]
Chile Pulp and Paper (CyA, CC)	10	−53% (1958–1978)[e]
Spain Steel (Aceralia)	0	−19% (1965–1985)[f]
Spain Shipbuilding (Barreras)	0	−47% (1965–1985)[g]
Chile Steel (CAP)	0	−95% (1965–1985)[h]

[a] Raw steel in tons. (CIS 1996).
[b] Oil production in cubic meters. (Instituto Argentino de Petróleo y Gas database, Buenos Aires)
[c] Oil refined in tons. PETROLIBER oil producer in Spain is included in private sector. (*Enciclopedia Nacional de Petróleo Petroquímica y Gas* 1970, 1974, 1979, and 1984)
[d] Basic chemicals in tons. (IPA 1999b and *Tendencias Económicas* various years)
[e] Paper pulp in metric tons. (Mamalakis 1996: Table 8.60)
[f] Raw steel in tons. (Martín Aceña and Comín 1991: 648)
[g] Ships delivered in gross tons. (Martín Aceña and Comín 1991: 649)
[h] Raw steel in tons. (Hachette et al. 1993: 62)

firms. The growth in the share of production prior to reform not only signals that domestic companies are becoming "bigger," but also – given that state enterprises are their main competitor in these sectors – that state companies are becoming "smaller" relative to them. Hence, the chances for a market-insider takeover become greater.

CONCLUSIONS

As argued in Chapters 3 and 4, national models of adjustment can indeed be identified. However, this chapter suggests that, in the end, national models amount to the aggregation of the sectoral dynamics that are prevalent in each

Exceptions That Prove the Rule

country. The study of restructuring in petrochemicals in Argentina and oil in Spain poses an interesting puzzle because both are heavy ISI sectors that deviate from the national pattern of industrial reform in both countries. As I have argued, alternative models of adjustment in these sectors (state imposition and subsidies in Argentine petrochemicals, concertational policymaking and market-share deals in the Spanish oil industry) are rooted in different prereform trajectories. Whereas oil was the single heavy industrial sector in Spain in which the military-founded INI could not undermine the influence of domestic private capital prior to reform, petrochemicals was the single sector in which the military (and therefore the state) consolidated relative industrial power in prereform Argentina. Indeed, the underperformance of local petrochemical groups under ISI and their weakness in relation to the state in Argentina did not suppress their political contacts and lobbying when liberalization took off. It just largely determined the type of compensation they were in a condition to claim – a subsidy to pay off debts rather than market concentration via privatization.

Besides, the story of the Spanish oil sector demonstrates that it was perfectly possible to administer protectionist deregulation safeguarding established companies even in the context of Spain's accession to the EU and the pressures emanating from the commission. As shown previously, neither the persistent lobbying and complaints from international oil majors such as Shell and Conoco nor the cases opened by the European Commission were able to alter the process of accommodation with insiders in the oil deregulatory framework. Indeed, the oil industry in Spain also witnessed a statist strategy in the construction of a national champion – Repsol – out of previously scattered state assets in the sector (see Etchemendy 2004a). But it was one that took into account the interests of private business insiders – especially CEPSA. In short, when the Spanish government confronted the single powerful group of domestic private companies in heavy industry, the result was neither a top-down reconversion plan, nor of course naked liberalization, but rather concertation and protection.

Finally, this chapter reinforces the notion that only powerful capitalists – those who had been taking market share, building expertise, and performing efficiently under the inward-oriented model – tend to lobby for market-share compensation to confront the harsher world of competition. In other words, neoliberal reformers tend to bestow protection and market reserves not on politically well-connected capitalists, but rather on the economically powerful.

PART III

THE POLITICAL ECONOMY OF LABOR ADJUSTMENT

6

Compensating Labor Insiders

The Origins of Statist and Corporatist Models in Spain and Argentina

INTRODUCTION

On November 23, 1984, Pablo González Larrazábal, a worker from the Spanish shipyard Euskalduna, was killed in Bilbao amid clashes between the police and union-led protesters opposing the government's decision to close down the yard. Another worker was wounded by a police bullet, and a third seriously burned as a consequence of the riots. A few days before, in what some local newspapers called "an urban guerrilla exercise," workers from the same plant had tried to seize Bilbao's major banks and had occupied the Basque television station, forcing it to air their demands. In early 1984, as part of what came to be known as the "Battle of Sagunto," steelworkers almost cut off the city of Valencia from the rest of Spain by occupying the airport and the train station and by setting up blockades in the main highways.[1] But massive industrial conflict during economic liberalization and labor restructuring in Spain was not restricted to Euskalduna and Sagunto; nor was it limited to the early 1980s. During the adjustment period 1982–88, there were more strikes, and more workers participated in strikes, than in any other period since the civil war (Wozniak 1991: 2), and Spain consistently ranked at the top of strike activity in the European Union until 1995.[2]

In Argentina, by contrast, no major industrial conflict arose during the heyday of market reform and industrial adjustment in the 1990s. No significant riots took place, either in populated urban areas similar to Bilbao or in company towns that were decimated by downsizing and unemployment. Big sectoral strikes were sporadic and generally faded away before they had gathered momentum. Widespread popular mobilization would only reemerge in the late 1990s, in the postadjustment period. However, it would take the

---

[1] For the Bilbao incidents see *El País*, November 16, 1984 and November 24, 1984, and Wozniak (1991: 324–25); the Sagunto protests are taken from Wozniak (1991: 312) and Olmos 1984.

[2] Rigby and Aledo (2001), who gather European data after 1990, show that Spain had, by far, the highest strike average (measured as days not worked per 1,000 employees per year) in the European Union in the period 1990–95.

153

154   *The Political Economy of Labor Adjustment*

form of street protest by the organizations of the unemployed rather than industrial action.[3]

The contrasting patterns of industrial conflict in neoliberal Argentina and Spain are even more striking if one considers that Spain was hailed by the scholarly literature as a model case of consensual transition to democracy only a few years prior to adjustment. Political, business, and labor leaders converged in a series of settlements that underpinned democratic consolidation.[4] Conversely, Argentina was almost the archetypal example of conflict-ridden democratization, marred with party disputes, military coup attempts, and serious labor conflict. Yet, when democratic transition was soon followed by economic reform, industrial adjustment in "consensual" Spain triggered massive urban riots and industrial action, whereas it flowed almost peacefully. in unstable and divided Argentina.

Chapters 3 to 5 analyzed the business dimension of industrial adjustment in Argentina and Spain. Chapters 6 and 7 will focus on the labor reactions to market reform in general, and industrial restructuring in particular. While the current chapter primarily explores the general determinants of the Statist and Corporatist models of labor adjustment in Spain and Argentina, case studies in Chapter 7 examine more closely industries that were paradigmatic of these alternative modes of restructuring. In both Argentina under the Peronist government (1989–99) and Socialist Spain (1982–96) – parallel to the logic of business restructuring already analyzed – labor-based reforming parties did not leave the consequences of trade reform, sectoral deregulation and adjustment for the working class to the operation of market forces but shaped it through essentially political payoffs. In Argentina's Corporatist mode of labor adjustment, the government included the traditionally hegemonic and Peronist-led union movement in the neoliberal coalition by providing it with market-share compensation. This type of compensatory policy involved the partial deregulation of both the labor law and the union-run health system, as well as the union control of employee-ownership programs and other state assets. The logic underlying market-share compensation catered to labor leaders in Argentina was very similar to that directed at business: it sought to protect the role played by unions in the newly liberalized markets, whether as unique representatives of labor in collective bargaining, as health care providers, as administrators of pension funds, or as members of the boards of privatized companies.

In Spain, the union movement was divided among the Socialist UGT (General Union of Workers), the Communist-influenced CCOO (Worker's Commissions), and regional unions. After a brief period in which the UGT was able to exert some influence in social and labor policy, the government

---

[3] For the divergent evolution of strike activity in Argentina and Spain see Graph A.2 in Appendix; on strike activity in Argentina during the 1990s see also Gómez's (1997) study.

[4] See Gunther (1992) and Linz and Stepan (1996). The Spanish consensual democratic transition also looms large in the O'Donnell and Schmitter (1986) classic volume.

Compensating Labor Insiders

TABLE 6.1. *Labor Adjustment in Argentina and Spain: Central Features of Statist and Corporatist Models*

Pattern of Labor Adjustment	Spain 1983–1996 Statist	Argentina 1989–99 Corporatist
Nature of Policymaking	*Dirigisme*: Centralized Formulation, Decentralized Implementation	Concertation with National/Sectoral unions
Compensatory Measures	Subsidy Allocation (targeted primarily at laid-off industrial workers and local unions)	Market-Share Compensation (targeted primarily at sectoral and national union leaders)
Industrial Conflict	High	Low

began excluding union leaders from the policymaking process. At the same time, the Spanish Statist mode of labor adjustment involved the implementation of top-down sectoral restructuring plans, which included subsidies and special job-placement programs targeted at laid-off workers. Unions challenged and confronted adjustment policies at the national level. Yet, the government and local (i.e., factory-based) union sections were prepared to implement workforce reduction policies jointly at the plant. As we shall see, monetary compensation targeted at laid-off industrial workers in Spain reached exceptionally high levels, not only for Iberian-American countries, but also by European standards.

As in the case of business liberalization, the chapter argues that the models of adjustment and their patterns of labor compensation are rooted in the type of regime and in the nature of the ISI actors:

> **Hypothesis 1:** *Both Argentina and Spain were plainly democratic countries during the adjustment period, and therefore market-oriented governments prioritized compensation to the "insiders" of the working class, that is, unions or union-represented workers.*

Again, the democratic nature of the polity in both countries is crucial for understanding the commonality. Argentina and Spain pushed forward marketization under plainly competitive and democratic regimes. Unlike other cases of thorough economic liberalization, such as Chile, Peru, or Mexico, repression or coercion was not an option in dealing with all or parts of the labor movement. When, in view of tariff liberalization, spending cuts, and privatization, unemployment reached levels of around 20% or more, and sectoral downsizing amounted to more than 50% of the workforce, the democratic governments of Spain and Argentina could not simply sideline or ignore – much less repress – unions. The labor movement could use mobilization threats and lobbying to contest adjustment and – eventually – receive compensation. Thus, not

156 The Political Economy of Labor Adjustment

surprisingly, democratic market reformers prioritized the organized workers in their quest to attenuate adjustment costs.

> **Hypothesis 2b:** *In Argentina's Corporatist model, organizationally strong national unions (monopolistic and centralized) made negotiated/concertational policymaking more likely and lobbied for market-share compensation (state assets and partial deregulation especially of the labor law). In Spain's Statist model organizationally weak (i.e., plural and decentralized) unions contested adjustment and demanded subsidies for the laid-off base.*

The strength of ISI unions in Argentina, built upon monopoly and centralization (understood as the institutional powers of national and sectoral leaders over shop-floor union bodies), favored concertation and market-share compensation during adjustment in three defined ways. First, monopoly makes concertation with neoliberal reformers easier as unions did not fear being outflanked by more radical unions. Second, the system of Corporatist inducements (within which union monopoly and centralized collective bargaining valid for both union and non-union members are the most central) provided national union leaders with something to bargain in the new order, namely, the preservation of those institutions that privileged their position in the labor market in terms of both finance and workers' representation. Indeed, monopoly also secured a base of members (or "consumers") for the ventures opened or retained by the market-share compensation bargains, such as the management of employee share ownership programs, of health services, or of pension funds. Finally, centralization and the low degree of autonomy of union bodies at the firm ensured governance at the shop floor. Workplace union leaders in Argentina depended heavily on the national federations and were not legally entitled to bargain autonomously or call strikes. Thus, despite workforce reductions of 50% or more, national labor leaders were able to restrain militancy at the firm through the lack of support for national/sectoral or local strikes, through simple pressure from above, and through the inclusion of firm-level union leaders in the ventures opened by market-share compensation.

By contrast, the institutional milieu of labor relations in Spain provided none of these incentives for both unions and market reformers. First, the plural and decentralized nature of Spanish unions made negotiations over adjustment more difficult from the outset. Moderate leaders were subjected to strong pressures from more militant national unions. Second, unions with a low level of state-granted inducements under ISI had fewer incentives to negotiate the preservation of the old labor law in the new liberal order. Furthermore, as will be shown later and in the case studies of Chapter 7, bureaucratic payoffs such as stock options or the managing of social services were much less attractive for union leaders, who – given low affiliation and high competition for members – lacked a secure base of contributors to those programs. Finally, rebellious shop-floor union leaders, institutionally empowered during the democratic transition and loosely connected with the union national structures, had more leverage to contest adjustment from below. They were not lured by bureaucratic payoffs,

Compensating Labor Insiders

but by generous job-loss and relocation programs oriented to protecting their base.

The first part of the chapter shows the high costs that adjustment and market reform entailed for the working class in both neoliberal Spain and Argentina. The second part gives a brief overview of government-union relations in the adjustment period and describes the policymaking process and dominant pattern of labor compensation. The third part systematizes and compares the patterns of payoffs directed to alternative segments of the working class in each country. Subsequently, I show that fiscal resources involved in compensation targeted at union leaders and formal-sector workers in Argentina and at dismissed workers in Spain were roughly similar and that, as a result, the state fiscal revenue fails to explain variation in the target and modalities of labor compensation. The last part of the chapter offers an explanation of the alternative outcomes based on how organizationally strong and weak unions coalesced under the inward-oriented model. I focus on the two central organizational dimensions that define each type of union, the "horizontal" of monopoly and the "vertical" of centralization, and on how they shaped the pattern of negotiations and payoffs during market reform.

INDUSTRIAL ADJUSTMENT AND THE COSTS FOR THE WORKING CLASS

As shown in Chapter 3, both the Menem and González administrations embarked on a bold project of market transformation. Deficit spending was curbed, tariffs were liberalized to an unprecedented degree as countries integrated into regional markets, and monetary supply was contained with zeal. The costs of economic restructuring for the working class would soon become clear. As adjustment policies advanced, unemployment rose substantially in both countries, reaching peaks of 18.5% in Argentina and 24% in Spain. Bankruptcies, plant closures, privatization, and downsizing hit the labor force hard. Although in both cases the industrial sector had undergone a gradual workforce reduction in previous years, it was under the Menem and González administrations that the majority of downsizing took place. Table 6.2 summarizes the degree of workforce reduction in the sectors subjected to some type of restructuring plan in Socialist Spain. The numbers are quite dramatic. The Socialist government pushed forward a reduction ranging (with the exception of textiles) from 20% to 80% of the workforce in the industrial sectors under reconversion plans.

Unfortunately there are no comparable data on the industrial sectors and subsectors most affected by economic restructuring and downsizing under the Menem government. Yet general figures are equally impressive. According to Census data the number of workers in the industrial/manufacturing sector diminished 42% between 1991 and 2001 and passed from 16% to 8% of the Economic Active Population in the same period.[5] Data provided by sectoral

---

[5] 1991 and 2001 Census in www.indec.gov.ar.

158 The Political Economy of Labor Adjustment

TABLE 6.2. *Spain: Evolution of the Workforce in the Sectors under State-Supported Reconversion Plans*

	Initial Workforce 1982 (number of workers)	Workforce Reduction to 1991–96 (number of workers)	Percentage of Workforce Reduction
Shipbuilding (public)	26,797	21,124	78.8
Shipbuilding (small firms)	11,764	8,168	69.4
Integrated Steel	35,149	22,583	64.2
Common Steel	9,497	4,336	45.7
Special Steel	11,000	6,145	55.9
Chemicals	20,497	10,481	51.1
Home Appliances	23,869	11,597	48.6
Textiles	108,844	9,925	9.1
Automobile Components	6,720	1,451	21.6
Electronic Components	19,877	10,168	51.2
Copper Processing	4,503	1,102	24.5
Nonferrous metals	1,277	362	28.3
Oil (refining)	5,543	1,891	34.1
SEAT	25,235	11,547	45.8
Total	310,572	120,880	38.9

Note: Oil, Shipbuilding, and Steel Adjustment to 1996, SEAT to 1994, rest to 1991. SEAT and Repsol did not establish formal plans under the framework of Law 27/1984 but reached similar restructuring agreements with state support.
Source: Ministry of Industry and Energy, Spain (1991: 228; 1993: 290); SEAT data, Ortiz (1999: 344); and *Anuario El País* (1995). "Chemicals" includes workforce reductions in ERT, and "electronics" the Alcatel group.

chambers in the industries studied in this book indicate, for example, a 47% workforce reduction in the steel sector and a striking 85% downsizing in the oil sector (see Chapter 7). These downsizing numbers highlight the different impacts of economic liberalization in ISI economies such as Argentina and Spain and in the advanced industrial world: in her book on industrial job loss based on case

Compensating Labor Insiders 159

studies from advanced countries, Golden (1997: 2) defines as "mass workforce reductions" those involving only around 10% of the workforce.

GOVERNMENT-UNION RELATIONS UNDER ECONOMIC LIBERALIZATION: A GENERAL OVERVIEW

In Spain, the labor movement was dominated by two unions, the Socialist UGT (General Union of Workers) and the Communist-oriented CCOO (Worker's Commissions). Affiliation was low (around 16% of the workforce), and, by 1982 – when the Socialists took office – the UGT and CCOO each accounted for about 40% of total affiliation (Zufiaur 1985: 229). UGT had been founded by PSOE members in the nineteenth century and had strong ties to the party at both the organizational and ideological levels. Initially, when adjustment policies began to be implemented, the UGT espoused a policy of "critical support" (Burgess 2004: 101). CCOO, on the other hand, abandoned the moderation adopted during the final stages of the transition to democracy and contested the PSOE's policy turn from the outset. In addition, important regional unions such as the Basque Worker's Solidarity (ELA-STV) and Inter-Union of Galician Workers (INT-CIG) strongly opposed those restructuring projects that affected their provinces.

In Argentina, the Peronist unions represented by the General Workers' Confederation (CGT) dominated organized labor. Affiliation in the mid-1980s has been calculated at 42% of the labor force (Feldman 1991: 97). The CGT initially split between a moderate and a militant faction in reaction to Menem's market-reform agenda. It did not formally reunify until February 1992, when it sought to present a stronger opposition to deregulation of the union-controlled health system.[6] Only a minority of unions – one of the two state workers' unions and the teachers' federation – resisted reunification and soon formed the Left-leaning CTA (Congress of Argentine Workers) as a separate confederation. Thereafter, the traditionally Peronist labor movement suffered only minor splits[7] and, despite successive rounds of privatization and deregulation, backed the Peronist party in elections and President Menem's pursuit of a new term as president in 1995.

By contrast, in Spain the old alliance between the UGT and the PSOE soon began to crumble. As the Socialists pursued the project of European integration and maintained the pace of monetary restraint, pension reform, and industrial downsizing even during the boom of the second part of the 1980s, the UGT

---

[6] On this period see Levitsky and Way (1998), Falcón (1993), and Senén González and Bosoer (1999). The initial division was between unions mostly in the service sectors in the Menemist faction (General Workers' Confederation [CGT]-San Martín) and the industrial (basically metalworkers) and state unions (CGT Azopardo). In 1992 the industrial unions rejoined the CGT.

[7] In 1994 the teamsters' and bus drivers' unions formed the MTA (Movement of Argentine Workers). Although it occasionally joined forces with the Congress of National Workers (CTA) to mobilize against the government, it was never formally established as a separate confederation and in 1996 would reintegrate into the CGT leadership.

160   *The Political Economy of Labor Adjustment*

joined CCOO in the opposition. In the context of this strategy of "unity of action," in 1988, both CCOO and UGT called for the first general strike since the civil war. The strike paralyzed the country and would be followed by two more general strikes staged in 1992 and 1994. Yet the government refused to change the fundamentals of its orthodox economic policy. In this context, the UGT, led by its secretary general, Nicolás Redondo, finally abandoned the party. The few loyal union leaders who sided with the government were expelled from the organization. A century of "fraternal relations" between the PSOE and its sister union had come to an end, and the UGT would only return to the national bargaining table under the center-Right government that took office in 1996.[8]

CORPORATIST AND STATIST MODELS OF LABOR ADJUSTMENT

Labor adjustment in Spain can be termed Statist because, aside from social compensation to laid-off industrial workers, the union movement had very little leverage over the policies of economic reform in general and the state-driven plans of industrial restructuring in particular. As analyzed in Part II, the Spanish government designed a series of top-down restructuring plans in a variety of industrial sectors declared "under reconversion." Only unions that had consented to the sectoral plans could join the Control Commissions that essentially oversaw adjustment implementation, that is, downsizing, mergers, and technological updating. By contrast, the mainstream Peronist union movement became part of the neoliberal policy coalition from the outset, although its ability to exert substantial influence was restricted to a specific set of policies, such as labor, health and pensions, and some sectoral restructuring initiatives (oil, steel, and autos). It should be noted, however, that the label *Corporatist* refers in this book to a type or mode of adjustment and economic liberalization. It conveys, first, that dominant national unions (and business groups) had privileged access to, and were included in, policy formulation.[9] Second, it underscores that compensation, by essentially preserving Corporatist inducements, protected the unions *as organizations* more than any other group within the working class. However, as a mode of economic liberalization the concept here does not involve the formal, peak level wage bargaining associated with the European experience of the 1980s and 1990s. Indeed, Corporatist as a model of labor adjustment is closer to the more recent notion of "Competitive Corporatism" that Martin Rhodes (2001) and others have applied to social pacts in Europe, in which unions accept adjustment and monetary integration in exchange for the preservation of some minimal protections and inclusion in the policymaking process.

---

[8] For UGT-PSOE relations in this period see Paramio (1992), Burgess (2004), Wozniak (1992), and Astudillo (2001). These authors agree that the UGT started to distance itself decisively from the government in 1985. For the 1988 general strike see the interesting analysis in Espina (1991).

[9] Indeed, Falcón (1993: 98) defines as "Corporatist" the relationship between Menem and the allied union movement.

Argentina's Corporatist Labor Adjustment

The Policymaking Dimension: Labor Inclusion and Concertation

Labor inclusion in the reformist coalition in Argentina may be assessed on three levels: union appointments as part of the government, the role played by the union parliamentary group, and labor participation in policy formulation. A union leader was appointed as labor minister during the first years of the administration (1989–91), when many of the crucial adjustment measures were passed. Other ministers of labor with union links were Rodolfo Díaz (1991–92) and Enrique Rodríguez (1993), and a politician very close to the Peronist unions was again named in 1997 (Erman González). Caro Figueroa (1994–97) was the only labor minister who openly sided with Cavallo and the more neoliberal wing of the government. Furthermore, the labor movement controlled a key governmental agency during the entire Menem period: the National Administration of the Health System (ANSSAL). This agency was in charge of managing the health system for formal sector workers – which is run by organized labor – and channeled state subsidies to the unions.

Second, the unionist representatives within the Peronist parliamentary group, for their part, voted for all of the main legislative bills (privatizations, exchange rate anchor, central bank independence, etc.) that pushed through economic liberalization (Etchemendy 1995: 146). Finally, the unions exerted influence on two levels of policy formulation. First, they helped shape national policies that most directly affected their interests, such as labor, health, and pension policy. Indeed, the most important deregulatory initiatives in these areas, the labor reform of 1994–95 and the partial deregulation of the health system, were drafted at the bargaining table with the CGT leadership and presented in formal protocols signed publicly (see Etchemendy and Palermo 1998: 569, 577, and Alonso 2000: 182). The second level of union intervention in policy formulation was sectoral. It was mainly restricted to the industries in which privatization was taking place and to the automobile industry, where the sectoral union joined business to lobby for a special tariff regime. Of course, government-union relations were not always smooth, and conflicts arose occasionally – as one would expect in any liberalization coalition that has both a capital and a labor wing. The following statement by Armando Caro Figueroa, minister of labor between 1994 and 1997, which describes the way in which Menem preserved union control of the state agency that oversees the health system, is eloquent.

I recall that one time I planned a big restructuring of the ministry. I changed secretaries, undersecretaries, and modified administrative divisions. When I took the decree for Menem to sign it, he only asked: "Does Lingieri [the union leader in charge of the Office for the Health System] stay?" I said "Yes," although Lingieri's office was not even in my area, and then he promptly signed all the changes without even looking at them. The president was only interested in ensuring that Lingieri remained in his position. He was a very important guy; he guaranteed Menem a fluid relation with the

162 *The Political Economy of Labor Adjustment*

unions. Nobody could have removed Lingieri. Lingieri was the right hand of the president.[10]

The Compensatory Policies

Side payments to unions in Argentina fall under the two now-familiar types of market-share compensation: partial or limited deregulation and the awarding of state assets. As noted, these compensatory measures were aimed at enhancing the future position of union leaders in more open markets, specifically as representatives of labor in collective bargaining, as health care providers, as members of the boards of privatized companies, and as administrators of pensions funds.

THE SYSTEM OF INDUSTRIAL RELATIONS. Three features of the Argentine labor law framework were a major concern for the unionist old guard. First, established labor leaders sought to maintain the union's monopoly (i.e., the ban on forming multiple unions) at the plant level, especially in newly privatized sectors such as utilities, in which state companies were divided into more than one firm. The State Reform Law guaranteed the traditional unions' representation in their respective privatized sectors.[11]

Second, labor leaders sought to preserve the centralized framework of collective bargaining, that is, the provisions by which only national/sectoral union leaders, and not plant-level works councils, are entitled to negotiate contracts in the name of both union members and non-members. In the episodes of labor reform of 1991 and 1994–95, the logic of the negotiation between the government and the CGT was the same: the unions accepted some flexibility in individual contracts (i.e., fixed-term contracts with lower dismissal costs) in exchange for the maintenance of centralized collective bargaining and monopoly at the plant level (Etchemendy and Palermo 1998).[12] Most varieties of fixed-term contracts were, however, rolled back in 1998, again in a labor reform jointly drafted with unions that also strengthened the position of national/sectoral leadership in collective bargaining (Murillo and Schrank 2005: 990). The third and final concession to the unions in the area of labor law was the automatic renewal of collective agreements. In Argentina, a collective agreement is automatically valid beyond its expiration date if business and workers do not negotiate a new one (the so-called *ultractividad*). The unions sought to preserve

---

[10] Author's interview, Buenos Aires, November 29, 2000.

[11] Author's interview with Luis Vidal, cabinet chief of the Ministry of Labor 1993–97, Buenos Aires, December 12, 2000. In 1991 the government presented a bill that allowed for the creation of firm level unions. It was voted in the Senate but later blocked in view of the negotiations between unions and the government.

[12] A bill sent by the government in 1991 to recast the system of centralized collective bargaining died in Congress. The government sought to decentralize collective bargaining via administrative decrees. Though the number of firm-level agreements increased throughout the 1990s, the national or regional union leadership retained control of contracts signed at the firm level – i.e., the national union or federation bargained with individual firms. See Marshall and Perelman (2004).

Compensating Labor Insiders 163

this provision because they wanted to protect the validity of the prereform collective agreements, which were generally more favorable to unions and workers.

HEALTH REFORM. The reform of the health system during the Menem administration constitutes a model case of compensation to labor "insiders" via partial deregulation. Health services in Argentina had traditionally been provided by public hospitals and a complex system of health insurance. The latter was divided between private health maintenance organizations (HMOs), which covered only about the wealthiest 15% of the population, and the so-called welfare funds (*obras sociales*), which covered about 53% of the total population (FIEL 1995: 24). Welfare funds are agencies that provide health care to formal-sector workers and retirees. They are financed by compulsory payroll contributions from employers and workers. At the outset of neoliberal reform, approximately 60% of the welfare-fund-insured population was covered by funds run by the unions.[13] Unions traditionally used their welfare funds – and the compulsory payroll contributions of *both* unionized and nonunionized workers – to finance a whole variety of union activities, ranging from strikes and mobilization to union-run hotels for tourism.

The more pro-business and neoliberal wing of the Menem government targeted the union-run health system from the outset, for both political and economic reasons. A reform and deregulation of the health system would serve the twofold aim of fundamentally weakening Argentina's traditionally powerful union movement and providing private HMOs and insurance capital with an expanded market. In 1991, an important conservative think tank financed by big business, FIEL, presented a project for health-system reform that included free competition among union welfare funds and HMOs for the affiliation of workers. In 1992, the government submitted a health legislative bill that echoed the FIEL project and deprived unions of compulsory worker affiliation with their welfare funds.[14] These initiatives encountered fierce resistance from both the CGT and the legislative Peronist party (Alonso 2000: 161; Belmartino 2005: 200). Finally, in 1993, the administration enacted a decree that established the partial deregulation of the system: union welfare funds were allowed to compete among themselves for workers' membership and their social security contributions, but HMOs were formally excluded from the market of compulsory payroll-based health insurance. In 1995, the government and the leaders of the CGT consolidated this agreement in a new round of health policy decrees that essentially formalized limited deregulation, created a joint commission to implement it, and spared the union welfare funds from social security tax reductions

---

[13] The rest of the welfare funds was organized by universities, provincial governments, managers, and the single state-run welfare fund for retirees. Data in FIEL-CEA (1995). The union-controlled welfare funds either managed their own medical facilities or subcontracted health services from private clinics.

[14] The business chamber of HMOs hailed the project. Its president declared that health deregulation was "the fall of the Berlin wall, a revolution. It is as important as the privatizations" (Alonso 2000: 162).

164   The Political Economy of Labor Adjustment

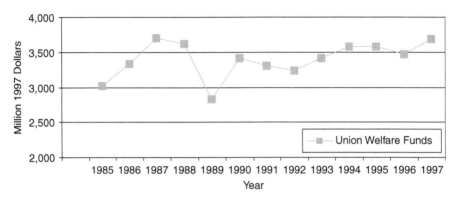

GRAPH 6.1. Consolidated Public Expenditures in Health Insurance: Union Welfare Funds. *Source*: Ministry of Economy Argentina (1999). Includes a minority of welfare funds for upper-level and state employees not administered by unions.

(Belmartino 2005: 208). In practice, this partial deregulation would not be fully implemented until 1997.[15]

With deregulation restricted to competition among labor welfare funds, unions managed to retain substantial control of the system. Indeed, contrary to what many would have expected, the amount of money that union leaders managed to retain in the welfare funds increased remarkably during neoliberalism and overall, measured in 1997 dollars, remained at levels similar to those of the 1980s. High economic growth and the increase in tax and social security revenues seem to have compensated for losses stemming from unemployment (Graph 6.1).

However, the partial reform did have distributive consequences *inside* the union-run system of welfare funds. The unions with stronger and more efficient welfare funds were in a position to poach affiliates from traditional large unions in declining sectors such as metals or textiles. The impact of partial reform during the 1990s for a group of traditionally powerful unions in former state-owned companies can be seen in Table 6.3. Welfare funds of the natural gas, oil, and water utilities unions actually thrived in the new health market and gained membership in the initial period of deregulation. The trajectory of the traditional oil union SUPE is telling in this respect. With the privatization of the oil monopoly YPF, the union suffered an astounding loss of 85% of its members between 1989 and 1997 (see Chapter 7). However, its welfare fund almost doubled its membership (i.e., incorporated workers from other unions) and gained 50% in revenue in 1997–2000 (Table 6.3). By 2008 it boasted around

---

[15] As the health policy analyst Claudia Danani (2003: 241) argues, referring to the mainstream unions, "the delay to implement deregulation was not simply that of someone on death row who wants to gain days alive, but the re-adaptation to new conditions in order to soften or revert the reform's pernicious effects."

Compensating Labor Insiders

TABLE 6.3. *Membership and Revenues of the Union Welfare Funds in Privatized Companies: Variation in the Period of Partial Deregulation (1997–2000)*

Union	Membership 1998 (workers affiliated)	Change in Members to September 2000	Percentage of Change Membership 1998–2000	Percentage of Change Revenues 1998–2000
Electricity workers (FATALyF – national)	24,137	–2,095	–8.68%	–10.21%
Electricity workers (FATALyF – Buenos Aires)	6,757	340	5.03%	–8.83%
Telecommunication (FOETRA)	23,649	–805	–3.40%	–12.13%
Water (FNTOS)	5,482	–249	–4.54%	60.67%
Oil Workers (SUPE)	6,830	5,905	86.46%	49.08%
Natural Gas Workers	1,767	573	32.43%	107.02%
Steel Workers (UOM – San Nicolás)	2,749	650	23.64%	–5.85%
Total	71,371	4,319		

Source: Superintendencia de Servicios de Salud (Office for the Health Services, Argentine Government), with data from the AFIP (Argentine Tax Collection Office). Revenue refers to wage payroll taxes collected January–November.

150,000 members including workers and their families.[16] In other words, union leaders were much more effective in doing business in the health market than in defending their workers from layoffs. In short, among the union-run welfare funds, certain small and medium unions and some larger unions in privatized companies (in which the privatization bargain often included subsidies oriented to improve the union welfare funds) or in the service sector reaped most of the benefits in partial deregulation of the health system.[17] Still, the loss of income and of members with higher wages would have been much worse for the largest unions had they been forced to compete openly with HMOs.

---

[16] Data from http://www.ospesalud.com.ar.
[17] In fact, data from the Office of Health Services (not shown in the table) indicate that the union welfare funds of relatively small unions, including insurance workers, building maintenance workers, and private teachers, strongly benefited from partial deregulation. Many of these smaller unions were allowed to subcontract health services with HMOs. In other words, private HMOs could enter the market if they reached an agreement with a union. Thus, some unions formed joint ventures with powerful private HMOs with the goal of recruiting workers (particularly those who earned higher wages) affiliated to other welfare funds, generally run by bigger unions.

EMPLOYEE SHARE OWNERSHIP PROGRAM AND OTHER STATE ASSETS. As in the case of the powerful ISI business players, compensatory policies for unions were also bestowed in the form of state assets. A handful of unions participated in some of the privatization rounds. For example, FATLyF (electricity workers) bought a number of electricity generators and SUPE (state oil workers) purchased YPF's former fleet (Murillo 1997: 86). In addition to the direct awarding of assets, as Chapter 2 underlined, the awarding of stock options in privatization was another form of market-share compensation suitable for unions and workers. In Argentina, the Employee Share Ownership Program (ESOP) became a vital side payment targeted at the union structure. The State Reform Law, which structured the legislative framework that governed privatization, granted a percentage of the stock share of each privatized company to the workers. The stocks reserved for sale to the workers would be reimbursed by the profits that those same shares would yield after privatization. In practice, the price paid by workers for those stocks was negligible. Two aspects of the ESOP should be emphasized. First, the law and the series of decrees that regulated the program established that only insiders, that is, workers who remained in the company after privatization, were eligible to participate in the program. Second, although there is not a single mention of the unions in the entire legislative body that regulates the ESOP, in almost all the cases the program ultimately was administratively managed by the monopolistic union in each company. In fact, the government negotiated the percentage of stocks included in the ESOP with each sectoral union. After some time, workers could subsequently sell the shares or keep them and collect future dividends. Both options involved important benefits as the value of these stocks generally soared after the early 1990s.

PENSION FUNDS. In 1993, the government partially privatized the state pension system through the creation of a capitalization market. In the negotiation of the reform bill, unions successfully lobbied to maintain a state-run system that could compete with private pension funds for the workers' affiliation. At the same time, they obtained the right to create their own pension funds to compete in the market. When the system was launched, sixteen unions controlled or were participating in three pension funds. Taken together, these three pension funds ranked fifth among the initial twenty-two pension funds (most of them run by major banks), with around 10% of the market in terms of workers' affiliation. By the year 2000, however, most unions had sold their stakes in the system, and only one union-run pension fund remained – Futura – holding less than 2% of the market and managing $292 million in assets.[18]

To summarize, trade liberalization, privatization, and downsizing inexorably weakened the structural position of unions in the economy during the Menem

---

[18] Data from the Regulatory Office for Pensions (SJP), Buenos Aires. This compensation was in the end much less important than the others in terms of resources involved and expansion of the unions' role in the market. Plus, the whole pension system was renationalized by the Kirchner government in 2008.

Compensating Labor Insiders

period. Business was on the offensive during the heydays of market reform in the 1990s.[19] In fact, Levitsky (2003) shows that the Peronist unions' political retreat had already started in the 1980s, when they were excluded from the dominant positions in the Peronist Party. Yet after complicated negotiations, and as part of the neoliberal coalition, mainstream Peronist unions did not lose their essential sources of organizational power: representation monopoly, centralized collective bargaining, automatic renewal of prereform collective agreements, and the system of welfare funds.

Spain's Statist Labor Adjustment

The Policymaking Dimension: National Labor Exclusion and Decentralized Bargaining

In Spain, except for a brief initial period, organized labor was excluded from the arena of decision making. In effect, at the national coalitional level, Spain witnessed a shift from partial labor inclusion to outright exclusion after 1985. As mentioned, while the Communist CCOO and regional unions confronted the government from the outset, the Socialist UGT adopted a position of "critical support." In fact, the bargains between the government and UGT during the first few years of Socialist administration resembled the logic of the government-union political exchanges in Argentina just analyzed. As Burgess (2004: 103–05) shows, an implicit trade-off took place between the consolidation of collective rights of unions (i.e., measures favoring unions through collective bargaining and the provision for union sections in the plant) and decreased employment security.[20]

The most important agreement between the UGT and the government, however, concerned the situation of the workers laid off by the industrial restructuring plans. The ministries of Industry and Economics advocated the termination of the contracts of dismissed workers. The UGT (and sectors of the Socialist Party) proposed "suspension," meaning that employees who joined relocation programs would have their contracts suspended and could eventually claim the right to reenter the firm. After tough negotiations with the UGT during the first months of 1984, Prime Minister Felipe González sided with the union, and the

---

[19] As the former labor minister Caro Figueroa – an ally of the pro-market wing of the government and hardly a sympathizer of the Peronist unions – asserts: "The business sector thought it was 'their time'; in the meetings they asked for everything. They thought they could get whatever they wanted, free dismissals, individual wage bargaining, and complete liberalization of the welfare-funds system ... They wanted to deregulate the welfare-funds system not because they wanted to fix the health system but because they wanted to liquidate the Argentine labor movement." Author's interview, Buenos Aires, November 29, 2000.

[20] In 1984, the government, the UGT, and business signed the AES (Acuerdo Economico y Social), which allowed for the expansion of temporary contracts as a way to cope with unemployment. In 1985 the government, with UGT support, enacted the Organic Law of Union Liberty, which gave juridical status to union sections in the enterprise and granted bargaining rights to unions in the public sector.

168 *The Political Economy of Labor Adjustment*

legislation sanctioned only the suspension of the contracts of workers expelled by adjustment.[21] Yet, these types of negotiation would not last. Most analysts of union-government relations in Spain assert that, after 1985, UGT's influence in policymaking waned (Paramio 1992, Burgess 2004, Espina 1991). As noted, in the context of a hardening of the orthodox orientation of the government, the UGT joined the CCOO in the opposition.

In Chapter 3, I argued that the role of unions in the initial formulation of the industrial reconversion plans was limited. Still, at the same time that unions were contesting the government neoliberal turn nationally, they never ceased negotiating the implementation of industrial restructuring at the local, decentralized level. Unions held key positions in the Employment Promotion Funds (EPFs), which were agencies created in industrial sectors subjected to reconversion plans and whose main goal was to administer a system of compensation to laid-off workers and help them find alternative jobs. At the national level the EPFs were formally managed by a board with equal representation by the government, unionists, and the firms in the given sector under restructuring. But the practical operation of the sectoral EPFs was decentralized to the regions and firms in which extensive restructuring was taking place. At this level, the sections of the unions that had consented to the sectoral reconversion plans (and were therefore represented in the Control Commissions of implementation) essentially managed the EPFs: local unions helped organize the placement programs and agreed upon the workers who would be dismissed and included in the EPFs – Chapter 7 studies the operation of these funds in more detail.[22] Significantly, cooperation between state technocrats in charge of reconversion plans and base-level unions, which was restricted to the implementation of workforce reduction policies (i.e., largely excluded industrial plans, etc.) at the local/factory level and other practical issues, such as internal mobility and training, was not incompatible with outbursts of union militancy and protests. Indeed, it was parallel to strongly adversarial and conflictual relations nationally, that is, at the level of federations and confederation leaderships.

The Compensatory Policies

Monetary subsidies and special retraining and relocation programs became the main compensation aimed at the working class during industrial adjustment in Spain. Generally speaking, subsidies took one of the following forms: severance

---

[21] Author's interview with José Corcuera, secretary general of the Metals Federation of UGT 1984–85, Madrid, September 4, 2001, and Alvaro Espina, employment secretary of the Labor Ministry 1985–91, Madrid, September 15, 2001.

[22] Author's interviews with Nestor Alvarez, secretary general of Workers Commisions (CCOO) at the steel mill AHV and representative of CCOO to the steel Employment Promotion Fund (EPF), Bilbao, March 18, 2001; Pedro Morales, president of the Sagunto Factory Council, Madrid, March 25, 2001; and Angel Guido, member of the works council of the steel mill Ensidesa, Gijón, March 12, 2003. Wozniak (1991: 330) asserts that union leaders were "gatekeepers to the Employment Promotion Funds."

Compensating Labor Insiders

payments, early retirement, or inclusion in the aforementioned Employment Promotion Funds. The EPFs provided the most extensive social coverage to dismissed workers. EPFs received employers' contributions but were largely funded by the state. They paid a monthly compensation to workers and performed as a job placement agency. In addition, many EPFs offered job-training schemes. The fund granted the worker 80% of his gross wage (i.e., before payroll taxes) – almost his old salary in cash (Navarro 1990: 157). Early retirement programs, on the other hand, granted 75% of the worker's gross wage for five years before the legal age of retirement, which in Spain was sixty-five.

Workers' stays in the EPFs were, in theory, limited to three years, but in practice they were much longer than planned because, as stated previously, the government had established the "suspension" rather than the "termination" of dismissed workers' contracts. As the worker could theoretically claim the legal right to return to his position – which was impossible in the context of permanent downsizing – the state had few options but to keep workers in the EPFs. Furthermore, the percentage of workers placed in new jobs through EPFs was minimal. Although the conditions for relocation were later made more restrictive for workers in EPFs, in principle, the worker could claim the same wage level he had enjoyed in the old job and could reject geographical relocation. In fact, workers often joined EPFs and early-retirement programs consecutively. According to data from the Ministry of Industry, for the period 1983–91, 26.5% of those laid off under industrial reconversion plans participated in early retirement, 30.1% were included in EPFs, and 43.5% were "voluntary" departures with severance payments (Ministry of Industry and Energy, Spain: 1991, 1993).

THE WORKING CLASS AND COMPENSATION UNDER NEOLIBERAL ADJUSTMENT IN ARGENTINA AND SPAIN: TARGET AND FISCAL COSTS

Target

In a seminal article on Argentine labor's reaction to economic reform, Murillo (1997) argued that union leaders in Argentina sought to preserve their *organizational* resources in a context in which their *political* (influence in the Peronist Party) and *structural* resources (members, wages) were dwindling. Building upon this notion, it can be argued that the partial deregulation and state assets (i.e., the market-share compensation) through which the government rewarded unions in Argentina constitute *organizational* or *bureaucratic payoffs*. This type of labor compensation has two main features. First, as stated earlier, it is intended to support the *economic role* played by unions in future open markets, be it health services, the board of privatized companies, or wage bargaining. Second, this type of payoff tends to privilege the union leaders who command the organization and their associates rather than the rank-and-file workers. The bargain between government and unions in Argentina's labor reform, by which

The Political Economy of Labor Adjustment

TABLE 6.4. *Scoring the* Relative *Level of Compensation to Working-Class Segments: Argentina and Spain under Market Liberalization*

	Union Leaders	Formal Sector Workers	Laid-off Workers	Unemployed
Spain (Statist)	Low	Low	High (large firms)	Medium
Argentina (Corporatist)	High	Medium	Low	Low

protection against layoffs was traded for the preservation of corporatist inducements in both the labor law and the health system, is the most blunt example of this type of exchange. Union leaders are obviously the first beneficiaries of organizational survival.

Still, as Pizzorno (1978) argued in his classic study, concessions that protect unions and hurt workers in the short run could also be taken as favoring workers in the long run (at least those who kept their jobs) by strengthening their class organization. By the same token, compensation targeted at laid-off industrial workers in Spain also helped union leaders (especially factory council activists) to legitimize their role as protectors of workers' interests. Nonetheless, it is undeniable that both types of side payments – bureaucratic payoffs and job loss subsidies – are primarily oriented to safeguarding the interests of different subsectors of the working class.

Table 6.4 presents a general comparison of Argentina and Spain in the target of labor compensation and scores different subsectors of the working class in each country. We can consider four different aggregates within the working class experiencing the strains of adjustment and economic downturn: the leaders of the unions, the workers who remain in the formal sector (i.e., those who are not expelled by adjustment), the workers who are dismissed as a consequence of privatization and industrial restructuring, and the (increasing) general mass of workers who are unemployed but are not necessarily laid off in the process of industrial privatization/restructuring.

Few would dispute the idea that the leaders of the traditional sectorwide unions in Argentina were the most privileged in the government attempts to soften the impact of adjustment. National labor leaders would be the main beneficiaries of maintaining the traditional union role in centralized collective bargaining and in the health system. They benefited also from the union administration of ESOPs and, in a few cases, of pension funds. The preservation of the *ultractividad* (the prereform automatic renewal of collective agreements explained earlier) provides yet another good example. Most of these collective agreements date back to 1975. The wage levels and many of the working conditions included in those agreements were barely enforced in the factories

Compensating Labor Insiders 171

during the 1990s.[23] Yet, through *ultractividad*, union leaders preserved the employers' and workers' contributions to their unions or welfare funds that were included in those prereform collective agreements.

It could be argued, though, that some of these benefits also accrued to the workers who were not fired during adjustment and stayed in the formal sector. Workers who remained in privatized companies received handsome benefits either from the dividends or from the sale of the ESOP's shares, whose value almost always soared in the 1990s. In the oil company YPF, for instance, some workers who sold their ESOP shares received $70,000 or more; in the steel mill SOMISA individual workers could eventually sell their ESOPs for around $18,000. Likewise, the partial deregulation of labor law and the (relatively) higher protection from layoffs, when compared to other cases of extensive neoliberal reform such as Peru or Chile, also prioritized the interests of the mass of workers who remained in the formal sector. Finally, laid-off workers and the unemployed were the segments most hurt during Argentina's adjustment. Most of the layoffs were implemented through a "voluntary-departure" mechanism, which essentially meant a one-shot severance payment. Additionally, although by 1993 unemployment had reached 11% in the industrial areas of greater Buenos Aires (peaking at 18.5% nationally in 1995), national unemployment subsidies or targeted employment programs were extremely limited during the Menem government and would only expand decisively after 1999 (Golbert 1998: 67–68; Cortés and Marshall 1999). Indeed, Lodola (2005: 516–17) notes that during the Menem presidency the "portion of social policy allocated to the marginal population was minimal and showed no major change."

Working-class compensation in liberalizing Spain presents a very different picture. As noted before, negotiations between the government and UGT leaders over bureaucratic payoffs took place in the first two years of Socialist administration. Still, before long, the situation turned into one of aggressive confrontation between organized labor and the government. Formal-sector workers were affected by the government initiatives for reduction in layoff costs and benefited less from ownership programs than in Argentina.[24] However, laid-off workers from companies under industrial restructuring were, unmistakably, the most compensated working-class segment in neoliberal Spain. Table 6.5 compares compensation to workers dismissed under restructuring plans and

---

[23] "Go to a metal or steel factory and ask who enforces the 1975 Collective Agreement. Nobody does." Author's interview with Carlos Tomada, main adviser and lawyer to the metalworkers' union Union of Metal Workers (UOM), Buenos Aires, November 3, 2000. As Luis Vidal (chief of cabinet of the Ministry of Labor 1993–97) revealed, "The economic subsidies to unions were, in practice, the only surviving features of the old collective agreements." Author's interview, Buenos Aires, December 12, 2000. The lack of negotiations over new contracts was often complemented with informal agreements between companies and local or factory unions; see, for example, the work of Freytes Frey (1999) for the steel sector.

[24] After seven years of market reforms in both countries, the percentage of workers under fixed-term contracts in Spain was twice that in Argentina (Etchemendy 2004b).

172   *The Political Economy of Labor Adjustment*

TABLE 6.5. *Compensation to the Unemployed and Workers Laid Off under Reconversion Plans in Spain, 1983–91*

	General Unemployment Benefits	Early Retirement (Industrial Reconversion)	EPFs (Industrial Reconversion)
Extension of Coverage	From 3 months to 2 years (depending on previous contributions)	5 years, from age 60 to 65 (legal age for retirement)	3 years, with an extension of 1.5 years if there is no job relocation Full coverage until early retirement for workers aged 55–60
Income	1st to 6th month 80% of regulatory base[a] 7th to 12th month 70% of regulatory base 13th to 24th month 60% of regulatory base	75% of gross average income last 6 months before dismissal	80% of gross average wage of last 6 months before dismissal
Finance	Worker's prior contribution	State	State and employers

[a] The regulatory base is determined by the worker's previous contributions to the unemployment fund; it was far lower than the wage before dismissal.
Source: Navarro (1990: 158, Table 10), Garcia Becedas (1989: Table 22), and Sergio Santillan, "Marco Legal para el tratamiento de las empresas en crisis" (internal UGT publication), UGT Confederal Secretary (2001).

that granted to the general mass of unemployed in Spain. Benefits to workers under restructuring plans were more generous, in terms of both the extension of coverage and monetary compensation.

Workers under EPFs obtained 80% of their gross wage, which in practice meant their old wage in cash, irrespective of their previous contributions to the unemployment fund. The EPF compensation formally lasted for three years with an extension of one and a half years if relocation was not successful. Younger workers who were not relocated ultimately received compensation from the EPFs for five years or more, often until they obtained early retirement. The unemployment benefit subsidy was far less generous, was limited to two years or less, depended upon worker's previous contributions, and was calculated according to a "regulatory base" that was far lower than the workers' previous wage.

Even union leaders acknowledged this huge inequality in the benefits granted to workers hit by adjustment in Spain. Manuel Puerta, secretary general (1984–88) of the Metals Federation of the UGT, asserted:

If you worked in a sector under industrial reconversion, and you were 52, you went home as part of an early-retirement program. If you worked in a company that was not under an industrial reconversion plan and you were fired, God help you! In some sense the reconversion process created discrimination within the working class. It created an aristocracy of workers.

Compensating Labor Insiders

TABLE 6.6. *Steel Industry in Europe: Comparing Work Reduction Compensatory Policies (1979–85)*

	Spain		France		Germany		United Kingdom	
	Early Retire	EPF	Early Retire	EPF	Early Retire	EPF	Early Retire	EPF
Coverage	Age 55–65	4.5 years	50–60	2 years	55–60	No	No	1 year
Income % Gross Wage	80% age 55–60 75% age 60–65	80%	75% age 50–55 70% age 55–60	70%	80–90%			100%
Main Finance	State	State	State/EC	Idem	State/EC	Idem		State/EC

Source: Spain, García Becedas (1989: Table 22); other countries, Houseman (1991: Chapter 3 and Tables A.1, A.2, and A.7).

Those workers [under reconversion plans] got very different treatment from the rest of workers, and that was done – we must admit it – with the taxes of all Spanish people.[25]

It could be argued that the Spanish government was simply replicating workforce-reduction policies that are more common in Europe than in Latin America. Yet compensation to laid-off industrial workers in Spain not only was more generous than in Argentina, but was also among the most generous in Western Europe. Table 6.6 compares workforce-reduction policies in the steel sector in Spain, England, Germany, and France. Steel is the archetypical industry hit by global competition and overcapacity after 1980. It also tends to be concentrated in company towns and is home to generally militant labor unions. Therefore, the steel sector provides a good lens through which to assess compensation programs to industrial workers laid off in Europe during the peak years of liberal adjustment in the 1980s.

France, the United Kingdom, and Germany were part of the Davignon Plan whereby the EU tried to reduce capacity and employment in the steel sector for the period 1979–86. This program received generous support from the EU (Houseman 1991). As the Spanish steel sector intensified adjustment after 1982, when Spain was still not a member of the EU, it was not included in the Davignon Plan. Therefore, Spanish worker compensation was essentially financed by public coffers. The only country in the table that is close to Spain in terms of the benefits granted to steelworkers laid off by adjustment is France. Indeed, more French workers across industries were included in the Employment Funds schemes, which were regional rather than sectoral (Levy 1999: 251). However,

---

[25] Author's interview, Madrid, September 29, 2001. It should be noted that workers under reconversion plans were a minority of the labor force, around 300,000 workers, and that the unemployment during these years amounted to around 2.5–3 million workers.

174 *The Political Economy of Labor Adjustment*

employment-reduction policies in France were largely based on early-retirement programs rather than on the more generous relocation programs (Houseman 1991: 36; Rand Smith 1998: 169; Daley 1996). In brief, though encompassing an important minority of dismissed workers (see Chapter 7), the benefits entailed by the Spanish EPFs were among the most generous in Western Europe. As one worker asserted regarding the handsome benefits granted to workers while they remained under the Spanish job-placement program: "In the end, the worst thing that could happen to a worker in the Employment Promotion Fund was to get a job."[26]

Fiscal Costs

This section analyzes what for many would be the most intuitive explanation for the different pattern of compensation aimed at the working class in the different models of adjustment, namely, the question of state resources. Unlike Spain, Argentina suffered hyperinflation in 1989, and, since the early 1980s, the state had been burdened by heavy foreign debt. Thus, workforce reduction policies based on monetary subsidies would be less likely.

As mentioned, the ESOP constituted almost an ideal type of compensation targeted at "insiders," that is, unions and formal sector workers who were not dismissed. However, it involved a mass of resources – privatization income – that did not depend on the budget and that the state could disburse relatively easily. The cost of the ESOP can be measured by the market value of the shares carved out for the workers had the stocks been publicly sold during the first day that they were listed on the Buenos Aires Stock Exchange. Put differently, one can take the hypothetical value of those stocks (hypothetical because those stocks were not sold in the market but given to the workers for a symbolic price) if they had been traded in the market together with the rest of the stocks that each state company floated after privatization. Table 6.7 calculates the market value of each ESOP implemented during adjustment in Argentina by multiplying the number of shares allocated to the program by the value of the share on the first day of its quotation. Thus, the ESOP market value in Argentina (i.e., the money the state could have collected by trading those shares instead of allocating them to unions and workers who remained in the firm) was around $2,200 million (in 1997 dollars).

For Spain, Mikel Navarro (1990: 248–49) has estimated the total costs of what he calls "labor adjustment," that is, the workforce reduction policies included in all reconversion plans,[27] as $3,381 million in 1997 dollars for the period 1982–92. In short, although they were targeted at different segments of

---

[26] Author's interview, Madrid, February 23, 2002.

[27] The figure may underestimate the resources in Spain because it does not include the autoworkers and other sectors revamped but not subjected to formal reconversion plans or compensation after 1992. But one could also argue that the estimate of the monetary value of compensation in Argentina does not include some other state assets directly awarded to unions through privatization, other ESOPs in firms not listed in the Buenos Aires Stock Exchange (and therefore not included in Table 6.7), and pension funds run by unions.

Compensating Labor Insiders

TABLE 6.7. *Employee Share Ownership Program in Argentina: Market Value*

	Percentage of Shares in Privatization	Absolute Number of Shares	Price Stock[a] (in dollars)	Market value of ESOP (in dollars)
Siderar (steel)	20%	57,243,146	2.35	134,521,393
Aguas Argentinas (water)	10%	12,000,000	1.00	12,000,000
Metrogas (gas distribution)	10%	51,253,029	1.18	60,478,574
Telecom (telecommunications)	10%	98,438,098	4.33	426,236,964
Edenor (electricity distribution)	10%	83,161,020	0.97	80,250,384
Edelap (electricity distribution)	10%	28,322,004	0.50	14,161,002
Distribuidora Gas Cuyana (gas distribution)	10%	20,333,300	1.25	25,416,625
Banco Hipotecario (banking)	5%	7,500,000	7.65	57,375,000
YPF (oil)	10%	35,000,000	21.65	757,750,000
Telefonica (telecommunications)	10%	117,875,738	2.87	338,303,367
Edesur (electricity distribution)	10%	99,298,399	1.01	99,993,488
TGS (gas transportation)	3%	23,834,850	2.71	64,592,444
TGN (gas transportation)	4.4%	15,465,964	1.12	17,321,880
Central Puerto (energy generator)	10%	8,401,589	5.60	47,048,898
Central Costanera (energy generator)	10%	13,468,600	2.87	38,654,882
TOTAL				2,174,104,901

[a] First quotation in the Buenos Aires Stock Exchange.
Source: Buenos Aires Stock Exchange, company balances and monthly reports.

the working class, both the ESOP and the workforce-reduction policies in Spain entailed relatively similar amounts of resources. The cost of labor compensation measured in this way was 1.14% of the GDP in Argentina and 0.8% of the GDP in Spain (GDP at the outset of reform in both cases – 1989 and 1982, respectively).

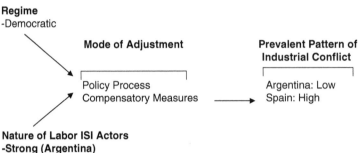

FIGURE 6.1. A Stylized Causal Assessment of Labor Restructuring in Argentina and Spain.

EXPLAINING THE OUTCOME: REGIME AND POWER OF ISI LABOR ACTORS

Why was the Spanish union movement, which was organizationally among the weakest in Europe – in 1985 it had the lowest affiliation among all Organization for Economic Cooperation and Development (OECD) countries[28] – able to obtain compensation packets for laid-off industrial workers that, as shown earlier, were not only unmatched in Ibero-America but among the most generous in all of Western Europe? Why did the most powerful union movement in Latin America become part of a liberalizing coalition whose policies decimated its membership? I have shown that the amount of state resources available from compensation does not provide an adequate explanation of the alternative patterns of labor adjustment and coalitional alignments in Argentina and Spain. As in the case of business analyzed earlier, I argue that the democratic character of the polity and the prereform configuration of economic actors – in this case, unions – shaped both the *politics* (i.e., the procedural formulation) and specific *policies* of compensation (Figure 6.1).

Democracy and Compensation to Labor Insiders

Unlike in Mexico, Peru, and Chile, which could be considered cases of sweeping marketization and were all more authoritarian or repressive at the time reforms were undertaken, democratic and nonrepressive regimes in Spain and Argentina

---

[28] In the peak adjustment year of 1985, Spain had a union density of 16% (Organization for Economic Cooperation and Development Done [OECD] *Employment Outlook*, July 1991).

Compensating Labor Insiders

could not completely ignore potential working-class reactions during an adjustment process that trimmed 50% or more of the workforce in some sectors. As analyzed in Chapters 8 and 9, nondemocratic neoliberal governments in Chile and Peru could use, and did use, coercion to thwart reaction from the working class and to avoid dealing with, and compensating, organized labor. Mexico and Bolivia were not as repressive as Chile and Peru, but neoliberal governments did use force to cope with dissident sectors of the organized working class. In Argentina and Spain, by contrast, in the context of plain democracy and civil liberties, coercion was not an option. Thus sizable compensation to at least certain segments of a mobilized labor movement became inevitable. This was evident in most interviews I conducted with officials in charge of labor policy.

In short, it seems scarcely disputable that a democratic system tends to bias the majority of compensatory policies during market reforms toward the more organized segments of the working class, or the ISI "insiders": unions or union-backed laid-off workers. The rebellious unions in Spain (particularly in sectors that led the industrial expansion of the 1960s and early 1970s, such as steel and shipbuilding) and the traditional Corporatist unions in Argentina had both been central actors in the semiclosed economies and had relatively more resources to deploy in the face of adjustment than did the atomized mass of unemployed. Even in hostile times, those resources (be they mobilization capacity or bureaucratic strength) can be better applied under democratic conditions. Indeed, building on the Chilean and Peruvian cases, Chapters 8 and 9 will argue that authoritarian neoliberal governments tend to bestow *relatively* more compensation on the unemployed and/or poor informal workers.

As pointed out in Chapter 2, it is obviously essential to distinguish the explanatory variable (type of regime, in this case, governments based on popular legitimacy subject to institutional accountability) from the outcome (compensation and deals with alternative segments of the working class). A democratic regime simply increased the costs and availability of coercion in dealing with established unions – the primary foe of economic liberalization within the working class in view of the protections and subsidies received under the ISI model.

Organizational Power of Labor and Compensation to Insiders

Antecedent Conditions: The Emergence of Strong and Weak ISI Labor in Argentina and Spain

FROM STATE CONTROL TO POWER AT THE BASE: ORGANIZED LABOR UNDER THE ISI MODEL IN SPAIN. In Spain, the traditional confederations that dominated labor politics under the Spanish Republic, the Socialist UGT and the anarchist CNT, were bloodily repressed in the postwar period.[29] In the early 1940s, during its "fascist" period the Francoist regime created an official

---

[29] Between 1939 and 1954, the members of seven executive committees of the UGT were arrested (Maravall 1978: 24). Tomás Centeno, secretary general of the Socialist UGT, died under torture in the headquarters of the regime's secret police in Madrid in 1953.

unionism through the so-called Vertical Syndicates, organized in the different areas of the economy, under the general command of the CNS (Center of National Syndicalism). Affiliation was compulsory, and, of course, independent unions and the right to strike were banned. However, as has been widely argued by Spain specialists, the fascist features of Francoism were more formal than real. Indeed, Franco hastily purged the more plebeian, secular, and revolutionary cadres of the Falange early on and replaced its leadership with loyalists. As Linz (1964: 308) noted in his classic essay on authoritarian systems, after its initial consolidation, the Franco regime eschewed any significant mobilization of the lower strata. More important for my argument is the fact that, although the regime established a series of welfare provisions to be channeled by the CNS, "the control of these services was almost completely divorced from the officials of the 'representative' lines," that is, the official unions (Amsden 1972: 75). In short, the official union movement would be centralized and *state controlled* yet organizationally weak and already deprived of resources under Francoism.

After 1960 the regime introduced a new system of collective bargaining as part of a general stabilization packet and allowed for more or less free elections of workers' representatives to shop-floor factory juries or councils (*jurados de empresa*). Thus, bargaining became quite extensive, as a result of both economic growth and the regime's attempt to legitimize itself in the eyes of the working class (Fishman 1990: 92). However, floor bargaining spawned a series of autonomous workers' commissions and assemblies in the largest factories. This grassroots movement spread primarily throughout the most developed regions of Madrid, the Basque Country, and Catalonia and gradually coalesced in a more or less organized union movement of the so-called *comisiones obreras* (workers' commissions), or CCOO, throughout the country.

By the late 1960s, CCOO was in practice dominated by the PCE (Spanish Communist Party), which devised a careful strategy of infiltrating the official union movement by electing representatives to the factory councils that were formally part of the Vertical Syndicates.[30] This new breed of union militants defended workers' rights in the economic bargains that occurred inside the official union structures, yet, at the same time, shaped a broad movement of working-class contestation that would shake the authoritarian regime. After the democratic transition, the "Worker's Statute" (1980) democratized the labor relations framework, formalizing the former factory juries (now called works councils) as the main organ of worker's representation at the local level.[31] Thus, the initially state-controlled labor organization under the inward-oriented

---

[30] However, the CCOO was also home to important non-Communist groups of a Socialist, Maoist, or Catholic bent. The literature on the surge of CCOO and its successful strategy of infiltrating the official unions is extensive. For indispensable accounts see Fishman (1990: Chapter 4) and the essays compiled in Ruiz (1993).

[31] For the way in which developments under Francoism shaped labor legislation under the newly democratic regime see the excellent account in Dubin (2002).

model gave way to a union movement strongly oriented to the workplace and well established in the large industrial companies that buttressed secondary ISI in the 1960s. The factory-based and clandestine assembly culture that virtually created a new union movement from below deemphasized formal affiliation and generated initially weak national structures. In short, the legacy of state-controlled unionism under most of ISI in Spain was a plural labor movement with relatively weak bureaucratic-financial power and institutionally empowered shop-floor bodies.

FROM POWER AT THE BASE TO POWER AT THE TOP: LABOR POPULISM UNDER THE ISI MODEL IN ARGENTINA. Modern organized labor in Argentina was decisively shaped under the regime of Juan Perón (1946–55), a military leader who crafted an alliance with the unions to win the 1946 elections and eventually created the Justicialista Party. The Peronist state enacted a series of institutional "inducements" (Collier and Collier 1979) that boosted the organizational strength of unions. Among the most important were the passing of the Law of Professional Associations, which granted a monopoly and the right to bargain (on behalf of union and nonunion members alike) to a single and officially registered union for each sector of production, and a framework for collective labor relations that strongly favored centralized bargaining at the sectoral level.[32]

Peronism, became, therefore, a model case of *labor populism*, a working class fully incorporated in political life through a populist party in which organized labor was the central constituency (Collier and Collier 1991). A less frequently invoked feature of union development under the early stages of Peronism is, however, the extraordinary expansion of worker organization at the shop-floor level. The new wave of collective contracts signed by the unions in the period 1946–49, amid high industrial conflict and state support for their offensive, almost always sanctioned the creation of "internal commissions" at the plant, with the goal of overseeing the enforcement of contracts at the workplace (James 1988). Before Peronism, employers had reigned supreme in the factory.

The internal factory commissions empowered during the early days of Perón emerged as the central locus of resistance of the unions against repression after the 1955 coup. However, after the defeat of the Peronist unions in some crucial strikes during the modernizing government of Arturo Frondizi (1958–62), the new collective agreements signed after 1960 severely limited the internal commission's role in the factory. In fact, James (1981: 401) is careful to point out that the new contracts did not fundamentally weaken the administrative and bargaining function of national unions, but were *aimed at shop-floor power*, which union sectoral leaders were also interested in curtailing – provided their role as the main social interlocutors was not affected. In brief, it was in the 1960s that mainstream union bureaucratic power soared, parallel to the demise of the

---

[32] Union affiliation skyrocketed in these years. The bibliography on the formation of Peronist unionism is vast. See the chapters in the book edited by Torre (1988), also Torre (1990), and McGuire (1997).

internal factory commissions.[33] The union bureaucracy was fed essentially by three main sources: union dues boosted by monopoly, extraordinary quotas assigned to the union each time a wage increase was granted in collective bargaining, and a variety of employer subsidies to union-run welfare funds. Furthermore, in 1970, the Onganía dictatorship formalized union control of health insurance through welfare funds financed by a mandatory payroll contribution of union and nonunion members (McGuire 1997: 159).

The union organizational framework consolidated in the 1960s would not be essentially modified until the beginning of liberalization in the 1990s.[34] The military government (1976–83) suspended labor legislation, intervened in some unions, and "disappeared" countless unionists, particularly base-level activists. However, the traditional union leadership managed to recover the bureaucratic apparatus and legislative framework almost intact during the Radical Civic Union (UCR) government of 1983–89, configuring at the outset of reform a labor movement powerful in terms of income and affiliation and centralized, that is, with relatively weak shop-floor bodies.

Union Organizational Structure and the Politics of Compensation to the Working Class

A culture of militancy and a foundational memory of heroic struggles – the Peronist years and the *Resistencia* (resistance) to the dictatorships in Argentina, and the Third Republic's Popular Front in Spain – galvanized the development of the union movement in the decades prior to neoliberal reform in Argentina and Spain. In both cases, the labor movement had played an important role in bringing about democratization in the 1970s and 1980s (R. B. Collier 1999: 118–32). Yet trade unions under ISI developed quite different organizational structures. Organized labor will be, therefore, assessed along two axes familiar in the literature on labor politics, the *horizontal* dimension, which measures the extent to which single unions organize potential constituents, and a *vertical* dimension, which concerns the power relations between plant union activists and their industrial federations.[35] As I have analyzed, both dimensions coalesced

---

[33] In words of Torre (1974: 79), after 1960, "Labor agreements prudently stopped short of big business' gates"; i.e., they concentrated almost exclusively on the sectoral level and downplayed shop-floor organization.

[34] The power of union leaders at the top of the organizations was not, however, always unchallenged. The series of worker revolts in the areas of Córdoba and Rosario that shook the 1966–73 dictatorship was led by plant-level workers, internal commissions, and local unions in the most modern industries of autos, steel, and electricity. Yet, with the return of Perón to power in 1973, the authority of the Peronist union leadership over local unions and the rank and file was reasserted. For the origins and development of labor contestation in Córdoba, with special attention to internal union organization, see the excellent works of Gordillo (1999) and (1991). Torre (1989) provides the essential account of the recasting of traditional union power in the 1973–76 period.

[35] Though they tend to go together, there is not a necessary overlap between corporatism or union monopoly and low shop-floor union autonomy; see Golden et al. (1999: 215). For example, in

Compensating Labor Insiders

in particular ways under the inward-oriented model. Both were decisive in shaping the variation in the models of labor adjustment.

THE HORIZONTAL DIMENSION OF UNION ORGANIZATION: MONOPOLY AND MEMBERSHIP. Monopoly of representation at the national level and in the main sectors of the economy helped to bring about labor cooperation under market reforms in Argentina. Murillo (2001: 151) underscores that sectoral monopoly, the reunification of the CGT in March 1992, and, later, the single national strike against the first Menem administration in October both increased the bargaining power and signaled the value of the restraint of the national union confederation. Thereafter, despite occasional skirmishes, a unified labor movement traded some flexibility in individual labor law for the maintenance of pro-union inducements in collective labor law and for the partial deregulation of the system of welfare funds.

Union pluralism in Spain, by contrast, made concertational policymaking more difficult. In the context of plural and competitive unionism, with nationwide union elections taking place every two years in the workplace until 1985 (and every four years thereafter), the moderate UGT had to face challenges not only from CCOO but also from regional unions. Therefore, a cozy relationship with the government in times of adjustment could undermine its electoral base. Indeed, although the Socialist union won the 1986 union elections, the gains of CCOO in large firms reinforced UGT's increasingly militant stance vis-à-vis the government (Paramio 1990: 77; Royo 2000: 89; Burgess 2004: 103). It is worth remembering that workplace elections in Spain were open to both union members and non-members, and, therefore, competition and accountability to workers (see Burgess 2004) were considerable despite low levels of formal affiliation. As noted, the UGT representatives broke with the Socialist parliamentary group in 1985 and would soon join CCOO in open confrontation with the government.

However, the degree of union monopoly and competition not only affected national cooperation with the reformist government, but also decisively shaped the type of concessions that the government was willing to afford. In the first place, in Argentina the mere existence of a system of Corporatist inducements (among which state-sanctioned union monopoly is the most central) brings to the table an issue over which labor leaders can bargain: once the general course of market reforms seems inevitable, Corporatist unions may have something to win, namely, the preservation of at least some aspects of their monopolies in the labor market. Thus, unlike labor negotiations in more pluralist settings, the bargain with reformers over Corporatist institutions can be more easily turned into a positive-sum game.[36]

---

both Corporatist Sweden and plural Italy until 1968 federations enjoyed significant statutory authority over lower levels.

[36] As Carlos Tomada, lawyer and adviser to the UOM – and future minister of Labor in the Kirchner government – asserted: "The unions did not want to lose what they considered essential in the Argentine union model: centralized collective bargaining, the prereform collective agreements, and the system of welfare funds. For them the liquidation of Argentine unionism was at stake, and they knew that those were the demands of the business sector." Author's interview, Buenos Aires, November 3, 2000.

182 *The Political Economy of Labor Adjustment*

In addition, monopoly of representation under the inward-oriented model had generally resulted in high union affiliation rates.[37] Compensation such as the limited deregulation of the health market, the management of pension funds, or the administration of the ESOP depends on the future ability of unions to encourage workforce participation in those businesses. Unions need to assume that there is a reasonable probability that they will be able to control or retain workers' individual resources in a variety of markets (stock options in the case of the ESOP and social security contributions in the case of the health system and pension funds). Monopoly at the plant level and high union density reinforced those expectations. As Caro Figueroa, former minister of labor and crucial broker in these negotiations, pointed out, referring to ventures such as the pension funds or the employee share ownership program: "They [the unionists] calculated that the loyalty of the workers and the weight of the unions would carry a lot of affiliates to those businesses."[38] It is not surprising, therefore, that negotiations over market-share compensation were constantly interwoven with those of labor law reform: for sectoral union leaders, the loss of the union monopoly and their reign in the factory would have made market-share compensation much less appealing.[39] Other unions or labor leaders could have claimed to profit from those businesses and disputed the workers' contributions to them. Of course, the loyalty of workers proved to be more resilient in areas such as the ESOP or the welfare funds than in the management of pension funds, in which union leaders could hardly compete with the marketing of big banks.

In Spain, by contrast, the absence of significant institutional labor inducements embedded in labor law, such as a state-granted monopoly of representation or centralized collective bargaining, inevitably narrowed the scope of negotiations, even among partners initially prone to cooperation such as the PSOE and their allies of the UGT.[40] In addition, any market-share compensation offered by government negotiators, such as the management of stock options or social services, would hardly be appealing to a union leader in an environment of union competition and an evasive rank and file. Indeed, the Spanish modern labor movement was, as explained, essentially constructed from below under ISI. Not only was it institutionally fragmented; it lacked any experience in

---

[37] Feldman (1991: 97) shows that in the run-up to reform (1985) Argentine unions were at the height of their affiliation rates: union density was above 42% compared to 30% in 1965.

[38] Author's interview, Buenos Aires, November 24, 2000.

[39] Carlos Lefort, the official in charge of the administration of the ESOP at the state National Bank, was eloquent (and ironic) about the overlapping of the dual role of unions as class representatives and as single administrators of the ESOP: "Once, in the act of an assembly of stockholders of the ESOP the union inserted a claim on extra hour pay and things like that. I told them that they could not debate the pay of extra hours in an assembly of stockholders! That could not happen. I told them to organize different assemblies ... It was in some sense contradictory that stockholders were supporting a demand against the firm." Author's interview, Buenos Aires, May 15, 2001.

[40] Indeed, Burgess (2004: 43) defines the Spanish labor code that resulted from democratization as "anticorporatist."

Compensating Labor Insiders

managing economic resources. As a former CCOO union leader of the works council at the Ensidesa steel mill argued:

The problem is that we started as a sociopolitical movement in the context of a clandestine struggle. We were enormously wary of bureaucracy! I remember I was the secretary general of CCOO at Gijón in the late 1970s and did not even have an office. I spent all day in the halls of the factory talking with people until a comrade would tell me: "Perhaps you should have an office." Once we had an hours-long debate in the executive commission to vote on whether we should buy a typewriter or not.[41]

In a nutshell, pluralistic unions socialized in a clandestine culture that deemphasized formal membership, in which leaders did not have offices and debated in an assembly over whether to buy typewriters, would hardly be attracted by market-share compensation deals, involving, for example, stock programs or pension funds, which require both experience in managing businesses and a relatively secure base of loyal/affiliated workers for those ventures. Indeed, the government did distribute stock options to employees in the steel and oil privatizations in Spain. The stock distribution constituted an excellent opportunity for unions to expand their economic resources and their leverage over the decision-making structures of the company, as their counterparts have in Argentina. Nevertheless, unions in Spain did not attempt to seize that payoff. When I asked factory union leaders in the steel mills of Basque Country and Avilés and the oil refineries of Tarragona and Puertollano about the possibility of managing the stock programs as a union rather than leaving the issue to the individual choice of workers, the answer was invariable: "Unions should not manage stocks"; "We never thought about that possibility." Many union leaders and base activists – even a number who belonged to CCOO and the Communist Party – would admit *privately* that they held stock options offered by the government in privatization. However, their incapacity to manage the stocks *as unions*, that is, as a "collectivity of workers," was simply the result of a particular culture of militancy, and most centrally, of a set of institutional incentives: it was enormously difficult for individual unions to control the stocks program and manage it efficiently as a result of both union competition and low levels of bureaucratization.

THE VERTICAL DIMENSION OF UNION ORGANIZATION: CENTRALIZATION AND THE GOVERNANCE OF THE WORKPLACE. The political management of labor adjustment under a democracy did not only involve conflict or cooperation between the government and national union leaders, be they monopoly or plural unions. When downsizing affects more than 50% of the workforce, the most immediate concern of both government officials and union leaders is to prevent, or (in the case of unionists) eventually be able to lead, the mobilization of the rank and file. This workplace governance dimension has been

---

[41] Author's interview with Francisco Prado Alberdi, secretary general of the CCOO section in Ensidesa company, 1982–86, Gijón, March 13, 2002.

largely neglected in comparative studies of labor in transitional economies.[42] The general assumption is that union leaders coping with adjustment will encourage or restrain mobilization, depending on whether they get government or employer concessions. However, mobilization is not simply driven by labor leaders' incentives to respond to government initiatives. It is also shaped itself by a set of institutions and historical practices that mold the relations between leaders and the rank and file. National or federation union leaders cannot always spur or control mobilization at will. Workers' mobilization (or the lack thereof) in the advent of massive workforce reduction largely derives from what I have called the *vertical* dimension of union organization, namely, the capacity of shop-floor militants to organize and exert pressure on the upper echelons of their organizations.

As a result of the organizational developments under ISI noted previously, the degree of centralization of unions greatly differed in the two countries. Shop-floor union organization has two main aspects. The first is the electoral and signals whether plant workers can vote out both factory union delegates and national/federation leaders relatively easily. The second concerns the institutional powers of shop-floor union activists and delegates (1) to resist intervention and removal from the upper echelons of the organization and (2) to conduct autonomous strategies and negotiation with employers over wages, working conditions, and eventually adjustment implementation.

In Argentina both dimensions denoted a high level of centralization. The democratic character of union elections varied notoriously across sectors, but in all of them minority factions find enormous hurdles to present electoral slates, and uncontested elections are common. Most importantly, as shown earlier in the historical account, the power of internal factory commissions in Argentina had been waning in the two decades prior to reform. National/sectoral federation leadership in Argentina is legally allowed to intervene in local unions and factory internal commissions and to remove dissident leadership.[43] Plus, workplace leaders were not entitled to conduct autonomous negotiations with employers or to call for strikes and were largely controlled by the sectoral bureaucratic union.[44] Local, factory-level union organization in Spain is the mirror image of Argentina's. Largely as a result of the workers' movement that took over the factory union organization from below under Franco, the works councils became the institutional locus of union organization in the recovered democracy. Works councils are broadly accountable to union and nonunion

---

[42] See, for example, the studies of Murillo (2001), Robertson (2004), and Tafel and Boniface (2003). An exception to this neglect is Burgess (2004), who assesses the influence of union accountability from below on party-union alliances.

[43] Of course, in the case of important union sections or local unions in federations intervention from above is not always easy.

[44] Members of the factory internal commission in Argentina are not entitled to bargain autonomously with employers, must have been affiliated with the sectoral union for more than one year to be elected, and depend financially on the union – they cannot collect dues. Chapter 7 discusses these organizational features in more detail.

Compensating Labor Insiders

members in open elections, and delegates do not need to be members of the sector's unions. Its members are entitled to conduct negotiations with employers and call strikes, and though of course its leaders generally belong to the main unions, they cannot be removed by the upper-level federations or by any union decision.[45]

The dynamics of this vertical organizational dimension and its centrality for the governance of the workplace in times of adjustment will be analyzed in more detail in the sectoral studies of Chapter 7, all based on extensive fieldwork at the factories. For the big picture, it should be noted that in the four main labor conflicts that erupted over adjustment and privatization in the first half of the 1990s in Argentina – in telecoms, railways, steel, and oil – top-level union leaders benefited by market-share compensation either openly sided with the government or passively tolerated adjustment and downsizing. The telecom conflict in September 1990 has been taken as a showdown case in the Menem administration (McGuire 1996: 114). Buenos Aires, the largest regional union, waged a one-month strike against privatization. The section was led by a dissident faction that had displaced the unionists loyal to the national leadership in the 1989 elections. Though the strike was massive in the city of Buenos Aires, the local union was "isolated and hampered by the national Federation. When they wanted to extend the strike nationwide, FOETRA [the national union] undermined mobilization and the struggle" (Dávolos 2001: 74). At the same time, the national union obtained from the government the administration of the ESOP and full control of the welfare fund previously shared with the company (Murillo 2001: 160). The strike was defeated, the company was privatized swiftly, its workforce of 45,000 reduced by around 40%, and the national federation recovered the control of the rebellious local section.

In the oil and steel industries, conflicts over privatization and adjustment witnessed similar dynamics: significant spurts of strikes and mobilization lost momentum as the national/sectoral union leadership deactivated conflict from above (see Chapter 7). Moreover, *local* (i.e., plant level or regional) union leaders – scarcely accountable to the base and financially dependent on the sectoral organization – often joined national bosses in the ventures initiated by market-share compensation. The factory activists opposed to privatization, abandoned by the national federation and often by the local union and not even legally entitled to negotiate with employers, were powerless to rally the rank and file against privatization and adjustment. In short, in Argentina centralization, that is, the capacity of top-level leaders to control the shop floor from above reinforced the initial negotiation pattern: the progressive flow of bureaucratic payoffs induced national leaders to contain conflict at the base. As Chapter

---

[45] Wozniak (1992: 78) argues that council leaders in Spain "are not legally bound to the unions. Practically they follow independent courses." Fishman and Mershon (1993: 68) write that "workplace union leaders enjoy significant decisional autonomy." Though Wozniak may have overstated the council leaders' independence (see Chapter 7), the contrast with Argentina is nevertheless striking.

186   *The Political Economy of Labor Adjustment*

7 shows in more detail, conflict was curbed by a combination of a lack of support (or even hostility) from sectoral union leaders and the defection of local union activists lured by bureaucratic side payments such as the managing of stock options programs or other state assets.

In Spain, the national union leaders who coped with restructuring (whether from UGT, from CCOO, or independent) hardly possessed the freedom of their Argentine counterparts to negotiate adjustment and bureaucratic payoffs with government and employers. Not only were they accountable in regular union elections with high levels of participation, but plant-level works councils were always represented in, and often led, the negotiations over restructurings with the government and employers. Moreover, the practice of general factory assemblies of workers, inherited from the struggle against Franco and typical of a union environment with low formal affiliation, was still common in the 1980s. Manuel Puerta was a key actor in the Spanish industrial restructuring; as secretary general of the Socialist Metals Federation he oversaw the unions most affected by reconversion plans in shipbuilding, steel, and autos. He reported:

We would finish a meeting at 3 am at the Ministry of Industry and at 8 am we were at the assembly of workers in the shipyard. You had to defend your position in an assembly with a lot of workers. It was hard; people were sometimes very aggressive. Rank and file mobilization was really intense; they would threaten to "burn" this or that leader. You had to have balls to be there. And you could not simply leave everything adrift.[46]

Indeed, pressure from base workers and mobilization by factory works councils were mutually reinforcing: works council activists were highly accountable to workers and therefore carried incentives to spur industrial action in the face of adjustment plans that often trimmed the workforce by a half. The decision over the contracts of the workers subjected to reconversion plans was a direct consequence of this pressure from below. I noted earlier that the government finally ruled in favor of the "suspension" of the contracts of redundant workers, rather than their "termination," which greatly enhanced compensation. Since it was, in practice, impossible for dismissed employees to return to the factories, workers with "suspended" contracts could claim to continue under the state-sponsored employment programs for a much longer time than formally allowed. The decision over the situation of dismissed workers was reached in the first months of 1984. The former minister of industry and economics Carlos Solchaga asserted:

Of course, the "suspension" [of contracts] did not work.... Felipe González [the prime minister] was under a lot of pressure from the UGT in the places in which reconversion was taking place. I am convinced that if he had held on a little bit more we would have won [i.e., the "termination" option]. We were about to win a big strike that had

---

[46] Author's interview, Madrid, September 29, 2001.

Compensating Labor Insiders

become symbolic at the time at Sagunto and other big labor conflict in the specialty steel sector.[47]

Though the former minister of industry thinks that they "could have won," his words evince the only aspect in which reformist industrial planners in Spain lost, namely, the amount of worker's compensation at the base. His statement reflects that the pressure from below and collective mobilization are central to explaining the decision over the termination/suspension of contracts – in particular, the conflict in the Sagunto steel mill, in which the factory works council, out of the control of national union federations, led a prolonged struggle against the plant closure (see Chapter 7). This mobilization cannot be understood without underscoring the institutional power of plant-level works councils (especially at large firms) and the worker's assembly culture associated with them, still widespread in the Spanish factories by the 1980s. The ruling proved decisive in making the compensation for laid-off workers under state plans for reconversion in Spain one of the most generous in Europe. In short, in Spain the scarcity of bureaucratic payoffs targeted at federation leaders, coupled with the strength of plant-level union bodies, underpinned the spiral of conflict. Neither top-level leaders nor, of course, workplace activists institutionally empowered prior to neoliberal reform had any reason to restrain militancy in the hostile (but openly democratic) environment of market reforms.

CONCLUSIONS

This chapter has shown that either at the national or sectoral leadership level (Argentina) or at a more decentralized level (Spain) organized labor became a crucial actor in the implementation of industrial adjustment in the Corporatist and Statist models of economic liberalization. The chapter stresses the need for a better conceptualization of the concessions granted to labor in the process of market liberalization. Important comparative studies of labor in a context of massive industrial adjustment tend to focus analytically on either self-interested union leaders or their organizations (Golden 1997, Murillo 2001, Tafel and Boniface 2003) or plant-level workers and the different types of labor militancy and workforce reduction policies (Houseman 1991, Wozniak 1991). This book argues that both levels of analysis should be combined and that, in contexts of massive downsizing, governments (and employers) may use different types of policies to compensate different segments of the working class, be they union leaders and their organizations or laid-off workers and factory-based local unionists. The Market path in Chile, analyzed in Chapter 8, shows that a neoliberal government can also target compensation primarily at the atomized mass of unemployed and informal poor.

In Argentina the mainstream labor movement became part of the reformist coalition and ultimately obtained important concessions in the form of

---

[47] Author's interview, Madrid, October 8, 2001.

bureaucratic payoffs and protection of their economic role in future reregulated markets. At the same time that laid-off workers were practically left to their fate, industrial conflict (paradoxically) almost disappeared at the national level. In Spain's Statist model, by contrast, most of the union movement was by 1986 in the opposition and contesting adjustment through industrial action. Though labor did not fundamentally alter the state reconversion plans, local industrial unions managed to control the implementation of workforce reduction programs at the factory level. The compensation to laid-off workers that unions obtained not only was much more extensive than ordinary unemployment payments, but was also among the most generous in Western Europe.

I have argued that alternative patterns of conflict and types of compensatory policies, which define Statist and Corporatist paths of labor adjustment, are rooted in the democratic nature of the regime and in the way in which organized labor became embedded in the ISI model. In Argentina a union movement built around sectoral monopoly and low autonomy of shop-floor bodies welcomed market-share compensation. National federations accepted bureaucratic payoffs and deactivated industrial conflict at the plant. In Spain, strong shop-floor union bodies demanded job-loss subsidies and pressured national federations for industrial action from below. At the same time, union pluralism and low rates of affiliation made concertation and bureaucratic payoffs less attractive for Spanish national labor leaders.

The dynamics of labor adjustment in Argentina and Spain also point to the limits of partisanship in the explanation of alternative liberalization paths. Most of the workers and base-level activists whom I interviewed in Argentina, and many of those I met in the factories of Spain, carried deep Peronist and Socialist identities that made them initially sympathetic or tolerant vis-à-vis the government despite adjustment measures. Most of them probably voted Socialist or Peronist, respectively, during or after adjustment heydays. However, Socialist labor activists and leaders in Spain finally engaged in prolonged industrial action, whereas Argentine Peronist national union leaders and often firm-level cadres acquiesced to massive downsizing. My argument is not meant to deny that their working-class roots and labor loyalties may have helped governing parties in both cases to navigate the rough waters of liberalization. However, partisanship can hardly account for the main outcome analyzed in this book, namely, the alternative patterns of policymaking, compensatory mechanisms, and winners and losers within the working class.

7

Statist and Corporatist Models of Labor Adjustment in Spain and Argentina

Sectoral Case Studies

INTRODUCTION

Over the course of the 1980s and 1990s, labor-based parties in Spain and Argentina embarked on bold projects of market restructuring that hit the working class hard. Neither in Argentina nor in Spain were the consequences of neoliberal reform for the formerly protected industrial workforce left entirely to the whims of the market. Rather, they were shaped through essentially political payoffs. Chapter 6 showed, however, that Corporatist and Statist pathways to labor adjustment in Argentina (1989–99) and Spain (1983–96) diverged on three main levels: in policy formulation (labor inclusion and national concertation in Argentina vs. state *dirigisme* and decentralized bargains with local unions in Spain), in the type and main target of compensatory policies oriented to the working class (bureaucratic payoffs that primarily benefited union leaders vs. job loss subsidies for laid-off workers), and in the level of industrial conflict (low in Argentina vs. high in Spain).

Chapter 6 argued that the democratic nature of the polity in both countries is crucial for understanding the commonality: adjustments paths that were made politically viable through compensation bestowed primarily on the organized actors of the working class or insiders, that is, unions or union-backed laid-off workers. The main variable driving the difference in compensatory schemes and policymaking patterns concerns the organizational configuration of unions at the outset of adjustment. In Argentina, an organizationally strong (i.e., monopolistic and centralized) union movement was less likely to face collective-action problems in negotiations with the government and found market-share compensation, such as the partial deregulation of the pro-union labor law or the managing of state assets, attractive to weather the storm of marketization. In Spain, conversely, an organizationally weak labor movement, plural and decentralized, made sustained concertational policymaking more difficult from the outset and was not lured by bureaucratic payoffs but by generous jobless programs targeted primarily at base unionists and workers.

Thus, the organizational structure of unions was assessed along two axes familiar in the literature on labor politics, the horizontal dimension, which measures the extent to which single unions organize potential constituents, and the vertical dimension, which refers to the power relations between plant union activists and their industrial federations (see Thelen 1991, Golden et al. 1999). The horizontal dimension of union monopoly is crucial to understanding the appeal of market-share compensation for national union leaders. In Argentina, state-enforced union monopoly and labor control of health services under ISI had helped structure a union movement with high levels of membership and experience in managing economic resources. In the eyes of the union leadership their traditional, if downsized, base of affiliated workers became a relatively secure base for the business opened or transformed by marketization, such as their ventures in the health and pension markets and in the administration of stock programs in privatized companies. In Spain, the plural organizational structure of unions made the bargains around market-share compensation (which in the labor domain I have also labeled bureaucratic payoffs) quite difficult to sustain. Any reward targeted at federation and national leaders, such as the management of workers' social services or stock options, was by definition uncertain in a context of low affiliation and strong union competition at the workplace.

In addition, this study calls attention to the second, "vertical" organizational dimension, which is also crucial to understanding the alternative modalities of labor adjustment. In Argentina, the price of government bureaucratic concessions to labor had to be the governability of the adjustment process. The ability of union leaders to control or restrain industrial conflict at the base – in contexts in which the workforce was being reduced by a half or more – was decisive to upholding the negotiations over market-share compensation. Lower-level union bodies in Argentina (especially factory internal commissions) lacked the institutional and financial power to challenge the strategy of top-level leaders – that is, did not have statutory powers to bargain autonomously, collect funds, or strike. In Spain the reverse was true. Plant-level union activists, institutionally empowered during the democratic transition, could contest control of the workplace. In this case, the price paid by democratic reformers was generous job-loss programs oriented to appeasing shop-floor activists and curbing workplace rebellions, especially, as will be argued later, in the sectors with higher concentration of workers per firm.

The following case studies, based on fieldwork at steelworks, shipyards, oil refineries, and auto companies in Argentina and Spain, intend to illuminate the crucial question of shop-floor governance in (extremely) hard times – rarely studied in scholarship on labor in transitional economies. Beyond the assessment of alternative patterns of labor adjustment, a more general question looms large in the chapter: how was it possible to implement adjustment measures that trimmed 50% of the firm's workforce or more and sometimes threatened to destroy the social world of company towns, under fully democratic governments and with labor movements previously activated by democratic transitions?

Statist and Corporatist Models of Labor Adjustment 191

Fieldwork evidence reveals a key aspect of the answer: in Argentina the low degree of autonomy of union bodies at the plants' shop floor meant that territorial union sections (often representing a group of firms in the area or region), rather than factory-based internal commissions or works councils, led negotiations over adjustment at the local level. Section activists were more connected to the union bureaucracy than were their factory counterparts. Therefore, they would be more likely to embrace bureaucratic payoffs at the cost of workers' general demobilization. By contrast, in Spain factory-based works councils and shop-floor activists rather than territorial union sections were the key brokers in the negotiations over adjustment at the local level. Shop stewards and works councilors were more accountable to workers and enjoyed more statutory powers than their Argentine counterparts. Thus, they were much more likely to be appeased by job-loss subsidies that helped them maintain legitimacy in the eyes of workers than by bureaucratic payoffs that appeared very uncertain for a base activist loosely connected with the union bureaucracy.

The following sections examine the adjustment process in the ISI sectors already studied in business. Thus, in Spain I study steel and shipbuilding, which, as argued by several Spain specialists (e.g., Navarro 1990, Segura and Romero 1992), formed the core of industrial restructuring in terms of both resources poured into the sectors and manpower. In Argentina, the steel, oil, and auto sectors were home to industrial unions that were among the most numerous in the country and were paradigmatic of the market-share deals that define Corporatist labor adjustment. The first part of the chapter describes in more detail the organizational structure of unions at the outset of reform, stressing the vertical dimensions of union organization outlined previously and the way in which alternative labor institutional frames shaped the politics and policies of compensation directed to the working class. I will then illustrate the general mechanisms driving labor adjustment paths through sectoral case studies. The last section reassesses the comparative perspective on labor adjustment in Argentina and Spain in the light of the alternative explanations that scholars have presented for both countries.

INDUSTRIAL ADJUSTMENT AND EMPLOYMENT REDUCTION

Table 7.1 shows the evolution of the workforce in the five sectors studied in this chapter in Argentina and Spain. All are core ISI sectors in which employers and workers were severely challenged by tariff liberalization, international economic integration, and privatization. Adjustment was roughly equally dramatic in all the case studies in this chapter and ranged between 50% and 80% of the total workforce. Among the sectors analyzed, only autos in Argentina increased employment because of the very compensation that the government targeted to the "ISI coalition" of employers and workers in the industry, namely, a special tariff regime that largely spared the sector from international economic liberalization.

The Political Economy of Labor Adjustment

TABLE 7.1. *Spain and Argentina: Industrial Adjustment and Workforce Evolution in Case Studies*

	Initial Workforce (number of workers) 1982 (Spain) and 1989 (Argentina)	Workforce Reduction to 1996 (Spain) and 1995– 97 (Argentina)	Percentage of Workforce Reduction
Spain			
Shipbuilding	38.561	−29.292	−76.0
Integrated Steel	35.149	−22.583	−64.2
Argentina			
Steel	32.148	−15.406	−47.9
Oil (state monopoly YPF)	37.046	−31.821	−85.9
Autos	19.281	7.005	36.0

Source: Spain, Ministry of Industry and Energy, Spain (1991: 228; 1993: 290), Union of Steel Industries (UNESID), and Cerezo (2005). Argentina, Steel: CIS (1996); Oil: YPF, "The Argentine Petroleum Industry," institutional presentation at the Rio Oil & Gas Expo Conference, October 7, 1998; Autos: ADEFA (1997).

THE ORGANIZATIONAL STRUCTURE OF TRADE UNIONS AND THE GOVERNANCE OF THE WORKPLACE

As a result of the organizational developments under ISI analyzed in Chapter 6, both the horizontal (i.e., pluralism vs. monopoly) and the vertical institutional structure of unions greatly differed in both countries. Figure 7.1 illustrates the vertical institutional configuration of unions in Argentina and Spain, in three main aspects: elections, finance, and capacity of top-level leaders to "intervene" from above and displace lower-level unionists.[1] It also shows the statutory powers of each organizational level. In Argentina, all workers at the plant level elect a series of shop stewards, who in turn select an internal factory commission. All shop stewards must belong to the single sectoral union. Union-affiliated

---

[1] The organizational scheme in both cases is based on the metalworkers' union – CCOO has been chosen as the main model in Spain though the two unions are relatively similar in this respect. The figure is based on the formal capacities and relations among the different organizational levels set by the labor law and union's statutes, as well as on the informal workings of the organization that I investigated in fieldwork. In Argentina there are two legal organizational types of sectoral unions, the "First Grade Federations" (composed of regional unions) and the "First Grade Industry Unions" (nationally centralized). Figure 7.1 depicts the "Industry Unions," which are the most common among the main manufacturing sectors. However, many formal "Federations Unions" have become with time equally centralized. The literature on internal union organization is negligible in Argentina. A central historical source is Torre (2004). For Spain, Escobar (1993) is an indispensable source; see also Fundación FIES (1985).

Statist and Corporatist Models of Labor Adjustment

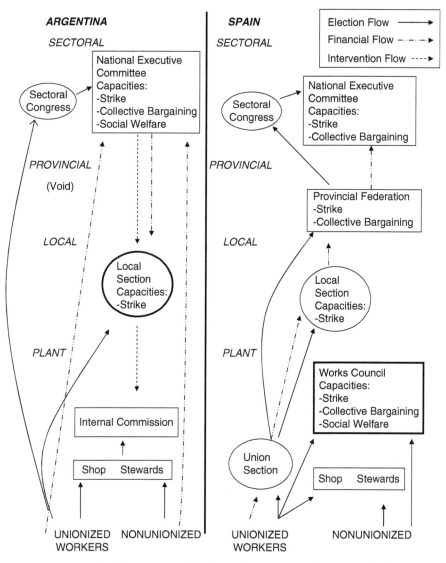

FIGURE 7.1. Vertical Organization of Industrial Unionism at the Outset of Adjustment.

workers also elect a local/territorial union section, which may include representatives from multiple plants or firms in the area. The local union section serves as a mere delegation of the national executive of the organization, which is elected by the national/sectoral union congress. Strike mobilization, collective bargaining, the collection of union dues, and the administration of welfare funds are all in the hands of the *national* executive committee, although the union section can occasionally call for strikes. Significantly, in Argentina both unionized (through the affiliation quota and welfare dues) and nonunionized workers (through welfare dues and mandatory "solidarity" quotas included in collective contracts) contribute directly to the coffers of the National Executive Committee or Secretariat. Finally, in Argentina labor law allows for the upper levels of the organizations to remove the leadership of lower-level bodies.[2] The local leaders of the territorial union section and the national union also tend to control the internal commissions informally at the plant level.[3]

In Spain, the locus of base-level union organization and power is the works council, which is set up *in the plant*. In Argentina, by contrast, it is the local section organized at a broader territorial level (Figure 7.1). Indeed, internal factory or firm workers' commissions are not regulated by the Argentine labor law – they are mentioned only once in the text and their organization is left to collective contracts (which are controlled by national unions and federations) and union statutes. In Spain, the Worker's Statute regulates firms' works councils in fifteen articles and forty-three subsections within them. Unionized and nonunionized workers in Spain directly elect shop stewards and a works council in medium and large firms. The works council – as noted in Chapter 6 the institutional legacy of the autonomous workers' commissions that fought the dictatorship – is entitled to call strikes and bargain and sometimes delivers social services to the workers in conjunction with employers. At the same time, unionized workers affiliated with the competing unions elect sections of those unions: that is, union sections also reside in the firm. In the bottom-up structure of Spanish unionism, the plant union section collects union dues,[4] which then climb to local, provincial, and sectoral/ national federations (Figure 7.1). Moreover, the Spanish labor law establishes the workers' assembly rights within the firm, that is, the right of workers to organize meetings at the plants, which can be legally convened by the firms' works council, by shop stewards, or by at least 33% of the firm's workforce.

This set of vertical relations largely determined the likelihood and forms of worker mobilization under massive employment reduction in two respects: the

---

[2] Even though intervention can be contested in the national courts, once the measure is adopted by a coalition of national leaders, section leaders are suspended automatically for 90 days. It is quite difficult, however, to carry out interventions in large union sections with strong affiliation.

[3] For instance, one leader from the Villa Constitución section of the metalworkers' UOM asserted that "to be a member of the internal commission you have to have good relations with the union section." Author's interview, April 23, 2001. A former member of the internal commission of SOMISA/Siderar argued that "the internal commission is in practice controlled by the section." Author's interview, December 22, 2000.

[4] Article 38 of the 1977 UGT statute mandated that "collection of dues will be done in the firm union section" and that 40% of the dues go to the local unions, and the rest to the national organization. In CCOO, by contrast, the upper-level union organizations "are the last to receive their quota, which climbs all the ladder from below to the top" (Fundación FIES 1985: 239). UGT had been traditionally more centralized than CCOO, though both were thoroughly decentralized in comparative perspective. Indeed, a 1985 report on union internal organization by a private foundation stated that "sometimes all the money is spent at the local level, without any control of the union federations."

power of plant-level union leaders to contest adjustment and their relationship with the base. First, in Spain, plant-based leaders possess more leeway for autonomous organization and mobilization, since the works council is institutionally empowered to bargain and call strikes, and they receive funds directly collected by the firm-level union section. In Argentina, the national leadership can starve a rebellious territorial section (let alone an internal factory commission) of funds by its decisions to cut remittances for welfare and union administration, and local leaders may always fear displacement from above.

Second, the institutions of workplace union organization had created powerful habits and routines at the plant that shaped the relationship between local labor activists and their base. Crucially, in Argentina, a good portion of base-level union life develops outside the plant. Local leaders generally start out as shop stewards, yet they often leave the plant to lead the regional union section. The section distributes the resources locally and has the final word in everyday bargaining with employers. In other words, the powerful local leaders are found in the executive committee of the territorial section and *not* in the internal commission of the plant – which, as mentioned, is not even directly elected by workers. In fact, in some cases, local section leaders had never been part of the factory internal commission. In Spain, conversely, the actions of a local or base union leader take place almost entirely within the plant. Emerging local leaders must be popular, not only among unionized workers, but also among the general mass of workers, in order to be elected to the works council. In fact, all the powerful leaders of the plant union sections are simultaneously leading work council members (Escobar 1993: 39). The works council emerged as the center of union activity in democratic Spain, because of both its statutory powers and its capacity to convene factory assemblies. In short, in Argentina the (low) power of base-level union organization resides *outside* the factory. In Spain it is built from the very center of the industrial plant.

This contrast has important implications. Massive downsizing in Spain implies a direct attack on the source of material power and legitimacy of base union activists, whereas in Argentina, even under the threat of massive downsizing, the loyalties of the base union leader – who had often left the firm to the local section bureaucracy years before – are more divided between shop-floor workers and the union. Moreover, in Spain, employees have been historically socialized in workplace habits in which the factory works council solves problems. In Argentina workers are socialized in a plant culture in which the local/territorial union section is in charge of the most important questions. Therefore, in Argentina the internal factory commission would have, a priori, a much harder time leading workers autonomously. When the neoliberal period began, all of these well-established patterns of behavior combined with the workplace leaders' actual institutional and material resources for mobilization.

In sum, the vertical relations that organized labor consolidated under the ISI model are crucial for understanding variation in the governance of labor adjustment. As the next case studies aim to show, government-union organizational bargains in Argentina were not only effective because monopoly and financial

196 *The Political Economy of Labor Adjustment*

power provided incentives for concertation and bureaucratic payoffs. It was also understood, by both government officials and national union leaders, that the corollary of the bargain had to be the restraint of mobilization at the workplace. Conversely, in Spain, national negotiations failed not only because pluralism and organizational weakness narrowed the scope for bureaucratic payoffs for unions, but also because plant-level-union activists could deploy a set of institutional resources and practices that challenged workplace governance.

COPING WITH RESTRUCTURING: LABOR ADJUSTMENT IN MAJOR ISI SECTORS

Spain: Steel and Shipbuilding

Integrated Steel: From the Sagunto Battle to Cooperation at the Shop Floor
The closures of the AHM (Altos Hornos del Mediterráneo, the state mill located in Sagunto, Valencia) and the private AHV (Altos Hornos de Vizcaya, located in the Basque Country) blast furnaces, already analyzed in Chapter 4, were the main episodes of labor adjustment in the sector and would result in a reduction of more than half of the workforce in each company. In March 1983, the Socialist government launched a restructuring plan that contemplated the revamping of AHV's and Ensidesa's (the other large steelworks) main plants and mandated that AHM close down its facilities for raw steel production, which meant around 70% of reduction in a workforce of 4,000. The CCOO national Metals Federation contested the closure and adopted a militant stance, whereas the UGT Metals Federation accepted the plan but demanded more generous labor compensation. However, works councils in each plant were united: in Ensidesa and AHV they supported (or tolerated) the restructuring plan that spared them from the worst downsizing, while the works council in Sagunto rebelled. In other words, the decentralization and national disarticulation of the labor movement in Spain at the time is evinced by the fact that local unions of CCOO at Ensidesa and AHV broke with their national federation's militant policy, whereas the local UGT section at Sagunto broke with the more conciliatory approach of its federation.[5]

What ensued at Sagunto was a one-year conflict between the local unions (in particular, CCOO, which was the strongest in the plant), acting through the works council, and the national government. Since the mid-1970s, Sagunto had

---

[5] Francisco Alberdi, secretary general of the CCOO union section of Ensidesa (1982–86) and leading member of the works council, asserted, "The Federation had a too radical position, total confrontation with the government plans for reconversion. But we knew that restructuring would come no matter what we did. So we had a big fight with the Federation; they wanted to mobilize and we wanted to negotiate." Author's interview, Gijón, March 13, 2002. The radical struggle of the CCOO-led works council and section in Sagunto, however, quickly challenged their own National CCOO Federation. Pedro Morales, union delegate of CCOO Sagunto, affirmed that "the Federation was incapable of aligning the main union sections and works councils; in the end they left us alone." Author's interview, Madrid, February 25, 2002.

Statist and Corporatist Models of Labor Adjustment

developed as a classic company town, heavily dependent on employment in the mill. Therefore, the works council could garner a variety of local forces to support its struggle, such as the city council and other community centers. Saguntinos led a bold battle, which included almost weekly strikes, demonstrations in Madrid and in the regional capital Valencia, and clashes with the police, in the most serious of which a worker was wounded by a police bullet.[6] In January 1983, the company's president had formally ordered the closure of the blast furnace for raw steel. Yet, the workers kept the facility working in spite of shortages of supplies and a threat to cut off the electricity. By February 1984, however, after a year of mobilization and failed negotiations, workers' resistance had started to fade. In March, the firm works council accepted (after the approval of workers in referendum) a government offer that involved the closure of the mill but included the creation of the generous Employment Promotion Funds for the sector studied in Chapter 6. Miguel Campoy, the CCOO president of the works council, who regularly reported to workers on the negotiations in massive assemblies during 1983, closed the final agreement in Madrid with the government and the Metals Federations of CCOO and UGT.[7] Significantly, once the settlement over layoff compensation and relocation programs was reached, the works council and the union sections of the CCOO and the UGT cooperated with the implementation of these redundancy policies at the local level, particularly by managing the EPF in the company.[8] Led by sections in AHV and Ensidesa, CCOO joined UGT in the Control Commission for the plan of the steel sector.

The second major episode of labor adjustment was the closure of the traditional steel mill of AHV located on the outskirts of Bilbao, a company that had been the cradle of Spanish industrialization in the nineteenth century. As shown in Chapter 4, in this new round of restructuring, the government took over private AHV and merged the Basque steelworks and Ensidesa into a new company, named CSI, in 1991. This plan included the replacement of the blast furnace at the AHV works with a modern minimill, which would entail a job loss of around 70%, as well as further reductions of capacity and employment at Ensidesa. The plan sparked the reaction of unions, which mounted a wave of strikes that culminated in the so-called Iron March on Madrid in October 1992. UGT, CCOO, and ELA-STV (the nationalist Basque union with strong representation in that province) supported mobilization, and on this occasion (unlike in 1983–84) the *vertical* fractures of unions were avoided: both federations and local union sections of the CCOO and the UGT (in addition to the ELA-STV) contested employment reduction. A final settlement was reached in January 1993 between the government and unions, built around heavy compensation to laid-off workers in the form of relocation and early-retirement programs.

---

[6] For good accounts of the sequence of mobilization in Sagunto see Wozniak (1991) and Olmos (1984).

[7] See, for example, *El País*, October 1, 1983.

[8] Author's interview with Pedro Ramon Morales, February 25, 2002.

The overall dynamics of negotiation over labor adjustment was similar in Sagunto and AHV: the unions contested (and had very little to say in) the government's industrial plan (plant closures, capacity cuts, formation of a single steel group, and modernization projects) but acquiesced to restructuring *once* they succeeded, through mobilization and strikes, in expanding compensation considerably. A quite paradoxical situation that emerged in this respect was that of the union Patriotic Workers' Commissions (LAB), a radical Basque union affiliated with Batasuna (the political wing of the ETA guerrilla group). This union, which had a minority share in the AHV works council, was in the front line of the street battles against adjustment, often being accused of promoting industrial guerrilla action. However, it ultimately participated in the implementation of the government-sponsored workforce reduction program at the mill. The leader of LAB in the AHV works council asserted:

It was in some sense contradictory that we participated in the negotiations over the implementation of the blast furnace closure. But once the closure was decided, we had to deal with it in the best way possible for the workers, protecting them as much as we could. If a union had not been involved in that, its affiliates would lack protection, no matter what they say. Today all the unions are together trying to get from the company the best layoff conditions for our workers.[9]

Thus, even a radical anticapitalist and Basque nationalist union accused of supporting violence would eventually, in a sense, cooperate with a general adjustment policy designed by the Spanish government. Given the firm's works council's centrality in the implementation of redundancy policies at the local level, the union, in order to protect its own workers, could not afford to renounce its position in it.

Steel adjustment was shaped by the industrial relations framework in important ways. First, the autonomy of union sections in Sagunto, AHV, and Ensidesa (particularly in the case of CCOO) to pressure upper-level federations and eventually push forward mobilization was a consequence of the power of works councils crystallized in the 1980 democratic labor law, and of the relatively late institutionalization of sectoral federations in each union as a result of authoritarianism. The works council of Sagunto and the other steelworks had developed workplace practices and financial resources that helped them to break with, or challenge, national federations. In the case of Sagunto, the works council carried well-established assembly traditions and led workers into a broad community coalition in a one-year struggle relatively isolated from the rest of the labor movement.[10]

Second, the role played by local unions and works councils that occasionally broke with their national federations is essential for explaining the flow of

---

[9] Author's interview, Bilbao, February 20, 2002.

[10] Asked about what was the main mobilization mechanism, Pedro Morales, former CCOO shop steward in Sagunto at the time of the conflict, replied, "Assembly. It was pure assemblies at the factory, in the soccer field. The families went with the workers." Author's interview, Madrid, February 25, 2002.

Statist and Corporatist Models of Labor Adjustment

compensation to the base in the process of industrial restructuring. In Chapter 6, I examined how the issue of dismissed workers' contracts affected labor compensation under reconversion plans. The government ruling in favor of the "suspension" of the contracts of redundant workers, rather than their "termination," was essentially determined by the conflicts in the steelworks of Sagunto and Reynosa, in which local unions led virulent reactions from below against downsizing.

Steel restructuring cost Sagunto a loss in employment of around 6,000 in the mill and related industries. By the year 2000, however, the city of 60,000 had recovered well after the Statist reconversion described in this book. Arcelor (the firm that resulted from the merger of the public steel group formed under reconversion and the French USINOR; see Chapter 4) invested heavily in the remaining facilities for the cold-rolling mill and set up two plants for galvanized steel. It uses its Sagunto port as a doorway to supply automakers through the Mediterranean. Fiscal incentives and state subsidies that were part of the reconversion plan generated about 1,000 positions for formal metalworkers in the industries of glass, chemicals, and transport materials.[11]

Shipbuilding: From the Euskalduna Battle to Cooperation at the Shop Floor

An episode related to adjustment in the shipbuilding sector that occurred two years before the Socialists took power is illustrative of the bottom-up structure of the labor movement that faced neoliberal restructuring in Spain. In January 1980, CENSA, a company associated with the shipyard Duro Felguera, located in Asturias, dismissed 200 workers in order to reduce costs. Duro Felguera's workers, led by the CCOO union section, rose in solidarity with their fellow workers at CENSA. Mobilization included wildcat strikes and the erection of barricades, which sparked violent clashes with the police in the streets of Gijón. The CCOO Metals Federation of Asturias, although backing the workers' struggle, adamantly criticized the tactics and violence employed during the conflict and decided to intervene in the Duro Felguera section and to expel its leader from the CCOO.

Yet the section mounted successful resistance against the federation's measures. First, the CCOO section proposed and reelected to the Duro Felguera works council the base activist who had led the conflict. Second, the section, together with CCOO sections from other Gijón plants that had joined in solidarity, decided to retain the workers' dues that should have been channeled to the regional federation. The lower-level sections had the capacity to retain dues (see Figure 7.1) and, in practice, began to function autonomously of the national structure.[12] What is more, at some point it was the plant union section that sanctioned the Asturias Metals Federation organization secretary, Joaquín

---

[11] See *El País*, June 11, 1999.

[12] The section militants hired three labor lawyers and continued to collect dues at the plant. In sum, the union section "did not accept its dissolution and continued to function under the same union label" (Vega García 1991: 143).

Fernández – aligned with the provincial federation but a worker from the Duro Felguera yard – for not paying his union dues at the factory during the conflict. In the end CENSA's workers were not dismissed.[13]

The majority of adjustment in the shipbuilding sector, however, would be carried out under the Socialist government after 1982. Among the largest yards in Spain, the government's reconversion plan contemplated the closure of the Euskalduna factory of the state yard AESA in Bilbao and significant manpower and capacity cuts in the factories of Asturias, Andalucía, and Galicia. CCOO and the Galician nationalist union INT-CIG Federations were soon joined by nationalist Basque unions in launching widespread mobilizations against the restructuring plan. UGT joined the government plan under the conditions of the "suspension" of contracts and extension of the EPFs.[14] The final reconversion decree was issued in September, but since mid-1984, the shipbuilding sector in Spain had been in a state of virtual upheaval. Unions carried out several regional strikes, occupied factories and yards, and converged on Madrid in sectoral demonstrations organized by a coordinated group of opposition unions in the shipbuilding industry. The violence of the protests surpassed that of steelworker demonstrations months before. In October, a student who supported the workers was killed in the midst of a barricade at Gijón.

However, the most violent battle during the shipbuilding adjustment (and arguably of the whole process of industrial restructuring in Spain) was waged by the workers of the yard Euskalduna, located at the heart of the Basque city of Bilbao. Two factors converged to make Euskalduna the symbol of workers' resistance to adjustment. First, the yard was situated a few blocks from downtown Bilbao, beside one the main bridges over the Nervión River, which divides the city. Workers could easily block the traffic over the bridge and launch street demonstrations that disrupted the city. Second, the majority of the works council was controlled by Basque nationalist unions (ELA-STV, LAB, and the independent Autonomous Collectivity of Workers [CAT]). In fact, Euskalduna, home to around 3,500 workers, carried great symbolism for the nationalist camp in the Basque Country, a fact conveyed by its name (which means "from Euskadi") and by its past ownership by Basque nationalist families.

From October to December 1984 the workers of Eusakalduna, led by the works council, waged a prolonged struggle. They routinely blocked streets; occupied Bilbao's banks, train stations, and government offices; and clashed with the national police almost daily. In November the national police attempted

---

[13] The incident gave birth to CSI (Corriente Sindical de Izquierdas), a radical leftist union currently based in Gijón, and is detailed in Vega García (1991: 139–45; 1995: 140–56).

[14] My summary account of labor adjustment in Spanish shipbuilding is based on interviews with Pedro Rodriguez, CCOO member of the AESA works council at Sestao (1988–2000), Bilbao, February 20, 2002; José Merino, former member of the same council and later UGT official in charge of overseeing the naval sector, Bilbao, February 20, 2002; Candido Carnero, CSI (radical Left) representative from the works council of Naval Gijon (formerly Duro Felgueras), Gijón, March 12, 2002; and Eduardo Lafuente, UGT representative in the Control Commission for restructuring the naval sector, Madrid, October 11, 2001; and newspaper accounts from *El País*.

Statist and Corporatist Models of Labor Adjustment

to seize the factory, causing the death of one worker and injuring several. From late November on, the works council led the occupation of the factory, but increasing divisions among unions, basically between the CCOO and the nationalist camp, undermined the struggle. In late December, the works council acquiesced, and, as in the case of Sagunto, most workers faced redundancy through early-retirement programs or EPFs.

Again, even relatively minor radical unions such as CAT joined the organization of the workforce reduction program. As one of their publications asserted, "In spite of our will we had to accept what we had rejected again and again" (CAT 1985: 17). The logic of plant-based unionism (which left to factory unions the administration of employment programs) proved to be, once more, stronger than entrenched ideological commitments. The yard was closed down, and around 1,500 workers remained in the EPF for the sector, which, as stated in Chapter 6, almost covered their salaries in cash. By 1988 redundant workers still demonstrated and occasionally clashed with the police, demanding their implausible return to the Spanish yards.[15] Today, the modern Guggenheim Museum of the city of Bilbao, designed by the celebrated architect Frank O. Gehry, dominates the area once occupied by the traditional Basque shipyard on the margins of the Nervión River. A picturesque restaurant at the Olaveaga wharf, two hundred meters from the museum, is named Euskalduna Shipyard.

After 1987, the government pushed forward a second wave of restructuring in the shipbuilding industry, but this time, although strikes broke out occasionally, the major unions CCOO and ELA joined the UGT both in the Control Commission overseeing the sectoral plans and in the administration of the EPFs. By 1995, around 75% of employment in the Spanish shipbuilding sector had been eliminated. The economist Jesus Valdaliso (2003: 65) of the Basque Country University writes that industrial reconversion in the sector "enabled a drastic employment adjustment without a great social cost" and that "workers in the sector were among the most privileged in the reconversion." The strength of union bodies at the plant and, as argued later, the concentration of workers per plant in the shipyard industry largely explains that "privilege."

To summarize, after the Sagunto and Euskalduna episodes it became quite clear to unions that, although they could not break the government's will to carry out its industrial adjustment plans, militancy was essential for expanding compensation for layoffs. In this point I disagree with the interesting study of Wozniak (1991: 7), who argued that works councils *instead* of national unions led the struggle against adjustment in Socialist Spain. Situations in which works councils led a persistent and relatively isolated struggle, such as at Sagunto and Euskalduna, only occurred in the early 1980s in an adjustment process that lasted until the mid-1990s. Rather – though occasional rebellions of lower-level unions occurred, particularly in the steel sector – works councils were involved in negotiations over labor adjustment *in conjunction with* their industrial

---

[15] *El País*, May 6, 1988.

202 *The Political Economy of Labor Adjustment*

federations.[16] In other words, federation leaders' bargain with state officials was conditioned by both sectoral union competition and the plant-centered organization of trade unions in Spain. On the one hand, the constant challenge from more radical organizations in a context of union pluralism made some degree of mobilization unavoidable even for the moderate federations. On the other hand, the financial and organizational autonomy of unions at the plant sparked a type of mobilization from below that was very difficult to control for national federations, making compensation to the base essential for the governability of their own unions.

Argentina: Steel, Oil, and Autos

Integrated Steel: From Union Militants to Owners

The state mill SOMISA, located on the outskirts of the city of San Nicolás on the Paraná River, was the sole fully integrated steelworks – whose activities range from the reduction of iron in blast furnaces to manufacture of semifinished steel – and the major industrial company in Argentina, home to around 12,500 workers. In May 1991 Menem named the unionist Jorge Triaca (a leader from the plastics sector and former labor minister) as supervising auditor in charge of SOMISA, and he soon presented a plan that included a 40% employment reduction (around 4,500 workers), the closure of one of the two blast furnaces, and significant cuts in production.[17]

In June 1991, in reaction to the restructuring plan, the San Nicolás section of the metalworkers' union UOM – the leadership of which was almost entirely from SOMISA – launched a series of strikes and demonstrations. In October, they organized a workers' campsite outside the plant, in practice controlling access to the mill, along with a series of mobilizations to Buenos Aires. Meanwhile, workers kept the blast furnace operating. The government reacted by sending the national guard to occupy the plant while workers maintained control of the surroundings and the blast furnaces inside the mill. In late October tension mounted. The UOM section leader Naldo Brunelli was abducted from the plant, harassed by the police, and eventually released.

Nevertheless, after several rounds of negotiations, a settlement was reached. The union agreed to a formula of "negotiation with participation" in the

---

[16] Pedro Pérez, former base activist from the CCOO works council of AESA-Sestao and participant in these negotiations, describes well the dual character of a union structured nationally, but also strongly decentralized as shown in Figure 7.1: "We coordinated action with every shipyard, Sestao, Valencia, Cadiz, through Federations. People from the eleven yards [*los centros*] surrounded our federation leader in the national table of negotiations, though of course there were reduced and hall meetings. But we also participated in all the [local] mobilizations, because it was one thing to negotiate the reconversion plan, and a different one to abandon workers in the factories." In other words, base activists had delegates in the national negotiations and largely felt free to push local mobilization. Author's interview, Bilbao, February 20, 2002.

[17] On the circumstances that led to SOMISA restructuring and privatization see Rofman and Peñalva (1995).

Statist and Corporatist Models of Labor Adjustment

restructuring process and some increase in redundancy payments. Between June and December 1991, around 6,242 workers (about 50% of the firms' workforce) enrolled in the programs of "voluntary departures," which meant dismissal with a one-shot severance payment, and in fewer cases, early retirement.[18] One of the two blast furnaces was to be shut down, and in 1992 SOMISA was taken over by the local group Techint and eventually renamed Siderar (see Chapter 4). "Negotiation with participation" involved two important side payments for the union: the granting of 20% of stock shares to workers after privatization (to be administered by the union) and the incorporation of the union in the company-controlled administration of the welfare fund for SOMISA workers.[19]

The institutional framework of union life is decisive in explaining this outcome. First, the local (San Nicolás) section of UOM was unable to pressure the metalworkers' national federation and was left in isolation to lead the struggle. While the conflict was taking place, the UOM's longtime national leader, Lorenzo Miguel, was bargaining with Menem over a set of bureaucratic payoffs concerning the welfare fund of the national UOM and the government's labor reform package.[20] Second, and more crucially, the conflict and negotiations over adjustment were led by the San Nicolás union section and *not* by SOMISA's internal factory commission (see Figure 7.1).[21] The local section already administered a clinic, a funeral service venture, and other community centers in San Nicolás. Section leaders would be, therefore, much more attracted to the idea of controlling a stock-options program and the workers' welfare funds than were ordinary union militants from the internal factory commission, whose life as activists took place at a greater distance from the union bureaucracy – and in closer everyday contact with the workers. Seen in this light, the emphasis on bureaucratic payoffs over a struggle for relocation programs for laid-off workers becomes more understandable.

The union negotiated with government and business over the implementation of the ESOP in a rigorous way, achieving a degree of control over the program

---

[18] The summary account of the mobilization is taken from my various interviews at San Nicolás, including with the section leader Naldo Brunelli, and from *Página 12*, October 20–31, 1991. The downsizing numbers are from UOM-San Nicolás.

[19] Until that point SOMISA's workers were not covered by the national UOM-managed welfare fund but by one managed by the state company.

[20] Lorenzo Miguel, leader of the metalworkers, met with Menem in September 1991, precisely when SOMISA workers were mobilizing, in order to bargain state relief for UOM's welfare fund debts and prevent the decentralization of the collective bargaining framework. See *Página 12*, September 13, 1991. One leading negotiator of the San Nicolás UOM section asserted, "The national union did not support us resolutely. They did not call a sectoral strike against privatization and that was a demand of our union section. It could have made a difference." Author's interview, Buenos Aires, December 22, 2000.

[21] The following statement by a shop steward member of the factory internal commission at the time is illustrative: "Brunelli [the section chief] and the executive board [of the section] carried out all the negotiations. When the meetings were over, they would come and tell us." Author's interview, San Nicolás, April 23, 2001.

The Political Economy of Labor Adjustment

that was unmatched in other privatizations in Argentina. First, they obtained 20% of the shares, twice what other unions had received in other privatized companies. Second, in most ESOPs, the state would hold workers' stocks until they were paid out of future dividends. In the case of the UOM, the union managed to obtain a loan from the company's welfare fund (now jointly administered by the company and the union) and immediately bought workers' stocks from the state at a very low nominal price, because "we wanted to get rid of the state from the outset, get rid of government surveillance."[22] The UOM section formed an investment company, Argentine Steel Investment (ISA),[23] which would lawfully own the workers' block of stocks – almost all workers who remained in the company joined the program. Any worker who wanted to sell those stocks could only transfer them to other workers in the ISA fund. In this way, the union prevented the company or its managers from tempting the workers with handsome offers for their stocks that would reduce the overall participation of the union in the shareholding. ISA managed the program and undertook secondary investments with the stock dividends.[24]

In addition to the fact that the local section and not the internal commission led the conflict, the union's takeover of the ESOP was facilitated by UOM's absolute dominance at the factory, where affiliation levels were more than 90% with the union both before and after privatization. The local/regional section negotiators did not fear that an alternative union – or even the internal factory commission – would challenge their control of the ESOP and could reasonably expect that their affiliates (those who remained after privatization) could be lured into a program that in fact benefited both the workers and the union. In short, both the "vertical" (lack of sectoral union competition) and "horizontal" (low autonomy of union bodies at the factory level) dimensions of union organization paved the way for bureaucratic compensation targeted at labor insiders.

The trajectory of one local UOM activist, whom I will call "Juan," is telling. Juan became a shop steward at SOMISA in 1982. In 1986 he advanced to the bureaucracy of the union section. Soon he was sent to the national UOM to join the union's administrative team for national collective bargaining. Significantly, although he would become an important cadre at the local level (section), Juan was *never* a leader at the factory: that is, he was never part of the factory's internal

---

[22] Author's interview with Carlos Herrera, member of the executive commission of UOM-San Nicolás and top union negotiator of the ESOP, San Nicolás, April 24, 2001.

[23] In theory, UOM-San Nicolás and ISA are separate entities. Many unionists I interviewed rejected any connection with ISA, saying, "Those are the stocks of the workers." Yet ISA's offices are located in the same building, beside the union's headquarters in San Nicolás. The founders and managers of ISA were or had been on the union board. As a former activist of UOM-San Nicolás puts it, "Formally ISA and UOM have nothing to do with each other; informally, UOM owns ISA." Author's interview, Buenos Aires, December 22, 2000.

[24] By the mid-1990s, ISA-UOM owned a 20% stake in Siderar (valued at $134 million, measured by the price of the share in the Buenos Aires Stock Exchange in 1996), the largest manufacturing company in Argentina. Workers earned more than $5,000 in dividends and could sell their share of the ESOP to ISA for about $20,000.

Statist and Corporatist Models of Labor Adjustment

workers' commission. When privatization took place in 1992, Juan had left the factory six years earlier. He was obviously still a local union activist much more than a national leader. Still, he spent his union life amid the administrative tasks at the national UOM and at the San Nicolás section, rather than at his original factory. My days of fieldwork at San Nicolás indicate that Juan sided with the most moderate union wing during the conflict over adjustment and privatization, resolutely defending the option of "negotiation with participation." Indeed, Juan became one of the architects of ISA at UOM and was deeply involved in the technical organization of the program, the hiring of administrative lawyers, and the negotiations with the government over setting up the investment company. When I interviewed him in 2001, the former shop steward and UOM-San Nicolás section activist was a strong defender of the privatization model, and of the business group that took over the company – his fellow shareholders. He asserted:

María Julia Alsogaray [the last state supervising auditor before privatization] kept her word and did not hand the company to some guys that would shut it down, but to a business group like Techint [the dominant Argentine steel-based group studied in Chapter 4], who, although they got it for nothing, have invested more than $800 million since 1991. They bought another steel mill in Venezuela; they are working to create a monopoly in the steel market. Today, if you are not big, you lose. They have a strategy of competition that consists in concentration. We unionists used to fight against monopolies. Now we want to be a monopoly![25]

It would be misleading and simplistic, however, to take Juan and the whole episode of SOMISA's privatization as evidence of a "sold-out" or "yellow" union. In fact, the union was a tough negotiator during the process. Neither the government nor the employers were happy about having the union as future owners. The ESOP was a concession that the union pursued systematically. Indeed, the union was quite successful in making the program work, in the sense that the union bureaucracy did not cheat workers (as some unions did in other privatizations), and the ESOP was not disarticulated by business pressure.[26] Certainly, it could be argued that local union activists in both the cases of SOMISA and the Sagunto mill in Spain opposed adjustment and pursued mobilization to some degree. The fact that the latter would end up collaborating with the job placement programs through the plant works council and that the former would become partial owners cannot be explained (at least entirely) by personal moral qualities or wisdom. Rather, this outcome is more likely to be explained by a set of established labor institutions, and by past habits that decisively shaped workers' behavior at the critical moment of adjustment.

[25] Author's interview, San Nicolás, April 24, 2001.
[26] Indeed UOM-SOMISA/Siderar militants claim that at the time they would try to convince workers *not* to accept the one-shot severance pay layoff. At the factory internal commission of SOMISA/ Siderar, one militant told me, "I swear on my daughter that I took out from this room 15 workers that came to quit. They are still thanking me. But a lot thought that with $30,000 they would leave and *hacer la América* [Spanish expression similar to fulfill the American Dream]." Author's interview, San Nicolás, April 24, 2001.

The Oil Industry: Market-Share Compensation and Restraint from Above

As analyzed in Chapter 3, the deregulation and privatization of the semimonopoly YPF meant the first major opening of the oil sector in a developing country. The government viewed workforce adjustment at YPF, home to around 37,000 directly hired workers and 15,000 under fixed-term contracts, as indispensable to the company's efficiency in deregulated markets. At the outset of reform, SUPE, the sectoral union, was a powerful and wealthy organization that had traditionally profited from the high wages paid by YPF and from its management of tourism services for workers. Unlike most industrial unions, however, SUPE was not a "First Grade Union" according to Argentine labor law – the type of Argentine union represented in Figure 7.1 – but rather a "Federation Union." The essential difference is that in the "Federation Unions," the model generally adopted in regionally decentralized sectors, local unions are the main collectors of funds (a percentage of which they eventually send to the National Federation) and occasionally have the right to bargain, thus having more autonomy vis-à-vis the national federation.

In September 1991, the company announced the divestiture of the refinery in Campo Durán, in the northern province of Salta. The rank and file at Campo Durán led a takeover of the refinery and blocked a national highway. The National Federation called a national strike for September 13. The government reacted bluntly: it declared the strike illegal (which by Argentine law can be a first step for depriving a union of its legal recognition and monopoly) and dismissed every striker. The SUPE National Federation quickly backed off and returned to the negotiating table. Once the government opened the channels for negotiations over market-share compensation, the national federation tacitly accepted the September layoffs and further downsizing and curbed any mobilization attempt led by the local sections.[27]

The main targets for downsizing were the Ensenada refinery, close to the city of La Plata in the province of Buenos Aires, and Comodoro Rivadavia in Patagonia, the two largest and traditionally most militant SUPE sections. Peronist factions of a more combative bent, traditionally opposed to the National Federation, led both the Ensenada and Comodoro unions. In Ensenada, the September strike was highly successful, paralyzing the flow of gas to Buenos Aires. During the strike 2,100 workers of a total of 4,000 were dismissed. After the dismissals, workers from the Ensenada section continued strikes and demonstrations. One day they marched to the headquarters of the National Federation, denouncing Secretary General Ibañez, who could only escape protected by his bodyguards.[28]

Nevertheless, the government and the union National Federation put pressure on the Ensenada union. They proposed a solution that consisted of severance

---

[27] Diego Ibañez, SUPE's national leader since 1970 and longtime friend of the president, met with Menem three days after the dismissals and declared that the whole strike episode "had been a mistake on the part of both the union and the company." *La Prensa*, September 17, 1991.

[28] *La Prensa*, September 27, 1991.

Statist and Corporatist Models of Labor Adjustment

payments and the formation of so-called small ventures (*micro-emprendimientos*), firms that would organize dismissed workers and carry out subcontacting work for YPF, often utilizing former YPF equipment. Workers were told that the offer was only temporary and that the alternative was outright layoff.[29] As in the case of SOMISA analyzed earlier, section union leaders became strongly involved in this bureaucratic payoff and mobilization subsided. Among the 5,000 workers of the Ensenada YPF facility in 1989, only 650 remained by the end of the decade.

The control of mobilization from above at the second largest SUPE section, located in the city of Comodoro Rivadavia in Patagonia, followed a similar pattern.[30] The Comodoro section had adopted a very militant stance against Menem's initial plan for sectoral deregulation. From the time of the September strike discussed earlier to December 1991, the SUPE local section led a bold struggle against privatization, which included repeated strikes, mobilizations in the city of Comodoro Rivadavia, and the occasional blockade of the main national highway in the region, almost in isolation. The section launched a series of strikes as early as 1990 and the first months of 1991,[31] when the first bidding for YPF oil fields was opened. The national federation backed neither of these strikes. Yet, the local section would finally give in to the pressure from the national federation and the YPF managers: as in the case of Ensenada, the choice given was between outright layoffs and severance payments plus inclusion in the YPF subcontracting ventures.[32] Many leaders of the Comodoro SUPE section, in spite of having led a prolonged struggle against adjustment, ended up joining the SUPE Federation in the creation of PEXSE, a drilling company that would perform subcontracting services for YPF and other small companies. Meanwhile, workforce reduction continued steadily. Of around 4,000 workers

[29] "They would tell you today you get this; tomorrow you don't know. And you'll keep the job in this other company. That led to a division in our struggle; the money was very tempting and they told you that you would have shares and become a business owner." Author's interview with Ramon Garaza, secretary general of the Ensenada section after 1992 and shop steward during adjustment, February 10, 2001.

[30] My summary account of adjustment at YPF-Comodoro is based on *El Patagónico* and *Crónica* newspapers; on interviews with Mario Diaz, secretary general of the SUPE-Comodoro at the time, and one section activist and five shop stewards involved in the conflict, all conducted in the Comodoro area during February–March 2001.

[31] See, for example, *El Patagónico*, November 23, 1989.

[32] The account of Mario Diaz, leader of the Comodoro union section, is eloquent on how the union and company restrained conflict from above through bureaucratic payoffs: "They called me to the headquarters of the company when I was negotiating in Buenos Aires and they offered us YPF equipment and that we use it to work for the company. I called Comodoro and told them 'this is the offer' but that if they reject it, I would go back, put myself at the head of the troop, and we would burn everything. They told me that they wanted the equipment. If I had joined the Federation in this I would be in a good position and not living in this house." Author's interview, Comodoro, February 27, 2001. A former shop steward reported: "There was tremendous psychological pressure. They would offer you 50 or 40 thousand dollars, and a position in the new subcontracting company. And they would convince you that you were now an owner." Comodoro, March 3, 2001.

208 *The Political Economy of Labor Adjustment*

in Comodoro and the surrounding oil fields, only 1,200 were left by April 1992. By 1997, the SUPE Comodoro section had 257 affiliates.[33]

In sum, in both Ensenada and Comodoro Rivadavia, the largest and most traditionally militant sections of SUPE, the restraint of mobilization in the face of extreme downsizing displayed two components that provide a useful contrast with the case studies on labor adjustment in Spain. The first is the role of the sectoral federation leadership: specifically, the absence of national coordination in the struggle[34] and even the pressure it exerted to curb mobilization. It was clearly difficult for militant sections, even powerful ones, to organize a national struggle in a regionally decentralized union such as SUPE without the cooperation of the central union bodies in Buenos Aires.[35] The second is the defection of the local union in the struggle. In Argentina, as stated in Figure 7.1, local union organization is built around a territorial section bureaucracy and not around plant-level union bodies. Since SUPE was a "Federation Union," sections possessed more financial autonomy and were regionally quite powerful, with affiliation levels well above 70%. Indeed, when regional sections led the struggle, as in the strike of September 1991 at Ensenada and the continued industrial conflicts at Comodoro Rivadavia, the local unions demonstrated strong leadership of the mass of workers. However, as in the case of the steel industry, industrial action essentially waned when the local union section decided to join the small ventures offered by the company and the National Federation. Ostensibly, local section leaders were more malleable to those payoffs than shop stewards who spent their life among the workers. As a shop steward from the drilling area of YPF-Comodoro Rivadavia characterized it:

I think that an important question was the type of militants leading the conflict. We did not have people formed in the everyday struggle. Most of the people in charge were administrative cadres rather than workers. They worked all day in the union office and were promoted by administrative decisions not because of their combative attitude. Those who played a leading role in the conflicts and negotiations were not linked to the wells and plants.[36]

Most of the workers' ventures were short-lived. Daniel Márquez (1999: 101) notes that twenty-eight YPF contractor firms were created in the Comodoro Rivadavia area between 1991 and 1993, employing around 25% of laid-off workers. In the context of a thoroughly deregulated oil market and YPF's drive

---

[33] A shop steward from the El Tordillo oil field is eloquent about the magnitude of YPF's downsizing: "We were 256 working in the area 'El Tordillo.' From one week to the next, we were 6." El Tordillo was a YPF central area awarded to the Techint group; see Chapter 4. Author's interview, Comodoro area, February–March 2001.

[34] One combative shop steward asserted: "Some of us told the local union to take the money from the national union and organize commissions that would travel to other sections in the country. But the union did not contribute what we needed: organization." Author's interview, Comororo Rivadavia area, March 3, 2001.

[35] Mario Díaz, secretary general of the SUPE-Comodoro section, commented: "Yes, Ensenada and we were the strongest unions. But YPF had 37,000 workers; we were 8,000. Without national support we were isolated." Author's interview, Comodoro Rivadavia, February 27, 2001.

[36] Author's interview with Jorge García, former shop steward from the drilling area, Comodoro Rivadavia, March 3, 2001.

Statist and Corporatist Models of Labor Adjustment

to lower costs, few would survive. The drilling firm PEXSE, which had been an important carrot in the hands of the Comodoro SUPE union at the time of adjustment, was bankrupt by the mid-1990s. In addition to its participation in the subcontracting companies created out of YPF, the SUPE National Federation obtained the control of the welfare fund (until then run by the company) of the newly privatized firm, which was allowed to offer health services to the outsourcing companies and the oil private sector; 10% of the shares of the privatized YPF (whose voting rights would be represented by national SUPE leaders); and the preservation of SUPE's monopoly in both the privatized YPF and the newly created subcontracting companies (Murillo 2001: 154; Orlansky and Makón 2003: 10).

By the late 1990s, the once-powerful and massive SUPE had turned into a relatively small company union mostly restricted to the privatized Repsol-YPF and surpassed in importance by the union of private oil workers. However, their newly created welfare fund thrived as a result of the partial deregulation of the union-run health system studied in Chapter 6 and its capacity to enroll workers from other companies: it covered around 20,000 workers and their families in 1999 and around 157,000 in 2008, an impressive eightfold increase that signals their plain conversion into business unionism.[37]

The Auto Sector: The ISI Coalition Survives the Market

Market-share compensation in the auto sector took the form of a protectionist deregulation, that is, a special tariff regime that spared the sector from import liberalization and downsizing. SMATA, the autoworkers' union, secured, in addition, two other concessions: the jurisdiction over the new TNCs established in Argentina, lured by the tariff regime and MERCOSUR, and the formation (jointly with electricity workers and other minor unions) of Futura, a successful pension fund. To be sure, in this case, the main compensatory policy is also explained by the pressure from the business sector. However, the central role played by SMATA in the lobbying and formulation of this type of market-share compensation should not be underestimated. In early 1990, the government had created the Concertation Committee for the Reconversion of the Auto Industry. Concurrently with the initiation of negotiations, the SMATA union sided with the moderate faction of the divided CGT and appointed its leader, Raul Amín. The "Motor Vehicle Regime" passed in 1991, setting a special tariff of 35% and other privileges for domestic automakers, born of a joint agreement between the union and the firms in the sector. SMATA's cadres drafted the project in conjunction with the automakers' association ADEFA and served as a privileged channel of communication with President Menem and the Peronist Party.[38]

---

[37] Data from http://www.ospesalud.com.ar/.

[38] Enrique Federico, head of institutional relations of Mercedes Benz Argentina, stated that "without the active role of SMATA the whole bargain with the government would have been more difficult." Author's interview, Buenos Aires, March 27, 2001.

210 The Political Economy of Labor Adjustment

Of course, the restraint of industrial conflict at the workplace was, overall, less of an issue for SMATA national leaders because the tariff regime preserved employment levels. Yet, the case of SMATA is illustrative of the way in which the two essential features of labor development under ISI, monopoly and low autonomy of union shop-floor bodies, underpinned the Corporatist path of labor adjustment. First, the fact that a handful of businessmen had to bargain with a single monopolistic union reduced collective-action problems on both sides. Second, the price that national leaders paid for market-share compensation, that is, forgoing agreements that contemplated more flexible working conditions – especially for the new TNCs established in the country – was facilitated by the reduced role of internal plant commissions in the collective bargaining of those contracts. The Argentine labor relations analysts M. Novick and A. Catalano (1996: 87) already made this point clear in their analysis of the new collective contracts signed by individual auto assemblers and SMATA national union in the 1990s:

The firms enjoy the benefits of "tailored" negotiations without the risks of governability entailed by decentralized bargaining. *The firm's partner in these negotiations is not the internal commission but the Executive Committee of the Section or the National Executive Committee* [my emphasis; see Figure 7.1]. This arrangement guarantees the company a distance that undermines the power and autonomy that a radicalized internal commission may develop, while at the same time it makes negotiations more attentive to the specificities of the firm.

Two negotiations reveal the way in which the low degree of autonomy of union shop-floor bodies facilitated SMATA's adaptation to adjustment. When Toyota, Fiat, General Motors, and Chrysler invested in Argentina, the union agreed to more flexible collective agreements than those enforced in the already established plants in exchange for its jurisdiction over the workers of the new companies.[39] In a kind of extreme version of low shop-floor autonomy, the national union negotiated the collective agreement of the new company over wages and working conditions *before* the internal factory commission was even set up – with the approval and encouragement of the Ministry of Labor. In other words, incoming workers were locked into a collective contract for which they never voted or bargained. Manuel Pardo, number two of SMATA national union at the time, describes the negotiations when Fiat was about to be established in Córdoba and demanded lower labor costs:

UOM [the metals union] in Córdoba had signed an agreement with Fiat [involving clauses of flexibility and lower costs] but the National UOM blocked it. They feared

---

[39] As a shop steward from Toyota said, "For example, the old contracts [those of the established auto companies in Argentina] in the painting section include a 15 minute break per hour; in Toyota we have a break of 10 minutes each two hours." Author's interview, Zárate, March 9, 2001.

Statist and Corporatist Models of Labor Adjustment

that SEVEL (Peugeot), the other plant in which they represented workers, would demand the same conditions. In our case, we had the necessary strength to prevent other firms from claiming the same conditions we were giving to Fiat. But in Fiat we gave them all the warranties to set up the new plant. You have to bargain with each company individually, but in the context of a national union strategy.[40]

So SMATA benefited from its greater centralization (and from its tradition of company bargaining involving national SMATA and each company under ISI) to sign "contracts with no workers" and obtain the affiliation of the new workers of the TNCs that invested in Argentina in the 1990s.[41] Despite the inclusion of team or cluster work amid a generally new and young labor force – which sometimes resents union solidarity – by the early 2000s SMATA had achieved complete dominance in all the new TNCs established in Argentina.

The second episode illustrative of the way in which union centralization facilitated SMATA's alliance with the government based on bureaucratic pay-offs occurred when a production downturn affected the sector in 1998. The recently established Fiat reacted with a wave of layoffs and suspensions. Discontent expanded among the rank and file and a few factory assemblies took place. Yet, the Córdoba section (whose bureaucracy represented a group of factories in addition to Fiat) backed the firm's policy of layoffs and suspensions and quickly curbed any initial sign of mobilization. As a shop steward from Fiat asserted:

The majority of shop stewards followed the line that flowed from the Córdoba union section, which was to negotiate and avoid confrontation. But the union protected its affiliates, and the majority of people who left were workers not affiliated with the union.[42]

The preconditions that underpinned SMATA's negotiation of market-share compensation in the context of economic liberalization would have been unthinkable in the Spanish institutional setting. The negotiation of flexible labor contracts for newly established companies without any intervention of the factory union bodies would have been impossible in a country where plant works councils, by law, have to approve any collective contract. Plus, the union acceptance of a policy of workforce reduction would have been more difficult to implement in a context in which plant works councils elected by union and

---

[40] Author's interview, Buenos Aires, October 19, 2000.

[41] The fact that national SMATA signed the contracts before setting up a factory internal commission does not mean that future workers were opposed to that deal. As one shop steward of the newly installed Toyota asserted: "Toyota got started in the country, and the people they target, they are 20 or 21 years old; they don't even know what a collective contract is. So the company presented the contract saying, 'This is the contract you will have for the next four years; take it or leave it.' We renewed the contracts again in 2000." Author's interview, Zárate, March 9, 2001.

[42] Author's interview, Córdoba, April 4, 2001.

nonunion members, rather than territorial union sections, were the central brokers of local union power.

COMPARATIVE PERSPECTIVES ON LABOR ADJUSTMENT IN ARGENTINA AND SPAIN: A REASSESSMENT

In Argentina, modern trade unions initially expanded in the years of Peronism in the context of primary ISI production, for example, the food industry, textiles, light metals, and consumer nondurables. Sectoral unions, therefore, originally developed in a context of industrialization based in small and medium plants. Although factory commissions acquired an unprecedented degree of power in the initial years of Peronism, from the outset the national and territorial organization of unions was more important than their power *within* certain factories. Indeed the factory commission never became fully entrenched in the Argentine labor legislation. When secondary and more complex ISI sectors (steel, chemicals, transport materials) developed in the 1960s, the new large-scale plants were taken over by the original bureaucratic/territorial structures, with the short-lived exceptions of the strong plant-oriented unionism in Córdoba and the Paraná industrial belt during the late 1960s and early 1970s noted in Chapter 6.

In Spain, by contrast, modern trade unionism essentially developed in the 1960s in the long night of the civil war aftermath, in the context of secondary ISI production. The modern labor movement was born in the large shipyards, steel mills, and auto assembly plants through scattered and independent workers' commissions that fought the Franco dictatorship. The emergence of trade unionism from below out of big firms with a high concentration of workers sowed the seeds for a strongly plant-oriented union movement with weak national structures. In addition, in Spain, the permanent repression of independent national trade unions reinforced the plant assembly culture and the low bureaucratization, while in Argentina the political role of unions as the representatives of the Peronist Party helped them to consolidate the bureaucratic power of the national leadership until the 1980s.

As argued in Chapter 6, in both countries, the evolution of union politics under ISI was reflected in the labor laws passed or revalidated shortly before the period of market reforms began. Sectoral monopoly and the reduced role of plant union bodies in Argentina became formalized in the labor law reforms of 1974 and 1988. The Worker's Statute passed in 1980 in Spain sanctioned labor pluralism and the power of plant-level works councils as the core of union organization. Thus, in a democratic environment in which unions cannot be simply ignored or repressed, labor adjustment paths were thoroughly affected by these labor institutions and the historical practices associated to them. Indeed, in Spain, the generation of large firm-based works councilors and shop stewards who confronted adjustment in the 1980s was essentially the same who had undermined the Franco dictatorship from below. A shop steward who participated in the one-year struggle against the closure of the Sagunto blast furnace facility describes it this way:

Statist and Corporatist Models of Labor Adjustment

We were the last generation who had participated in the struggle under Franco. We were a unionism of participation and assembly. That will not be repeated again. When we confronted the closure we were as much an assembly movement as a union.[43]

Of course, this factory "assembly culture" was not to be found in Argentina, which witnessed precisely the opposite prereform trend, that is, the progressive demise of shop-floor union organization. Table 7.2 shows the distribution of compensatory programs for laid-off workers in Spain in the sectors with available data. The power of works councils in Spain can be measured by the concentration of workers per plant: the higher the average of workers per plant, the more powerful and representative the works council is in terms of both their influence in the respective union's industrial federations and their capacity to promote mobilization. In fact, only firms with more than fifty employees have works councils and, therefore, meaningful union representation. The table shows that the share of workers who went into EPFs (as argued in Chapter 6, by far the most generous compensatory mechanism) was the highest in the three most concentrated sectors in terms of workers per plant at the outset of reform. Indeed, EPFs were developed *only* in those sectors: steel, shipbuilding, and home appliances.[44] In sectors with a less concentrated workforce (which on average would tend to have less powerful works councils and less influential base-level union organization), redundancy policies were based on somewhat less generous early-retirement programs or much less compensatory severance payments. It is no accident that the two sectors that placed the highest percentage of workers into EPFs witnessed the most emblematic battles against adjustment in heavily concentrated factories described earlier, Sagunto (steel) and Euskalduna (shipbuilding).

The importance of the concentration of workers per firm and the way in which it drove compensation was clear to many protagonists of industrial adjustment in Spain. For example, Alvaro Espina, employment secretary between 1985 and 1991, who suffered the strains of labor conflict in office, asserted:

The crucial question for the industrial reconversion plans was not the number of workers involved – they were a minority within the entire working class – but the number of workers in each firm. These were large firms that were geographically concentrated.[45]

José Corcuera, leader of the UGT Metals Federation until 1984, is even more blunt:

If we see what has occurred in Spain, we would realize that traumatic adjustment took place in the small and medium firms. But there was no traumatic adjustment in the big industrial sectors – Why? Because, unfortunately, in the former there was no union strength at all, and in the latter there was.[46]

---

[43] Author's interview, Madrid, February 25, 2002.

[44] According to the data presented in the table, shipbuilding should have had even more workers in EPFs given that it has a more concentrated workforce than steel. Yet the subsector of common steel, which did not have an EPF, is not included in the ministry data on redundancy programs, thus driving up the percentage of workers included in the steel EPF.

[45] Author's interview, Madrid, September 14, 2001.

[46] Author's interview, Madrid, September 4, 2001.

TABLE 7.2. *Spain: Distribution of Compensatory Program by Sector (1982–93) and Factory Concentration of Workers (1982)*

	Plants (1)	Workers (2)	Workers/ Plant (2/1)	EPFs Percentage	Early Retirement Percentage	Rest Percentage[a]
Shipbuilding	102	51,493	505	50.3%	12.3%	37.4%
Steel (integrated and special)	332	69,825	210	49.8%	28.6%	21.6%
Home Appliances	121	20,722	171	28.0%	11.2%	60.9%
Chemicals (fertilizers)	162	11,770	73	0.0%	57.8%	42.2%
Textiles	3,809	136,580	36	0.0%	31.2%	68.8%
Electronic Components	65	4,903	75	0.0%	0.5%	99.5%
Autos: Components	618	36,635	59	0.0%	9.0%	91.0%

[a] Layoff with severance payments and direct relocation in other firms.
Source: Distribution of compensatory programs, Ministry of Industry and Energy, Spain (1991: 229; 1993: 291); Industrial data, Instituto Nacional de Estadísticas (INE) (1990).

In brief, the logic of plant-based trade unionism in Spain described in Figure 7.1 implies that those sectors with the highest concentration of workers per plant tended to get the better deals. What is more, since the degree of union pluralism was very similar across sectors, the power of plant-level union bodies, that is, the *vertical* dimension of union organization, is more central than union competition for explaining the flow of compensatory policies in Spain.

The origins of job-placement programs and base-level compensation in Spain provide a useful contrast with Argentina. Important studies have shown the dire consequences of downsizing and unemployment for Argentine industrial communities studied here, such as San Nicolás (Rofman 1998, Rofman and Peñalva 1995), Comodoro Rivadavia (Paura 1995, Cicchiari 1999, Márquez 1999), and other places such as the oil enclaves of Cutral-Có (Constallat 1997) and Mosconi. Rofman (1998: 62–65), for example, noting the extensive resources poured into severance payments (and, one could add, into the ESOP), blames the failure to enact any meaningful employment programs in these communities on the negligence of state officials, the quality of the state apparatus, and the exclusionary nature of the economic model imposed in Argentina. Yet this type of approach fails to capture what in my view is the central reason for the absence of any meaningful layoff compensation in neoliberal Argentina: the type of union organization, particularly at the local level, and the pattern of labor

Statist and Corporatist Models of Labor Adjustment 215

conflict/negotiation that it produced. The Spanish example shows that consistent compensatory programs targeted at laid-off factory workers did not need a large amount of administrative capacity and are better explained by violent local industrial conflict and the strength of union factory councils than by the moral quality of state officials.

Furthermore, this analysis casts doubt on common views that posit Peronist identity and/or anomie among workers brought about by hyperinflation as the primary causes of the absence of social conflict under neoliberal adjustment in Argentina (see, for example, Palermo and Novaro 1996, Ostiguy 1998). In fact, industrial conflict did erupt when adjustment was implemented. The case studies have shown that often the rank and file did not seem paralyzed by anomie or a Peronist identity but was rather quite willing to resist. To be sure, most conflicts remained essentially restricted to the local level and, as a result, are often not captured by national statistics on industrial strikes. Yet, they were contained and repressed by a combination of a lack of support by the national/sectoral unions and the defection of local section leaders lured by bureaucratic payoffs. I am not arguing that Argentine workers are intrinsically combative and union leaders are not. Nevertheless, the willingness of the rank and file to resist downsizing in communities that had been at the vanguard of the industrial workforce, where affiliation rates were above 70% and workers spent a good part of their social life in the organization, is fundamentally shaped by the union, and more specifically by the *local union section*.[47] In this sense, my research concurs with Fishman and Mershon (1993: 72), who stress the indispensability of workplace union leaders in any enterprise of collective labor mobilization. As a shop steward from a Comodoro Rivadvia oil field argued:

Imagine, if the unionist was telling the workers that privatization was unavoidable, what can you expect from the people? The unionist should be there to change reality, to see who dominates the floor, the workers or the bosses. I think that if they [he refers to the SUPE-Comodoro local section] hadn't had the stocks and the subcontracting ventures they would have resisted a lot more.[48]

The statement suggests that the rank and file was not immersed in anomie but, rather, permeated by the discourse of local union leaders, most of whom abandoned confrontation to join diverse forms of market-share compensation. It also alludes to the fact that market-share compensation is important for explaining the (relatively) nonviolent path to sweeping labor adjustment in Argentina.

---

[47] A shop steward from the El Tordillo oil field puts it this way: "The lead of the [union SUPE] section among Comodoro workers was enormous. They would call an assembly and it would be massive. The section was thoroughly respected by the workers. And they did things. They denounced privatization. They presented lawsuits. What they did not do was to organize the workers to resist." Author's interview, Comodoro Rivadavia area, February 27, 2001. This inaction, however, was probably less the preference of the section leaders at the time than the consequence of workplace habits that had relegated assembly mobilization long ago and of the lack of institutional means to wage a struggle against the government and the national federation.

[48] Author's interview, Comodoro Rivadavia, March 3, 2001.

216 *The Political Economy of Labor Adjustment*

Finally, it reflects that the Argentine government was not a strong Leviathan but a democratic one from which unions could extract concessions. In short, privatization or downsizing in Argentina was, probably, unavoidable. But this was also true in Spain, a fact that did not preclude the struggle of plant works councils and of federations pushed by the local unions. In fact, a prolonged struggle did not stop industrial adjustment in Spain at all; it only led to a very different type of compensation, much more generous for laid-off workers.

CONCLUSIONS

In the context of sweeping market liberalization, blast furnaces at Sagunto (Spain) and San Nicolás (Argentina) steelworks were shut down in 1984 and 1991, respectively. The Sagunto workers led a one-year struggle that included frequent clashes with the police, whereas the SOMISA workers in Argentina undertook peaceful resistance that lasted less than three months. The Sagunto crisis was solved when a generous job-placement fund for laid-off workers was created. The SOMISA conflict came to an end when local labor leaders and the government negotiated the union control of 20% of the shares in the privatized company and of the workers' welfare fund. The contrasting outcomes are puzzling for a number of reasons. Both steelworks are located in company towns heavily dependent on employment in the mills. Workforce reduction affected around 60% of employees in less than a year in each firm. Both companies were home to the most militant industrial union in the country, the axis of working-class movements that carried with them a combative tradition.

This book has argued that alternative patterns of conflict and types of compensatory policies, which define Statist and Corporatist paths of labor adjustment, are rooted in the democratic nature of the regimes, and in the way in which organized labor became embedded in the ISI model that unfolded prior to neoliberal reform. In Spain, the competitive nature of unionism and, especially, the power of plant-level union bodies precluded any accommodation between National Federations and the government, and, after massive mobilization, paved the way for extremely generous compensation packages directed at laid-off (industrial) workers. In Argentina, case studies illuminated that important local union sections rebelled in the face of an adjustment that left thousands in industrial communities jobless. Yet rank and file and local rebellions were curbed by the unions' embrace of bureaucratic payoffs, and by the scarce institutional and financial power of the local union sections (and, most importantly, factory-level union bodies) to lead any revolt from below.

Thus, my analysis points to the importance of the *vertical* structure of unions for assessing labor reactions to market reform. When labor disputes move from the terrain of collective and wage bargaining (largely dominant under ISI) to the arena of massive downsizing, the relationship between sectoral leaders and shop-floor union bodies becomes much more central. It determines to a great extent the patterns of negotiation and compensation that eventually unfold.

Statist and Corporatist Models of Labor Adjustment 217

Generalized labor downsizing in heavily protected economies is, if anything, a question of shop-floor governance.

My research runs counter to some myths regarding labor adjustment during neoliberalism in both Argentina and Spain. In Argentina the reason for the absence of any meaningful workforce reduction policies and the consequent decimation of industrial communities in the 1990s should not be sought in the anomie of a working class hit by hyperinflation, the lack of state administrative capacity, or the strength of the Peronist identity of the working class. Rather, it should be explained by the type of union organization at both the local and national levels, and by the consequent absence of lasting industrial conflict. Similarly, the broad character of compensation targeted at dismissed industrial workers in particular sectors in Spain has less to do with a "social-democratic"[49] approach to economic reform than with the struggle of previously empowered plant-level unions that led to continuous industrial conflict and violent clashes with the police.

Arguably, both labor movements in Argentina and Spain adapted to neo-liberalism and used the democratic context to extract concessions from committed pro-market governments that threatened their foundations. Indeed, it could be argued that individual unions in Argentina, such as UPCN (national administration state employees), Private Oil Workers, or SMATA, which did not suffer massive downsizing and profited from the opportunities opened by market-share compensation, were arguably stronger after neoliberalism than before. Through different types of compensation – massive subsidies directed at laid-off workers backed by local unions in Spain and bureaucratic payoffs in Argentina – the case studies have shown how unions sought, and achieved, organizational survival in a structural environment radically different from the one in which they thrived under ISI. Peronist unions in Argentina generally preserved and even increased their dominance among their (downsized) base after reform. Current affiliation rates exceed 80% to 90% in the refineries, oil fields, auto assembly plants, and steelworks of the country. Likewise, virulent industrial adjustment in Spain did not generate massive changes in the affiliation or in the electoral support of the two main unions – though the price UGT paid was its divorce from the Socialist Party. In short, even if affected by adjustment legacies (see Chapter 10) and ongoing internationalization, labor unions, with their defined traits – concentration and centralization in Argentina, pluralism and decentralization in Spain[50] – continue to be key players in the liberalized political economy.

---

[49] See Maravall (1993).

[50] It is entirely possible that, if not formally by law – the union law has not been essentially changed in Spain – in fact the unions in Spain are today more centralized as a result of their bureaucratic consolidation over time and the progressive prevalence of the dominant factory union sections over the more plural works councils. Evidence of this may be the attitude of CCOO, once the leading supporter of firms' works councils in Spain, which is increasingly eschewing the mediation of works councils and privileging direct negotiations with employers and UGT.

PART IV

THE MARKET MODEL

8

Compensating Outsiders

Chile's Market Model in the Comparative Framework

INTRODUCTION

This chapter analyzes the Market path to economic liberalization, which in this book is embodied by Chile under Pinochet (1973–89) and Fujimori's Peru (1990–2000). The essential features of the Market model are unilateral imposition and marginalization of ISI insiders, that is, protected industrial business and labor actors, and an explicit national strategy to compensate, and eventually politically mobilize, the atomized poor in the informal sector, or ISI outsiders. The "Market" label indicates that the state did not develop any major form of political payoff (neither a system of subsidies nor market-share compensation) aimed at mitigating the cost of adjustment for industrial firms, and their workers or unions, in the way that it did in the Statist or Corporatist models. Sectoral readjustments in industry were largely left to the market. In both Chile and Peru the financial sector, international investors, and multilateral institutions were clearly prevalent in the initial liberalizing coalition. While unions and other independent popular actors were sidelined, the neoliberal elite attempted to gain legitimacy and support for new pro-market parties through the compensatory policies targeted at the informal poor or outsiders.

In Chile, the critical stage of "Market" adjustment took place between 1975 and 1982 when the economic team led by the "Chicago Boys" implemented a bold stabilization plan and sweeping financial, commercial, and structural reforms. Although after the 1982 debt crisis a more pragmatic approach to economic policy prevailed, Market restructuring had already taken a considerable toll: state downsizing, currency overvaluation, and radical tariff liberalization had provoked massive bankruptcies in industry and a peak of 30% unemployment. The chapter argues that the Market path to industrial and labor adjustment in Chile had its main sources in the authoritarianism of the regime, and in the weak nature of the ISI actors that unfolded prior to reform – especially business but also labor.[1]

---

[1] The outright suppression of labor reaction via authoritarianism, however, makes prior labor weakness less relevant to the explanation of the Market path. Thus, the explanatory account concentrates on the weak nature of the domestic industrial bourgeoisie.

Following the explanatory scheme laid out in the first part of the book, the chapter conveys two main hypotheses:

> **Hypothesis 1:** *Under an authoritarian regime, neoliberals in Chile could bypass (costly) compensation to the organized ISI actors and were left with the informal poor (e.g., ISI outsiders) as the main arena to cultivate some form of mass support. Authoritarianism also eased the construction of a popular base in the poor areas through the top-down implementation of targeted social policy by a web of allied majors.*

Authoritarianism in Chile is essential to understanding both the repression and marginalization of ISI actors, and the effective regime penetration of the *poblaciones* (shantytowns) and poor areas flooded with informal and unemployed workers, or ISI "outsiders." In view of its frontal attack on the ISI actors and mass organizations, the less politicized and nonunionized informal sector remained the only arena in which the government could organize some form of popular support. This task was accomplished, first, through political decentralization and a web of regime-appointed majors in charge of the implementation of targeted social policy, and, since the early 1980s, through the construction of the pro-regime party Independent Democratic Union (UDI) and its municipal apparatus in those areas. The radical redistribution of welfare within the popular sectors that this approach entailed would have been much more difficult under a democratic or competitive regime.

> **Hypothesis 2:** *In Chile, weak ISI business groups/firms had been relentlessly losing ground against the state under the inward-oriented model, especially within basic and intermediate industry. Thus, they were more likely marginalized by the neoliberal technocratic elite.*

The relative weakness of the private industrial sector vis-à-vis the state was not only the obvious result of the nationalization policies of the 1970–73 period under Allende. It can be traced back to the pattern of industrial development that took shape in the late 1930s. A powerful state industrial holding, Corporation for Development (CORFO) – similar to the state industrial holding INI in Spain – was the main engine of industrial growth under the inward-oriented model, and its market dominance accelerated during the 1960s, especially in the area of intermediate goods and basic industry (e.g., steel, chemicals, cement, oil, paper pulp). A private industrial sector thoroughly debilitated by a historic pattern of state-led development and by the nationalization policies of the 1970–73 period had neither the economic weight nor the organizational means to thwart radical economic liberalization. In short, in Chile the weakness of the main capitalist foe of economic liberalization – protected private industry – also paved the way for market imposition.

Thus, the chapter analyzes the Chilean neoliberal experience in the light of the two main components of the comparative explanatory framework developed in previous chapters. First, I stress the importance of the politics

Chile's Market Model in the Comparative Framework

of compensation in *any* project of neoliberal restructuring, even in one carried out under a bloody dictatorship. Although my emphasis on the authoritarian character of neoliberalism in Chile is hardly a new approach, the linkage among the specific nature of its authoritarianism, one that was fundamentally concerned with achieving institutionalization and popular legitimacy; compensation to ISI outsiders; and the political and electoral sustainability of the pro-market governmental elite has been less clearly established in the scholarly literature. Second, I argue that, seen in comparative perspective, the relative weakness of the domestic industrial bourgeoisie in relation to the state prior to neoliberal reform (in stark contrast to cases such as Argentina, Portugal, or Mexico) is an essential and overlooked feature of the Chilean market transformation.

The first part of the chapter presents well-known facts about the extent of of trade reform and industrial adjustment in Chile between the mid-1970s and early 1980s. I stress the lack of any state-sponsored compensation policy targeted at affected businesses, unions, or dismissed workers. It also introduces the single compensatory strategy developed by the regime: the expansion of unemployment subsidies and antipoverty policies aimed at the informal sector and the poorest segments of the working class. I show that this strategy was quite different from the labor compensation modalities found in the Corporatist and Statist models, that it involved significantly fewer resources than traditional welfare entitlements, and that it was a top priority for the civilian wing of the Pinochet coalition from the outset.

The second part of the chapter explains how authoritarianism and the development of weak ISI actors prior to neoliberal reform, most crucially in business, shaped the market path to industrial adjustment in Chile. First, I underscore that the compensatory approach of the regime was intimately connected with the goals of political survival and institutionalization of the dictatorship, which were eventually advanced through the creation of the Pinochetista UDI party. The top-down, uncontested construction of a web of municipal institutions and committees in charge of social policy served to strengthen UDI's support among the popular sectors. It also established the basis for an organizational and electoral presence of the Right in the poor areas unknown prior to 1973. Next, I argue that the progressive undermining of the Chilean industrial bourgeoisie under ISI in general, and before 1973 in particular, is essential to understanding radical marketization with a comparative lens. Finally, I examine the two largest industrial privatizations in the steel and paper pulp sectors, in which established ISI business actors were largely excluded. These case studies illustrate the way in which the combination of authoritarianism and prereform state industrial power underpinned the main strategies of the Pinochet regime to cement a coalition with business: the empowerment of financial conglomerates during the 1970s and the creation of "private" business groups associated with the regime through insider privatization in the 1980s.

THE MARKET PATH IN COMPARATIVE PERSPECTIVE: STATE "NEUTRALITY" IN INDUSTRIAL RESTRUCTURING AND COMPENSATION TO THE UNEMPLOYED AND INFORMAL POOR

The Macroeconomics of Neoliberalism in Chile: An Overview

Pinochet seized power after the bloody 1973 coup. In the context of persistent inflation, the military government turned to shock therapy in 1975. The economic team led by the Chicago School–trained ministers Cauas (finance) and De Castro (economics) reduced fiscal expenditures, implemented a flat-rate value-added tax of 20%, and, most centrally, instituted a very tight monetary policy. In the context of the liberalization of both finance and trade, the government turned to exchange-rate stabilization mechanisms (Edwards and Cox 1991: 35–39; Foxley 1983: 59–61). In June 1979 Minister De Castro fixed the exchange rate at thirty-nine pesos per dollar and announced that the parity would be upheld "forever."

The new stabilization strategy was initially successful, giving way to a boom of growth and consumption. In this context, the government launched more ambitious reforms, such as the privatization of pensions and health services. However, the combination of a fixed exchange rate, which led to overvaluation with the strengthening of the dollar after 1979; trade liberalization; and a financial reform that caused interest rates to soar proved disastrous. Unrestrained financial inflows in the context of the world liquidity paved the way for speculation and a cascade of bad loans in the domestic market. The debt crises that broke out with Mexico's default in 1982, and the consequent hike in world interest rates, only made conditions worse. Unemployment figures, already high as a result of the shock treatment of the mid-1970s, reached unofficial rates of 30% by 1982, while the GDP plummeted by 14% in the same year. In the context of mounting recession, the government finally gave up and devalued the peso by 18% in June 1982 (see Whitehead 1987).[2]

In 1983, the government appointed a less orthodox economic team. Capitalist support of the regime had been threatened by the crisis and the surge of the moderate opposition of the Alianza Democrática, an alliance between the Christian Democrats and Democratic Socialists (E. Silva 1996: 182–85; Kurtz 1999: 419–21). The 1984–89 period was characterized by what E. Silva (1996) calls "pragmatic neoliberalism." The new approach was based on periodic devaluations and sectoral and microeconomic polices that bolstered the industrial sectors that had emerged victorious from the phase of radical adjustment: food processing, paper pulp, and fishmeal.[3] It was complemented by a rapprochement with the major business associations, in particular the economy-wide Confederation of Production and Commerce (CPC) and the industrial association Society for

---

[2] The administration had already begun to take over banks and *financieras* in 1981. In 1983, aside from the official bank of the state, the government was holding more than 65% of the reserves in the entire financial system (Whitehead 1987: 126).

[3] For an excellent account of the new type of sectoral intervention under neoliberalism see Kurtz (2001).

Chile's Market Model in the Comparative Framework

Industrial Development (SOFOFA), which were now consulted periodically (Schneider 2004a: 165).

In sum, the basic policy package originally developed in Chile was not very different from the neoliberal macroeconomic menu implemented under the Statist and Corporatist episodes of market adjustment analyzed earlier in Spain and Argentina. In the context of liberalized financial regimes, stabilization was based on a tightening of monetary policy combined with fiscal retrenchment and trade reform. Moreover, in order to tame inflationary pressures in increasingly open economies, the three governments would seek ways to anchor the exchange rate – a currency board in Argentina, a fixed exchange rate in Chile, and integration into the European Monetary System in the case of Spain. The process of industrial adjustment underlying similar macroeconomics was, however, remarkably different in the three cases.

Absence of Compensation to ISI Actors: Market Adjustment in the Industrial Sector, 1975–82

The De Castro team took the average rate of effective protection in manufacturing from 151.4% in 1974 to 13.6% in 1979 (Edwards and Cox 1991: 114). By the early 1980s, Chile's foreign trade regime "corresponded quite closely to the neoclassical ideal" (Edwards and Cox 1991: 109). Of course, trade reform was not the only challenge for manufacturing. Financial liberalization took negative real interest rates to 30% for the period 1975–82 (Mizala 1985: 1), and the index of the real exchange rate went from 40.3 in 1973 to 105.1 in 1978 (Edwards and Cox 1991: 116). The industrial sector tripled its share of total bankruptcies from an average of 8.4% per year during the period 1965–70 to 24.6% per year in 1974–82 (Gatica Barros 1989: 40).

The almost unrestrained flows of trade and private investment and the comparative advantages of certain sectors shaped sectoral readjustments in Chile.[4] As a top leader of the industrial association SOFOFA at the time stated with respect to this period, "The government was not close to the business sector; it was close to the neoliberal technocrats."[5]

Yet the leading members of the De Castro team shared not only a background as students at the University of Chicago, but also experience as executives of the largest finance-based conglomerates, Cruzat and BHC/Vial, which played the dominant role in the policy coalition of radical neoliberalism in Chile (Silva 1996, Dahse 1979) and benefited enormously from financial deregulation.[6] De Castro himself was linked to the Cruzat group (Silva 1996: 140). Unlike in

---

[4] The devastating impact of liberalization on the industrial sector is well documented; see, for example, Gatica Barros (1989) and Muñoz (1989).

[5] Author's interview, Santiago, June 7, 2002.

[6] According to Silva (1996: 107) the Chicago economists were "allies of the radical internationalist conglomerates by ideology and by employment." See also Schamis (2002). For the history of the Chicago School in Chile and its determinant influence on the Pinochet regime, see Valdés (1995).

TABLE 8.1. *Chile: Privatization of State-Owned Stock among the Largest Conglomerates, Share of Financial and Traditional ISI Groups (1974–78)*

Type of Economic Group	Amount (millions of 1978 dollars)	Percentage
Organized around Banks		
Cruzat	164.93	46.8
BHC-Vial	90.81	25.8
Total Financial	**255.74**	**72.6**
ISI Traditional Groups		
Angelini	36.39	10.3
Luksic	21.89	6.2
Edwards	17.3	4.9
Galmez	14.56	4.1
Matte	3.43	1.0
Briones	2.95	0.8
Total Traditional ISI	**96.52**	**27.4**
Total	352.26	100

Source: Elaborated from data in Schamis (2002: 57, Table 2).

Argentina, privatization during this first stage of adjustment in Chile was not compensatory: that is, the government did not encourage industry-based groups subjected to liberalization to expand market share through privatization.

Indeed, financial groups were the main beneficiaries of privatization. Though supporters of the 1973 Pinochet regime, the largest private industrial groups – for example, Angelini (fishing and forestry), Luksic (food and others), and Matte (pulp and paper and others) – would only emerge as dominant actors after the 1982 debt crises swept the local financial groups that were the key players in the initial Pinochet coalition (see Fazio 1997: 138; also Majluf et al. 1997). Table 8.1 indicates that the groups essentially organized around banks and financial societies – Cruzat and BHC/Vial – and that had provided key economic cadres to the regime benefited with the lion's share of privatized stock.

Despite the more pragmatic approach to economic policy put in place after the 1982–83 crisis, the main components of the orthodox neoliberal model, that is, trade openness, broad industrial and social service privatization, and fiscal and monetary restraint, were maintained and even broadened. Indeed, after a brief interlude the neoliberal Chicago-trained economists regained the dominant positions in economic policymaking, led by Minister Hernan Buchi (1985–989).[7] The new state interventions at the micro- and exchange rate levels were not

---

[7] As Martínez and Díaz (1996: 98) argue, after the 1982–83 crisis, "both Pinochet and the civil neoliberal technocracy regained incontestable power."

Chile's Market Model in the Comparative Framework

"compensatory" in terms of this study's framework: that is, they were enacted *once* the main adjustment period of liberalization and fixed exchange rate had already passed with its tale of deindustrialization and industrial bankruptcies. Fernando Aguero, former president of the national industrial association SOFOFA (1987–91), is eloquent on this point: "When Buchi came in, the same guys from before returned, with the same ideology, but the 'dirty work' had already been done."[8] For the sake of analytical clarity and because essential traits of the Market model, such as authoritarianism and sustained compensation to the informal poor, lasted until 1989, this book considers the whole Pinochet period as a crucial instance of the "Market path." Yet the pattern of sweeping and non-compensatory business adjustment essentially corresponds to the 1974–82 period of radical neoliberalism.

Compensating the Unemployed and Poor Workers in the Informal Sector: Chile in Comparative Perspective

Parallel to the relentless imposition of a market-driven restructuring in the industrial world, the Pinochet regime did target a particular segment of the population to help it weather the harshness of liberalization: the unemployed and poor workers in the informal sector. The government undermined each of the pillars of the welfare state that Chile had developed before 1973. State support for public education (particularly at the university level), the health system, and housing was severely curbed (Raczynski 1988: 66; Castiglioni 2001: 44–45). Family allowances and social security quotas of both employers and workers were also reduced. The assault on unions was carried out through the legislation that promoted sweeping deregulation in both individual and collective labor law.[9] Predictably, this reform triggered a huge fragmentation of organized labor in Chile.

This major attack on the ISI actors and institutions was accompanied by the aforementioned targeting of the "poorest among the poor," as Morales (1987: 384) described it. The new orientation had two main components: means-tested unemployment compensation based on direct subsidies and targeted antipoverty policies – see the typology of compensation in "Compensation under Neoliberal Adjustment: A Framework for Analysis" in Chapter 2. The latter covered diverse programs that principally catered to the poor households with children, such as family subsidies and nutritional intervention aimed at pregnant women, mothers, infants, and children. The regime also established a program of assistance pensions that benefited the elderly who qualified as poor and had not been able to obtain regular social security benefits. These programs often reached vulnerable sectors that had been relatively abandoned by traditional welfare policies, and even

---

[8] Author's interview, Santiago, June 7, 2002.
[9] The regime's Labor Plan allowed employers to dismiss workers without just cause and allowed for the formation of alternative unions with only a few workers in the same company, and permitted collective bargaining only at the plant level. For the Chilean neoliberal labor reform in comparative perspective see Etchemendy (2004b) and Cook (2007).

228   *The Market Model*

TABLE 8.2. *Chile: Per Capita Public Social Expenditures, 1970 = 100 (in 1978 pesos)*

	Education	Health	Social Security	Housing	Employment	Other	Total
1970	100	100	100	100	100	100	100
1974	113	97	69	131	83	62	92
1975	87	76	65	78	994	65	76
1976	87	67	60	56	2,533	132	72
1977	93	77	66	70	2,250	203	79
1978	98	87	69	53	1,733	171	80
1979	100	86	75	54	1,556	230	84
1980	91	84	77	60	1,644	367	84
1981	100	89	78	53	717	454	85
1982	103	92	84	37	1,428	381	88
1983	89	79	83	29	3,278	249	84

Source: Elaborated from Raczynski (1988: 67, Table 3.6).

scholars opposed to the dictatorship acknowledged that they were in certain cases effective (Vergara 1990: 24–25; Raczynski 1988: 87, 1994: 78). In the domain of labor, the two main programs oriented to the unemployed were the Minimum Employment Program (PEM) and the Occupational Program for Heads of Households (POJH). The PEM was more extensive and created as early as 1974. Both programs involved public works, such as the painting of state buildings, street cleaning, or the construction of sanitation facilities in poor areas. The POJH was aimed at heads of households and only began to be implemented during the crises of 1982. In brief, Chile pioneered the strategy of targeting the informal poor in the context of widespread market reform, that is, a compensation scheme that shifts subsidies and resources away from the middle and working classes in the formal sector of the economy to the extreme poor, which has been strongly advocated (and funded) by pro-neoliberal international institutions like the World Bank and the Inter-American Development Bank (IDB).[10]

The PEM and the POJH became central in the overall strategy of social compensation developed by the dictatorship. Table 8.2 shows the priority that the dictatorship placed on employment policy within the domain of social expenditure. Whereas the share of most traditional sectors dwindled in the period 1970–82, targeted employment expenditure soared. Despite its relatively broad coverage (see later discussion) a key element should be underlined regarding the compensation to outsiders in Chile: its costs were less burdensome for the state than traditional welfare entitlements. Table 8.2 shows that total per capita social expenditures decreased compared to those of 1970.[11] The income provided by

[10] For Chile see Graham (1991) and Vergara (1990); more generally see also Graham (1994).

[11] Data on social expenditure in authoritarian Chile, like most socioeconomic statistics produced at the time, have been the object of heated debates between scholars and analysts, largely because of governmental manipulation. The most thorough analysis of social spending statistics is probably

Chile's Market Model in the Comparative Framework

TABLE 8.3. *Scoring the Relative Level of Compensation to Working-Class Segments: Argentina, Spain, and Chile under Market Adjustment*

	Union Leaders	Formal Sector Workers	Laid-off Workers (Industry)	Unemployed/ Informal Sector
Spain (Statist)	Low	Low	High	Medium
Argentina (Corporatist)	High	Medium	Low	Low
Chile (Market)	Repression	No	Low	High

PEM, for example, was negligible and could only serve for the most elementary needs of survival. It was about 33% of the minimum wage between 1978 and 1982 (Morales 1987: 382). Considering that the state used PEM workers for its own program of public works, its cost-saving character is even more evident. The lower cost of the compensation to outsiders is of course coherent with the smaller size of residual welfare states that has been repeatedly noted in the scholarly literature on advanced countries.

Table 8.3 compares the patterns of compensation to alternative segments of the working class under the Statist, Corporatist, and Market models. Union leaders got the best deals in Argentina, where they became part of the liberalizing coalition; were marginalized and relatively excluded in Spain; and were severely repressed in Chile. Formal sector workers in Chile did not fare very well either. The sweeping deregulation of labor law, which eliminated barriers to layoffs and significantly reduced severance payments, combined with the reduction/ privatization of traditional welfare services (for example, health), meant important costs. In Argentina Corporatist adjustment meant attenuated labor law deregulation, and traditional welfare entitlements were not diminished in the same way. Laid-off industrial workers in Argentina (mostly abandoned by their unions) and in Chile did not receive any other major form of compensation aside from one-shot severance pay. In Spain, by contrast, rebellious shop-floor-based unions obtained generous compensation packets for laid-off industrial workers, especially in large firms, as analyzed in Chapters 6 and 7.

In relative terms, the atomized poor/jobless were most benefited in Chile. It is important to understand that, unlike in Spain, employment subsidies (PEM and POJH) were aimed at workers by taking into account their poverty, regardless of whether the individuals had been recently employed in the formal sector or not.[12] The Spanish unemployment compensation, though generous, did not

---

that of Cabezas from CIEPLAN (1988), who revises different sources and concludes that, except for 1982, in the period 1974–86 social spending per capita was below that of 1970, and that in 1986 it remained 13% below 1970 figures. Cabezas's numbers do not differ significantly from those provided by Raczynski (1988) in Table 8.2, but Cabezas does not disaggregate spending on labor programs.

[12] Indeed, according to survey data in Morales (1987: 385), half of the PEM workers had not been employed previously.

cover individuals who had made no contributions to the unemployment fund, that is, who had had no previous formal sector employment. To be sure, in Argentina, both unemployment compensation and a variety of means-tested antipoverty programs were put in place in the first half of the 1990s, many of them with World Bank funding. Yet analysts of Argentine social policy in the 1990s such as Repetto (2002: 185–209) and Cortés and Marshall (1999) agree that those programs and the agencies that implemented them never achieved centrality within the Menem administration. Moreover, Lodola (2004: 519, 2005: 517–19) shows that low Argentine spending in national targeted social programs witnessed virtually no change during the 1990s.[13]

Graph 8.1 compares the degrees of compensation of the mass of unemployed people. In all three cases unemployment reached double digits after the third year of market reform. Officials cared about delivering subsidies to the jobless in Spain and Chile. In Argentina, by contrast, this type of compensation remained negligible as liberalization unfolded.

It could be argued that in Argentina jobless subsidies were lower simply because unemployment during adjustment did not reach the levels of Spain and Chile (see unemployment figures in Graph A.3 in the Appendix). Graph 8.2 shows, however, the evolution of what could be called the "unprotected labor force during reform," that is, the percentage of the labor force without any employment *or* unemployment compensation. Measured in this way, after the fifth year of reform the general cost of adjustment for the working class was larger in Argentina's Corporatist adjustment than in the Statist or Market models.

Employment programs – especially POJH – expanded considerably during the 1982–83 crisis, when the government sought to restrain popular protest. Indeed, skeptics could contend that there was no genuine strategy of social compensation in neoliberal Chile. This view would hold that officials simply reacted to mass unemployment and to the series of monthly street demonstrations that the opposition staged throughout 1983, which shook the regime. Yet the fact is that compensating the jobless and the informal poor through employment and other targeted policies emerged as a prominent strategy soon after the smoke of the 1973 presidential palace bombing settled. The dictatorship launched the PEM in August 1974, and, as shown in Table 8.2, employment spending had already soared by the mid-1970s. As early as 1974, ODEPLAN (State Planning Office) designed and carried out a broad survey, called the "Map of Extreme Poverty in Chile," to determine the population to be targeted. This measurement was perfected with the CAS (social stratification measurement) survey in 1978, which attempted to identify those in extreme poverty to whom employment plans and other targeted programs would be channeled (Vergara

---

[13] The neoliberal government in Argentina did create a special fund for social use, the Greater Buenos Aires Promotional Fund. This initiative was vital to enhance the patronage ties and the new territorial strategy of the Peronist Party in the main province of Buenos Aires (see Levitsky 2003), but it hardly constitutes an example of an informal sector–oriented national compensatory policy scheme such as the one pioneered in Chile.

Chile's Market Model in the Comparative Framework 231

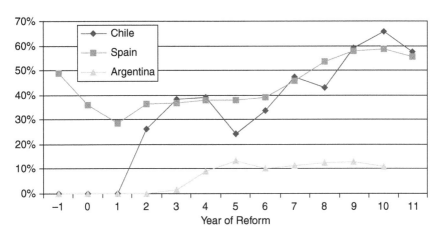

GRAPH 8.1. Percentage of Unemployed Receiving Compensatory Subsidy during Adjustment (Year 1: Spain 1983, Argentina 1990, Chile 1974). *Sources*: Spain, Elaborated with data from the *Anuario Estadístico de España* 1989, 1990, and 1995, INE (Insitituto Nacional de Estadística) Madrid, annual means. Chile, Labor Force Statistics from CIEPLAN in French Davis and Raczynski (1990: 30); Employment programs PEM and POJH from *Indicadores Económicos y Sociales, 1980–1988*, Dirección de Estudios del Banco Central de Chile, Santiago, 1989 (figures for December each year). Argentina, Labor Force Statistics from Ministry of Labor and Social Security, Argentina 2003a. Employment Programs from Golbert (1998) and *Plan Jefas y Jefes de Hogar Descupados, Un Año de Gestión*, Ministry of Labor and Social Security, 2003. Includes workers receiving both employment programs and unemployment subsidy, annual means.

1990: 52–56; Graham 1991: 9).[14] In fact, Graph 8.1 shows that in 1976, well before the protests of 1982–83 and in the wake of a consumption boom and of increasing government euphoria, with unemployment figures growing but yet far from the extreme numbers of 1983, the regime's targeted unemployment compensation already covered around 40% of the jobless.

THE MARKET PATH TO ECONOMIC LIBERALIZATION: EXPLAINING THE OUTCOME

The following sections argue that a causal explanation of the Chilean Market model of neoliberal adjustment in comparative perspective should focus on two factors: the authoritarian nature of the liberalizing government – more precisely, the centralization of coercive mechanisms and the project of authoritarian institutionalization – and the type of business actors shaped by prereform industrial development.

---

[14] "The definitive eradication of extreme poverty constitutes one of the fundamental goals of our development program" (ODEPLAN [Office Development and Planning], Government of Chile, 1976: Introduction).

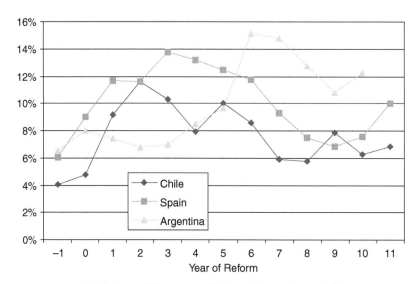

GRAPH 8.2. Evolution of Unprotected Labor Force during Adjustment Percentage of Labor Force without Employment or Compensation (Year 1: Spain 1983, Argentina 1990, Chile 1974). *Sources*: Spain, Elaborated with data from the *Anuario Estadístico de España* 1989, 1990, and 1995, INE (Insitituto Nacional de Estadística) Madrid, annual means. Chile, Labor Force Statistics from CIEPLAN in French Davis and Raczynski (1990: 30); Employment programs PEM and POJH from *Indicadores Económicos y Sociales, 1980–1988*, Dirección de Estudios del Banco Central de Chile, Santiago, 1989 (figures for December each year). Argentina, Labor Force Statistics from Ministry of Labor and Social Security, Argentina 2003a. Employment Programs from Golbert (1998) and *Plan Jefas y Jefes de Hogar Descupados, Un Año de Gestión*, Ministry of Labor and Social Security, 2003. Includes workers receiving both employment programs and unemployment subsidy, annual means. Reprinted with permission (slight changes) from Sebastián Etchemendy, "Repression, Inclusion, and Exclusion: Government-Union Relations and Patterns of Labor Reform in Liberalizing Economies," *Comparative Politics* 36 (April 2004): 273–90.

Authoritarianism: Centralization and the Search for Popular Legitimacy

Centralized State Terrorism and Market Adjustment

The authoritarian nature of the government is essential for explaining the Market path of adjustment in Chile. The major attack on the ISI institutions and actors launched by the Chilean dictatorship would have been unthinkable under a democratic government. However, since other dictatorships in Latin America, such as the Argentine military government between 1976 and 1983, attempted – and failed – to impose a similar model of neoliberal reform, it is necessary to state the defining features of authoritarianism that brought about the Market model in Chile. This study focuses on two: the centralization of power (including state terror mechanisms) in the person of Pinochet and the

Chile's Market Model in the Comparative Framework 233

regime's early project to institutionalize and build a political base, adjustment costs notwithstanding.

The importance of the centralization of authority in the person of Pinochet cannot be underestimated and has been well documented in the literature.[15] The Pinochet regime operated as a personal dictatorship rather than as a typical military junta. Centralization of power in the figure of the dictator stemmed from two interrelated sources: the purge of rivals in the junta and other top governmental bodies that the general carried out between 1974 and 1978 and the early (1974) creation of a new secret-service agency, the feared DINA (National Intelligence Agency), which was under direct presidential command. The DINA – and its successor, CNI (National Agency of Intelligence) – led by the infamous General Contreras, became the embodiment of state terror in Chile, quickly overshadowing other state intelligence agencies.[16]

It is no accident that the heyday of market adjustment imposition, the 1975–82 period, coincided with both Pinochet's consolidation as the strongman of the regime and DINA/CNI's peak years of power. E. Silva (1996: 123) notes that the strengthening of one-man rule aided the expansion of radical neoliberalism in this period. Authoritarianism is linked to the absence of compensation, first and most obviously, because it hindered the emergence of protest by organized labor, the most likely actor to launch unrest in the face of downsizing and layoffs. In this sense, the murder of the union leader Tucapel Jiménez is emblematic of the way in which state terror was at the service of economic and labor reform. Jiménez, the leader of a union of state employees, belonged to the moderate wing of the Radical Party. As a middle-class-leaning employee group, his union had been opposed to the Popular Unity government and had shown a conciliatory stance vis-à-vis the military regime in its initial years. Indeed, Jiménez met a number of times with government officials. Nevertheless, when Jiménez began to contest the imposition of labor law deregulation, and to sponsor an incipient united labor front against the regime, the CNI agents simply assassinated him.[17]

State terrorism and centralization of power are also related to market adjustment in the domain of capital. Almost every government official, military or otherwise, was under surveillance by the DINA/CNI – which, as mentioned earlier, reported directly to Pinochet. Therefore, in view of the reluctance of radical neoliberals to moderate the pace of adjustment and trade opening, affected business lacked alternative ways of exerting pressure on other government circles, sidelining economic authorities. In brief, the meticulous undermining of central ISI actors in the domain of labor and business – extending even to their physical elimination – cannot be assessed without considering defining features of the

---

[15] See Huneeus (2000: Chapter 3), Remmer (1989), and Valenzuela (1991).

[16] For the hegemony of the DINA and its successor the CNI within the regime structure, and its direct control by Pinochet see Huneeus (2000: 103–07) and Cavallo et al. (1989: 57–70). The latter is probably the most thorough journalistic account of the military regime in Chile.

[17] The CNI authorship of the assassination of Tucapel Jiménez is exhaustively documented; see Cavallo et al. (1989: 509–11).

234   *The Market Model*

liberalizing regime: its nondemocratic quality and the centralization of power and state terror mechanisms in the figure of the president, who consistently backed neoliberal reformers.

Indeed, these features differentiate the Chilean experience from other analogous dictatorships in Latin America that attempted to impose radical marketization, notably the military government in Argentina of 1976–83. Although it constituted the other major example of state terror in the region, political authority was always divided among the branches of the armed forces that controlled the junta. Many capitalists, within-state actors, and even unionists utilized those divisions to exert pressure and undermine economic deregulation attempts (see especially Munck 1998, and Palermo and Novaro 2003).[18] Moreover, state terror organs were fragmented among different agencies that responded to alternative groups within the armed forces and were not, as in Chile, essentially at the service of the pro-liberalization faction.

Is Coercion Enough? Institutionalization and the Search for Legitimacy among the Popular Sectors

In addition to the centralization of authority and mechanisms of state terror, a second defining feature of the Chilean authoritarian regime was its plan of institutionalization and the eventual creation of a pro-regime party. In 1977, the dictator launched the project of a "protected democracy" in the so-called Chacarillas speech. The new institutional framework contemplated a strong presidentialism and a semidemocratic legislature – which combined legislators elected through universal suffrage and those directly appointed by the regime.[19] These general ideas were formalized in the 1980 Constitution, which established the institutional umbrella under which the democratic transition would be carried out. Not every group within the "families" of the regime supported a project of institutionalization that would eventually allow for the departure of the dictator.[20] In particular, the nationalist Right, epitomized in the former Patria y Libertad (Fatherland and Freedom, a fascist/paramilitary group very active before the coup) leader Pablo Rodríguez, and sectors of the military envisioned a more permanent and traditionally Corporatist dictatorship led by the armed forces. By contrast, Jaime Guzmán, leader of the so-called *gremialista* faction and an ideologue of the 1980 Constitution, was aware of the succession problems inherent in every dictatorship and of the need to safeguard the main institutions of the regime in a future democratic or semidemocratic order.[21]

---

[18] In fact, Munck (1998: 171–73) notes that regime institutionalization and the centralization of power and state terror organs were the crucial differences between the two bureaucratic-authoritarian regimes.

[19] On the Chacarillas plan, see Vergara (1985: 106–15).

[20] The concept of "families" to refer to more or less loosely organized groups within an authoritarian coalition is from Linz (1964) and is applied to Chile by Huneeus (2000: 66).

[21] See Vergara (1990: 118–23), Huneeus (2000: 293–306), and Barros (2002).

Chile's Market Model in the Comparative Framework 235

Crucially, the same civilian group that promoted regime institutionalization, the controlled transition, and the 1980 Constitution most vigorously, the *gremialistas*, was in charge of designing and implementing the compensatory policies targeted at the poor and the unemployed in the informal sector described previously. The *gremialista* group was born out of the struggle of right-wing students against Allende's Popular Unity coalition at the Catholic University in the late 1960s.[22] Jaime Guzmán, its undisputed leader, would become the main civilian adviser to Pinochet. Significantly, in that fight against university reform and Popular Unity, the *gremialista* movement crafted an alliance with the Chicago-trained economists who had dominated the Economics Department at the Catholic University since the 1950s. Although the *gremialistas* carried a background of a traditional, Catholic Corporatism with interventionist overtones and the Chicago economists embodied free market ideology, as a Chicago-trained economist turned *gremialista* summarized, "In the struggle against Allende subtleties disappeared."[23]

The alliance would endure and constitute the main civilian political base of the Pinochet regime. Whereas Guzmán progressively embraced the ideas of radical marketization, leaving behind his communitarian integralism, a group of Chicago economists, particularly among the so-called second generation of Chicago Boys – such as Miguel Kast and Cristian Larroulet – became aware of the necessity to cultivate mass support for the regime. In other words, they saw the need to turn to politics. In the words of a former director of the state planning office ODEPLAN under Pinochet:

The [Chicago] economists influenced Guzmán in his economic thought, but Guzmán in some sense introduced them to the idea of politics, of the need for political support and representation.[24]

---

[22] As a young college activist in the turbulent early 1970s, Guzmán had articulated a political philosophy by which the *gremios* (guilds), the interest/functional groups in civil society, were called to contain the advance of a totalitarian/Marxist state.

[23] Author's interview with Cristian Larroulet, a Chicago-trained economist, former *gremialista* student leader, planning director of ODEPLAN, and chief cabinet adviser to Minister of Economy Hernán Buchi, Santiago, June 14, 2002. For the origins of the alliance between the Chicago Boys and the *gremialistas* in the struggle against the Popular Unity see Valdés (1995: 203). For an intensive analysis of Guzmán's political thought and his role as main ideologue of the 1980 Constitution, see Cristi (2000).

[24] Author's interview with Luis Larraín, former ODEPLAN subdirector, Santiago, June 17, 2002. Federico Willoughby, one of the leaders of the nationalist Pinochetista faction, fiercely opposed to the *gremialistas*-Chicago economists axis, was less benign about the alliance. On UDI he stated, "I call it the *gremialismo* employment agency [he refers to the numerous positions of the group in the Pinochet state] and the Chicago Boys the demolition company [he alludes to their economic policy], and both groups have now gathered in an organization with the name of a lady." Quoted in Moulián and Dujisin (1988: 34). Pollack's study of the New Right in Chile repeatedly uses the notion of "ideological fusion" to refer to the blend of *gremialistas* and Chicago Boys within the Pinochet regime; see Pollack (1999: 116). As Moulian and Dujisin (1988: 57) argue, in each critical moment of the regime, Pinochet always favored this neoliberal alliance over the nationalists.

Compensation to poor workers and households in the informal sector should be, therefore, read both as a device to soften the costs of radical adjustment and as a means to promote the *gremialistas'* instinct for political survival and institutionalization of the regime. The *gremialistas* were attentive to the political consequences of reform policies that undermined the formal sector and its main organizations in a way not seen in the Corporatist and Statist models of neoliberal adjustment. Therefore, the unemployed and the atomized informal sector remained the only base for the construction of regime legitimacy and mass support. A top official at the ODEPLAN office at the time and prominent *gremialista* leader put it this way:

There is obviously a political interpretation of our policies toward the working class. If one is going against the "established interests" [by which he refers to unions and protected business], you need to seek support somewhere else; we had to do something.[25]

Building Regime Support: Authoritarianism, Compensation to Outsiders, and the Organization of the UDI Municipal-Patronage Apparatus
The whole enterprise of organizing popular support for the regime was carried out with zeal by the *gremialista* cadres (see Huneeus 2000). The *gremialistas* controlled a number of key governmental offices well suited for the task. First and foremost, they seized the office in charge of implementing social policies, the Office for National Planning (ODEPLAN). The aforementioned Miguel Kast became the leader of the agency for the crucial period 1974–80. A true embodiment of the regime and *gremialista* mystique, Kast began to recruit for ODEPLAN a set of cadres with a Chicago ideology in economics and a *gremialista* political view, that is, the need of the organization for social support and for regime institutionalization.[26] The group also came to influence and control the Ministry of Interior and a series of offices at the level of the secretary of the presidency – a ministry-rank office where Guzmán acted as main adviser – most centrally the secretary of youth, which was in charge of organizing a series of pro-regime social activities and political rallies. The secretary of women, which set up the Mothers' Centers in charge of providing primary needs and "civic orientation" to women, also fell in this area. Finally, a large number of *gremialistas* were appointed mayors, a position that became increasingly important after the administrative decentralization that greatly enhanced the responsibilities of local governments (see Eaton 2004a).

Figure 8.1 summarizes the main structure of *gremialista* political power from the national to the local level, highlighting the offices that played a prominent role in implementing the employment programs targeted at the informal poor,

---

[25] Author's interview with a prominent former official of ODEPLAN and member of the *gremialista* movement, Santiago, June 22, 2002.

[26] Kast commanded the team that designed the "Map of Extreme Poverty" in 1974, which served as the basis for the design of targeted social policies. Kast was born in Catholic Bavaria, Germany, son of an army lieutenant who left Germany after the war. He was a fervent Catholic and anti-Communist. His mystique and zeal in recruiting civilian cadres for the regime are well described in the apologetic, but informative, biography by Lavín (1986).

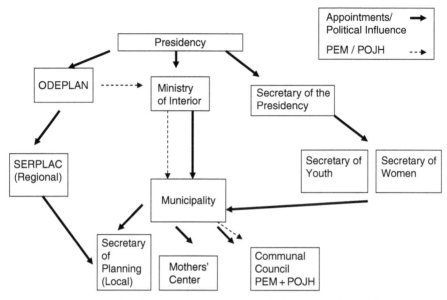

FIGURE 8.1. Organizing Consensus: Gremialista Political Network and Compensatory Policies. *Sources*: Author's interviews with former officials, Huneeus (2000), Morales (1987), and Ruiz Tagle and Urmeneta (1984).

the PEM and POJH, described earlier.[27] At the peak of their power (and of the employment programs' development), during the 1974–82 period, the *gremialistas* controlled all offices for the implementation of compensatory policies aimed at the working class. ODEPLAN undertook the general design of both the employment programs and the antipoverty policies, based on its relatively sophisticated poverty surveys. The Ministry of Interior, also in the hands of a *gremialista* close to Guzmán, was in charge of the *distribution* of employment programs nationwide – a role that provides a hint of their political character.[28] The municipalities, where *gremialistas* had concentrated their cadres, implemented the program at the local level, through a communal council in which (subordinated) nongovernmental organizations (NGOs) participated.[29] At the same time, the *gremialistas* controlled the powerful SERPLACs (Planning Regional Offices),

---

[27] Although the subsidy offered by the employment programs was meager, the subsidies were important in the survival strategies of the poor. See Raczynski (1994: 84) and, especially, the qualitative studies of poor households in Raczynski and Serrano (1985).
[28] In his description of the implementation of the PEM and POJH, Eduardo Morales (1987: 379) argues that "since the program depended on the Ministry of Interior, it was completely in the orbit of the political authority, which enabled it to exert a strict control both over the users and over the municipal apparatus."
[29] "Workers under PEM were under complete dependency with respect to municipal officials" (Ruiz Tagle and Urmeneta 1984: 132).

where local infrastructure and social projects were jointly formulated between regional agencies set up by ODEPLAN and municipal governments. Finally, the secretary of youth, also in the hands of the *gremialistas*, carried out important political organizing at the local level.

During the second half of the 1970s this official network was in charge of administering social policy and organizing support for the regime on certain occasions. In the early 1980s, in view of the transition timetable established by the 1980 Constitution, and after the first talks on political opening had started, the Guzmán group decided to form the Democratic Independent Union (UDI). The party was launched in 1983 out of the Nueva Democracia group in which Guzmán had rallied the *gremialista* state cadres since the 1973 coup. The main goal of the party was to transform this established web of support for the regime into a formal political organization that would eventually be able to compete in democratic politics. Given the entrenched position of the *gremialistas* in the municipalities and their access to the social policy resources, not surprisingly the penetration of the poor areas and *poblaciones* became a major goal of the party. Carlos Huneeus (2000: 373), the foremost Chilean scholar on the Pinochet regime, notes:

The municipality became an important center of power with significant clientelistic capacities to pursue the support of the poorest, one of the primary goals defined by Guzmán [the UDI leader] in order to construct the movement of the right to which he was determined .... The presence of *gremialismo* in ODEPLAN and in the Secretary of Youth facilitated the penetration of the municpalities, as the former agency could influence local governments through planning and social policy.[30]

Indeed, the UDI began to organize within the poor areas and the homeless movement, which carried a great historical tradition of popular activism in Chile. A prominent researcher of the shantytown movement in Chile, Philip Oxhorn (1995: 128), describes how, after most leaders of the land seizures organized in 1982 and 1983 – in the context of virulent anti-government protests – were arrested and sent to internal exile, UDI militants took control of the governing body of one of these "illegal" camps, in large part because of the welfare resources that the organization could funnel from the government. Hipsher (1994: 221) notes that UDI built its base in the poor areas upon *existing* shantytown organizations such as the Mothers' Centers (see Figure 8.1) and neighborhood councils, "which were already dominated by Pinochet supporters and soon developed a large electoral base."

---

[30] Carlos Huneeus (2000: 373) also points out that "Targeted social policies were designed at ODEPLAN under the command of Miguel Kast and they carried the goal not only of achieving better results but to construct a web of relationships and power within the poor, which served the political project of *gremialismo*." Luna (2010: 343) argues that resources channeled through targeted social policy under Pinochet served UDI mayors to "resurrect patronage and clientelism."

Chile's Market Model in the Comparative Framework

By the late 1980s, when the transition to democracy began, this patronage network was well established, and UDI had become "a significant actor in national politics and in shantytown organizing" (Hipsher 1994: 218). Prior to the democratic transition it could not be considered a typical patronage machine, given the absence of free elections and legal competitors in the municipalities – in fact, Luna (2010: 343) calls UDI's initial strategy "authoritarian clientelism." By 1988, however, with the advent of competitive elections the more traditional exchanges of local state favors for votes became more common.[31] Indeed, scholars such as Huneeus (2000: 373), Hipsher (1994: 404), and Pollack (1999: 191) also employ the terms "patronage" and/or "clientelism" to refer to the political machine created by UDI, building upon its control of municipal governments and social policy under Pinochet. Buoyed by its successful electoral performance in 1989 in these areas, UDI continued to organize the residents of the shantytowns after the transition. The party even sponsored land seizures with the goal of challenging the new democratic government and galvanizing its shantytown support.[32]

Authoritarianism enabled the new "popular-oriented" organizational strategy of the neoliberal Right in several ways. First, and most obviously, the use of coercion helped the government to prevent the mobilization of ISI insiders excluded from compensatory policies. Second, the phenomenal redistribution of welfare resources within the popular sectors would have been much more difficult to carry out in a democracy.[33] Finally, the numerous bureaucratic reforms that the establishment of this network of support entailed, such as political decentralization and the creation of powerful municipalities, the surveys of the poor population, the recalibration of social policy, and the channeling of massive resources to allied majors, could not be seriously hampered by any institution typical of functioning democracies such as Congress, the courts, or any other Executive accountability organ.

---

[31] For example, in the internal elections within the Right prior to the general elections of 1989, the Alianza repeatedly denounced UDI for pressuring PEM and POJH workers in their controlled municipalities to vote for their candidates (Pollack 1999: 97). Likewise opposition's accusations of patronage practices with state resources by the UDI at the local level were common in both the 1988 referendum and the 1989 presidential election.

[32] According to Oxhorn (1995: 268), UDI organized three illegal land seizures in August 1990. Its goals were to highlight the new government's inability to solve the desperate housing situation in poor areas. Oddly enough, the Communist Party played an important role in stabilizing the situation after UDI initially mobilized the land seizures. A sketch of the UDI organizational scheme within the homeless movement can be found in Hipsher (1994: 395, 405); an indispensable account of the homeless movement in Chile prior to the democratic transition is Cathy Schneider (1995).

[33] As Morales (1987: 384) argues, referring to this strategy, "This process of redistribution of income intra-popular sectors is only possible under the special repressive conditions of an authoritarian regime."

240   *The Market Model*

Neoliberal Authoritarianism in the Third Wave: Noncompetitive
and Competitive Elections and UDI's Patronage Machine
I have argued that authoritarianism in Chile enabled both the marginalization of
ISI actors and the construction of an important popular base for the neoliberal
elite among outsiders. Yet, one could ask why one of the harshest dictatorships
in Latin American history bothered to elaborate this latter mechanism of consensus in the first place. Given the extraordinarily ample coercion means at
government disposal, why would it develop the efforts in compensatory spending and political organizing described in this chapter? Why not simply rely on
force to pass draconian measures of economic reform?

Two points should be stressed here. First and most obviously, few governments in modern times have relied only on coercion. Classic modern political
sociology has underscored that stable domination requires mechanisms other
than force in the age of mass politics, be it legitimacy for Max Weber or hegemony
for Antonio Gramsci. The scholarly literature on authoritarian regimes is abundant on the alternative devices for organizing consensus that have existed even
under the most brutal dictatorial or totalitarian states. Pinochet's Chile did not
escape this pattern. In view of a UN resolution against the state of human rights in
the country, in January 1978 the government organized a referendum (*consulta*)
on the continuity of the regime as a means to contest this "international aggres-
sion." Two years later Pinochet instituted a referendum as one of the "legal" steps
to sanction the 1980 Constitution. Needless to say, in both instances the opposition denounced the elections as fake since it was denied the most elementary rights
for a fair campaign. Nonetheless, the two elections involved the mobilization of
five and seven million people, respectively, the broad majority of whom voted for
the government. Not surprisingly, the *gremialista* faction, the civilian wing of the
regime that engineered the compensation to outsiders, was in charge of promoting
and supporting the massive official mobilization. The secretary of youth and women
and workers' organization under the aegis of the civil organizations secretary
deployed "hundreds of activists" throughout the country, in particular in the
popular communes of Santiago and the periphery regions (Huneeus 2000: 150–51).

Second, if September 1973 in Chile signaled the dawning of neoliberalism
in Ibero-America, the Carnation Revolution in Portugal less than one year later
marked the birth of democracy's third historical wave (Huntington 1991). In
other words, few authoritarian leaders after the early 1970s in Ibero-America or
elsewhere could conceive of permanent or enduring dictatorships as Salazar,
Franco, or Stroessner had earlier in the twentieth century. True, in the case of
Chile, as stated previously, some factions – especially the more nationalist wing
linked to the precoup paramilitary Right – did envision a more permanent
regime. Yet, the hegemonic civilian group, that of Jaime Guzmán and *gremialismo*, was conscious that a democratic opening would be inevitable sooner or
later. Thus, it pushed the institutionalization goals of the regime to that end.
As just noted, among them the creation of a mass party, not restricted to elite
support, was essential. Thus, as ISI working-class actors and organizations were

Chile's Market Model in the Comparative Framework

TABLE 8.4. *Change in Votes for the Right in Lower Chamber Elections, Urban Area of Santiago, 1969–89*

Municipality	Poverty 1977	Right Vote 1969 Percentage	Right Vote 1989 Percentage	Percentage of Change
Renca	Extreme	13.55	27.65	104.06
Quilicura	Extreme	26.63	38.40	44.17
La Cisterna	Extreme	15.73	34.49	119.29
La Granja	Extreme	12.77	26.35	106.38
Conchali	Extreme	10.58	27.72	162.00
Quinta Normal	High	12.72	28.58	124.62
La Florida	High	37.06	30.82	−16.84
San Miguel	High	12.76	35.03	174.58
Maipu	High	24.36	33.52	37.60
Santiago	Medium	24.22	40.78	68.37
Nunoa	Medium	31.46	31.31	−0.48
Providencia	Low	50.17	56.02	11.66
Las Condes	Low	42.12	60.92	44.63

Source: Elections, 1969 from Mauricio Morales (2010 database), 1989 from Gobierno de Chile (2010); Poverty Municipality Index from Tomic and Gonzalez (1983).

inexorably doomed in the new order (because compensating them was more expensive and violated free market principles and because they were ideologically contaminated), the only sector in which it seemed plausible to create a popular base of support was that of the atomized poor and the unemployed.

The patronage machine created by the dictatorship met considerable success in the new democratic regime. UDI had built a popular base in the *poblaciones* surrounding Santiago and other major urban centers previously unknown for the Right in Chile, and with time, it became the most powerful party of the Right in electoral terms. Table 8.4[34] shows the evolution of the Right vote for the Chamber of Representatives between 1969 and 1989 – the first democratic

[34] The table includes all the municipalities (*comunas*) that remained as such between 1969 and 1989 within the province of Santiago. Municipalities created or eliminated by the Pinochet regime were excluded. I chose the 1969 and not the 1973 elections to avoid possible bias caused by the extreme polarization of 1973. The boundaries of the municipalities were changed in 1982, so the two years do not include exactly the same geographical areas, but they should be reasonably similar. For 1969 the Partido Nacional is considered "Right." For 1989, I consider "Right" the coalition Democracia y Progreso, which included the UDI, Renovación Nacional (RN) (National Renovation, heirs to the Partido Nacional, also pro-Pinochet), and independent candidates under list A. As both UDI and RN agreed to back each other's candidates in many districts to profit from the majoritarian bias of the electoral system, it was not reasonable to disaggregate votes between the UDI and the more traditional Right in Table 8.4.

242   *The Market Model*

parliamentary election since the transition – in the urban province of Santiago, the nucleus of Chile's popular sectors. The Right increased its vote massively, by more than 100%, in most of the municipalities that in 1977 had extreme or high poverty levels. Of course, these are not definitive data; elections are governed by many factors. However, it is hard not to link at least in part the phenomenal increase in votes for the Right in the poorest areas after the dictatorship with the patronage machine constructed by UDI based on the compensatory policies just analyzed. UDI did extremely well in municipal elections in the popular areas during the 1990s and replaced the national state with big business as its main source of patronage expenditures among the poor (Posner 2004: 73–74).

Weak ISI Actors in Chile and the Dynamics of Market Adjustment

The logic of most accounts of the political economy of marketization in Chile is built "from above": that is, scholars tend to focus on the authoritarian nature of the regime and on the ability of technocratic teams to insulate themselves from social pressures. My own explanation of the Market path in Chile spelled out in the previous sections stresses the state elite strategy of building a support network among ISI outsiders parallel to the relentless imposition of market adjustment. However, this book also argues that a complete comparative assessment of the Chilean model of adjustment should combine the perspective "from above" with an analysis constructed "from below," that is, one that takes into consideration the type of socioeconomic actors that emerged in Chile after decades of ISI development. The Pinochet regime not only deployed a high level of coercion and administered compensation to the informal poor to make adjustment politically feasible; it also confronted an exceptionally weak private industrial sector, which enabled its alliance with alternative business actors.

In fact, the weakness of social actors that eased the unfolding of the Market path was manifested in both the industrial business and labor domains. The Chilean labor movement has been historically pluralist and organizationally underdeveloped, close to what I have called a weak ISI labor actor in the book's framework (see Power of ISI Actors and Models of Economic Liberalization: General Measurement in Chapter 9). Nevertheless, since organized labor was repressed and its capacity to exert pressure curtailed, my analysis concentrates on the business configuration prior to liberalization and on business-state relations during market reform.

The Making of Weak ISI Actors in Chile: The Business Dimension
As in the case of Spain, industrial development prior to neoliberal reform in Chile was decisively shaped by a state holding created on the eve of World War II. CORFO (Corporation for Development) was established in 1939. It emerged from the interventionist desires of the Popular Front in Chile, a typical interwar coalition among Communists, Socialists, and middle-class parties. The holding was envisioned and constructed by sectors of the Radical Party linked to the state bureaucracy who saw the domestic bourgeoisie as incapable of leading an

Chile's Market Model in the Comparative Framework 243

autarchic process of industrial development. It was conceived as a financial source for private firms yet also entitled to set up companies or joint ventures with domestic businesses when deemed necessary.

As Cavarozzi (1975) has shown, CORFO symbolized the settlement between the Popular Front government (1938–52) and bourgeois parties and their allied interests. CORFO, although formally managed by a political board appointed by the Executive, was more informally placed in the hands of a set of technocrats strongly committed to economic development and business profits, with little connection to the Marxist parties that formed the Popular Front.[35] Toward the mid-1940s, Chile's manufacturing sector experienced the first bottlenecks after more than a decade of import-substitution. CORFO thus became a shield for the nascent industry, channeling soft credits to manufacturing and agricultural business and fostering investment in infrastructure. The late 1940s and 1950s witnessed the launching or substantial expansion of the major CORFO projects, that is, its companies or *filiales* (subsidiaries) in the sectors of steel (CAP), oil (ENAP), and power (ENDESA), which received the lion's share of public investment. The corporation also set up a large company in the sugar industry, IANSA, which was expected to become a catalyst for agricultural modernization due to the sophistication of its industrial beet processing (Mamalakis 1976: 308–10; Ortega Martínez et al. 1989: 139–43).[36] CORFO was far from being dominated by private-sector interests. Its leadership often decided to channel most finance to industry mainly in the form of capitalization and stock purchases (which meant control of or influence over the company boards), and not through direct loans.

After the election of the Christian Democrats in 1964, CORFO once again became the pivotal government instrument for industrial deepening. The state corporation acquired the majority of equity in the steemaker CAP, the largest industrial company in the country, and made important inroads in chemicals and petrochemicals, autos, and engines, as well as in sectors traditionally controlled by private business such as paper pulp.[37] For example, CORFO founded and became the principal shareholder of two plants, Celulosa Arauco and Celulosa Constitución, the latter of which, by the early 1970s, was the largest producer of unbleached chemical pulp. It is worth mentioning that the main private player in the paper pulp sector, CMPC, controlled by the traditional Matte group, actively lobbied against these projects (Alvarez 1993: 118; Stumpo 1997: 298).

---

[35] Furthermore, CORFO was financed largely by foreign loans and a tax on the mostly foreign-owned copper mining sector, therefore taking the burden off domestic business. For the creation of CORFO see Cavarozzi's (1975: esp. 113–50) analysis. Other excellent sources on which I base my account are Muñoz and M. Arraigada (1977), Muñoz (1986), Ortega Martínez et al. (1989), and Alvarez (1993).

[36] In addition, CORFO established important companies in the fishing (Tarapacá), tires (INSA), mining (ENAMI and Mantos Blancos), and agricultural equipment (SEAM and ECA) sectors.

[37] The firms were Chilean Petrochemicals (Petroquímica de Chile), SOQUMICH (in the nitrates subsector), CORMEC (engines), and Automotriz Arica (autos).

244 *The Market Model*

By 1970, CORFO-managed firms had displaced the private sector and dominated or were central players in the steel, oil, chemicals, cement, pulp, and fishing sectors, controlling around 50% of the total industrial exports of the country (Alvarez 1993: 90).[38] In sum, as in Spain, prereform industrial development in Chile was shaped by a state corporation that, although engaging in a variety of activities, was essentially geared toward promoting industrial deepening into the intermediate- and capital-goods sectors (chemicals, steel, oil, and machinery), transport equipment, and energy infrastructure. In both cases, the agencies developed complex relationships with the domestic industrial bourgeoisie, promoting partnership with the private firms but occasionally coming into conflict with domestic actors over control of the production process.

Assessing a Weak ISI Actor: Prereform Economic Power of the Chilean Industrial Bourgeoisie in Comparative Perspective

Although it obviously reached its zenith in the Allende period – CORFO was the central agency implementing nationalization policies between 1970 and 1973 – the role played by the Chilean state as owner and manager in the industrial domain increased markedly after 1939 and gained significant strength in the 1960s. In this way, Chile parallels the Spanish case and stands in stark contrast with Argentina, where no encompassing state industrial holding was ever created, and private *grupos*, more than state firms, performed as the main agents of industrial deepening. This section demonstrates that, in comparative perspective, the Chilean industrial bourgeoisie that confronted liberalization was structurally weak vis-à-vis the state. In the first place, I present data on sales as an indicator of economic power – the main relational measure used in the comparison between Argentina and Spain in Chapter 3. Second, I add two other indicators of industrial business structural power: distribution of production in more value-added sectors and sectoral concentration of the largest business groups in the country. I then spell out the logic by which this societal configuration facilitated the imposition of a Market pattern of adjustment.

As indicated in Chapter 3, sales volume is a typical measure of firm power in the business literature, signaling the size of a company and the resources it pours into the economy (Table 8.5). The year 1976 seems a reasonable year in which to score the economic power of the private industrial sector in Chile since most of the assets taken over in the 1970–73 period had been returned to the private sector, the privatization of the more traditional CORFO companies had not yet started, and the full-scale liberalization period was only beginning. To avoid bias, I have excluded from the table CODELCO, the state-owned company created out of the expropriation of U.S. mining interests under Allende, by far the largest company in the country, which the military refused to privatize. The data reflect the historical trajectory described in the previous section and the

---

[38] It is true that business associations, in particular SOFOFA, had representatives on the board of CORFO, but as Schneider (2004a: 159) argues, the internal bureaucracy of CORFO was "relatively professional and Weberian, and its decisions were rarely overturned."

Chile's Market Model in the Comparative Framework

TABLE 8.5. *Top 30 Industrial Firms by Sales at the Beginning of the Liberalization Period: Share of Top 30 Total Sales by Type of Producer*

Type	Sector	Argentina 1988 Percentage of Top 30 Sales	Spain 1984 Percentage of Top 30 Sales	Chile 1976 Percentage of Top 30 Sales
State	Total	28% (2 firms)	55% (11 firms)	52% (10 firms)
	Oil/Mining	23% (1 firm)	40% (4 firms)	25% (2 firms)
	Manufacturing	5% (1 firm)	15% (7 firms)	27% (8 firms)
Foreign	Total	33% (11 firms)	25% (13 firms)	16% (6 firms)
	Oil/Mining	13% (3 firms)	0%	9% (2 firms)
	Manufacturing	20% (8 firms)	25% (13 firms)	7% (4 firms)
Private	Total	39% (17 firms)	20% (6 firms)	31% (14 firms)
Domestic	Oil/Mining	3% (2 firms)	14% (3 firms)	14% (3 firms)
	Manufacturing	36% (15 firms)	6% (3 firms)	17% (11 firms)
	Total	100% (30 firms)	100% (30 firms)	100% (30 firms)

Note: State ownership implies state control of more than 50% of shares. Numbers may not total 100 because of rounding.
Source: Argentina, *Mercado Review* (August 1989); Spain, *Anuario El País* (1985); Chile, World Bank (1980).

contrasts drawn with Argentina and Spain. In Chile, state industrial companies, among them CAP (steel), SOQUIMICH (chemicals), ENAP (oil), INSA (tires), Celulosa Constitucion and INFORSA (pulp), INACESA (cement), IANSA (food), and ENAMI (mining) shared more than half of the total sales of the top thirty companies in the country, a similar level to that in the Spanish case. If we focus on manufacturing – the sector hit hardest by liberalization – according to this measure, the Chilean state had five times the power of the Argentine state. Likewise, the Chilean industrial bourgeoisie proved to be structurally much weaker than the Argentine: in manufacturing, its share of sales among the thirty largest companies was less than half of its Argentine counterpart.

A second measure of the power of industrial interests is provided by the share of value added by the industrial subsector (ISIC three digits) in consumer goods, intermediate goods and complex transport equipment (steel, oil, chemicals, plastic/rubber, automobiles, shipbuilding, and others), and capital goods (electrical and nonelectrical machinery). In Table 8.6 consumer goods are divided between those most directly manufactured out of natural resources (food, beverages, leather, pulp and paper, wood, nonferrous metals), in which developing economies tend to be more competitive, and more "autonomous" sectors (textiles, apparel, glass, metal transformation, printing, and publishing), in which a semiclosed developing economy tends to enjoy less of a comparative advantage in a neoliberal age. The most vigorous foes of liberalization are located in intermediate, capital goods, and in the more autonomous consumer goods, all of which will

TABLE 8.6. *Industry: Structural Conditions at the Outset of Adjustment*

	Argentina 1985	Spain 1980	Chile 1975
Industrial Production as Percentage of GDP	29.6	28.4	26.0[a]
Share of Value Added in Industry (percentage)			
Competitive			
Natural Resource–Based Consumer Goods	29.1	25.7	44.8
Noncompetitive			
Autonomous Consumer Goods	20.0	27.6	15.8
Intermediate Goods/Transportation Equipment	43.7	31.1	31.9
Capital Goods	6.7	14.3	7
Total Noncompetitive	70.4	73	54.7
Total	100	100	100

[a] Refers to 1973 and is taken from ECLA in Alvarez (1993: 69).
Source: United Nations Industrial Development Organization (UNIDO) (1985, 1990).

be presumably more challenged by international competition. Table 8.6 indicates that these "potential losers" generated 70.4% of the industrial GDP at the outset of reform in Argentina, 73% in Spain, and only 54.7% in Chile. Chile had an overall concentration in the more competitive, natural resources–based industry before economic liberalization.

Finally, it could be the case that although the sector of intermediate and heavy industry is structurally smaller, the largest and more powerful Chilean capitalists are still found in that domain. Table 8.7 compares the sectoral concentration of the five largest private business groups in Chile and Argentina at the outset of reform, including tradable and nontradable sectors.[39] According to these data, of the five largest business groups in Chile in 1977, that is, when liberalization was about to reach its heyday, only Angelini can be taken as fully industry-based: that is, it had an overall industry concentration of around 87%. Cruzat, BHC, and Edwards were essentially financial/real estate groups. Moreover, only Matte, the largest paper producer in Chile, appeared to have sizable concentration outside the food industry.

In Argentina, by contrast, at the outset of reform (1) the largest domestic capitalists were based in industry rather than in nontradable sectors, and (2) four of the five

[39] For reasons of data availability, I used assets in Chile and sales in Argentina to measure the sectoral concentration of the large domestic business groups. Although these measure different aspects, they both provide reasonable hints about the sectoral concentration of domestic groups and are therefore comparable. In the Argentine case, the score of Pérez Companc concentration in industry may be inflated because the CEPAL database in Bisang (1996) does not include its bank (Banco Río). Still, Pérez Companc was the only one of the five largest groups that owned an important bank.

TABLE 8.7. *Argentina and Chile: Sectoral Concentration of Five Largest Domestic Business Groups during Economic Liberalization (Percentages)*

Sector	Chile 1977[a]					Argentina 1992[b]				
	Cruzat	BHC	Matte	Angelini	Edwards	B&B	Techint	SOCMA	Cofal	P. C.
Real Estate	13.9	25.4	18.05	0	41.94	0	0	0	0	0
Bank/Insurance	2.6	20.8	7.02	0.7	11.51	0	0	0	0	0
Agriculture/Forestry	18	13.9	12.63	10.3	7.67	15.06	0	0	0	3.7
Mining	3.8	4.7	7.26	0	0	0	0	0	0	0
Construction	3	0	0	0	0	0	11.88	1.63	0	16.54
Other Nontradable	7	2.47	2.68	2.32	17.51	5.63	5.75	24.08	0	4.9
Food Industry	16.74	2.19	0.37	67.41	21.25	53.14	0	0	0	0
Rest of Industry[c]	**34.9**	**30.4**	**52**	**19.45**	**0.12**	**26.17**	**82.38**	**74.3**	**100**	**74.86**
Total	100	100	100	100	100	100	100	100	100	100
Selected industries:										
Autos								74.3	100	
Chemicals						20.74				
Steel							34.5			
Oil	11.8									56.26
Electronics		10.79								
Paper			41.71							
Wood				11.1						

[a] Asset value in millions of dollars from Dahse (1979: Tables 1, 5, 10, 11, and 14).
[b] Sales in million of dollars, database of CEPAL Argentina in Bisang (1996: table 2).
[c] Within energy subsectors, electricity is considered nontradable and oil and gas are included in "rest of industry."

248 *The Market Model*

TABLE 8.8. *Industry: Initial Conditions at the Outset of Full-Scale Liberalization*

	Argentina Corporatist	Spain Statist	Chile Market
Position of Private-Domestic Industrial Interests in Relation to State in Production	Strong	Weak	Weak
Degree of Industrial Deepening into Intermediate/Heavy Industry	Strong	Strong	Weak

largest business groups were concentrated in heavy industry/intermediate goods, such as steel, autos, and oil, rather than in the food industry – and would eventually be compensated, as shown in Chapters 3 and 4.

To summarize, the argument in this study assumes that industrial opening in middle-income, mixed, semiclosed economies will be eased under two conditions, both of which put the Chilean state in an ideal position to impose liberalization when compared to Spain and, especially, to Argentina (Table 8.8):

1. The state dominates the production of substantial sectors. It tends to be easier for policymakers to impose adjustment on their own state managers than to face powerful local capitalists lobbying against the liberalization plan. In addition, an important role of the state as supplier and producer in crucial segments of industry (as in the Spanish case) hampers the organization of collective action and associations in the industrial private sector.

2. The ISI sectors that harbor firms that are at the same time economically powerful – that is, that tend to be capital intensive and generate more production value – and less internationally competitive are not well developed. As hypothesized in Chapter 2, firms in heavy and intermediate industry, especially when they are domestic-owned and therefore lack the support of mother companies in developed countries, will deploy lobbying more forcefully against the liberalization plan.

Thus the Pinochet regime was in command of a state that was exceptionally powerful vis-à-vis local private industrial interests in economic terms. At the same time, overall, the noncompetitive sectors of heavy industry and intermediate goods were comparatively smaller. On top of this, nationalization policies of the Socialist 1970–73 government severely hit the ISI private sector as a whole. Manuel Feliu, president of the economy-wide capitalist association CPC, referred to the situation of domestic industry by 1973 in the following terms:

The traditional sectors of industry had lost their economic power. Thus, having lost their economic force, they lost their political force to pressure for the preservation of the system of protections. Most of SOFOFA [the Chilean industrial national association] companies were either nationalized or bankrupt; what could they say?[40]

[40] Author's interview, Santiago, June 17, 2002.

Chile's Market Model in the Comparative Framework 249

Indeed the main business components of the Pinochet initial coalition, though some of them powerful in economic terms, had been relatively minor players under the inward-oriented model and as stated previously, were mainly associated with the financial and real estate sector. As one scholar argued with respect to the economic groups that cemented the initial business support of Pinochet:

The main groups are newcomers and they are nothing like their predecessors, they have no historic roots and they do not have their origin in the control of one or several firms linked to the productive goods sector, but rather in the control of financial activity.[41]

Though the BHC group, a central ally of the dictatorship, structured around the banking industry, was already a massive conglomerate by 1970, the Cruzat group did not even exist as a separate entity, and other later ascendant financial groups such as Aetna or Concepción were relatively minor players before Allende. All of them had banks and financial societies that brokered international loans and would greatly expand during the financial liberalization of the 1970s.

At the political level SOFOFA, the Chilean industrial association, carried considerable bureaucratic capacity in the wake of neoliberalism. It encompassed medium and large firms, had a strong technical staff, and had been quite active in the fight against Allende (Schneider 2004a: 163). Indeed, the fact that despite organizational strength, ISI large and small players were largely marginalized by the Pinochet initial coalition points to the importance of the direct relations between the state and the main economic conglomerates in the politics of compensation under neoliberalism.

The Noncompensatory Character of Industrial Privatization in Chile: The Paper Pulp and Steel Industries

Privatization during the Pinochet regime took place in two rounds. The first unfolded between 1974 and 1978 and was largely restricted to industrial, financial, and agrarian assets, which had been seized by the state during the Allende period. The second round of privatization took place between 1985 and 1988; it involved state-run services and utilities, along with the major industrial companies traditionally owned by CORFO. The following case studies examine the two largest industrial privatizations in each round: the paper pulp companies Celulosa Arauco and Celulosa Constitución and the steelmaker CAP. Though one took place during radical neoliberalism in the 1970s, and the other occurred during the industrial commodity boom of the 1980s, both cases illustrate well how the weakness of established ISI business players shaped the economic coalitional strategy of the government in each period: the empowerment of financial groups in the early phase of the regime and the creation of new Pinochetista economic groups through insider privatization, that is, the distribution of stock to regime managers and associates, in the 1980s.

---

[41] Ricardo Lagos, cited in Martínez and Díaz (1996: 88).

The Privatization of Paper Pulp Industries in the 1970s

As mentioned, Celulosa Arauco and Celulosa Constitución were the central CORFO projects for the forestry-based industry during the 1960s. By the time of privatization, the two CORFO-managed companies, together with INFORSA (also owned by CORFO), produced 53% of the paper pulp in the country; the rest was in the hands of CMPC, the flagship company of the powerful Matte group (Mamalakis 1996: Table 8.6). Celulosa Arauco and Celulosa Constitución were singled out for privatization in 1976 and 1979, respectively. The government implemented the divestiture through competitive bidding for controlling stock. Two groups bid for the control of Celulosa Arauco, the finance-based Cruzat and the industrial group Angelini, with stakes in the related timber industry. The company was eventually awarded to the Cruzat group after the Angelini group refused to make a better offer. In the case of Celulosa Constitución, the main bidders turned out to be Cruzat and the other main player in the sector, the Matte group, through its pulp and paper company CMPC. The sale was again awarded to the Cruzat group.[42] Finally, the third largest CORFO company in the sector, INFORSA, went to the BHC/Vial financial group in 1977.

Thus, established industrial actors were displaced from the most important industrial privatizations in this first round, which were awarded to the two largest finance-based groups. The financial/real estate–based groups Cruzat and BHC/Vial, together with the Edwards group, constituted the main coalitional base of the regime at the time, and, in fact, most of the Chicago economists were from within their ranks. It is true that the private company CMPC was mostly competitive in the heavily natural resource–based pulp industry and, therefore, was in less need of compensation. Yet, its paper business was oriented toward the domestic market and was seriously affected by liberalization and currency appreciation.

Had it been successful in the privatizations of the mid-1970s, CMPC would have controlled most of the pulp and cellulose business in the country. However, CMPC was in a relatively weak position when privatization took place. It had been constantly losing ground to the state in the years prior to reform, and its share in paper pulp production had declined from 100% in 1960 to 47% in the mid-1970s. As one analyst of Chilean business argues, at the time of privatization "the position of the *grupo* Matte [the owners of CMPC] was relatively weakened by the socialist government of Allende and by the predominance of the financial groups" (Montero 1997: 269).[43]

---

[42] See Hachette et al. (1993: 70–73) and Mamalakis (1996: 354).

[43] Manufacturing Company of Paper and Cardboard's (CMPC) revenge would occur only in 1986 with the reprivatization of INFORSA after the financial groups succumbed to the 1982 crises and the period of industrial liberalization was well behind. Indeed, the Matte group and the other major natural resource–based traditional industrial groups became important beneficiaries of the second round of privatizations in the mid-1980s.

The Privatization of the Steel Industry in the 1980s

Whereas direct bids for controlling stakes predominated in the first round of privatization between 1974 and 1979, the second was carried out mostly through sequential public offers in the stock market. In the early 1980s, the steelmaker CAP was the largest industrial company in the hands of the state after CODELCO, the nationalized copper giant. Although it had been hit by the sweeping tariff deregulation carried out between 1974 and 1982 and was burdened by a high level of debt, the government had carried out a sound employment and financial rationalization plan that had yielded positive cash flows (Hachette and Luders 1993: 135). Furthermore, the company controlled more than 80% of the domestic market.

CAP became a quintessential example of a divestiture mechanism through which the managers of the state companies and political associates of the Pinochet regime became owners and capitalists. In 1986, the government decided on a capital reduction plan through which the company was entitled to acquire its own stocks. In fact, only CORFO sold its shares to the company, reducing its equity share to 51%. Therefore, private stockholders (who did not sell their shares and were mostly managers and regime insiders with privileged information) went from sharing 11.6% of equity to controlling 47% of the reduced equity. Subsequently, the remaining 51% of the company was sold to the employees and institutional and private investors through the stock exchange. But in a context of a repressive dictatorship, unlike the example of the Argentine steelmaker SOMISA/SIDERAR – where, as shown in Chapter 7, the union eventually controlled the workers' stock programs – employees could not organize autonomously and were easily co-opted by the managers. In the end, CAP remained in control of the Pinochet-appointed managers and a series of institutional investors. Roberto Andraca, the president of the company appointed by Pinochet, became CEO and strongman of privatized CAP in the 1990s.[44] Crucially, no local business group or steelmaker would hamper the path to insider privatization. As shown in Chapter 5, local steelmakers had been wiped out by the strong expansion of the CORFO-managed CAP after 1965.

Many other large privatizations of the period in both the industrial and utility sectors were organized in ways that enabled the Pinochet associates (many of them members of or close to the official party UDI) and managers to become owners. A series of public offers and credits from the state banks biased in favor of regime insiders, who occasionally shared ownership with institutional investors and foreign interests, constituted the essential mechanism. For example, Julio Ponce Lerou, the Pinochet-government-appointed head of SOQUIMICH – the largest chemical company in the country – became its first president and main equity investor after privatization (Fazio 1997: 277–82). Carlos Yuraszeck, an

---

[44] For a detailed account of CAP's privatization, see Sáez (1987). Huneeus (2000) and Fazio (1997) stress the way in which regime insiders were favored. For a useful and more benevolent vision of economists close to the regime see Hachette and Luders (1993).

official associated with UDI who had served in ODEPLAN since the initial years of Pinochet, organized the privatization of the main electricity generator (ENDESA) and distributor (Chilectra). He became CEO and main shareholder of the dominant business group ENDESA formed after privatization. Indeed, regime insiders became CEOs of the three largest electricity corporations emerging from privatization: Bruno Philippi, head of Gener, was a former state regulator of the sector under Pinochet, and Gonzalo Ibáñez, CEO of the new Chilquinta, was a former collaborator of the UDI leader Guzmán in the drafting of the 1980 Constitution (Murillo 2009: 113).

In brief, whether they were awarded to a single buyer or to insiders of the regime, the important point is that, unlike in Argentina, in both rounds the government did *not* allocate the most important state-owned industrial assets to established private ISI business players in the sector. In the first round, assets were awarded to the main coalitional base of the regime at the time, the financial conglomerates; in the second, industrial privatization became a means to reward regime insiders and officials, though the industry-based groups that had weathered the financial crisis of 1982–83 also received important assets. Private interests in the steel and chemical sector were negligible or nonexistent when CAP and SOQUIMICH were divested, a fact that facilitated the regime insider-biased privatization fully carried out in the second half of the 1980s.

CONCLUSIONS

Building upon insights provided by comparative analysis, this chapter ultimately fuses two traditional currents in the interpretation of the politics of radical neoliberalism in Chile. The first can be traced back to the literature on the politics of economic adjustment of the 1990s and focuses on the cohesiveness of Chilean authoritarianism, the unabashed support that the Chicago-trained economic team received from the dictator, and the insulation it achieved from societal economic interests.[45] More recently, it has been most effectively represented by the work of Huneeus (2000). Unlike his predecessors, though, this scholar stressed the crucial role played by Guzmán and the *gremialista* faction in the consolidation of the Market model, in the regime institutionalization, and in the creation of the official party UDI. The second strand of scholarship emphasizes the socioeconomic coalition that underpinned radical adjustment, which is seen as essentially backed by a handful of finance-based conglomerates close to the Chicago economists and is most notably embodied by the work of E. Silva (1996).[46]

---

[45] For analysis in this vein see Haggard and Kaufman (1995: 42–43) and Nelson (1990: 341).

[46] The precursor of this line of research is Dahse (1979). The work of Schamis (2002) and Fazio (1997) can be also placed within this camp. However, although his main focus is business coalitions, Silva also pays attention to the state-level variable of authoritarian centralization and cohesiveness.

Chile's Market Model in the Comparative Framework

Regarding the first interpretation, although I underscore the importance of authoritarian centralization to explain the Market path, I have also stressed how the type of authoritarianism established in Chile, which aimed to achieve radical adjustment and institutionalization *simultaneously*, determined its compensatory strategy: when traditional ISI actors were sidelined or repressed, the informal sector and the atomized poor and unemployed remained the only arena in which the alliance of Chicago economists and *gremialistas* could cultivate mass support and, therefore, enhance the prospects for political survival through the creation of a regime party.[47]

This book concurs with the second approach in rejecting the view of Chile as a case in which the neoliberal authoritarian state remained thoroughly autonomous of social interests. It can hardly be argued, however, that radical neoliberalism was essentially driven by the financial bourgeoisie. Domestic financial groups were not among the main economic players before 1973 – they were offspring, more than parents, of the dictatorship. The Pinochet market reform project can thus be aptly conceptualized as a capitalist revolution from above. Yet, it can be equally naive to deny the social basis of the initial Pinochet coalition, that is, the financial groups from which it took most of the neoliberal cadres and that it helped to empower.

Indeed, amid the specific initial process of industrial reform and liberalization, the state did remain formally neutral in the sense that it did not seek to privilege most ISI players and left sectoral adjustment largely to market forces. In any case, the question in the end is not *how much autonomy* but *autonomy from whom*. The Chicago-trained economic teams, as Silva shows persuasively, were closely linked to the finance-based conglomerates, particularly during the 1974–82 period of radical adjustment, but remained aloof from most traditional industrial interests. That autonomy, I argue, was enhanced not only by authoritarianism, but also by the weakness of the Chilean industrial bourgeoisie, in terms of both its economic power relative to the state and its sectoral composition. It was ultimately rooted in a type of ISI development in which the state was the main agent of industrial growth. In brief, seen in comparative perspective, the Market path in Chile was the result of both a type of centralized authoritarianism that sought popular legitimacy and the extraordinary weakness of the main capitalist foe of economic liberalization in a mixed developing economy.

---

[47] For an analysis that combines the business coalitional basis of the Pinochet regime with its strategy of winning mass support in the countryside see Kurtz (2004).

PART V

COMPARATIVE PERSPECTIVES IN IBERO-AMERICA

9

Models of Economic Liberalization in Brazil, Portugal, Peru, and Mexico

INTRODUCTION

The rest of Ibero-America appears as the ideal setting to further test the main hypotheses of this book: all the largest countries in the region share the Iberian-Catholic cultural background, all had undergone Import Substitution Industrialization (ISI) since the 1930s, all had generated private labor and business actors relatively autonomous of the state (the potential losers from market reform), and all had developed mixed (i.e., private and state-owned) industrial sectors protected by high tariff walls when the strongest international pressures for liberalization arose. This chapter extends the analytical framework to study adjustment trajectories in the other major countries of the Iberian world that underwent extensive neoliberal reform in roughly the same period: Brazil (1990–2002), Peru (1990–2000), Portugal (1985–95), and Mexico (1982–94).

As argued in the introductory chapter, the major Iberian-American countries can be essentially grouped into three models or paths to economic liberalization. The models are based on the policymaking strategies and compensatory measures (or lack of thereof) employed to make adjustment politically viable. Governments rewarded some of the "potential losers" of market liberalization: protected firms, unions and union-backed workers in the formal sector (ISI insiders), or the atomized poor in the informal sector (outsiders). Compensatory mechanisms were broadly divided into two types: subsidies, such as monetary infusions and soft credits, and market-share compensation, that is, those arrangements, such as the direct handout of state assets, the sanction of tariff regimes, barriers to entry, or the preservation of labor laws inducements, that grant market niches and serve to strengthen the role of established ISI business and labor actors in future open markets.

Statist and Corporatist variants focused compensation on what I have called ISI insiders (protected businesses and formal workers), though in different ways. In Brazil, as in the Spanish Statist model, the administrations of Presidents Collor, Franco, and Cardoso (1990–2002) redesigned strategic industrial sectors from above in a *dirigiste* manner and aided ailing firms using subsidy compensation principally channeled through the developmental bank BNDES.

Comparative Perspectives in Ibero-America

TABLE 9.1. *Extending the Argument: Models of Economic Liberalization in Ibero-America*

	Statist Spain (1982–96) Brazil (1990–2002)	Corporatist Argentina (1989–99) Portugal (1985–95)	Market Chile (1973–89) Peru (1990–2000)	Mixed Mexico (1982–94)
Policymaking Style	State *Dirigisme* (centralized formulation, negotiated implementation)	Concertation	Unilateral State Imposition	Concertation/ Imposition
Main Compensatory Measure	Subsidy	Market Share (partial deregulation/ state assets)	Subsidy	Subsidy/ Market Share
Main Actor Compensated	ISI Insiders (industrial firms/ groups and laid-off workers)	ISI Insiders (industrial firms/groups and national unions)	ISI Outsiders (atomized informal poor)	ISI Firms/ Groups, Unions, *and* Atomized Informal Poor

Neoliberal reformers developed adversarial relations with most ISI actors, particularly organized labor. Though reconversion plans in selected strategic sectors were largely formulated in a technocratic manner, the government was willing to negotiate implementation, especially regarding amount of compensation to affected workers and firms. Ostensibly, privatization in Brazil was not used to reward domestic, industry-based business groups massively. Rather, ownership was fragmented among local banks, construction groups, pension funds, and other institutional investors. As in Spain, sequential privatization (i.e., the gradual flotation of stock) allowed the state to achieve great leverage over emerging national champions such as the plane manufacturer Embraer, the flagship oil company Petrobras, and the mining-industrial giant Vale.

In a pattern that closely resembles Argentina's Corporatist path, the Portuguese adjusting government of Anibal Cavaco Silva (1985–95) administered market-share compensation (i.e., the allocation of state assets through privatization and the partial reform of the labor law) in the context of different forms of negotiation with local ISI business groups and national labor confederations. Domestic ISI business groups were largely empowered through privatization, and adjustment was accompanied by several rounds of concertation in which mainstream unions sought to protect past regulatory gains.

The political underpinnings of economic liberalization and industrial adjustment in Fujimori's Peru (1990–2000) essentially followed the Market path

Economic Liberalization: Brazil, Portugal, Peru, and Mexico

pioneered initially by Chile: unilateral imposition of liberal reforms by an Executive strongly backed by the financial sector, multilateral institutions, and international investors; little or no compensation to ISI insiders (domestic, industry-based business groups or companies and organized labor); and the deliberate and massive search for political support among the informal poor through targeted social programs. In short, the Market model in Peru excluded ISI insiders, while it focused its compensatory measures on the atomized poor. Mexico, finally, witnessed a Hybrid or "Mixed" strategy. The market-share deals and concertation with certain ISI business groups and unions were *combined* with the repressive imposition of adjustment on portions of labor and the courting of the informal poor through an extended antipoverty program, PRONASOL. Thus, while Statist, Corporatist, and Market models of economic liberalization concentrated compensation either on ISI insiders or on outsiders, Mexico is a Mixed case because neoliberal governments directed compensation to sectors of both.

The first part of the chapter introduces further methodological considerations in the general cross-country comparison. The second part analyzes the adjustment trajectories of Brazil, Portugal, Peru, and Mexico in the light of the compensation framework already presented in this study. The last part provides evidence to support the main hypotheses used earlier to analyze the three principal cases, namely, that the type of regime and the power of the prior ISI actors were decisive factors that conditioned policy choice and models of adjustment. For the analysis of the power of prior ISI actors, I proceed in the same way as in previous chapters. First, I analyze historically the qualitative evolution of both business and labor under the inward-oriented model and the causal factors that helped launch the countries on different liberalization paths. Subsequently, I propose a general quantitative assessment of their economic and organizational power at the onset of adjustment.

EXTENDING THE COMPARISON: METHODOLOGICAL CONSIDERATIONS

The theoretical framework presented is essentially constructed for cases of *extensive* market reform in mixed semiclosed economies, that is, those that carried out successful price stabilization, wide financial and commercial opening, and vast privatization. It is in these contexts where the question of political survival (in the case of state officials) and the need for compensation (in the case of private industrial firms, independent unions, and workers) arises more forcefully. A combination of initial recession and downsizing, the abrupt end of high tariffs and promotional regimes, and currency overvaluation threaten established business and labor groups, and neoliberal reformers may have incentives to compensate potential losers. What methodologists call the domain of causal homogeneity or frames of comparison (Munck 2004: 110; Collier and Mahoney 1996: 66–69) – that is, the range of cases to which the researcher presumes that hypothesis may have the same form and significance – would be given, then, by mixed,

260   *Comparative Perspectives in Ibero-America*

semiclosed economies that underwent at least a minimum of domestic market-oriented industrialization and, eventually, substantive neoliberal adjustment.

In a recent article on case selection, Mahoney and Goertz (2004: 660) distinguish between "scope conditions," that is, the assumed domain of causal homogeneity among units to be analyzed, and what they call "the possibility principle," the range of cases in which the outcome is simply possible, that is, there is a chance of having at least a "positive" result. In East Asia, late industrializers such as Taiwan and Korea developed domestic business groups that were largely export-oriented *before* the strongest pressures for liberalization arose – and depended less on the control of domestic markets. Therefore, the need for compensation was much less pressing. Eastern European economies, on the other hand, did not generate private unions or protected business groups independent of the state with analogous potential capacity to challenge incumbents or disrupt the neoliberal process.

Thus, following Mahoney and Goertz's approach, in Eastern Europe we may find positive and negative cases of compensation under neoliberal reform. Yet, private and independent ISI actors were almost nonexistent. Thus, the replication of the theory would fail to fulfill the assumption of unit homogeneity – despite the obvious theoretical relevance of the post-Communist experience for this book noted in Chapter 2. East Asian high-growth countries, in which there was no need for extended compensation given that the outward-oriented model was established before the 1980s, would be less relevant cases according to the possibility principle.

The most relevant cases to extend the comparison are, consequently, the other economies that had experienced widespread market liberalization in the Iberian world in the last two and a half decades, Brazil, Portugal, Mexico, and Peru, which, together with Argentina, Spain, and Chile, configure the major economies in the area.[1] Other good cases to test the explanatory framework further – following criteria of both scope conditions and the possibility principle – would be Greece and the Asian cases in which ISI was more extensive during the postwar period, such as Turkey or India.

As explained previously, this study argues that Spain, Argentina, and Chile constitute model cases of each adjustment path or type in terms of the policy-making strategy, the compensation scheme, and the actors targeted. In other words, they deploy more comprehensibly the features of each model, in the same way that in the advanced world Sweden often constitutes the model case of the social democratic welfare state or Germany and the United States exemplify more fully coordinated and liberal market economies, respectively (Esping-Andersen 1991, Stephens and Huber 2001, Hall and Soskice 2001). The cases of Brazil, Portugal, and Peru can be aptly taken as instances of the Statist, Corporatist, and Market models of adjustment, respectively. It could be argued,

---

[1] In the Index of Economic Freedom constructed by Gwartney et al. (2001) for the year 2000, all these cases are the major market reformers in Ibero-America measured on a 0–10 scale with scores that range from 5.8 (Brazil) to 7.5 (Chile).

Economic Liberalization: Brazil, Portugal, Peru, and Mexico

for example, that in Brazil Statist reconversion from above involved fewer industrial sectors than in Spain, or that in Portugal the divestiture of state assets as a compensation mechanism to national unions was less extended than in Argentina. However, these cases draw together the crucial elements in terms of the policymaking strategy, the type of compensation, and the potential losers targeted, to be placed in each category. One can identify nominal cutoff points that help in assigning cases to alternative types.[2] Essential criteria are whether privatization was compensatory vis-à-vis established ISI industrial groups or not, whether the government gave out significant subsidies to workers and industrial companies affected by liberalization, whether it negotiated bureaucratic payoffs with national unions, and whether the informal poor were massively targeted for national government–directed compensation or not.

Among the major Iberian-American countries, the adjustment trajectory of Mexico, however, does not fit any of three types constructed. In fact, Mexico under the presidencies of De la Madrid and Salinas presents not a uniform compensatory strategy or target, but a combination of unilateral imposition of adjustment policies, concertation with certain established ISI insiders, and alternative patterns of payoffs – that is, both market-share deals with organized actors and extended subsidies to the informal poor.

MODELS OF ECONOMIC LIBERALIZATION: BRAZIL, PORTUGAL, PERU, AND MEXICO

The Statist Path in Latin America: Subsidy Compensation and *Dirigisme* in Brazil (1990–2002)

Brazil's pattern of adjustment is an instance of the Statist model. The Statist path to economic liberalization, epitomized by Spain, includes a *dirigiste* style of policymaking – the reconversion from above of selected industrial sectors – and compensatory measures based on subsidies rather than on market share. Statist adjustment also involves a noncompensatory privatization process, that is, one in which ownership is more diversified among banks and institutional investors, and public assets are *not* deliberately geared to reward the established industrial business groups (or unions). The state empowers privatized national champions through golden share mechanisms and management supervision. Finally, this mode of adjustment is defined by an adversarial (but not openly repressive) relation with national unions, which tend to oppose the state-driven

---

[2] The idea of distinguishing cutoff points in typologies is discussed by the methodologists George and Bennett (2005: 236). As Mahoney (1999: 1158) argues, strategies of comparison based on the most similar systems design, such as the one presented in this book, involve nominal comparisons in which the alternative categories – in this case, mode of adjustment – are mutually exclusive. Of course, an ordinal comparison could also be introduced to measure the *degree* to which each mode is present, for example, Statism in Brazil and Spain. The book, however, concentrates primarily on assessing whether each case carries the minimal features to be conceptualized as generally Statist, Corporatist, or Market.

plans for industrial liberalization, combined with specific negotiations with base-level unions and workers on the conditions of plant closures or downsizing.

Economic liberalization and industrial adjustment in Brazil took off with the Collor administration (1989–92) and gained momentum under the Cardoso presidencies between 1995 and 2002. Under the administrations of Collor and Cardoso the government employed subsidies, channeled by the state developmental bank BNDES, as a way to soften the costs of adjustment for firms. Although a Spanish-style broad series of sectoral reconversion plans was not established, core ISI industrial sectors were transformed by the state in a *dirigiste* manner. In these strategic sectors the government established the number of future players and largely preserved state management and leverage in privatized "national champions."

Two important horizontal programs of industrial reconversion based on subsidies were the Brazilian Program of Productivity and Quality (PBQP), launched in 1990 as part of Collor's Industrial Competitive Program (PCI), and Finame, a program run by BNDES and oriented to financing capital goods purchases of firms undergoing reconversion (Carvalho and Bernardes 1998: 161, 210; Kingstone 1999: 214). Additionally, in 1996 BNDES opened a $1 billion credit line for firms undergoing the strains of adjustment in the sectors of shoes, textiles, auto parts, and furniture (Kingstone 1999: 222). More ad hoc but generous subsidized credits catered to important sectors under liberalization, especially to ISI secondary or basic industries such as pulp and paper (Bonelli 1998: 247). According to Kingstone (2001: 1004), "Collor and Cardoso used state finances to design policies that facilitated competitive adjustments." Similarly, Finchelstein (2010: 22) notes that "the Brazilian government used the bank [BNDES] as a tool to compensate for the more moderate role that the state should play under market reforms."

Graphs 9.1 and 9.2 show the evolution of BNDES lending during neoliberalism. The growth of the Brazilian National Development Bank's subsidized credits allocated to manufacturing, agriculture, services, and infrastructure during neoliberalism is remarkable (Graph 9.1). BNDES was lending around R$7 billion in 1995 (about $7 billion) when Cardoso took office and implemented a successful stabilization plan, and close to R$35 billion at the end of his second period in 2002, an outstanding 386% increase in real terms. Graph 9.2 shows the growth in disbursements for the manufacturing sectors in the years available, which is equally impressive.

Comprehensive, top-down reconversion and rationalization plans were put in place in industrial sectors considered strategic by the government such as steel, aluminum, pharmaceuticals, mining and related industries, oil, and aeronautics. The steel sector reconversion is probably the paradigmatic example of the Statist industrial adjustment in Brazil, well analyzed in Montero (1999). Montero argues that the steel privatization of 1990–94 represented "a deliberate strategy by a neo-developmentalist state to implement industrial policy" (p. 27). He notes the "very active role" (p. 32) of the state planners at BNDES in restructuring the public steel firms. Officials injected funds and carefully selected the pool of

Economic Liberalization: Brazil, Portugal, Peru, and Mexico

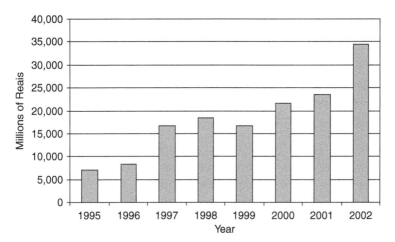

GRAPH 9.1. Brazil: Total BNDES Subsidized Lending during Neoliberalism (in millions of reais deflated by CPI). *Source*: BNDES, CPI from World Development Indicators Database, World Bank.

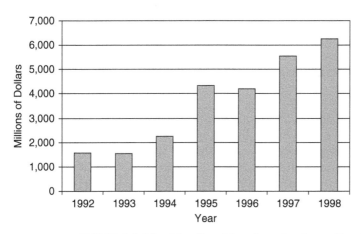

GRAPH 9.2. BNDES Subsidized Lending, Manufacturing Sector (in millions of dollars). *Source*: Andrade, Unpublished manuscript (2000).

prospective buyers, in an attempt to maximize the generation of domestic capacity and the competitive potential of the local steel mills. Unlike in Argentina, steel privatization was far from being driven by the interests of established private producers. In fact, in the largest privatizations, Usiminas and CSN, ownership was diversified among a group of investors with no previous stake in the sector such as the financial group Bozano and Nippon Steel (Usiminas), and the Vicunha group and the bank Bamerindus (CSN) (Montero 1999: 45; Manzetti 1999:

208).[3] Likewise, the government subsidized, through BNDES and other programs, the reconversion and downsizing of the state aeronautics giant Embraer, which had enormous potential for civil regional aviation and military training planes but was burdened by debt. Total subsidies to Embraer amounted to around $142 million from 1993 to 2000 (Schneider 2009b: 169; Goldstein 2002).

Indeed, the fact that privatization in Brazil, unlike in Argentina, Mexico, or Portugal, *was not* primarily geared to strengthening the main local ISI business groups in the context of economic opening has been repeatedly pointed out by analysts.[4] Some Brazilian industrial groups did, of course, participate as partners in some privatizations. However, the point is that unlike in the aforementioned countries, the neoliberal government did not cement an alliance with the main private ISI groups based on massive control of former state assets. Manzetti (1999: 167), for example, underscores the absence of market-share compensation in the Brazilian privatization process in the following terms: "Whereas in Argentina Menem clearly used privatization to reward supporters from big capital and some sectors of the labor movement, this is not quite as clear the case in Brazil."[5]

Very much as in Spain, the state carried out a sequential and gradual mode of industrial privatization, based on gradual stock offers. The major state industrial companies, such as the steel holdings, the aircraft manufacturer Embraer, the mining-industrial giant Vale Company (CVRD), and the oil monopoly Petrobras, were part of the National Program of Privatization (PND), started by Collor and continued by Cardoso. The divestiture program was heavily centralized at BNDES, which set the privatization plans in a technocratic manner, largely insulated from business and labor pressures (Goldstein and Schneider 2004: 55). The program diversified ownership among the main Brazilian banks and financial groups; some domestic industrial and, especially, construction-based groups; and the pension funds of the workers in the largest state companies. Thus, Embraer was acquired by a consortium formed by the financial group Bozano, the pension fund of Banco do Brasil, and the state company Telebras (Goldstein 2002). Indeed, the state, through BNDES (and its investment arm BNDESPar), remained an important actor in business. It still owned $34 billion in portfolio shares in thirty-one listed firms by 2008 (Schneider 2009b: 180). State intervention and empowerment through BNDES of these companies continued after

---

[3] The most powerful prereform domestic steel group, Gerdau, did acquire certain assets, yet "it was completely absent from the privatization of the largest companies" (Bonelli 1998: 274) and only marginally increased its market share beyond the steel subsectors in which it was operating before reform.

[4] Goldstein (1999: 673) notes that, unlike in Brazil, "in other countries of Latin America, such as Argentina and Mexico, the sell-off program led to the expansion of a limited number of business groups, whereas domestic banks and institutional investors played a much more subdued role." For arguments in the same vein see also Manzetti (1999: 193) and Bonelli (1998: 281).

[5] Schneider (2009b: 175) notes that, though certain family-owned Brazilian groups have invested in stakes in privatized firms, "they do not have the absolute control characteristic of group acquisition elsewhere."

Economic Liberalization: Brazil, Portugal, Peru, and Mexico 265

privatization. Unlike in Spain – where would-be internationalized national champions were mostly, though not only, built in the energy and telecom sectors – Brazilian bureaucrats focused on industrial commodities with the exception of Embraer.[6]

The Brazilian neoliberal governments faced the occasional reaction of private business[7] and the consistent opposition of labor. The main national labor confederation CUT ([Unified Central of Workers] union arm of the Workers' Party) contested the process of industrial adjustment and privatization from its onset in 1990. After three national strikes called by CUT in the first half of the 1990s, industrial action largely subsided. However, major episodes of labor conflict occurred in 1995 (when CUT workers on strike occupied the oil producer Petrobras subjected to partial privatization), in the state divestiture of the mining-industrial complex CVRD – where workers held a sixty-seven-day strike – and during the privatization of steel companies (see Rands Barros 1999: 46–55; Riethof 2002: 235).

Market-share compensation or bureaucratic side payments targeted at organized labor were largely absent in the political implementation of adjustment in Brazil. Attempts to involve the CUT in the privatization process consistently failed.[8] In the steel, mining, computing, and aeronautics sectors, downsizing took place largely before privatization, and BNDES subsidized workers' compensation and employees' purchase of shares, against the will of unions. Moreover, as in the case of Spain, local unions often broke with national confederations to negotiate compensation to the laid-off base (Montero 1999: 49). The moderate and small Workers' Force (FO) union did support privatization in exchange for shares in the privatization of the steel mill CSN – one of the few examples of market-share compensation that catered to organized labor in Brazil. But even this move was severely contested by CUT (see Montero 1999 and esp. Riethof 2002: 241). In brief, the Brazilian market reformers confronted national unions and only attempted special compensation for the downsized workforce at the base, administered largely through BNDES. As in the Spanish case, the amount of compensation to laid-off workers ultimately depended on the alternative contestation capacity of the local unions from below. Finally, no major national,

---

[6] The Brazilian government established a tariff regime for the auto industry, which departs from the more general subsidy-based reconversion. However, as Laura Gómez Mera (2007) shows, the Brazilian automobile policy was largely a response to the protectionist regime enacted in Argentina in 1991 and was driven by the developmentalist wing of the Brazilian bureaucracy as well as by TNCs. Unlike in Argentina, it was not a market-share compensation essentially lobbied by domestic business from below. This case shows, however, that occasionally Statist liberalization can be combined with tariff regimes.

[7] Statist adjustment in Brazil included episodes of conflict with business, mainly around the pace of commercial liberalization. In 1996, business organizations staged an unprecedented demonstration in Brasilia demanding state aid in the context of adjustment and import liberalization; see Kingstone (1999: 215).

[8] Tafel and Boniface (2003: 327) write that organized labor "was denied compelling incentives (that is government inducements) to cooperate with economic reforms. Not surprisingly, the CUT remained a consistent obstacle to the reform process in Brazil."

266   *Comparative Perspectives in Ibero-America*

informal sector–oriented antipoverty program of the significance of PRONASOL in Mexico, FONCONDES in Peru, or the PEM and other targeted programs in Chile was put in place during neoliberalism in Brazil, despite relatively minor welfare reforms (Draibe 2002: 122–23).

The Corporatist Path in Southern Europe: Concertation and Market-Share Compensation in Portugal (1985–95)

The Corporatist mode of market adjustment is defined by formal or informal concertation with ISI insiders in business and labor with market share as the main compensatory tool. Argentina is arguably the embodiment of this path. Portugal is the other Iberian country that is closest to the Corporatist pattern. In Portugal, Prime Minister Aníbal Cavaco Silva (1985–95) carried out a broad process of economic adjustment and structural reform as the country joined the European Union in 1986. After heading a minority government, Cavaco and his conservative Social Democratic Party (PSD) earned an absolute majority in 1987. The administration pushed forward constitutional reforms that revoked the nationalization principles dating from the 1974–75 revolution and paved the way for the largest privatization drive in Western Europe (measured as proceeds relative to GDP) for the period 1990–2001 (Clifton et al. 2003: 99). As in Spain, EU Structural Funds were used more in infrastructure investment in backward areas than in industrial reconversion and only arrived massively after 1994, when the worst part of adjustment was behind.

Indeed, analysts of the Portuguese neoliberal reform agree that the Cavaco government used privatization to strengthen the main national industrial business groups in the context of EU accession. Very much as in Argentina and Mexico, state divestiture in Portugal was a means to empower portions of the domestic industrial class in hostile times. Though some biddings and stock flotation were formally competitive, Clifton et al. (2003: 71–72) argue that through privatization the Portuguese government "helped to consolidate the main local economic groups." David Corkill (1999: 58) notes that the privatization disposals "proved extremely successful as large [local] economic groups vied to gain a position in profitable firms." Nunes and Montanheiro (1997: 70) go further to argue that privatization allowed for "the rebuilding of the Portuguese economic groups."[9]

The Champalimaud group, a large conglomerate originally based in the cement business under ISI, purchased an insurance company, an important state bank (Pinto & Soto Mayor), and a large stake of the state cement giant CIMPOR, and soon became a major player in the state oil monopoly Petrogal. The Mello group, originally based in the soap and petrochemical industries, obtained control of the

---

[9] The fact that privatization under Cavaco was fundamentally aimed at strengthening the domestic industrial groups has also been pointed out by Barnes (1995: 124) and Barreto and Naumann (1998: 404).

Economic Liberalization: Brazil, Portugal, Peru, and Mexico 267

shipyard Lisnave, the large state insurer Imperio, the tobacco firm Tabaqueria, and participation in Petrogal. SOGRAPE, a wine-based group, acquired the state-owned brewery Unicer. Furthermore, SONAE, a major group in the wood industry, expanded successfully into the pulp and paper sector through its participation in the state holding Portucel and took over state financial assets. Another prereform ISI group, Amorim (a world giant in the cork industry), was rewarded with the Banco Comercial Portugués and with a stake in Petrogal.[10] All these and other Portuguese family-owned ISI groups won assets in their former or related industrial sectors, as well as in financial or service companies. As we shall analyze later, all these Portuguese groups originated in the industrial sector under the inward-oriented model, though they later diversified, especially to finance. Some were dominant in the Salazar/Caetano authoritarian coalition (and were therefore more affected by the 1974 revolutionary attempt), some were newer, but all expanded market share and were equally empowered by Cavaco's privatization program.[11]

Economic liberalization in Portugal occurred in parallel to national concertation with organized labor around the partial reform of a heavily protective labor law. Between 1987 and 1995 Cavaco's neoliberal government and the dominant union General Confederation of Portuguese Workers (CGTP, linked to the Communist Party), plus the smaller General Workers' Union (UGT, independent), closed a series of agreements in the context of the Committee for Social Dialogue (CPCS). Unions negotiated an income policy and the preservation of a centralized system of collective bargaining (in particular, the provisions by which any agreement is in force until replaced by another more favorable to workers) in exchange for the tacit acceptance of flexibility of individual labor relations (i.e., rules governing layoffs) and acquiescence to the general marketization trend.[12] Plus, under the disadvantageous conditions of neoliberal restructuring, unions refused to revise prereform national/sectoral collective agreements. Most of them included significant advantages to unions and workers (Barreto and Naumann 1998: 416).

In other words, concertation with organized labor was cemented on the preservation of generous collective labor rights (bargaining centralization, state-enforced coverage and extension, automatic renewal of pro-labor prereform sectoral agreements) in exchange for the tacit consent to restructuring and

---

[10] In fact, a number of Portuguese traditional private groups (mainly Mello, Champalimaud, Amorim, and Espíritu Santo) formed an investment holding, Petrocontrol, and acquired 45% and veto power in the former state oil monopoly. Petrogal would later become the energy holding Galp and would be completely privatized.

[11] For the configuration of prereform Portuguese business groups, Rodriguez and Mendonca's "Os Novos Grupos Económicos" (1989) is essential. The traditional group Espíritu Santo, which also expanded via privatization, had financial origins but diversified heavily into industry and colonial commodity trade under ISI. The data on the results of privatization are taken from Clifton et al. (2003), Corkill (1994), and Barnes (1995) and company profiles of Amorim, Sonae, and Champalimaud.

[12] See Barreto and Naumann (1998) and Dornelas (2003).

268   *Comparative Perspectives in Ibero-America*

some degree of flexibility in the law on dismissals. Indeed, analysts underscore the rise of "neocorporatist" bargaining and the "institutionalization of social concertation" amid Portugal's process of neoliberal reform and the subsequent "maintenance of corporatist arrangements" (Stoleroff 1992: 119; Dornelas 2003: 136). Finally, as in Argentina, neoliberal restructuring in Portugal witnessed relatively low levels of industrial conflict, which was prevented by the concertation with national unions under the umbrella of the CPCS. In the words of the industrial relations analysts Barreto and Naumann (1998: 396) during this period, "Tripartite national negotiations . . . functioned primarily as a means of gaining political acceptance for the overall process of liberalization and restructuring."

The Market Path in the Andes: Unilateral Imposition and Subsidy Compensation to the Informal Poor in Peru (1990–2000)

The Market model of adjustment pioneered by Chile was defined by relentless and unilateral state imposition of economic liberalization, no compensation and marginalization of the ISI private actors in business and labor, and extensive compensation and political courting of the unorganized informal poor through targeted social policy. Peru's market transformation under President Alberto Fujimori between 1990 and 2000 closely resembles the Market model. Soon after taking office, Fujimori, who won the 1990 elections as an independent against both the populist Indo-American Popular Revolutionary Alliance (APRA) and the traditional Right, launched a harsh stabilization plan. This "shock therapy" (implemented in the midst of a hyperinflation spurt and a severe fiscal crisis) was later complemented by a sweeping tariff reform, by financial and exchange rate liberalization, and by an ambitious privatization program. Facing mounting opposition from Congress to his project of market reform, Fujimori staged a "self-coup" in April 1992 in close alliance with the military. Congress was shut down and replaced by one made up of supporters, and the judiciary was purged (Arce 2005: 35–40).

Few would dispute that "unilateral state imposition" aptly describes the policy formula under which adjustment was implemented in Peru. Overall, the business sector applauded Fujimori's policy turn and his tough stance against terrorism. Yet domestic capitalists had initially little leeway to protest the aspects of the plan that hurt them most, such as the radical tariff reform and the recession triggered by shock therapy. After the *autogolpe*, with the appointment of Jorge Camet – a man from the National Confederation of Private Business (CONFIEP), the national association which encompasses the main economic activities – as minister of finance in 1993, the business sector stepped in. However, CONFIEP was largely dominated by the banking association and by traditional exporters in fishing and mining. The industry associations that represented most sectors of ISI production were more critical of the government and increasingly marginalized from both policy circles and CONFIEP (see Arce

Economic Liberalization: Brazil, Portugal, Peru, and Mexico

2005: 46; Castillo and Quispe 1996: 60–61; Durand 2002: 328). Likewise, the support of international financial institutions continued unabated after the coup (Stokes 1997: 219).[13]

More crucially, as initially in Chile, privatization in Peru – the quintessential form of market-share compensation – largely bypassed domestic industrial interests and mainly privileged financial and international investors. As Manzetti (1999: 250) puts it, drawing a key contrast with Argentina: "To what extent Fujimori used state divestiture to reward supporters remains unclear.... Unlike Menem, the Peruvian President did not ally himself with the big economic groups and instead dealt with them from a position of strength." Domestic business was sidelined in the big industrial privatizations, such as the mining giant Hierro-Perú (awarded to a Chinese consortium), the Cerro Verde copper mine, the steelmaker SiderPerú, the oil fleet Petromar, and the largest copper refineries, which all became controlled by international investors. In the largest nonindustrial divestitures, the telecom and electricity monopolies and the state bank Continental, the role played by domestic business groups was almost nil (Manzetti 1999; see also Arce 2005: 43). Of course, the policy exclusion and undermining of organized labor were even more flagrant. As Cook's comparative study of labor reform under neoliberalism asserts, the constraints on labor rights in Chile and Peru were "among the most severe in the region" (Cook 2007: 116).

Still, as in Chile's Market model, economic liberalization in Peru was not simply a matter of financial capital imposition. Fujimori's government sought to mitigate the costs of adjustment through a massive poverty-alleviation program. FONCONDES was set up in 1991, and, along the lines of the Chilean antipoverty initiatives, it became a showcase of the "new" type of social policy targeted at the informal poor and backed by the World Bank. From 1991 FONCONDES invested more than $1.5 billion in community projects, which included nutrition, infrastructure, and credit and employment schemes (Arce 2005: 107). Though it is often praised for its capacity to reach the extreme poor, there is wide agreement among analysts that FONCONDES was manipulated to enhance the political and electoral prospects of Fujimori and his project of market transformation. The fund was created as an autonomous body outside the traditional line ministries, and the director and board reported directly to the presidency. Indeed, despite their different methodological assessment of the programs' politics, Schady (2000: 303), Roberts and Arce (1998: 233–34), and Graham and Kane (1998: 99) conclude that the program was exploited to Fujimori's political advantage.

---

[13] Indeed, after 1998 CONFIEP was increasingly divided as a result of the pressure of industrial interests and exporters of nontraditional goods, who began to distance themselves from the government. The situation by then was essentially similar to that of neoliberal Chile in 1982, when traditional industrial groups, sidelined and hurt by the exchange rate regime and prior adjustment, threatened to join the opposition. Of course, the Pinochet regime managed to achieve a new coalitional equilibrium, and Fujimori did not.

A "Mixed" Model of Economic Liberalization: Market-Share Compensation and the Targeting of the Informal Poor in Mexico (1982–94)

Mexico in the liberalizing period 1982–94 constitutes a "Mixed" case in terms of the framework constructed in this study. I have argued that both the Statist and Corporatist models of adjustment focus compensation (though in different ways) primarily on the organized actors of the ISI model. The Market model, by contrast, excludes and/or represses ISI insiders. It concentrates its compensatory measures on the atomized poor of the informal sector through national, top-down-run targeted programs. In Mexico, however, the political sustainability of neoliberal reform was sought through a mixed strategy. On the one hand, certain ISI actors (both allied labor and, particularly, domestic ISI business groups) were rewarded with market-share compensation. On the other hand, a massive poverty alleviation program oriented to the informal poor was combined with state repression on labor dissenters' factions.

Thus, Mexican reformers from the PRI (the hegemonic party in Mexican politics until 1997) seem to have used a *combination* of the compensatory strategies that prevailed in the other cases studied in this book. In the wake of the debt crisis, stabilization measures under the De la Madrid presidency (1982–88), which involved wage pacts and concertation with business and organized labor, were soon complemented by privatization and tariff and financial reform. The Salinas administration (1988–94) plunged ahead with even more widespread privatization and sectoral deregulation. Market reformers in Mexico opened the economy to unprecedented foreign commercial and financial flows. At the same time, however, they rewarded a number of domestic industrial groups in a way unmatched in the rest of Latin America with the exception of Argentina. Privatization was carried out under "very favorable" conditions for buyers among the large and traditional family-owned Mexican groups[14] such as Visa, Cemex, Alfa, Vitro-Cydsa, Minera Mexico, and Desc. These conglomerates were diversified but mostly based on consumer and intermediate goods and mining. The divestiture program and the partial deregulation of certain markets enabled the national business groups to concentrate their market share in the "same sectors in which they produced before reform" (Garrido 1998: 418), at the same time that they expanded to other businesses.[15] After privatization, the major established national groups became the dominant nucleus of the Mexican economy (Garrido 1998: 403; Teichman 1995: 187; Valdés 1994: 234).

The local industrial groups also dominated the main business associations and obtained favorable conditions and a number of protections (i.e., partial

---

[14] In the same way as in Portugal, but to a lesser extent than in Argentina, these family-owned industrial groups are often intertwined in a dense web of cross-shareholding and company boards.

[15] Some newer groups, notably the Carso conglomerate owned by the millionaire Carlos Slim, also climbed to the top in the midst of the reform process (Garrido 1998: 411). The Carso group, however, originated in finance and not in industry under ISI. It expanded massively after its control of the privatized telecom Telmex.

Economic Liberalization: Brazil, Portugal, Peru, and Mexico 271

deregulation) in the NAFTA agreements, in whose negotiations they had privileged access (Thacker 2004).[16] Some of these conglomerates had been deprived of their financial assets by the 1982 bank nationalization. Thus, privatization of the banking sector under Salinas enabled the restoration of their sundered ties with the financial world. For example, Visa (originally based on beverages and purchaser of state sugar refineries) and Vitro-Cydsa (glass and synthetic fibers) acquired Bancomer and Serfin, respectively, the second and third banks privatized in terms of purchase value. The owners of Minera Mexico, the largest private mining group in Mexico, which had taken over the historic Cananea state complex, became associated with Multibanco Comermex, the fourth bank in terms of privatization value. The petrochemical-based Desc took over the fifth bank, Banco Mexicano Somex (see Garrido 1998, Morera 2002).

The interaction with popular actors was more complex. Adjustment in Mexico involved repression and control from above of organized labor. The government utilized various mechanisms to quell labor dissent: it banned strikes, unilaterally broke prereform collective contracts, and harassed opposition labor dissenters. It also employed outright military repression to crack down on base-level protests in the cases of the steel mill Fundidora Monterrey and the Cananea mining complex. In a show of force intended to discipline labor, in 1989 the military occupied the PEMEX union headquarters and arrested the leader of the petroleum workers, La Quina, and more than forty of his cohort. The fallen leader had contested the opening of the petrochemical sector (Teichman 1995: 116, 124–25).

At the same time, however, the government employed various forms of market-share compensation aimed at the portions of the labor movement that aligned with the liberalization project: it negotiated with the CTM (the dominant PRI confederation) only minor reforms of the corporatist labor code and workers' affiliation with the official unions in many of the new FDI projects, especially in the booming auto sector (Middlebrook 1995: 275). It also expanded the Workers Bank, through which the CTM gained control of 400 firms, and only partially deregulated INFONAVIT, the state agency for low-cost housing, which after negotiations continued to be controlled by the CTM (Burgess 2004: 76, 87).[17]

Finally, political sustainability of neoliberal reform in Mexico crucially involved a massive poverty alleviation program. PRONASOL was modeled on the new type of "demand-driven" and targeted neoliberal social policy. As did the Peruvian FONCONDES (and, before, the Chilean antipoverty initiatives),[18]

---

[16] For the use of partial deregulation in the cement sector to protect the local group Cemex see the eloquent account in Schrank (2005).

[17] In words of Burgess (2004: 76–77) these "*organizational rewards* [my italics] ... came nowhere near to compensating workers for their generalized loss of income, but they provided CTM leaders with resources for sustaining the loyalty of key subordinates."

[18] Kurtz (2002: 307) explicitly links the redirection of antipoverty policy in Mexico with the prior Chilean experience: "In intellectual terms, it also borrowed from the Chilean military's approach to rendering social and economic policy consistent by utilizing private agents where possible and emphasizing the perfection of the market function."

it depended directly on the presidency, bypassing traditional bureaucratic agencies and party and union constituencies. PRONASOL implied a shift of resources away from the more urban-based and "universal" social policy to poorer and rural sectors. The program, set up in 1988, included a wide variety of projects in the domains of food support, infrastructure, and social services. In addition to providing a safety net in times of adjustment and distress, PRONASOL served the Salinas administration with two more specific goals. The first was to diffuse social discontent in the areas where the opposition had grown in the 1988 elections. Second, Salinas used PRONASOL to strengthen his technocratic, reform-minded project within the PRI, displacing both the regional elites[19] and the party "sectors" (e.g., labor) more wedded to the inward-oriented model (Dresser 1994; Cornelius et al. 1994: 12–14; Burgess 2004: 79; Magaloni 2008: 126). Judith Teichman (1995: 183) captures well the duality of the Mexican neoliberal government strategy vis-à-vis the popular sectors underlined in this book, when she asserts that "the new clientelism [i.e., PRONASOL] had to be supplemented with various forms of violent repression."

EXPLAINING ECONOMIC LIBERALIZATION PATHS: REGIME TYPE, ANTECEDENT TRAJECTORIES, AND POWER OF PRIOR ISI ACTORS IN IBERO-AMERICA

Two issues should be clarified at this point. First, as already mentioned in the overview chapter, I study the *dominant* strategy of compensation under neoliberalism in each case. In other words, Argentina and Brazil, for example, did develop some informal sector–oriented poverty alleviation programs partially funded by the World Bank during adjustment. But they were minor in size and impact. Indeed, both countries substantially expanded subsidies to the informal poor through national targeted programs in the *postliberalization* periods of Presidents Lula and Duhalde/Kirchner. By contrast, in the cases of Chile, Peru, and Mexico, massive antipoverty programs were developed extensively as safety nets – and became a central part of a national political strategy – *during* the main period of neoliberal adjustment. Likewise, one may find minor episodes of alternative forms of compensation (a differential tariff regime for a specific industry, an antidumping measure, or the subsidization of a certain firm) in various countries. Yet the main responses are clearly identifiable and produced alternative models of adjustment.

Second, the book focuses on the political winners in each case, that is, those groups directly favored by the state. The fact that local ISI business groups were not extensively targeted for compensation through market share in Spain, Chile, Peru, or Brazil in the way they were in Argentina, Mexico, and Portugal might not preclude the remarkable expansion of some of them

---

[19] For an excellent account of how Salinas utilized PRONASOL to wage the battle against the PRI old guard in different Mexican states see Kaufman and Trejo (1997).

Economic Liberalization: Brazil, Portugal, Peru, and Mexico 273

during neoliberalism. Economic liberalization tends to favor concentrated capital everywhere, and portions of it may win even without direct political compensation.

What accounts for each liberalization mode? The theory presented in Chapter 2 was summarized in the following hypotheses concerning the likely policy choices of neoliberal reformers and business and labor actors.

> **Hypothesis 1:** *Democratic reformers prioritized compensation (of any kind) to the organized actors of the ISI model, that is, protected business and unions or union-represented workers. Authoritarian neoliberals could bypass (costly) compensation to the organized ISI actors and were left with the informal poor as the main arena to cultivate some form of mass support.*

> **Hypothesis 2a:** *When domestic ISI business groups/firms were economically strong vis-à-vis the state and growing in the years prior to reform, they were more likely to engage in concertational/negotiated policymaking and lobbied for market-share compensation (state assets and partial deregulation) as the main compensatory measure. Weak domestic ISI business groups/firms in relation to the state, in decline before reform, were more likely to be subjected to state plans and could only demand subsidies or were left to their fate.*

> **Hypothesis 2b:** *Organizationally strong national unions (monopolistic and centralized) made negotiated/concertational policymaking more likely and lobbied for market-share compensation (state assets and partial deregulation, especially of the labor law). Organizationally weak, that is, plural and decentralized, unions contested adjustment and demanded subsidies for the laid-off base.*

These hypotheses combined to produce alternative liberalization models. Democracy is essential to understanding the Statist and Corporatist models in which most of the compensatory measures went to the ISI insiders. In plainly open and competitive polities, the organized actors of the inward-oriented model, business and unions, have the institutional means to pressure and lobby the government in the advent of adjustment. By contrast, authoritarianism allows neoliberal reformers in the Market mode to ignore costly demands from organized actors, to take resources from the established parties and unions linked to the ISI model, and to utilize them to compensate the atomized, informal poor.

In addition, the power of prior ISI actors (Hypotheses 2a and 2b) further shaped the compensatory mechanisms. In Argentina's and Portugal's Corporatist model, economically powerful ISI business groups and centralized national unions were rewarded with market-share compensation, that is, state assets and partial deregulation of certain industries and the labor law. Domestic, family-owned industrial groups had expanded heavily in relation to a relatively weak state in the run-up to neoliberal reform and boasted the financial power and economic scale to pressure for compensation in the form of privatized state assets. Relatively centralized and organizationally strong labor movements negotiated the preservation of generous collective labor rights (bargaining centralization, automatic renewal of contracts, pro-labor prereform collective agreements) in exchange for their general acquiescence to restructuring.

In the Statist models of Spain and Brazil, top-down plans and subsidies appeased ailing ISI firms. Family industrial groups were relatively weak in relation to a powerful state, which under ISI dominated core production sectors and had generated the bureaucratic capacity to direct industrial adjustment from above. At the same time, plural union movements made concertational policy-making more difficult to coordinate. The low levels of union bureaucratization and prior labor institutional inducements reduced the room for organizational payoffs of the sort that one finds in the Corporatist path. In Spain and Brazil the modern labor movement was essentially built bottom-up out of a clandestine struggle under ISI, and compensation depended on the capacity of local and plant-level unions to demand compensation to laid-off workers from below.

Finally, the weak nature of ISI industrial and labor groups in the Market model of Peru and Chile reinforced the pattern of authoritarian exclusion and emasculated any resistance to neoliberalism. In Mexico, however, we find a Mixed or Hybrid model, in which both ISI insiders and outsiders were compensated. Historically powerful family business industrial groups and portions of a heavily centralized and bureaucratized labor movement obtained market-share compensation. Yet, authoritarianism also enabled a repressive and selective imposition of adjustment on rebellious sectors of the labor movement and the establishment of a massive informal sector–oriented antipoverty program that largely bypassed the partisan and labor interests more associated with ISI.

In the next two sections I provide evidence to support the view that the political regime and the power of the prior ISI actors in labor and business are decisive factors that shaped each model of adjustment. I proceed in the same way I did in the analysis on Spain, Argentina, and Chile in previous chapters. First, I establish how the type of regime drove alternative patterns of compensatory schemes under neoliberal adjustment. Second, I trace historically the emergence of alternative patterns of economic actors (state firms, private business groups, and organized labor) in the postwar industrial development of each country. Finally, I propose a quantitative measure of the strength of the prior ISI actors, and I further analyze the influence of this variable in the configuration of alternative modes of adjustment. Table 9.2 summarizes the argument that follows.

Political Regime and Models of Economic Liberalization in Ibero-America

Under fully democratic and competitive regimes, such as those of Brazil, Argentina, Spain, and Portugal, neoliberals tend to prioritize and privilege the organized actors of the ISI model for compensation. In contexts of extended civil liberties, domestic business and organized labor – the ISI insiders – have a more developed potential to endanger the liberalization process through strikes and other forms of disruption and through lobbying. Even in Statist transformations (where I argue that business and organized labor were economically and organizationally weaker and more subordinated) democratic governments cannot

TABLE 9.2. *Models of Economic Liberalization in Ibero-America: Historical Trajectories and Explanatory Factors*

Models of Adjustment	Statist Spain (1982–96) Brazil (1990–2002)	Corporatist Argentina (1989–99) Portugal (1985–95)	Market Chile (1973–89) Peru (1990–2000)	Mixed Mexico (1982–94)
Antecedent Conditions (ISI)				
Mode of Late Industrialization	State-Led	Business Groups–Led	State-led	Business Groups–Led
Mode of Labor Organizational Development	State-Controlled	Argentina: Labor-Based Populism Portugal: State-Controlled (prior to 1974), Labor-Based Communism (after 1974)	Electoral/Partisan Leftist Radicalization	Labor-Based Populism
Explanatory Factors				
Power of Prior ISI Actors Business Labor	Weak: Subordinated Industrial Bourgeoisie Weak: Plural/Decentralized	Strong: Dominant Industrial Bourgeoisie Strong: Corporatist/ Centralized	Weak: Subordinated Industrial Bourgeoisie Weak: Plural/Decentralized	Strong: Dominant Industrial Bourgeoisie Strong: Corporatist/ Centralized
Type of Regime	Democratic	Democratic	Authoritarian	Authoritarian
Outcome	Rewards Domestic Industrial Firms and Laid-off Workers with Reconversion Plans and Subsidies	Rewards Domestic Industrial Firms and *National* Unions with Market-Share Compensation	Excludes/Represses ISI Actors and Rewards Informal Poor through Targeted Programs	*Combines* Market-Share Compensation to ISI Actors with Labor Repression and Programs Targeted to the Informal Poor

276 *Comparative Perspectives in Ibero-America*

simply let entire industrial sectors fall apart. In more authoritarian settings, neoliberal reformers tend to have more leeway to pay attention only to their "natural" allies in the financial sector and multilateral institutions and tend to avoid costly compensation to the main foes of neoliberalism: protected industry and organized labor. Death squads associated with the regime in both Chile and Peru assassinated top labor leaders who explicitly opposed neoliberal labor and economic reforms, Tucapel Giménez, head of the Chilean civil service workers, and Pedro Huillca, secretary general of the Peruvian workers' confederation (CGTP).[20] If murder is an option, compensation to those actors is obviously less likely to be on the table.

Naturally, the authoritarian neoliberal governments of Chile, Peru, and Mexico differed in their type and in their degree of repression. Yet the three of them fundamentally restricted democratic accountability, civil liberties, and competition. The authoritarian and repressive character of Fujimori's regime should not be underestimated. In the words of Durand (2002: 327), "What began as a delegative democracy degenerated into an undisguised dictatorship." With respect to Mexico, Teichman (2001: 191) asserts that "the most extreme case of authoritarian imposition of reforms (aside from Chile under military rule) is that of Mexico under the Presidency of Carlos Salinas."

That said, few governments tend to rely only on coercion. Indeed, the last quarter of the twentieth century was not only a period of economic internationalization but also of global democratization, a fact that did not escape the most lucid minds in these nondemocratic regimes. Moreover, in all these authoritarian neoliberal regimes some form of national elections took place – if obviously under various degrees of manipulation and coercion. Chapter 8 noted the referendums held in Pinochet's Chile in 1978, 1980, and 1988. Fujimori also sought to revalidate his authoritarian rule in the ballot box; elections were held for the Constitutional Convention in 1993 and for the presidency in 1995. Controlled elections were, of course, also the norm in Mexico until 1997. In Chile and Peru military-backed reformers knew that some form of popular and electoral support was (or would be) needed for eventual political survival and that they could not seek it in the domain they were excluding and repressing (formal labor). Therefore, they chose the informal poor to build a constituency for the regime parties (UDI in Chile and Fujimori's Cambio 90 in Peru). Chilean neoliberals, as shown in Chapter 8, were more successful in institutionalizing the party among the poor than their Peruvian counterparts. Unlike Fujimori's, the Pinochet regime enjoyed the support of an organized group of civilian cadres from the outset – the alliance between the *gremialistas* and the Chicago economists studied in Chapter 8 – but the motives behind the different outcomes in neoliberal party creation exceed the scope of this book.

---

[20] See Chapter 8 on Tucapel Jiménez. Pedro Huillca was brutally murdered by the infamous Grupo Colina, Fujimori's death squad, December 18, 1992. See the report by the Center for Justice and International Law at www.cejil.org.

Economic Liberalization: Brazil, Portugal, Peru, and Mexico

In short, authoritarian regimes in the last quarter of the twentieth century had a more pressing need to cultivate some form of mass support systematically than did more traditional dictatorships such as those of Salazar or Franco, especially in contexts of economic liberalization. The argument is not that democratic governments will be unable to pursue nationwide programs of informal poor-targeted social policy but that, in contexts of sweeping neoliberal adjustment, instability, and resource scarcity, democracies privilege the organized actors of the ISI model for compensation. Of course, democratic governments had even more pressing electoral needs. However, the "governability question" was prior to the "electoral question." In the democratic cases, compensation to the organized actors of the ISI model was important to govern the market transition, that is, to stay in office and preserve the general order (i.e., avoid labor strife and business lockouts or antigovernmental activity), rather than to win elections. Authoritarian neoliberals, less constrained by governability needs (at least in the short run), found it easier to deprive traditional ISI interests of the resources delivered to the extreme poor. This capacity to maneuver and divert resources away from the traditional popular actors is also seen in Mexico, where Salinas used PRONASOL both to strengthen his base within the PRI against the old "dinosaurs" and to seek new constituencies outside the PRI and formal labor. However, despite authoritarian controls, Mexican reformers (unlike their counterparts in Chile and Peru) were confronting relatively strong private actors in labor and, especially, in domestic industry, the loyalty of whom they could aspire to win through a different form of compensation. This takes us to our second decisive explanatory factor, the power of prior ISI actors.

The Power of Prior ISI Actors and Models of Economic Liberalization: Antecedent Trajectories

Industry: Family Business Groups or State Dominance?

The fundamental distinction that I draw in the business domain, already introduced in Chapter 2, is between those countries in which the state became a dominant actor as investor and owner in the industrial development under the inward-oriented model, or, by contrast, domestic private and family-owned business groups[21] performed as the main engines of industrial growth (see Table 9.2). In particular, the crucial question is whether industrial deepening away from the "easy" stage of ISI (food, textiles, and simple metal products) into basic or intermediate goods (e.g., oil, steel, petrochemicals and chemicals, cement, paper

---

[21] Leff's (1978: 663) classic article defines a business group as "a multicompany firm which transacts in different markets but which does so under common entrepreneurial and financial control." Most scholars agree that diversified economic groups emerge more typically in developing countries as a way to reduce uncertainty and cope with scarce capital. In the Iberian world they are typically family-controlled, and only a minor part of their shares are publicly traded. Most of the ISI business groups studied here originated in consumer or intermediate and basic goods but later diversified to a wide variety of sectors including finance.

278   *Comparative Perspectives in Ibero-America*

pulp, aluminum) and transport equipment (shipbuilding, cars, planes) was essentially pushed by the state or by private industrial *grupos*.[22]

Late industrialization in ISI economies can thus be classified as essentially state-led or business group–led. Though large industry-based business groups existed everywhere in the most developed countries of the Iberian world, they only became dominant in some countries. As implied by Hypothesis 2a, in those cases in which domestic private family groups became the hegemonic agents of industrial deepening during ISI (i.e., Argentina, Mexico, and Portugal), these local conglomerates would generate the economic power and political contacts to be compensated through market-share deals during neoliberalism. Conversely, where the state became the main force of inward-oriented industrialization, domestic industrial firms were either subsidized (Spain, Brazil) or largely marginalized (Chile, Peru) during neoliberalism. The "degree of dominance" of state and private industry will be measured quantitatively in the next section. Here, our task is to assess qualitatively the alternative historical configuration of business actors in the countries not studied in the previous empirical chapters: Brazil, Portugal, Peru, and Mexico.

PORTUGAL: THE HEGEMONY OF FAMILY GROUPS UNDER ISI. Baklanoff (1978: 178) has noted that under the Salazar/Caetano[23] dictatorship in Portugal (1928–74) state enterprises were notoriously absent from the manufacturing sector, and a handful of private business groups controlled industry in close alliance with the regime. In the same vein, Nancy Bermeo (1990: 139) observed that Salazar, unlike Franco, never backed the idea of state-led industrialization embodied in Spain by the public industrial holding INI analyzed in Chapter 3. The Portuguese industrial GDP rose significantly in the later stage of the Estado Novo, with growth rates that matched those of Spain.[24] But the tiny role of the state in production under ISI in Portugal was probably unmatched in the Iberian world.[25] The famous "seven families" dominated the economy. Economic groups such as CUF, Champalimaud, Borges, Espíritu Santo, Ultramarino, Fonseca, and Atlantico profited from their links to the regime, heavily expanded

---

[22] Classic works by Hirschman (1968), O'Donnell (1973), Collier (1979), and Evans (1979) have analyzed, particularly in Latin America, state intervention in late industrialization and the political determinants of the degree of "deepening." Though the role played by state, foreign, and local capital was central to many works, the issue was less systematically explored in comparative perspective.

[23] Salazar, founder of the Estado Novo authoritarian regime, suffered severe health problems and was replaced by Marcello Caetano in 1968.

[24] GDP grew at a yearly rate of 7.4% between 1968 and 1973 and industrial production by 9%. Between 1960 and 1973 the share of the labor force in the primary sector fell from 44% to 28%, while that of the secondary sector rose from 29% to 36% (Baklanoff 1992: 8).

[25] Baklanoff (1986: 257) writes that in postwar Portugal "not only were state enterprises conspicuous by their absence in the manufacturing sector, but private ownership totally dominated the railways, air transport, mining, electricity, petroleum refining and telecommunications."

[26] See Baklanoff (1978: 110) and Corkill (1993: 21). Borges and Espíritu Santo both had financial origins but held a substantial part of their assets in industry (see Rodrigues and Mendonca 1989). The major groups enjoyed direct access to the regime and largely bypassed the corporatist structures of Salazarismo, which essentially served as a buffer institution for the smaller and less modern sectors of business (Makler 1979: 159).

Economic Liberalization: Brazil, Portugal, Peru, and Mexico 279

into finance, and controlled the commodity commerce with the African colonies.[26] Paradigmatically, the largest ISI business group in Portugal, CUF (Union of Factories Company), owned by the Mello family, held interests in chemicals, petroleum refining, cellulose, tobacco, shipbuilding, and other industries. It was estimated to represent 20% of Portuguese manufacturing through its 186 subsidiaries and was the largest private business group in the Iberian Peninsula.

These groups would become dominant in the intermediate sectors of steel, petrochemicals and chemicals, glass, and cement. Thus, they were main targets of the nationalization policies of the revolution led by middle-rank military officers and the Communist Party that overthrew the Salazar/Caetano regime in 1974. Yet, the revolutionary impulse subsided in summer 1975, and by early 1976 the implicit alliance of the moderate Socialists of Soares and the conservatives consolidated power.[27] Thereafter, many industrialists who had fled to exile benefited from a policy of deintervention (Makler 1983). The old family oligarchy, however, had been partially broken up. Yet, a new breed of groups, "Os Novos Grupos Económicos" (see Rodriguez and Mendonca 1989), based in the nonnationalized sectors such as wood, cork, and wine, replaced the fallen families. In sum, the survivors of the nationalization of the mid-1970s (notably Mello, Espiritu Santo, and Champalimaud groups) plus the new economic groups such as SONAE (wood panels), Amorim (cork products), and SOGRAPE (wine), among others, would be largely rewarded by privatization policies as part of the Cavaco neoliberal coalition of the early 1990s.

MEXICO: THE RISE AND CONSOLIDATION OF THE MONTERREY ECONOMIC GROUPS. Mexico had experienced regional or cluster industrialization in the northern area of Monterrey since the late 1890s, before any Latin American country except Argentina. The Monterrey industrial base profited from its closeness to the U.S. market and access to cheap inputs (especially natural gas). Unlike most landholders in the area, as an urban and industry-based bourgeoisie, the Monterrey large industrialists weathered relatively well the winds of revolution between 1910 and 1920 (Cerutti 2002: 44–49). Thereafter, these northern groups became major beneficiaries of the strategies of growth predicated on tariffs and protection put in place by the PRI, the hegemonic party that grew out of the revolution. Mexican business groups evolved around mother companies in the consumer goods and incipient basic industries that could be traced back to the 1890–1930 period, and were linked by both family ties and interlocking directorates. Despite the protection granted by the state, the Monterrey groups would constitute the locus of the economic and often political opposition to the PRI in the second part of the twentieth century.[28]

---

[27] On the Portuguese transition to democracy and the defeat of the Communists in 1975 see especially Maxwell (1995).

[28] In the words of the historian R. Camp (1989: 212), in postrevolutionary Mexico "Monterrey personifies the private sector." From the 1950s the Monterrey groups actively supported the PAN (National Action Party), the right-wing political opposition to the regime.

280   *Comparative Perspectives in Ibero-America*

Yet the Mexican state also developed a sizable sector of parastate firms, articulated around NAFINSA (National Financial Company). NAFINSA was established in 1934 as a state developmental bank and became the major institutional arm of state production in industry. Though its initial goals were to foster public infrastructure and to supply cheap credit to the private sector, it soon invested in equity ownership and direct production. It encompassed important assets in the steel, fertilizer, motor-vehicle (DINA company), paper, sulfur, and sugar industries, among others.[29] Nevertheless scholars agree that state expansion never threatened the market leverage of the private *grupos*, which often lobbied successfully against NAFINSA's projects and never ceased to control most branches of basic industries with the exception of petroleum.[30] As Story's study (1986: 47, 67) of Mexican postwar economic policy asserts, in the late 1970s the domestic private sector enjoyed a "dominant position in relation to private foreign and public investment" and had "the edge" in most comparisons among these three sources of capital.[31]

What is more, the Mexican domestic industrial groups greatly benefited from a series of laws and regulations passed between 1970 and 1973 that controlled FDI, prevented foreign majority ownership in most joint ventures involving TNCs, and facilitated the formation of diversified holding companies with links to the banks.[32] In short, despite populist and expansionary measures of PRI governments before 1982 (especially during Luis Echeverria's presidency between 1970 and 1976), domestic economic groups became dominant in the run-up to the debt crisis. The largest ISI *grupos* had diversified heavily, especially to finance, since the 1950s. Among the most important were Visa (originally beer and food products), Alfa (flagship firm in the steel sector), Cydsa (primarily concentrated in chemicals), Cemex (cement), and Vitro (glass).[33] Mexican national groups were well represented by influential peak level organizations that often circumvented the Corporatist structures of representation mandated by law (Shadlen 2004: 92–100). Though some of the largest Mexican private

---

[29] For the origins of NAFINSA see Blair (1964); on its development as financier and owner see Bennett and Sharpe (1990), Story (1986), and Cypher (1990).

[30] The consistent lobbying of the private sector to counter NAFINSA's influence dates back to the period of President Miguel Alemán; see Blair (1964) and Cypher (1990: 49). For a more extensive, though partisan, treatment of this subject during the 1970s see the book by Rey Román (a former director of NAFINSA) significantly entitled *Business Offensive against State Intervention* (1987).

[31] Cypher's *State and Capital in Mexico* (1990: 97) notes that even though the number of enterprises created since the 1970s suggested a shift toward Statism, the value of those assets was modest, and most of the planning initiatives of the Echeverría and Lopez Portillo governments never took hold.

[32] These measures triggered a process of *Mexicanization*, by which domestic groups gained controlling stakes in numerous industrial companies formerly owned by foreign capital; see Cypher (1990: 96–101) and Story (1986: 58).

[33] In general, a single bank had ties with several economic groups through either equity shares or board participation. Traditional families such as Azcárraga, Garza Sada, and Zambrano were represented on the boards of various Monterrey holdings. The bibliography of the Mexican *grupos* is, of course, abundant; standard accounts are Camp (1989, esp. Chapter 8 for details of the family groups and sectors), Garrido (1998), and more recently Cerutti (2000).

Economic Liberalization: Brazil, Portugal, Peru, and Mexico 281

groups were affected by both the debt crises and the bank nationalization of 1982, they would be significantly empowered by market-share compensation in the neoliberal era.

BRAZIL: THE STATE AND BNDES ECLIPSE LOCAL INDUSTRIAL GROUPS. The ISI regime in Brazil deployed two characteristics that are not found in the rest of the Iberian world with the exception of Spain. First, the state engaged as direct producer in a wide variety of industrial sectors such as petroleum, petrochemicals, steel, aluminum, mining, complex transport equipment, pharmaceuticals and computers during the second part of the twentieth century. Initial public enterprise expansion in industry and mining took place during the Vargas era (1930–46), the original period of state consolidation and centralization in Brazil. In the early 1940s the Vargas government launched a series of ambitious industrial projects such as the state-owned steelmaker CSN (Companhia Siderúrgica Nacional), and CVRD (Companhia do Vale Rio Doce), which would become the largest mining company in the world. Petrobras, the oil monopoly, was created during the second Vargas presidency (1951–54). All these major initiatives were watersheds in the unfolding of economic nationalism in Brazil and were largely the result of the alliance between the centralizing elites of Varguismo and the military.[34]

Second, the ISI period in Brazil witnessed the rise of a powerful state development bank, BNDES, which performed both as financier and owner of industry and as an effective state planning agency. It was also established in the Vargas late period (1952) and would soon develop as a quite strong bureaucracy reputed for the quality of its cadres. Unlike the case of the Mexican NAFINSA just analyzed, BNDES enjoyed great bureaucratic autonomy both to recruit personnel and to decide which projects to finance.[35] In the first decades BNDES primarily funded state enterprises. Yet it also invested heavily in equity: in 1965 stock subscriptions accounted for one-third of BNDES operations and ultimately it would take over almost all the Brazilian steel sector. By 1978 BNDES supplied about 12% of total loans of the financial sector and was the second largest bank after the state-owned Bank of Brazil (Baer and Villela 1980: 430–31, 434).

These forms of state intervention through public holdings and through BNDES were carried to new heights by the military dictatorship of 1964–85. After the initial stabilization plan, the Brazilian generals put in place an expansionary economic policy based on the planning targets set by BNDES (which, as Baer and Villela [1980: 433] argue, under the military regime significantly increased its centrality in the state administration) and on the preeminent role

---

[34] See Wirth (1970) and Trebat (1983: 41–45). For a recent excellent review of the state role in those years see Kohli (2004: 152–65). As Wirth and others point out, many of these state initiatives were the result of the unwillingness of foreign private capital to invest. Yet they fit well with the pragmatic yet largely conservative-modernizing ideology of Vargas.

[35] Though its sources were debated, all main analysts agree on the great bureaucratic capacity and institutionalization of BNDES (before liberalization, BNDE) within the Brazilian state, and on its autonomy from the private sector. See Sikkink (1991: 201–02), Willis (1995: 627), and Schneider (1991: 36).

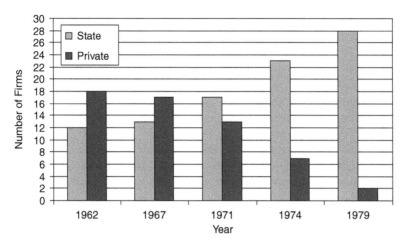

GRAPH 9.3. Brazil: Ownership Distribution of the 30 Largest Nonfinancial Firms, selected years. *Source*: Data from Trebat (1983: Table 3.6).

played by public enterprises. The military empowered state enterprises first and foremost by notably increasing managerial autonomy, especially for self-finance and price setting (Trebat 1983: 46–47). As described by Trebat (1983: 49), this period witnessed a revival of the alliance between public sector technicians and the military that was so important for the founding of state enterprises in the Vargas era. Embraer, the state producer of military and medium-sized commercial aircraft, became the embodiment of this new impulse.

The phenomenal increase in public ownership under the military regime can be seen in Graph 9.3. Most of it took place in the industrial sector through subsidiaries of CVRD (which by 1976 had expanded to shipping, paper pulp, aluminum, forestry, and other industries with about twenty-five subsidiaries and affiliates) and Petrobras (with about ten companies in the oil sector, petrochemicals, and fertilizers), and through BNDES's ventures. As Peter Evans (1979) notes in his classic study of Brazil, *Dependent Development*, during this period the rise of state enterprises vis-à-vis both foreign companies and, especially, domestic private groups stands out as the most important trend in manufacturing.[36]

Of course, ISI private economic groups also flourished in Brazil – among the main ones Votorantim (based in cement and metals), Cofap (motor vehicle parts), Vicunha (textiles), Klabin (paper and forestry), and Matarazzo (food). However, they paled in comparison with the growth of state industrial holdings in the run-up to the debt crises. Indeed, in view of the dominance of the state and

---

[36] The state share (percentage of assets) among the 300 largest manufacturing firms almost doubled between 1966 and 1972, from 17% to 30% (Evans 1979: 222). The dominance of the state in most branches of basic industry was almost complete. Indeed, Kohli (2004: 212) argues that Evans's model of dependent development based on the triple alliance of domestic, foreign capital, and the state "greatly exaggerates the role of Brazilian private capital."

Economic Liberalization: Brazil, Portugal, Peru, and Mexico

multinationals in Brazilian industry, large domestic private groups expanded more in the finance and construction sectors rather than in manufacturing (Evans 1979: 151). In his major book *Os Donos Do Brasil* (1984), the Brazilian researcher Geraldo Banas provides clear evidence of the central role that the Brazilian state played in heavy industry and of BNDES as *articulador da industrializacao*. Significantly, domestic business groups are barely mentioned in Banas's account of the economic weight of state, foreign, and domestic private industry.[37] These structural trends did not change significantly in the short period between the transition to democracy (1985) and the beginning of economic liberalization (1990).

In brief, the Statist Brazilian industrial adjustment in the 1990s, which included subsidies to ailing firms provided by BNDES, and a privatization model that diversified ownership to the local financial sector and preserved leverage of former state managers, should be understood in the light of this antecedent trajectory. Since the postwar period, and especially during the military regime of 1964–85, the main and most profitable public companies grew enormously in relation to the local industrial groups, making controlling takeovers by the domestic private sector during neoliberal reform more difficult.[38] Unlike in Spain – where private industrial groups were even weaker under ISI – some local prereform groups, notably Votorantim (based on cement) and Gerdau (steel), did expand with market reforms. Yet Schneider (2009b: 174) underscores the brokerage role of BNDES in facilitating and financing privatization to institutional investors (rather than to economic groups) as a key difference between Brazil and the other major countries of the region. BNDES and state companies consolidated their bureaucratic leverage over the public and private sectors under the inward-oriented model, setting the stage for subsidy-based and technocratic reconversion from above in core ISI sectors during the 1990s.

PERU: THE SUBORDINATION OF THE INDUSTRIAL BOURGEOISIE AFTER 1968. Finally, Peru is also a case where the ISI model generated relatively weak private industrial groups in relation to the state. Peruvian modern economic history prior to the neoliberal reform of the 1990s can be essentially divided into three stages. Until 1968, the economy was dominated by an indigenous landholding class of traditional exporters and by foreign companies that controlled most of the mining and oil sectors and portions of manufacturing.

---

[37] In a sample of local private business groups in 10 developing countries in 1990 (among them Korea, Mexico, India, and Turkey) constructed by Singh (1995: 45) Brazilian groups rank as the *weakest* in terms of Sales/Manufacturing Value Added ratio. Only two industry-based private conglomerates are mentioned as important in Banas's book, Votorantim, based on cement, and Matarazzo, based on food and agroindustry. However, Votorantim, unquestionably the major ISI Brazilian group, was probably not so large in relation to the local economy. For example, total asset value in relation to the domestic GDP for the major Argentine group Pérez Companc doubled Votorantim's numbers – calculated from Banas's figures and Pérez Companc's 1990 balance.

[38] For example, Coutinho and Rabelo (2003: 47) state that in the steel sector "the amount of capital required to purchase control blocks in the major firms was too large for the local investors alone." This argument could be easily extended to the case of the other state industrial giants.

284   *Comparative Perspectives in Ibero-America*

Though industrialization had spawned a local manufacturing class, foreign interests owned 40% of fixed assets in manufacturing and 62% of banking assets (Thorp and Bertram 1978: 295). This situation changed radically after the 1968 coup led by the reformist general Velasco Alvarado. The "Revolutionary Government of the Armed Forces" soon unveiled a massive program of state nationalizations and land reform, a project with both nationalistic and antioligarchic overtones that essentially sought to modernize Peruvian capitalism (Cotler 1975: 44).

The Velasco government virtually eliminated big private capital in agriculture, took over firms that belonged to international and domestic capital, and greatly expanded existing or newly created state companies. It established Petroperu after nationalizing International Petroleum and merging it with a small domestic refiner and created Hierro-Perú and Centromin out of the nationalization of foreign mining complexes. The state expansion in industry affected domestic owners more. The government took over the important fishing industry (extraction and transformation) and assumed control of almost all output in basic industries such as cement, paper, chemicals, and fertilizers, as well as shipbuilding and parts of the textile industry. It greatly expanded the state-owned facilities in the steel sector (Siderperú) and in the refining and marketing of mineral production. Finally, it strengthened public trading companies in the areas of industrial inputs and food and created a new state development bank, COFIDE (Corporation for Financial Development).[39]

Thus, if international and landholding capitalists were dominant in Peru until 1968, the state, not the local industrial bourgeoisie, replaced them as the leading economic player after 1968.[40] By 1975 the state was responsible for half of domestic investment, half of the mining output, half of the imports, and almost all exports in the country. The state controlled most basic and heavy industry. After the more moderate general Morales Bermúdez ousted Velazco in 1975, in a third stage of ISI development some of these trends were partially reversed, especially in the financial sector. Indeed, some scholars (Becker 1983, Durand 1994; see also Spalding 1994) claim that a new breed of domestic business groups was strengthened by the demise of traditional landholding families, the retreat of foreign capital before 1975, and the business-friendly policies of Morales Bermudez and his civilian democratic successor Belaúnde (1980–85). These domestic groups controlled the reprivatized financial system and diversified into the mining and manufacturing sectors. Yet they were essentially *financial* groups, and their diversified stakes in manufacturing were in light rather than in heavy industry, especially food and textiles (Durand 1994: 48, 62). According to Durand (1994: 74) the Peruvian Banking Association became the "organizational locus of the top Peruvian *grupos*."

[39] For the phenomenal state expansion in industry under Velasco see the detailed study by Fitzgerald (1979: esp. 191–95) and Durand (1994: 38–41).

[40] As characterized by a leading economic historian of Peru, E. V. K. Fitzgerald (1979: 136), "Asset ownership in Peru exhibited two distinct trends: the penetration of foreign enterprise and the retraction of domestic capital up to 1968, and the rapid expansion of the state sector to replace domestic capital after that date."

Economic Liberalization: Brazil, Portugal, Peru, and Mexico

To sum up, in Portugal and Mexico (as well as in Argentina), domestic industry-based family groups became crucial agents of inward-oriented industrialization, in particular in the industrial deepening into intermediate basic goods and occasionally mining and complex transport material. In Portugal, the Salazar/Caetano dictatorial regime, in contrast to that of Franco in Spain, simply eschewed state-led development from the outset, and the revolutionary coalition of 1974 was ephemeral in this respect. In Argentina and Mexico, the big domestic industrial bourgeoisie largely prevailed over successive populist and more ortho-dox administrations before the debt crisis. By contrast, in Brazil, Peru, and Chile, as well as in Spain, though private industrial groups had varying influence, the state took the lead and became the hegemonic agent of industrialization in the run-up to neoliberal reform, in particular in the same areas of basic industry mentioned. It is no accident that in the Latin American development literature of the 1970s, Peru (e.g., Cotler 1975: 53; Fitzgerald 1979: 190) and Brazil (Evans 1979: 270, 1982: 215) were central cases in the debates around the idea of "state capitalism," and Chile obviously became the embodiment of a Socialist developmental project.

The preneoliberal state dominance in industry that unfolded in Spain and Brazil was, however, qualitatively different from that of Chile and Peru. Indeed, Brazil and Spain, the two countries that implemented Statist models of economic liberalization in the Iberian world, share striking similarities in their ISI trajectories. Both countries had military-led and lasting bureaucratic-authoritarian (BA) regimes that held power until a few years before neoliberal reform. Plus, both successful BA regimes were strongly antilabor and had established a solid alliance with the United States that eased multilateral lending for their state-led industrial projects. Unlike Mexico or Argentina, where populism and polarization in the early 1970s erected more hurdles to TNC expansion, the friendly relation of Spain and Brazil's BA regimes with international capital helped to reinforce the penetration of foreign companies, and the corresponding relative weakness of domestic industrial capital. By contrast, the ISI statism that arose in Peru and Chile, especially under Velazco and Allende, was more populist in macroeconomic terms and socially inclusive rather than developmentalist. It was implemented in contexts of a smaller domestic market and industrial base. Though it also helped to weaken domestic private industry, it had less potential for Statist modes of neoliberal transformation.

Labor: Bureaucratic-Organizational Development under ISI
In the case of labor the central question concerns the type of organizational development under the inward-oriented model. Hypothesis 2b suggests that in countries such as Argentina, Portugal, and Mexico, in which labor movements grew centralized and achieved relatively high organizational power prior to reform, mainstream labor prioritized tripartite national concertation and market-share compensation (partial reform of relatively pro-labor collective

286 *Comparative Perspectives in Ibero-America*

labor laws and/or participation in privatization and other economic ventures) during neoliberalism. They also restrained industrial conflict at the base. Their fundamental goal was to preserve organizational capacity in hostile times. Conversely, where labor developed organizationally weaker, that is, more plural and decentralized during ISI, as in the democratic cases of Brazil and Spain, the relation with national union confederations was more adversarial in the period of market reforms. Weakly bureaucratized and bottom-up-structured national unions did not find organizational side payments so attractive. In these cases, compensation took the form of subsidies for the laid-off and essentially depended on the collective action capacity of unions at the local level. In Peru and Chile labor had also generated weak organizational structures under ISI, which made even easier the pattern of authoritarian imposition under neoliberalism. This section spells out the qualitative evolution of labor movements under ISI; the next section proposes a comparative quantitative measure of the organizational power of labor movements at the outset of neoliberal reform in the Iberian world.

I study labor movements under ISI in three dimensions that are key to understanding their organizational development and the eventual pattern of compensation during economic liberalization: (1) whether unions became central allies to a party that took effective control of state power prior to reform; (2) whether, as part of that governing coalition, labor obtained significant organizational inducements in the areas of collective labor law and financing;[41] (3) whether factory councils and shop-floor union bodies acquired some degree of institutional or factual power in the run-up to the liberalization period. In fact, the first two dimensions are closely related to what Collier and Collier (1991) have labeled "patterns of political incorporation," that is, the alternative ways in which governments addressed the inclusion of the urban working class in the national polity in the origins of industrialization.

MEXICO: LABOR-BASED POPULISM AND ORGANIZATIONAL CONSOLIDATION. The type of union organizational development under ISI in Mexico and Argentina (analyzed in Chapter 6) can be labeled as laborbased populism (Collier and Collier 1991). In Mexico, labor became a vital ally of the PRI, the hegemonic party that grew out of the revolutionary elites. The Federal Work Law passed in 1931 granted labor exclusion clauses that made union membership quasi-compulsory and the right to aggregate collective bargaining and to strike. Organized labor, active since the early days of the revolution, was largely empowered in the 1934–40 period, when President Cárdenas forged an alliance with unions in order to fight competing PRI leaders and the economic elite. Cárdenas fostered the creation of a new labor confederation, the

---

[41] Collier and Collier (1979: 969) have conceptualized the inducements that states can offer in terms of the "structuring" and "subsidy" of unions. Therefore, union structuring is shaped by the collective labor law and provisions such as monopoly or bargaining centralization, and subsidy refers to union capacity to obtain financial resources.

Economic Liberalization: Brazil, Portugal, Peru, and Mexico

CTM, which was assured a place in the PRI ruling coalition. As is well established in the literature, the labor framework originally enacted by the PRI also regulated several tools for union control: official recognition implied that the government could favor docile or pro-PRI unions, collective contracts were subjected to state approval, and strikes had to be allowed by tripartite "arbitration and concilia-tion" boards. Indeed, after the Cárdenas presidency the CTM became increas-ingly domesticated and labor demands were curbed in successive more centrist administrations.[42]

However, as Ruth Collier (1992: 50) has argued, though to some extent controlled from above and far from autonomous, labor was part of a populist settlement that had to be recrafted constantly under ISI.[43] As part of the "orga-nizational bargain" (Burgess 2004: 71) the PRI unions obtained financial benefits. In the first place, unions could collect mandatory union dues without direct state interference. Second, the CTM controlled two important sources of funds, INFONAVIT, a state agency in charge of popular housing construction, and the Workers' Bank, a financial outlet created by President López Portillo in 1977 to provide cheap credit for workers. In sum, despite official controls, the labor movement under ISI in Mexico was an important part of the ruling party: it could – occasionally – activate aggregate collective bargaining at the sectoral and national levels and managed important financial resources.[44] The counterpart to this national/sectoral bureaucratic activation was a very poor organization at the shop floor. Collective contracts were often negotiated by union leaders with-out workers' approval (and even before the majority of the workforce was actually hired). As in Argentina, unions under ISI consolidation in Mexico were largely external entities to the workplace. In the words of Graciela Bensusán (2000: 259), the fact that union representatives "were kept far from the places of work would be essential to impose unilateral decisions on restructuring in the 1980s."

PORTUGAL: FROM AUTHORITARIAN CORPORATISM TO LABOR-BASED COMMUNISM. Portugal also witnessed an organizational development under ISI that resulted in a labor movement relatively centralized and with weak shop-floor bodies. Portugal was initially a case of state-controlled unionism (Table 9.2). The Salazar dictatorship inaugurated in 1926 established one of the most institu-tionally complex Corporatist systems in the world. The system was based upon "syndical associations," a structure of licensed workers' organizations for the different occupations, which paralleled the *gremios*, the employers' associations for each branch of production. The goals of the *sindicatos* (in which membership was compulsory) were to control and depoliticize the workforce and to provide

---

[42] For comparative perspectives of labor empowerment under Cardenismo see R. Collier (1982) and Erickson and Middlebrook (1982).

[43] Two good examples are economic downturns of 1954 and 1976 in which the CTM pressured the PRI and the government and largely managed to extract wage concessions after currency deval-uations (Collier 1992: 47–48).

[44] Labor and the CTM also enjoyed representation in the management of the IMSS, the state agency in charge of social security and welfare for workers. Yet their control of INFONAVIT and the Workers' Bank was ostensibly higher (Burgess 2004: 66–67).

288   *Comparative Perspectives in Ibero-America*

welfare benefits. Of course, genuine national federations and confederations were outlawed, and strikes were legally banned.[45]

This organizational development began to change in 1969, when Salazar gave way to Caetano as head of the regime, and would be fundamentally altered with the 1974 revolution. In the context of industrial growth, Caetano established direct negotiations between employers and the *sindicatos*, although bargains remained subordinated to state decisions. Yet the promotion of some sort of genuine bargaining implied the need for meaningful labor representation, a fact that activated the dormant official unions (Williamson 1985: 113–14). By the early 1970s the opposition-sponsored Intersindical, a semiclandestine union confederation, was developed within the structure of the official unions. Intersindical soon became controlled by the powerful Portuguese Communist Party, basically the only social organization that had escaped repression and control under Salazar. Yet, unlike in Spain, where the Communists who controlled Comisiones Obreras were always marginal to state power under ISI, the Communist Party and Intersindical played a central role in the leftist coup that ousted the dictatorship in 1974 (Logan 1983: 144).

In the midst of a revolutionary upheaval strongly backed by the newly organized working class, the alliance between MFA (Movement of the Armed Forces) and the Communists ushered in a period of organized labor institutionalization. Labor legislation mushroomed: individual and collective dismissals were made very difficult, and strikes rights were tightened. Intersindical (later the CGTP, General Worker's Confederation of Portugal) won monopoly of representation and a compulsory check-off system of union dues, and constituted genuine industrial federations in place of the old official *sindicatos*. In addition, unionization was expanded to the public and agrarian sectors. The centralized system of collective bargaining was regenerated, now involving an independent and notably strengthened labor movement. Indeed a new series of sectoral collective bargaining rounds that favored labor was launched between 1977 and the early 1980s (Barreto and Naumann 1998: 409–09; Stoleroff 2001: 177). As Nataf (1995: 129) states, the Communist strategy "focused upon the union apparatus rather than the more decentralized organizations at the point of production." The contrast with the Spanish Communists, who, as analyzed in Chapter 6, essentially galvanized a decentralized, assembly-based union movement from below that eschewed bureaucratic-national organization, is remarkable.

Although some of the pro-CGTP provisions, such as monopoly of representation, were relaxed once the revolutionary impulse lost momentum, the legacy of the revolutionary period was a relatively centralized labor movement in which the dominant CGTP boasted the affiliation of 71% of unionized workers.[46] As in the other cases of Corporatism with high levels of inducements bestowed by a

---

[45] On the evolution of Portugal's Corporatism under ISI see Schmitter (1979) and Williamson (1985).

[46] According to Barreto and Naumann (1998: 418), "The role of government extensions [of collective contracts], the dominance of industry collective bargaining relative to company bargaining ... are legacies of the corporatist system."

Economic Liberalization: Brazil, Portugal, Peru, and Mexico 289

labor-based party in power, national-sectoral organizations largely prevailed over shop-floor bodies. Though plant-level works councils were legalized by the 1976 constitution, they remained largely ineffectual, becoming "a death letter in practice" (Barreto and Naumann 1998: 409). In Spain factory works councils legally enjoyed great independence from the national unions and financial autonomy – which, as shown in Chapters 6 and 7, is essential to explaining the flow of compensation to the base during the neoliberal transition. In Portugal, conversely, most internal factory commissions were inactive and depended on the sectoral trade union dominant in the company. Finally, the Portuguese labor movement was, however, less involved in the administration of social services than its counterparts in Argentina and Mexico under ISI, a condition that probably explains why the eventual pattern of market-share compensation was based more on the preservation of collective labor law inducements rather than business-type payoffs.

BRAZIL: INDEPENDENT UNIONISM FROM BELOW AND ORGANIZATIONAL WEAKNESS. As in Spain, in Brazil the labor movement had been tightly controlled by the state and depoliticized in most of the inward-oriented model (Table 9.2). Constraints on the formation of independent unions had precluded the structuring of a powerful national labor organization with at least *some* degree of autonomy vis-à-vis capitalists and the state. In the 1930s Vargas imposed an authoritarian Corporatist framework as part of his broader project of state power centralization. Scholars agree that Vargas never attempted to form a strong labor-based party as a vehicle for garnering popular support and confronting other elites (Ruth B. Collier 1982: 66; Erickson and Middlebrook 1982: 218). The Consolidation of Labor Laws Framework (CLT) passed in 1943 regulated unions with compulsory affiliation at the municipal, federal, and confederate levels that paralleled the organization of business interests by occupational category. Their mission was to provide social welfare services and collaborate with the government. Unlike in Mexico and Argentina (and Portugal after 1974), the state directly collected union dues and was legally empowered to freeze striking unions' accounts. It could also intervene in union internal affairs by appointing a delegate invoking minor legal pretexts (Erickson 1977: 36, 42).

Though in the late Vargas years, and especially under the presidency of Goulart (1961–64), some unions were politically activated from above when the government relaxed the more stringent controls, this heavily authoritarian institutional system of labor relations was never changed until the mid-1980s. What is more, it was actually reinforced by the 1964–85 dictatorship, which increased exponentially the number of unions that experienced intervention. In addition, the dictatorship unified the sectoral agencies for the administration of health services in which labor was represented into the single Instituto de Previdencia Social, depriving the already domesticated unions of a potential source of financial power (Malloy 1977: 57).[47]

---

[47] In the words of Malloy (1977: 57), "The new system eliminated an important source of labor's political power and contributed to the general weakening of organized labor as an autonomous political force."

290   *Comparative Perspectives in Ibero-America*

As in Spain, labor in Brazil witnessed a period of activation from below and increasing pluralism in the years prior to neoliberal reform. In the late 1970s economic growth, mounting government repression, and the high concentration of workers in the expanding heavy industry sparked the base movement known as "new unionism" (Seidman 1994: 159). In 1978 the workers of the industrial belt of San Pablo contested the wage freeze imposed by the dictatorship. Soon the wave of strikes expanded to other sectors (especially white-collar sectors such as banking and education) and regions, and spurred other demands such as political democracy and union autonomy (Keck 1992: 66–67; Seidman 1994: 150–54). This shop-floor workers' reaction galvanized a social movement that involved union militants, grassroots and church activists, and leftist intellectuals, which a few years later would give birth to the left-wing Worker's Party (PT) (Keck 1992: 78–79).

Yet the surge of autonomous unions in Brazil did not attenuate, and in some sense intensified, the general organizational disarticulation of the labor movement. The first classwide labor organization, the CUT, was organized by PT militants in 1983 and legally recognized in 1985 (only five years before the neoliberal transition). The unions more linked to the traditional official structure formed the CGT in 1986. In 1990, a new national organization, Forca Sindical, grew out of the CGT as an even more moderate and pragmatic national confederation. In short, in prereform Brazil organized labor was never firmly established in a partisan coalition that held power, it never developed a minimal capacity for genuine aggregate (i.e., sectoral or national) collective bargaining,[48] and it never achieved any form of financial autonomy. Local/factory organizations predated the creation of national bodies.[49] Though democracy and the constitutional reform of 1988 removed the most blatantly authoritarian aspects of this labor legislation – basically the state capacity to intervene in unions – the labor movement that would confront economic reform in Brazil was relatively plural and decentralized, and with recent and comparatively weak national bureaucratic structures.

PERU: ELECTORAL-LEFTIST RADICALIZATION AND ORGANIZATIONAL FRAGMENTATION. Finally, labor's organizational development in Peru during ISI would also appear as low in the dimensions of alliance with a labor-based party in power, collective bargaining, and financial capacity. The traditional Peruvian populist party, the APRA, dominated the main labor confederation CTP (Peruvian Workers' Confederation) from the 1940s until the mid-1960s. However, despite tactical alliances with military governments and the Right, the party founded by Haya de la Torre never attained firm control of state power

---

[48] M. Keck (1992: 62) writes that under the CLT "Labor contracts were mainly individual contracts; collective contracts negotiated between union and employers, while legally allowed, were rare." The lack of a duty-to-bargain provision for employers made aggregate collective bargaining unlikely.

[49] By the mid-1980s a series of de facto works councils, not recognized by the labor law, spread in the sectors where the new unionism insurgence had been more effective, particularly in the metals sectors of Sao Paolo (Keck 1992: 171; see also Rands Barros 1999: 84–85).

Economic Liberalization: Brazil, Portugal, Peru, and Mexico

during the period. As stated previously, Velazco Alvarado's inclusive military regime (1968–75) launched a mobilization project that garnered a variety of popular forces including labor, peasants, and shantytown dwellers (Collier 1976, Huber 1983). These initiatives included the massive creation of unions and new forms of worker participation in industrial ownership and profits.

Yet the complex mixture of popular mobilization from above and Corporatist controls backfired: industrial action increased significantly, and the official and old APRA unions were overtaken by the Communist-controlled CGTP (General Workers' Confederation of Peru). By the mid-1970s CGTP became the strongest labor confederation. Workers' militancy soared during the democratic transition in 1978–80. Labor was at the center of the social ferment behind the creation of Izquierda Unida (United Left), an alliance between the Communist Party and other Marxist parties and social movements, which became the most powerful electoral Left in Latin America by the early 1980s.[50] Yet, as in Chile, labor's impact on the political Left did not result in any lasting bureaucratic gains in terms of collective bargaining or financial resources, nor in a fundamental strengthening of shop-floor labor organization. Indeed, in view of the growing labor market informalization, and of the scarce institutionalization of past labor advances, the Peruvian labor movement that would confront adjustment in the early 1990s was "organizationally diminished and politically orphaned" (Roberts 2002: 22; see also Rosa Balbi 1997: 134).

In sum, following the logic of Collier and Collier's classic work, in virtually all major Iberian-American countries, states attempted some type of Corporatist control of the labor movement from above in the wake of modern industrialization. However, the results for the organizational power of unions were very different. In some cases (Argentina, Mexico, and Portugal) unions forged strong alliances with labor-based parties in government, which resulted in some degree of real and institutionalized collective labor rights and financial autonomy. Indeed, the preservation of these collective labor rights (especially regarding monopoly of representation, aggregate collective bargaining, and/or prereform sectoral contracts) and financial resources would be their main bargaining object during neoliberal reform.

---

[50] The radical Left parties jointly polled 29.5% of the vote in the 1978 constituent assembly elections, the highest vote obtained by the Marxist Left in Latin America except Chile. The legendary Trotskyite leader Hugo Blanco was the third highest vote getter. In the 1983 municipal elections the United Left (supported by the Communist Party and the CGTP) became the second party in the country and won 28.28% of the national vote. Though the United Left (IU) leader Alfonso Barrantes momentarily led the polls for the 1990 presidential elections, the electoral Left finally succumbed to endemic fractionalization (Roberts 1998: 221).

In Brazil and Spain, by contrast, the contemporary labor movement essentially emerged as a reaction from below to authoritarian modernization and depoliticized unionism controlled by the state. Local and factory unions that rebelled against dictatorships existed *prior to* national unions, configuring a union movement quite plural, decentralized, and organizationally weak at the national level. Thus, bureaucratic side payments would be largely absent during the neoliberal transition, and labor would focus on compensation to the base. Yet, unlike in Brazil, works councils in Spain were legalized during the democratic transition and were institutionally more powerful and widespread in the largest industrial sectors. Thus, Spain witnessed a greater reaction from below to economic adjustment, precisely from the big factories whose works councils pressured for compensation to the decimated workforce. Finally, in Peru and Chile organized labor became part of a powerful electoral (and in the case of Chile, governing) leftist coalition under ISI. Yet in the context of polarization, more fragmented labor markets, and smaller industrial economies, the Left was unable to stabilize unions' organizational development. Prior organizational weakness and authoritarian repression largely explain labor marginalization under the Market path.

Power of ISI Actors and Models of Economic Liberalization: General Measurement

I have argued that the strength of ISI actors – primarily economic in the case of firms, organizational in the case of labor – is the second decisive variable that helps explain the alternative models of adjustment. A complete causal analysis of compensation to protected industrial firms and the working class in the additional cases would entail the same strategy used in earlier chapters for Spain, Argentina, and Chile, that is, the measurement of the power of ISI actors at the outset of neoliberal reform and the national and sectoral narratives on how the type of actors conditioned the compensation politics in each particular case. Thus, for business we would need data on sales and profits for domestic, state, and foreign top nonfinancial companies, and on the evolution of prior market trends in core industrial sectors. For labor, each case would demand a detailed study of the horizontal and vertical organizational structures of unions of the sort presented in Chapters 6 and 7. These tasks cannot be accomplished in the scope of this comparative chapter. However, more general measures of the strength of economic actors relative to the state under ISI can help us to operationalize this variable in a broad comparative perspective.

Industrial Business

Table 9.3 assesses the economic strength of the state in the industrial sector prior to the neoliberal period in Argentina, Chile, Brazil, Portugal, and Spain.[51]

---

[51] Peru is not included in the table because I could not find reliable and comparable data on state participation in industry, especially its share of the manufacturing GDP prior to reform. A qualitative assessment of the strength of ISI private business actors was provided in the preceding narrative.

TABLE 9.3. *State Strength in Industry under ISI and Models of Adjustment Index 0–35*

Percentage State Firm's Share:	Argentina 1988	Score	Portugal 1985	Score	Mexico 1985	Score	Brazil 1988	Score	Spain 1982	Score	Chile 1973	Score
Manufacturing GDP	8.4 (1980)	2.1	12 (1976)	3	6.9 (1975)	1.7	22.2 (1983)	5.5	17.3	4.3	40	10
Steel Production	47	2.3	40.8 (1978)	2	59	2.9	72	3.6	40	2	100	5
Oil Production/Refining	62.2	3.1	100	5	100	5	100	5	45	2.2	100	5
Autos	0	0	0	0	8	0.4	0	0	26	1.3	100	5
Commercial Aviation	0	0	0	0	0	0	100	5	100	5	0	0
State Industrial Holding	No	0	No	0	NAFINSA	1	BNDES	2.5	INI	5	CORFO	5
Total "State Strength"		7.5		10		11		19.1		19.8		30
Mode of Adjustment	Corporatist		Corporatist		Mixed		Statist		Statist		Market	

Source: See Appendix.

294 Comparative Perspectives in Ibero-America

I constructed an index of "Prereform State Industrial Power." The index ranges from 0 (minimal state power) to 35 (maximal state power) and combines three dimensions: (1) the total share of the state in manufacturing GDP; (2) the share of the state in production in four core sectors representative of ISI deepening, two intermediate goods (oil and steel), and two complex transport equipment goods (autos and commercial airplanes) for which I could find data for all countries; (3) the postwar presence or absence of a state industrial holding or bank endowed with bureaucratic capacity (a) to engage in production as owner in various industrial activities and (b) to finance public and private industrial firms (see the Appendix for details on the sources of the index).

For the state firms' share of the manufacturing GDP I constructed a 0–10 scale in which 40% of state share (the maximum found in Chile) receives a score of 10 and the other cases are scored proportionately. For each of the four selected ISI sectors I use a 0–5 scale, in which a case of total control (100%) by the state scores 5, and the other cases are scored proportionally. Finally, I measured the role played by state industrial holdings/development banks in postwar industrial growth also along a 0–5 scale: a state industrial agency endowed with relative bureaucratic autonomy, and with capacity to launch its own firms in a variety of industries (especially in those ISI sectors, such as steel or petroleum, that require high initial investments) would receive a score of 5. If the state industrial holding or developmental bank was more oriented to finance than to engage directly in production, it scored 2.5. A lasting state industrial holding set up during ISI, but scarcely autonomous of the lobbying of private groups, would only score 1, and existence of no significant state industrial holding or developmental bank would score a 0. Of course, this assessment is subjective and based on the secondary literature reviewed in the previous section, but I am confident that country specialists would take it as relatively uncontroversial.

Admittedly, the table says nothing about the economic power of local *private* industrial firms or groups that would eventually be compensated (or not) during neoliberalism. However, in semiclosed economies it is reasonable to assume a zero-sum game between the strength of the state and that of private national groups in the industrial domain: where the state has dominated core ISI sectors (steel, oil, cement, petrochemicals, etc.) there would be less room for private sector expansion, and vice versa.[52] Power is a relational concept, and the variable "strength of ISI private business groups" is no exception: in mixed economies that reached a minimal degree of industrialization, in which FDI has not been massive in strategic sectors, and in which firms essentially dispute the *domestic* market, a strong state that expanded direct production generally implies weaker domestic ISI groups. Of course, other more general measures of state capacity in developing economies can be constructed (see, for example,

---

[52] Of course, the lack of state production in some sectors such as commercial aviation need not imply the strength of private firms, but just the absence of production in that area. In any case, the fact that the state engages successfully in complex industrial production such as commercial airplanes is a reasonable indicator of relative state industrial capacity per se.

Economic Liberalization: Brazil, Portugal, Peru, and Mexico

Sikkink's [1991] comparison of Argentina and Brazil, Migdal 1988, Evans 1995, Evans and Rauch 1999). Though this measure is restricted to the industrial sector, it gives a reasonable approximation of the relative strength of the state vis-à-vis private industrial actors in the wake of neoliberal reform.

The results support the expectations of the theory. Chile is the case of the most blatant imposition – policymaking exclusion and no compensation – on most ISI private producers during neoliberalism. Not only was it a case of violent authoritarianism, but in Chile the prereform state ranks as the strongest in industry relative to the private sector – it scores 30 of 35. It had expanded industrial production considerably in the run-up to reform (even before Allende's Socialist government, as described in Chapter 8). The Chilean state had developed a powerful industrial and infrastructure holding with stakes in various sectors, CORFO (Corporation for Development). In Spain and Brazil private local industrial groups and firms were also relatively subordinated during neoliberal reform (they received subsidies and were comparatively marginalized in the privatization process). These cases also display high state strength in the industrial realm before reform. Both states engendered autonomous developmental holdings that fostered public firms in the core ISI sectors. BNDES (National Developmental Bank) in Brazil, despite an important equity portfolio, performed more as a finance institution for public and private firms. The Spanish INI (National Industrial Institute) evolved more as a direct producer until it was dismantled in the neoliberal aftermath. Indeed, Montero (2001: 33) explicitly points out the similar role played by BNDES and INI under ISI in Brazil and Spain, and their key role in domestic industrial expansion.

Argentina, on the other hand, is the archetypical Corporatist case in which private ISI groups received important side payments in the form of market niches and state assets. As expected, Argentina had developed a very weak state in the industrial realm prior to reform according to this measure. Although a developmental bank formally existed (BANADE), its bureaucratic capacity and autonomy under the Argentine ISI model were almost nil (see Rougier 2004). In Portugal and Mexico domestic ISI business groups were also considerably privileged by privatization and/or partial deregulation. Both cases displayed relatively low prereform state industrial power, which left space for the expansion of industry-based family groups. In Mexico NAFINSA performed, as did BNDES, more as a developmental bank than a direct producer. Yet, it played a far less central role in the ISI political economy than its Brazilian counterpart. As analyzed previously, by the early 1970s pressures stemming from the private sector had seriously limited its autonomy and effectiveness. In Portugal, a state industrial holding was created in the revolutionary aftermath (1974), but it was soon closed down after the period of denationalization began. It is no accident that Brazil, Spain, and Chile, which, according to the qualitative analysis of ISI trajectories, generated relatively weak industry-based private business groups in relation to the state, rank high in the index of Prereform State Industrial Power (between 19 and 30). Conversely, those cases in which family-owned economic groups were the main protagonists of industrial

296   *Comparative Perspectives in Ibero-America*

deepening (and eventually received market-share compensation), such as Portugal, Argentina, and Mexico, rank relatively low (between 7 and 11).

Organized Labor

To restate the argument, Hypothesis 2b posited that labor movements that developed high organizational power prior to reform (i.e., those more concentrated and centralized) would tend to be appeased through concertation and market-share compensation – in particular the preservation of collective labor law inducements. Conversely, particularly in democratic settings, labor movements in which power was less centralized in national leaderships and that were more plural would tend to contest adjustment policies and seek subsidies for the affected base workers. Table 9.4 constructs an index of "Prereform Union Organizational Power" for the major Iberian-American countries under ISI, which ranges from 1 to 30 and is composed of three dimensions: (1) degree of monopoly,[53] (2) degree of centralization,[54] and (3) maximal union density during ISI.[55]

Again, this assessment supports the expectations laid out in this study. In Argentina, where unions had developed the highest organizational power prior to reform, labor would negotiate the most extended set of bureaucratic side payments (ownership programs and partial deregulation of the collective labor law and health system). As analyzed, in Portugal and Mexico the CGTP and CTM had been historically dominant (but not monopolistic), and centralization is relatively high – though unions are organized primarily at the sectoral level in Portugal, and local and sectorwide forms of organization are more balanced in Mexico. These countries also witnessed labor concertation and negotiated partial deregulation of the labor law and other forms of organizational side payments during neoliberal reform. All the cases in which labor movements received some form of bureaucratic payoff under neoliberalism (Corporatist and Mixed) rank between 16 and 30, well above the organizational power of the other cases.

In Brazil and Spain, by contrast, we find poorly organized labor movements, that is, relatively plural and decentralized, in terms of this index.[56] Accordingly, neoliberal reform would advance amid adversarial relations with national labor organizations and, especially in Spain, subsidy compensation (rather than bureaucratic payoffs) essentially negotiated with more rebellious local

---

[53] Monopolistic labor movements receive a score of 10, those with a dominant national union confederation score 5, and those plural, i.e., where more than one national union compete on relatively equal terms, score 1.

[54] "Industry" as the dominant pattern of union structure scores a 10, "industry and local" scores a 4, primarily "local" (i.e., regional or municipal) receives a 3, and "firm" or "craft" receives a 1 (scores given by Mcguire 1997: Table 10).

[55] Density is measured along a 0–10 scale in which 50% of peak unionization under ISI receives a score of 10, and the other cases are scored proportionately.

[56] CUT in Brazil competed with the remnants of the official unionism, CGT and Forza Sindical, and has become more dominant lately.

Economic Liberalization: Brazil, Portugal, Peru, and Mexico

TABLE 9.4. *Labor: Organizational Strength under ISI and Models of Adjustment Index 1–30*

	Argentina	Score	Portugal	Score	Mexico	Score
Monopoly-Pluralism	Monopoly	10	Dominant	5	Dominant	5
Centralization	Industry	10	Industry	10	Industry/Local	5
Top Density (percentage)	50.1	10	30	6	32.1	6.4
Total		30		21		16.4
Mode of Adjustment	Corporatist		Corporatist		Mixed	

	Brazil	Score	Spain	Score	Chile	Score	Peru	Score
Monopoly-Pluralism	Plural	1	Plural	1	Plural	1	Dominant	5
Centralization	Local	3	Firm	1	Firm	1	Firm	1
Top Density (percentage)	24.3	4.8	15	3	35	7	25	5
Total		8.8		5		9		11
Mode of Adjustment	Statist		Statist		Market		Market	

Source: Centralization (measured as dominant pattern of union structure) from Mcguire (1997: Table 10); Spain and Portugal, author's assessment. Peak density during ISI taken from Roberts (2002: 15), Spain and Portugal from Martínez Lucio (1998) and Barreto and Naumann (1998).

unions and workers. Plural union movements made concertational policymaking more difficult to coordinate, and the low levels of prior labor institutional inducements reduced the room for organizational payoffs. Finally, though the pattern of union organization in Chile and Peru is less important given the virulence of authoritarianism, liberalizing governments marginalized and repressed relatively weak labor movements.

CONCLUSIONS

This book has argued that Spain, Argentina, and Chile are model cases in the typology of economic liberalization paths. They display most fully the main traits of each model in the same way that Sweden is frequently considered as the embodiment of the social democratic welfare state, or Japan the main example of state-led strategies of growth. As shown in previous chapters, in the Spanish Statist mode, in the wake of tariff and financial liberalization the Ministry of Industry implemented a bold project of industrial reconversion from above that included sectoral plans for a number of key industries and subsidy compensation for affected firms and workers. In Argentina's Corporatist model, the most powerful industrial economic groups and unions obtained market-share compensation (i.e., state assets and partial deregulation) in a way unmatched in the rest of the Iberian world. Finally, Chile embodies the Market path with its violent exclusion of ISI actors and the wide implementation of targeted policies for the informal poor during neoliberalism.

This chapter extended the main research question – namely, which actors among protected firms and the working class were compensated, and in what way – to other episodes of sweeping neoliberal adjustment in Ibero-America. I argued that the Brazilian case under the Collor and Cardoso presidencies (1990–2002) shows important features of the Statist path – top-down reconversion plans for strategic ISI sectors, subsidies to affected firms and workers as the prevalent compensatory measure, and a privatization process oriented to diversify ownership among institutional investors rather than to reward the established industry-based conglomerates. In Portugal, the adjusting government of Cavaco Silva (1985–95) used privatization to empower the domestic ISI business groups and appeased unions through tripartite concertation and the partial reform of the labor law. Peru's (1990–2000) model of adjustment closely resembles the Chilean path: marginalization and/or repression of most ISI actors and massive national compensation to, and political courting of, the informal poor. Finally, Mexico under De la Madrid and Salinas (1982–94) constitutes a Mixed case. Several of the strategies prevalent in the other cases were used: market-share deals with important ISI business and labor groups, repression, and the political courting of the informal poor through a national social program. Of course, the general comparison has focused on the dominant patterns of compensatory arrangements under neoliberalism in each case. Further research may unveil sectoral exceptions similar to the ones analyzed in Chapter 5 for business in Argentina and Spain.

I have argued that the type of regime and the power of prior ISI actors (primarily economic in the case of firms, organizational in the case of unions) are decisive factors that help explain these adjustment trajectories. Although more research and better general measurement (especially of the power of industrial business groups) would be needed to test the theory beyond the three main cases studied in the book, the qualitative analysis of the evolution or the power of prior ISI actors, and the quantitative measures of their strength, suggest that these factors explain an important part of the variation in the models of neoliberal adjustment in Ibero-America.

Though this book does not aim to explain the variation in ISI developmental regimes among countries[57] – but rather the influence of those trajectories on the different adjustment models – it should be noted that the power of labor

---

[57] For variations in ISI strategies and the dilemmas of the transition to more export-oriented models see Haggard (1990) and Gereffi and Wyman (1990). For more recent iterations of this debate see Chibber (2004), Kohli (2004), and Schrank (2007).

Economic Liberalization: Brazil, Portugal, Peru, and Mexico 299

under ISI often mirrors that of the local business sector in these Ibero-American economies. For example, organizationally weak and decentralized labor movements matched private industrial groups relatively weak in relation to the state in both Spain and Brazil. By contrast, in Argentina and Mexico the development of relatively strong domestic business groups vis-à-vis the state was parallel to the configuration of organizationally powerful labor movements. Indeed, in the advanced world, for example, Statist forms of industrial growth in the postwar period (notably in France and Japan) have also resulted in organizationally weak national unions and in private business sectors comparatively more subordinated to the state. Thus, this "parallel development" in the structural and/or organizational strength of economic actors, frequently noted in the literature on varieties of capitalism for advanced countries (see Hancké et al. 2007: 24), is also a feature in the postwar development of the major countries in the Iberian world.

10

Conclusions

Legacies for the Liberalized Economies and Varieties of Capitalism in the Developing World

INTRODUCTION

The macroeconomics of effective stabilization and market adjustment evolved in a roughly similar way in all the cases analyzed in this study. All involved thorough financial and trade liberalization, monetary restraint and alternative ways to anchor the exchange rate to cope with inflationary pressures (e.g., modes of fixed parity to the dollar in Chile, Argentina, Mexico, and Brazil and integration into the European Monetary System in the cases of Spain and Portugal). Exchange-rate-based stabilization generally led to currency overvaluation and therefore to rising adjustment costs for the industrial sector.

Yet this book has shown that the modes of making economic liberalization politically viable, the patterns of compensation delivered, and the type of actors in business and the working class that benefited from them were remarkably different. In Argentina's and Portugal's Corporatist adjustment, important industrial business groups and national unions were rewarded with market-share compensation – that is, state assets and partial deregulation in the context of more or less formal concertational policymaking. In the Spanish and Brazilian Statist models, top-down restructuring plans in strategic sectors and a system of subsidies were used to placate industrial firms and unions. In Chile's and Peru's Market path, the state sidelined traditional ISI insiders, leaving industrial and sectoral readjustments largely in the hands of market forces. At the same time, the neoliberal governments targeted the unemployed and the atomized poor in the informal sector, or ISI outsiders, in a manner unrivaled in the Statist and Corporatist models. Finally, in the Mixed model of Mexico analyzed in Chapter 9, neoliberal authorities, unlike in the three models just depicted, did not concentrate compensation exclusively on ISI insiders or outsiders, but on a combination of both. Market-share deals with certain business groups and unions were parallel to a massive search for political support among the informal poor through the targeted social program PRONASOL.

These contrasting adjustment models were explained in terms of the type of political regime and the power of the ISI actors formed prior to neoliberal

300

Conclusions

adjustment. In cases of sweeping and far-reaching liberalization such as the ones analyzed here, major compensation to ISI insiders – the organized economic actors of the inward-oriented model – is found in the democratic Corporatist and Statist paths, under which firms, unions, and formal workers can deploy their lobbying or mobilization resources. In the Market path, authoritarianism enabled both the political marginalization of ISI actors and a significant shift of resources to social programs that targeted the extreme poor and unemployed in the informal sector.

In addition, the type of prior ISI actors also conditioned both the political process and the type of compensation awarded. In the Corporatist mode of Argentina and Portugal, the top echelons of a powerful industrial bourgeoisie relative to the state were able to expand their market share in the heyday of adjustment through protectionist deregulation and/or state assets awarded through extended privatization. Furthermore, once liberalization seemed unavoidable, relatively centralized and organizationally strong union movements with weak shop-floor bodies embraced bureaucratic payoffs and the preservation of collective labor law inducements in exchange for demobilization. In the Statist mode of Spain and Brazil, industrial business groups and firms that were relatively weak in relation to the state were subordinated to state *dirigisme* and generally sidelined in the major privatizations, compensatory subsidies notwithstanding. At the same time, poorly bureaucratized and bottom-up-structured, decentralized union movements did not find organizational side payments attractive but mobilized aggressively (especially in the Spanish case) for subsidy compensation targeted at shop-floor, laid-off workers. Finally, Mexico's Mixed model was explained in Chapter 9 as shaped by the more atypical combination of authoritarian neoliberalism and some strong ISI economic actors.

In this concluding chapter I evaluate, first, the results of this study in the light of the recent and expanding scholarship on institutions and institutional change. I also elaborate on the relation between choice and structure in the comparative historical approach presented here. In the last part of the chapter I argue that each model of adjustment left important institutional and organizational legacies for the liberalized political economies. Finally, I discuss the implications of these legacies for a research agenda based on the conceptualization of alternative varieties of capitalism in developing economies.

MODELS OF ECONOMIC LIBERALIZATION, INSTITUTIONAL CHANGE, AND PATH DEPENDENCY

Most of this book has dealt with conceptualizing and explaining different courses of neoliberal adjustment in the Iberian world. The comparative historical analysis spans from the logic of compensatory politics during neoliberalism between the 1970s and 1990s, to the original configuration of business, labor, and state actors since the initial expansion of industrialization on the eve of the Second World War or before. It follows a historical-institutionalist logic in its assessment of actors' preferences and interests as contingent upon domestic organizational and structural configurations as they have unfolded historically in each country. Indeed, it is not only the preferences of groups, but also the formation of actors, that were the subject of inquiry.[1] How business and labor groups were originally constituted under the inward-oriented model – for example, whether they became weak or strong ISI actors – had a fundamental impact on the definition of their interests once market reform was launched.

Models of adjustment also left decisive legacies for the future workings of these political economies in the contemporary liberalized order. Indeed, the course of liberalization in these countries can be understood as a "critical juncture," that is, "as a period of significant change, which typically occurs in distinct ways in different countries ... and which is hypothesized to produce distinct legacies" (Collier and Collier 1991: 30).

Thus, the alternative courses of neoliberal reform are path dependent in two ways. First, the diverse postwar industrialization trajectories – and the consequent configurations of economic actors – decisively influenced the modes of adjustment. Second, when a particular neoliberal path is taken, it is difficult to reverse: new power relations emerge, and, once reform has lost momentum, the window of opportunity for institutional change becomes increasingly narrow. The way in which actors use the reformed set of policies and institutions to deepen asymmetries of power is one of the "increasing return" mechanisms that make path-dependent phenomena difficult to reverse (see Levi 1997: 28; Mahoney 2000: 513; Pierson 2000: 252). For example, negotiated and partial labor law reform in Argentina preserved the organizational power of traditional unions for the postliberal polity, while thorough collective labor law deregulation largely hindered Chilean unions' role in the open economy. Extensive privatization in Argentina left the state out of the oil and gas sectors in the liberalized economy. By contrast, sequential and controlled privatization to national champions empowered the state for future domestic market energy production and/or regulation in Spain and Brazil.

The tendency in many methodological studies on critical junctures and path dependence has been to emphasize *contingency* and *rupture* in a certain historical setting rather than institutional continuity (Pierson 2004: 44–46; Mahoney 2000; Capoccia and Kelman 2007: 348). Mahoney, for example, emphasizes that "path dependence ... involves both tracing a given outcome back to a particular set of historical events, and showing how these events are themselves contingent occurrences that cannot be explained on the basis of prior historical conditions" (Mahoney 2000: 508). As Thelen (2003: 209) contends, this view has been prevalent in the historical approaches on institutional change and "tends to encourage a rather strict separation of the issues of institutional innovation and institutional reproduction." However, if the argument presented in this book is correct, the compensatory deals during adjustment were

---

[1] On this topic see Thelen (1999: 733) and Evans and Stephens (1988: 732). For a summary of the historic institutionalist research program see Pierson and Skocpol (2002).

Conclusions 303

historically more constrained than the dominant paradigm on critical junctures and path dependency would lead us to think. The policy preferences and compensation arrangements at the critical juncture of adjustment were largely shaped by the political regime and the alternative patterns of late industrialization and labor organizational development under the inward-oriented model. The critical juncture of neoliberalism was indeed a window of opportunity for major and enduring institutional change. Yet the scope and content of those changes, especially in the industrial and labor domains, were conditioned by ISI organizational and structural legacies.

This complex interplay of institutional change and continuity in the political economy of compensation under neoliberalism echoes the work of Weir (1992) and Thelen (2004) and a strand of the scholarship on economic and political transformations in Eastern Europe since 1989, such as Stark and Bruszt (1998), Grzymala-Busse (2002), and Ekiert and Hanson (2003). The compensatory deals studied in this book, for example, present elements of the two mechanisms of institutional change theorized by Thelen (2004): conversion and layering. The setting up of plant-level works councils under Franco in Spain, described in Chapter 6, can be taken as a paradigmatic example of institutional conversion: an institution originally thought to legitimize the authoritarian regime mutated in a vehicle of working-class contestation and subsequently became the institutional locus of a strongly bottom-up-structured and combative union movement. When confronting neoliberal adjustment, such a decentralized union would only be appeased through compensation at the base, not by bureaucratic payoffs. Drawing on the work of Eric Schickler, Thelen posits institutional layering as involving the grafting of new elements onto an established institutional framework. The partial deregulation of the health system in Argentina is an example. The system today is very different from the one established under ISI. Yet, as analyzed in Chapter 6, reforms were juxtaposed upon the old health regulatory scheme, and unions are still the main brokers. In short, in the same way that, for David Stark and Laszlo Bruszt (1998), it was in the ruins of the collapsed Communism that Eastern European societies found the materials with which to build alternative reform paths, so the alternative ISI institutional legacies established the foundations for coalitional crafting, market organization, and industrial reform in many Iberian-American economies.

MODELS OF ECONOMIC LIBERALIZATION: BETWEEN STRUCTURE AND CHOICE

The theorization of critical junctures and contingency takes us to the ever present question of structure and choice in the social sciences. In Chapter 2 I have tried to uncover the micrologic by which the political regime and certain endowments of actors shaped the policy choices during neoliberal adjustment. At the same time, the comparative historical analysis deployed in this book carries a considerable structural flavor. I have assessed certain macrosocial and institutional variables that predispose countries to different outcomes, configurations favorable or unfavorable to make adjustment politically viable in one way or the

304 — *Comparative Perspectives in Ibero-America*

other.[2] For example, in democratic environments, big private industrial groups and centralized unions induced modalities of neoliberal reform and compensation very different from those in contexts in which the state was a powerful industrial player under ISI, and unions were organizationally weak at the national level and generally decentralized. Certain institutions and economic structures made countries more prone to specific liberalization models. Yet this type of analysis may run the risk of structural overdetermination. In the same way that Katznelson (1997: 94) observed that Skocpol's classic work on social revolutions eventually portrayed "revolutions without revolutionaries," this study may run the risk of representing "neoliberalism without neoliberals."

That said, it is worth stressing that alternative ISI institutional and structural legacies and political regimes predisposed countries to certain outcomes, but they did not determine the final "success" (i.e., likelihood of implementation) of a certain neoliberal experiment. Nor did they shape, of course, all the dimensions of market reform. Liberal economic recipes after years of inward-oriented development required enormous political crafting, be it the myriad market-share deals with unions and business groups in Argentina, the elaboration of sectoral reconversion plans and negotiations with empowered local unions and works councils in Spain, or the construction of a new political base for neoliberals among the informal poor in Chile. The outcome of these interactions was not determined ex ante in any way. However, it is plausible to argue, for example, that Argentina could have followed the path of Venezuela, with its market liberalization stalled by vested interests before Hugo Chávez took power. Yet, it could hardly have carried out a neoliberal reform Chilean-style, because it was a democracy, and because ISI actors were too powerful to be sidelined. Likewise, Portugal was unlikely to implement state-guided adjustment the way Spain or Brazil did because it simply lacked the strong state industrial bureaucracy that these countries had engendered under ISI. Chilean authoritarian neoliberals were quite successful in creating a party out of compensation to the informal poor; Peruvian reformers were not. In short, the political regime and ISI organizational legacies did not decide the whole fate of neoliberal reform. But these factors made some strategies, deals, and coalitions more likely than others.

LEGACIES FOR THE LIBERALIZED ECONOMY

As stated previously, the models of liberalization, their sets of winners and losers and particular institutional arrangements, left decisive imprints for the workings of the marketized political economies. I examine four types of legacies in both the business and labor domains: (1) the reconstitution of the domestic business class and the degree of foreign control in the domestic economy, (2) the state role in the economy vis-à-vis local business, (3) the mobilization and coordination

---

[2] See Katznelson (1997: 89), Pierson (2004: 93), and Mahoney and Rueschemeyer (2003) for recent methodological discussions on this tradition, pioneered by Barrington Moore and successors.

Conclusions 305

TABLE 10.1. *Models of Adjustment and Legacies for the Liberalized Economies*

	Statist Model	Market Model	Corporatist/ Mixed Models
Business			
• Renewal of the Domestic Business Class	High	Medium	Low
• State's Role in the Economy vis-à-vis Business	Enhancing	Arms' Length	Specific Sectoral Protections
Working Class			
• Organized Labor's National/Sectoral Coordination Capacity	Medium	Nil	Potentially High
• Insider-Outsider Organizational Fragmentation	Low	High	High

capacity of organized labor in more open environments, and (4) the nature of the organizational insider-outsider divide within the working class. This section spells out the legacies of each model in these four dimensions (Table 10.1). Though the analysis is centered on the model cases of each path analyzed in most detail in the book – Spain, Argentina, and Chile – references will be made to the other cases studied in Chapter 9. The argument is not that adjustment paths determined all the main organizational qualities of the liberalized political economy. Rather, I argue that deals and exclusions forged during the period of adjustment influenced certain important features such as the power of the domestic industrial class, the state potential for collaboration with business, the coordination capacity of organized labor, and the strength of the insider-outsider cleavage within the working class. The final section discusses the implications of these institutional and structural legacies for the incipient extension of the varieties of capitalism theoretical discussion outside the advanced world.

Business

The Reconfiguration of the Domestic Business Class

The Statist model in Spain and Brazil and, to a lesser extent, the Market model of Chile triggered a substantial transformation and renewal of the dominant local business class. A defining feature of the postreform industrial landscape in these countries was the emergence of new local companies and business groups that have joined the top echelons of the country's private industrial class. Sequential and controlled privatization and the creation of national champions in the Statist mode essentially averted foreign takeovers and strengthened local control. In the Corporatist and Mixed models, by contrast, though local private groups expanded market share in the initial stages of reform, the lack of a national strategy to protect local companies coupled with ongoing liberalization

306   *Comparative Perspectives in Ibero-America*

prompted many compensated groups to sell assets and leave markets in which they had thrived.

Indeed, despite globalization and increasing FDI inflows, one could make the argument that Spain, Brazil, and Chile have a stronger *domestic* business class after economic liberalization than before. Through sequential privatization, the government gradually floated equity in the domestic stock exchanges and granted the control neither to a long-established domestic group nor to a foreign company. Rather, the resulting companies have a relatively fragmented ownership structure in which individual banks and investment funds play a significant role. Decision making resides in the hands of a small number of investor groups (in modern terms of corporate governance, "blockholders") and management. The rest of the stock is owned by "passive" pension funds and atomized shareholders.

In Spain, state-guided restructuring and sequential privatization have generated a new group of industrial holdings that are the main players in the domestic economy.[3] A similar process has taken place in Brazil. As we saw in Chapter 9, sequential privatization has spawned a series of companies that are at the vanguard of Brazilian industrial capitalism, such as the giant Vale (mining, aluminum, and forestry), Embraer (aircraft), Petrobras (oil and petrochemicals), and ACESITA, Usiminas, and CSN (steel), among others. In Chile, noncompensatory privatization of CORFO's industrial firms spurred a group of new and non-family-owned conglomerates that are leading players in some sectors: Pathfinder (based on electronics and explosives), Sigdo Koppers (food and wood), SOQUIMICH (chemicals), and CAP (steel).[4] In addition, Market adjustment in Chile, of course, strengthened the natural resource–based traditional groups, which were endowed with notable comparative advantages and powerful enough to expand in global markets without fearing hostile takeovers.

---

[3] Analyzing postadjustment Spain, the economists Carreras and Tafunell (1996: 87) argue that the most salient feature of the ownership structure of the leading Spanish firms is the "complete absence of foreign capital." Repsol (oil and petrochemicals), Ence (the largest maker of paper pulp in Spain), and Indra, a Spanish leader in electronics systems, were created out of government-controlled sequential privatization. Ercros, one of the largest holdings in chemicals, and the Mondragon group – the largest Spanish holding in home appliances and currently a power at the European level – also consolidated as the result of a series of government-backed mergers in the respective sectors. Together with the national champions ENDESA (electricity), Gas Natural (Energy), and Telefonica (telecoms) – also created through government-controlled sequential privatization – these companies constitute the locus of the Spanish nonfinancial industrial class.

[4] Sigdo Koppers was formed by a group of seven investors and consolidated after the privatization of the home appliances company CTI and the explosives manufacturer ENAEX. The Pathfinder group was bolstered by the acquisition of the state-owned sugar manufacturer IANSA and of the wood industry leader MASISA. CAP and SOQUIMICH grew out of the share-issue privatization process of the steel and chemical state companies that, as analyzed in Chapter 8, privileged managers and close associates and insiders of the Pinochet regime. Montero (1997: 268, 275) calls the new holdings in Chile "technical emerging groups," as opposed to the most traditional ones.

Conclusions

307

In the Statist model the thrust to create national champions was more remarkable. The fact that sequential privatization in both Spain and Brazil was heavily centralized in a relatively autonomous state institution that conducted the whole process (the Ministry of Industry and its subordinated INI in Spain, and BNDES in Brazil) facilitated the careful selection of prospective buyers and investors. Significantly, the capacity to prevent foreign takeovers in selected sectors and national champions continued once the majority of restructuring had taken place, through both formal and informal mechanisms. Formally, the state has retained preferential or golden shares that provide veto power over mergers and acquisitions in sectors considered strategic. Informally, the former state managers that continued in command after sequential privatization and ownership diversification often have close relations with government officials. In short, the possibility that the privatized national champions such as Vale, Embraer, and Petrobras in Brazil, or Repsol, Telefonica, and Gas Natural in Spain will fall under the control of a foreign group is quite low. The cases of ENDESA and Repsol, in which the Spanish government blocked, through both formal and informal means, hostile takeovers of Endesa by the German electrical group EON (in 2007) and of Repsol by the Russian Lukoil (in 2008) in broadly publicized battles for corporate control, are illustrative of this pattern.

The irony is that the spread of more modern, non-family-controlled forms of corporate governance – that is, ownership fragmentation, especially among banks and/or institutional investors – brought about by globalization in Spain, Brazil, and to a lesser extent in Chile contributed to strengthening the national business class and to preventing foreign takeovers. These companies' headquarters are locally based, and holdings are led by local managers with substantial decision-making capacity in view of the relatively diffused shareholding when compared to the traditional family groups. The newly emerging groups in Spain, Brazil, and Chile do not constitute a national bourgeoisie in the most traditional sense of family-owned business groups. Rather, the new local industrial bourgeoisie are the managers and CEOs who are independent of the largest prereform business groups but are not subjected to direct control by foreign interests or TNCs. In sum, this new industrial class emerging in Spain, Brazil, and Chile represents the most modern forms of corporate control in the Western world.[5]

Foreign takeovers among the largest industrial companies were eventually much more extensive in Argentina's Corporatist industrial adjustment, caught between traditional family-owned *grupos* and foreign multinationals' expansion in liberalized markets, during and after privatization. In fact, in Argentina, after the period of compensation in the first half of the 1990s, the main industry-based groups were left with two options: sell their assets in the tradable sector (whose value had significantly grown as a result of compensatory measures) or lobby

---

[5] Of course, although more dispersed ownership that empowers managers is the essential characteristic of the modern corporation, its features still diverge among advanced countries. The "blockholder" nature of these emerging groups makes them closer to Coordinated Market Economies forms of corporate governance (see Hall and Soskice 2001).

against the increasingly overvalued fixed exchange rate in order to improve their relative prices. Indeed the breakup of the consensus within the capitalist class over the exchange rate system in the second half of the 1990s arguably contributed to undermining its credibility and to its traumatic demise in the crises of late 2001 (see Etchemendy 2005). Of the six major sectors analyzed in Chapter 3 in which domestic hegemonic industrial groups were compensated via privatization and biased deregulation, in three – oil, cement, and autos – local families sold their assets after taking market share and gaining value.[6] In the other three – aluminum, steel, and pharmaceuticals – local groups remain key, sometimes dominant, players.

In Portugal and Mexico similar trends were reported by the business press, as traditional family groups privileged during privatization, such as the Portuguese Champalimaud conglomerate or the once-hegemonic Mexican Alfa group, struggled to prevent foreign takeovers in increasingly open markets. Indeed, in Mexico most of the nationalized banks that were part of the compensation packets directed to traditional industrial groups (see Chapter 9) were eventually sold to international investors by the year 2000. Plus, the only major domestic industrial company in Spain rewarded with market-share compensation, the oil group CEPSA, analyzed in Chapter 5, was also eventually taken over by the French ELF. The sale of CEPSA provides further evidence in the sense that market-share compensation for domestic companies in sectors dominated by advanced world-based majors is quite difficult to sustain. In short, the foreignization of the local industrial class has been much more pervasive, and a more hotly debated topic, in the Corporatist and Mixed cases than in the Market path of Chile and, especially, Statist models.

The State Role in the Liberalized Economy

State action may play an enhancing or a hindering role for business. The enhancing nature of the state vis-à-vis local firms is manifested in its capacity to support and finance ongoing industrial adjustment to globalization. As we have seen, the government played a central role in the subsidizing and financing of industrial adjustment and reconversion in both Statist cases of Brazil and Spain. In the postliberal order, these states have shifted their support from domestic adjustment to local firms' internationalization – understood as the growth in exports and/or outward FDI and foreign acquisitions. Indeed, in Spain the international expansion started when most of the "national champions" (e.g., Repsol, Telefónica, Endesa) were still controlled by the state. This task continued after full privatization, as demonstrated by the Spanish government's backing of Repsol's takeover of the oil monopoly YPF in Argentina in 1999. The support of government-empowered banks such as BSCH and BBVA, through both financing and cross-shareholding, has been crucial in the internationalization

---

[6] Among others, Astra (oil), Sevel and Ciadea (autos), IPAKO and INDUPA (petrochemicals), and the massive, cement-based group Fortabat were sold to foreign investors. Pérez Companc's energy division was sold to the Brazilian state giant Petrobras in 2001.

Conclusions 309

of Spanish firms. By the late 1990s Spain replaced the United States as the largest investor in Latin America. In 2010 Spain was severely hit by the world financial crisis initiated in the United States real estate market. Spanish business stakes in Latin America – basically banks and national champions empowered through the Statist model – were not affected by the crisis and were crucial to helping weather the storm.[7]

In Brazil, the state's support of domestic business adjustment is more direct. BNDES, the state developmental bank that shaped Statist industrial adjustment, remains a major player in the Brazilian political economy. It is in practice the only source of cheap long-term finance for Brazilian firms, and its equity investment arm BNDESpar accounted for about 8% of overall market capitalization by the late 1990s (Cassens et al. 2001: 11). BNDES continues to bolster domestic firms through two means, direct lending and securities subscription.[8] The bank has also supported the public works projects conducted by Brazilian companies abroad. Finchelstein (2010) shows eloquently how BNDES buttressed domestic companies' international expansion. He argues that "state intervention to create capital availability, added to other institutional variables such as state promotion of national champions, have encouraged the largest and deepest internationalization in the region" (p. 4).

This legacy of a proactive state in shaping adjustment makes these countries ideal settings for patterns of state-business collaboration that are well suited for a globalized economy, which scholars (despite differences in emphasis) have called "embedded autonomy" (Evans 1995) or, more recently, "embedded neoliberalism" (Kurtz and Brooks 2008; see also Schrank and Kurtz 2005). In effect, the Spanish state brokerage capacity with the merged and powerful local private banks and the spectacular growth of the Brazilian state developmental bank BNDES during neoliberalism (see Chapter 9) may be key drivers of the supply-side policies (cheap finance, infrastructure investment, R&D subsidies, labor skills upgrading) that enhance (and reduce costs of) capital and labor as factors of production in open economies. As Kurtz and Brooks argue (2008: 239), this type of open economy industrial policies (based on subsidies rather than on regulatory favors) rests heavily on a "compensatory logic," which, as this book

---

[7] While profits in the Spanish market stagnated or fell, they soared in Latin America. At the peak of the crisis, the chief of the American division of the Santander Bank, the largest global Spanish financial group, declared that 45% of the bank earnings were from Latin America in the first semester of 2010 (*El País*, July 13, 2010). The Repsol oil giant also reported that around 50% of profits were from its subsidiary in Argentina (*Página 12*, July 30, 2010). For the internationalization of Spanish business and the way it is inextricably linked to government backing see Guillén (2005), who notes that the largest Spanish multinationals – the banks BBVA and BSCH, Repsol, Endesa, and Telefónica –generated between 25% and 50% of their profits from Latin America (p. 122).

[8] For example, in September 2005 BNDES arranged an $80 million loan to the Brazilian meatpacker FRIBOI for the purchase of the Swift plant in Argentina and later subscribed equity for an additional $750 million for the purchase of the American Swift meatpacking plant. In July 2007 it granted a loan to ITAUTEC to strengthen the firm's subsidiaries in Lisbon and Miami (Sennes and Camargo Mendes 2007: 12–15).

has demonstrated, operated in the Statist model from the inception of the market transition.

The role of the state in relation to business, both in the domain of economic diplomacy and as midwife of embedded (neo)liberalism, in the postadjustment period is more restricted after the Corporatist, Market, and Mixed transitions. In Argentina and Mexico the state occasionally continues to support private giants that had consolidated during reform through market-share compensation, such as the Mexican Cemex (cement) or the Argentine Techint (steel). Yet these occasional interventions are more the result of special lobbying than of an articulated state industrial strategy. Plus, in these cases the extensive use of market-share compensation in the privatization process encouraged a broad diversification of local groups. Further international expansion, by contrast, generally requires specialization and competitiveness in specific product lines.[9] Finally the legacy of state-economy relations in the Market model of Chile can be characterized as arms' length. Except for the control of the major mining company in the case of Chile, the state has no major industrial policy to support business internationalization; nor does it control the allocation of investment in any way.

The Working Class

Organized Labor's Coordination Capacity

As argued earlier, the Corporatist and Mixed models of Argentina, Portugal, and Mexico have preserved collective labor rights and labor relations centralization to a larger extent. This may enhance labor's capacity to coordinate wage levels at a national or sectoral level and to manage industrial conflict. Indeed, in Argentina a centralized and monopolistic union movement has recently underpinned neocorporatist-type bargaining rounds. In the context of union revitalization and high economic growth after 2003, peak-level wage sectoral and national negotiations have been ongoing each year (see Etchemendy and Collier 2007). Likewise the reemergence of labor as an actor with national or sectoral coordination capacity has more potential in Portugal and in Mexico. Of course, organized labor's national or sectorwide bargaining potential does not depend only on institutional legacies. A pro-union government – as in Argentina after 2003 – as opposed to a pro-business government – as in Mexico after 2000 – obviously makes a difference for union activation. Still, inducements such as closed shop, union centralization, and provisions that enhance aggregate collective bargaining – all of which were central parts of the regulatory deals with unions under neoliberalism in these cases – remain important prerequisites.

In the Statist cases of Brazil and Spain, organized labor coordination capacity may be scored as medium: since the political and economic transitions the labor movement, historically tightly controlled from above, has increased autonomy

---

[9] See Finchelstein (2010). The reverse was the case in Brazil, where sequential and noncompensatory privatization did not encourage excessive diversification of domestic groups (Finchelstein 2010: 51).

Conclusions

vis-à-vis the state and traditional political parties and has participated in concertation councils as a legitimate actor. However, the union movement in these countries remains both vertically and horizontally divided among a plurality of national federations. Recent tripartism in Spain has sought to adapt the institutional regulation of labor markets and pensions to increasing Europeanization. Still, it has not involved extensive national or sectoral wage coordination, which in Spain remains largely restricted to provincial and firm levels.[10] Labor in Brazil has joined concertation councils under the Lula government, though its capacity to coordinate national or sectoral wage bargaining remains weak. Finally, repressive labor law deregulation and the boom in the weakly unionized natural resource–intensive industries inherent in Market transitions of Chile and Peru have seriously undermined organized labor's capacity for meaningful intervention in the postneoliberal period.

Working-Class Insiders and Outsiders: Bridging the Divide?

Working-class fragmentation accompanies changes in production systems and globalization. Thus, bridging the interests of insiders and outsiders of the labor market – be they informal, immigrant, or unemployed workers – becomes a central issue for the organizational configuration of modern labor movements.[11] In the Corporatist market transitions the organizational divide between these two groups is likely to be more intense. In Argentina, the unions' focus on bureaucratic benefits in the 1990s and their continuing reliance on state inducements make the dominant labor movement extremely dependent on government regulation and formal sector workers' contributions – such as health payroll taxes, collective wage bargaining "voluntary" contributions, and employee ownership programs. Indeed, this concentration on insiders and the lack of incentives to build any bridge to the jobless paved the way for the surge of autonomous and rebellious organizations of the unemployed in postreform Argentina.[12] Though the Left-leaning CTA (a splinter group of the CGT that mainly organizes public sector unions) has been a vigorous informal sector organizer (see Garay 2007), the mainstream and more politically relevant Peronist labor movement remains wedded to the formal sector. The insider-outsider divide between the Corporatist, former PRI unions and the informal working class is equally evident in Mexico (see Bensusán and Cook 2003).

In the Statist cases of Spain and Brazil, the legacy of autonomy and opposition to the neoliberal state and the more plural nature of the union movement in these countries may build more incentives for labor to court the unemployed or

---

[10] See Dubin (2008: 10) and Molina and Rhodes (2007: 236).

[11] Of course, the bridging of the insider-outsider divide is only one among the many organizational dilemmas posed by working-class fragmentation and the rise of what Collier and Handlin (2009) call the "associational networks." On the juxtaposition of old and new forms of working-class organization in Latin America see the essays compiled in Collier and Handlin's volume.

[12] For different perspectives on the surge of the organizations of the unemployed in Argentina see Svampa and Pereyra (2003), Delamata (2004), Garay (2007), and Schipani (2008).

informal workers. In their quest to confront employers and the state, these labor movements have more potential to narrow the insider-outsider cleavage in the labor market. In Brazil, the Worker's Party–affiliated CUT solidified its links with the landless movement during the antineoliberal struggle. In Spain the most tangible legacies of Statist labor adjustment were the organizational estrangement of the UGT from its sister party PSOE (see Chapter 6) and the emergence of a "unity of action" strategy between the two main unions, UGT and CCOO. Indeed, it could be argued that the main labor consequence of Statist adjustment in Spain was a reaction along class lines, which gave rise to solidarity between working-class insiders and outsiders. Unions confronting a hostile government and freed from the demobilization implications of bureaucratic payoffs put the expansion of unemployment benefits and other forms of compensation for outsiders at the top of their agenda.

Finally, the deepening of the insider-outsider organizational divide is also likely to be pronounced in the aftermath of Market transitions, but for reasons different from those found in Corporatist adjustment. First, in Chile and Peru organizational disarticulation, a legacy of repressive labor deregulation (see Cook 2007) and decimation without compensation of highly unionized ISI sectors, makes any union strategy more difficult, including, of course, the mobilization of outsiders. Second, in both cases the Right courted the informal poor through extended targeted policies during market reform. Neoliberal political activism among the poor is likely to diminish the potential for alliances with leftist unions. As studied in Chapter 8, an important legacy of the Market path in Chile has been the novel political and electoral influence of the Right in the poor areas, or *poblaciones*. The UDI, built largely upon the compensation mechanisms analyzed in Chapter 8, is today the major individual party in Chile. The construction of this mass base, and the conservative and promarket nature of UDI, may hinder the effective mobilization of the atomized urban poor. Although in Chile the postneoliberal governments of the Concertation have improved social inclusion, the prospects for an organized working-class mobilization of any kind remain meager after the Market transitions in both Chile and Peru. In short, though linkages between specific unions and informal sector associations have been established in a number of cases in postliberal Latin America (see Garay 2009), only in Spain and Brazil have mainstream unions – which contested adjustment from below and eschewed bureaucratic and regulatory payoffs – apparently built enduring alliances across the insider-outsider divide.

MODELS OF ECONOMIC LIBERALIZATION IN IBERO-AMERICA
AND THE VARIETIES OF CAPITALISM DEBATE

The debate around the alternative institutions that capitalist economies consolidate as they adapt to international pressures has a distinguished tradition in the study of advanced countries. In recent times, the debate has been decisively pushed forward by the publication of Hall and Soskice's (2001) *Varieties of Capitalism*, which hinges on the conceptualization of two polar types of

Conclusions 313

capitalism, Liberal and Coordinated Market Economies. However, economic internationalization and the emergence or expansion of private property and labor markets in Eastern and Southern Europe and in Latin America have prompted scholars to conceptualize the different institutions and actors that capitalist economies are producing outside the advanced world.

Though the debate is still incipient, some scholars (Amable 2003, Hancké et al. 2007, Molina and Rhodes 2007, Schmidt 2009) have defined a type of capitalism alternatively called Southern European, Mixed, or State-Influenced. For Molina and Rhodes (2007), the Mixed type, which encompasses Spain and Italy, has elements of both the Liberal and Coordinated models. Low levels of sectoral and national wage coordination and the weakness of labor and business organization resemble the Liberal Market Economy type. At the same time, nonmarket forms of coordination are evinced in the close links between banks and industry. Furthermore, the state enforces nonmarket forms of coordination through the compensation and subsidies it bestows on ailing firms and through the protection it grants against foreign takeovers, which, in the Spanish case, were analyzed in previous chapters. In sum, the Spanish political economy has become more inextricably linked to Europe after complete monetary integration and the transformations studied in this book. Nevertheless, its logic still departs from both the Liberal and Coordinated models prevalent in the advanced world.

In the case of Eastern Europe, Lawrence King (2007) identifies a "Liberal Dependent" capitalism, characterized by individualistic labor relations and TNC dominance. Andreas Nolke and Arjan Vliegenthart (2009) go further and argue that Dependent Market Economies in East Central Europe (Hungary, Poland, Czech Republic, and Slovakia) are defined by skilled but cheap and weakly organized labor, TNC hegemony, and FDI dependency, all of which yield comparative advantages for the production of relatively complex and durable consumer goods. Ben Ross Schneider (2009a) has distinguished a Hierarchical Market Economy (HME) type that includes the largest countries in Latin America. The principle of hierarchy is embodied by the hegemony of family business groups and TNCs over other and more diversified forms of corporate governance, by atomistic labor relations and the weakness of shop-floor union organization, and by the vertical control of suppliers by the largest firms.

How does this book speak to these efforts of conceptualizing capitalism in the less advanced world? What is the relation between this incipient theorization on the emerging organizational forms of capitalism and the institutional legacies of the alternative liberalization models? Both the Liberal Dependent and HME models are useful conceptual tools to capture the general logic of the political economy at a regional level. Schneider's, Nolke and Vliegenthart's and King's perspectives have two important strengths: First, they avoid the teleology of assuming that nonadvanced countries may evolve toward the models crystallized in the United States and Continental Europe. Second, they give decisive weight and attention to the role played by TNCs in the political economy, a theme that was largely ignored in the initial debates and is obviously even more central outside the advanced countries.

However, as may any general model, the Dependent and Hierarchical Market Economies may conceal relevant organizational differences. Even in Eastern Europe, where the dominance of international business and the weakness of unions are pervasive, some scholars have illuminated variation and the surge of coordinated capitalist relations, for example, in Slovenia (e.g., Feldmann 2007). In Latin America the conceptualization of a unified model for the largest countries may fail to capture important variation in the role played by the state in the postliberal period in the same way that critics charge that Hall and Soskice's original formulation undertheorizes the ongoing state interventions in the marketplace in France and other countries (see Levy et al. 2006, Schmidt 2009, also Howell 2003).

For example, the state performs a central role as financier in the Brazilian political economy, akin to the task of compensator and promoter that Molina and Rhodes (2007) and Schmidt (2009) describe in the "Mixed," or "State Influenced" market models in Spain and France. The Brazilian state influences market relations through the big (though formally autonomous) pension funds of state companies, through the massive BNDES (as both financier and equity owner), and through the energy giant Petrobras and the other infrastructure privatized companies in which the state maintains substantial leverage. In Chile the state is very far from performing analogous tasks, and its system of flexible labor relations and opaque industrial policy corresponds quite closely with the Liberal model. Likewise, though it is undisputable that unions in Spain and Brazil are fragmented, they still wield considerable power and are doubtless more relevant than their Eastern European, Chilean, or Peruvian counterparts. Though in Argentina firms' works councils are relatively weak, the centrality of organized labor as a sectoral economic actor in collective bargaining and as a coalitional base for the Kirchener governments of 2003–11 deviates to some extent from the HME model. Last, as argued earlier, the penetration of foreign TNCs seems to have been much more pervasive in the Corporatist or Mixed cases of Argentina, Portugal, and Mexico than in Brazil, Spain, or Chile, in which models of market transition preserved decision making in the local business class to a larger extent.

In sum, a fruitful theorization on the organizational features of capitalism in emerging economies may need both lines of research. On the one hand, we should work on general concepts and models that are able to capture the differences between the logic of liberalized capitalism in the advanced and less advanced countries. This perspective would emphasize the different economic institutions that are broadly similar and complementary *within* each region – for example, the reinforcing nature of the low-skilled, atomistic labor relations and hierarchical corporative governance that Schneider posits for Latin America. On the other hand, we need a comparative politics (and a comparative method) that, within specific emerging markets and regions, may contrast the politics of different adjustment strategies and economic institutions, one that avoids the alleged

Conclusions

absence of power politics and the static nature of the original *Varieties* approach given by – as Schmidt (2009: 520) argues – its largely equilibrium-focused analytical framework. What are the economic and political implications of the expansion of foreign control in Argentina's, Mexico's, and Portugal's business class when compared to that in Brazil and Spain? Does the "enhancing" role of the state for business internationalization in Spain and Brazil bring about more general benefits for the domestic economy? What are the consequences of the alternative role played by organized labor – central in Argentina, subordinated in Brazil, and irrelevant in Chile – in the governing coalitions of the "New Left" that emerged in Latin America after neoliberalism? In the Iberian world these questions and contrasts are likely to be shaped by the alternative pathways to economic liberalization analyzed in this book.

Appendix

Chapter 4

TABLE A.1. *Spain: Firms before and after Reform and Production of Raw Steel*

Integrated Steel (hot- and cold-rolled sheets, etc.) Before Reform (1984)	After Reform (1999)
Altos Hornos de Vizcaya (AHV – Private)	Merged in CSI (State) – Aceralia
ENSIDESA (state)	Merged in CSI (State) – Aceralia
2 firms (production 5.3 million tons)	1 Firm (production 4.2 million tons)
Common Steel (long products: tubes, bars, wires)	
Aceria de Santander SA	Sold to CELSA group
Aceros Corrugados SA	Shut down
Aceros de Andoain SA	Shut down
Altos Hornos de Cataluna SA (AHC)	Shut down
Arregui SA	Sold to CELSA group
Artierro SA	Shut down
Azma SA	*Sold to UCIN-Aceralia*
Cevether SA	Shut down
Compañía Española de Laminación SA (CELSA)	Survived
Construcciones y Aux. De Ferrocarriles SA (CAF)	Survived
Epifanio Eizaguirre Manterola	Shut down
Esteban Orbegozo SA	*Sold to UCIN-Aceralia*
Ferrerias de Arcade SA (ARCADE)	Shut down
Forjas y Aceros del Guadiana (FAGSA)	Shut down
Fundiciones Mos SA	Shut down
Hierros Madrid SA (HMADRID)	Shut down
Hierros y Aceros de Jaen SA	Shut down
Industrias de Besós SA (BESOS)	Shut down

TABLE A.1. (cont.)

Integrated Steel (hot- and cold-rolled sheets, etc.) Before Reform (1984)	After Reform (1999)
Jose M. Aristrain – SA (ARISTRAIN)	*Merged with Aceralia*
Laminadora del Sur SA	Shut down
Laminados Ibaizabal SA	Shut down
Laminados y Forjados SA	Shut down
Liberto Aizpurua SA	Shut down
Materiales y Construcciones (MACOSA)	Shut down
Marcial UCIN SA (UCIN)	*Merged with Aceralia*
Metalurgica Galaica SA (MEGASA)	**Survived**
Nervacero SA	Sold to CELSA group
Nueva Montaña Quijano Sa (NMQ)	Sold to CELSA group
Ramón Pradera e Hijos	Shut down
Rico y Echeverría Sa	*Sold to Aristrain-Aceralia*
Siderurgia de Galicia SA (SIDEGASA)	Shut down
Siderurgica de JACA SA	Shut down
Siderurgica Sevillana SA	**Survived**
Torras Herreria y Construcciones SA	Shut down
Union Cerrajera SA	*Sold to Aristrain-Aceralia*
35 firms (production 6 million tons)	**5 firms (production 8.3 million tons)**

Source: UNESID (Union de Empresas Siderurgicas), Madrid.

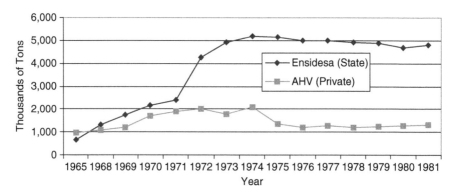

GRAPH A.1. Spain: Production of Raw Steel by Ensidesa and AHV, Prereform Period (in thousands of tons). *Sources:* Ensidesa and AHV Annual Reports and Aceralia (2001).

Appendix

Chapter 6

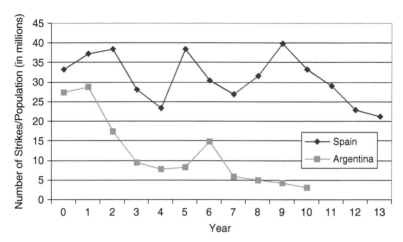

GRAPH A.2. Evolution of Strikes under Neoliberal Adjustment in Argentina (1989–99) and Spain (1983–95). Year 0 average of three previous years; Year 1 in Spain: 1983; Year 1 in Argentina: 1989. *Source:* ILO (various years).

Chapter 8

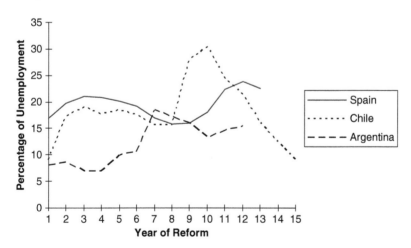

GRAPH A.3. Trajectory of Unemployment Rates during Reform.

320   *Appendix*

Chapter 9

The book takes the state share in manufacturing GDP as one indicator of state strength in the industrial arena under ISI (Table 9.3). Unlike other types of data, such as state revenues or public sector expenditure share as a percentage of the GDP, there is no general and common data source on the state share in the *manufacturing* GDP for the Iberian-American economies – and for developing economies in general – prior to the neoliberal era. The United Nations Industrial Development Organization's (UNIDO's) (1983a) *The Changing Role of the Public Industrial Sector in Development*, has no cross-national data on the state role in industry. The most comprehensive statistical source on the subject is Short's (1984) *The Role of Public Enterprises: An International Statistical Comparison*. However, his data set excludes all the countries I study except Portugal. Therefore, I privileged UNIDO's country reports in the *Industrial Development Review Series* when the data on state share of manufacturing GDP were available (Argentina and Mexico) and used national sources for Brazil, Spain, and Chile. In the following I list the rest of the sources for each country and sector in Table 9.3. In Portugal, Spain, and Chile, which do not produce oil, I used the state share in the refining industry.

Argentina

State firms' share in manufacturing GDP in United Nations Industrial Development Organization (UNIDO) 1984: 22, Table 5, Industrial Development Review Series, *Argentina*.

   Steel: CIS (1996: Table 17).
   Oil: Argentine Institute for Oil and Gas (IAPG). Production of State Company YPF Excluding Private Contractors. Database, Buenos Aires, retrieved in 2000.

Portugal

State firms' share in manufacturing GDP in R. Short (1984: 128, Table 2).

   Steel: Arminda Conceicao, Antonio de Sousa, and Adriano Rocha (1983: 258, Table 4.2).
   Oil: All production and refining were performed by Petrogal, a state monopoly created out of the nationalization of private refiners during the 1974 revolution.

Mexico

State's share in manufacturing GDP from United Nations Industrial Development Organization (UNIDO) Industrial Development Review Series, *The Role of the Public Industrial Enterprise in Mexico*. Vol. 428 (1983: Table A2).

Appendix

Steel: Instituto Nacional de Estadística, Geografía e Informática (INEGI) (1991: 28, Table 2.2.8).
Autos: Instituto Nacional de Estadística, Geografía e Informática (INEGI) (1986: 61, Table III.8). Data refer to Renault Mexico, in which the state held a controlling stake at the time.
Oil: Oil production and refining performed by state monopoly Pemex.

Brazil

Data on manufacturing refer to the public enterprise share of the sector's total capital value in Trebat (1983: 57, Table 3.4).

Steel: Schneider (1991: 101, Table 5).
Oil and commercial aviation sectors were monopolies of the state companies Petrobras and Embraer.

Chile

State firms' share in manufacturing GDP in Larroulet (1984: 148, Table 4).

Oil, steel, and auto industries passed to state hands beginning in the late 1960s.

Spain

State firms' share in manufacturing GDP in Farinas, Jaumandreu, and Mato (1989: 201).

Steel and autos: Martín Aceña and Comin (1991: 648, Table 6), Statistical Appendix.
Oil refining: *Enciclopedia Nacional del Petróleo, Petroquímica y Gas* (1984). State includes INI refineries and the state-owned refinery PETROLIBER.
Commercial aviation: State company CASA.

Bibliography

Aceralia. 2001. *Historia de AHV*. Madrid: Aceralia.

Acuña, Carlos. 1994. "Politics and Economics in the Argentina of the Nineties: Or Why the Future No Longer Is What It Used to Be" in W. Smith, C. Acuña, and E. Gamarra, eds. *Democracy, Markets and Structural Reform in Latin America*. New Brunswick, NJ: Transaction.

Acuña, Carlos and William Smith. 1994. "The Political Economy of Structural Adjustment: The Logic of Support and Opposition to Neoliberal Reform" in W. Smith, C. Acuña, and E. Gamarra, eds. *Latin American Political Economy in the Age of Neoliberal Reform*. New Brunswick, NJ: Transaction.

Agosín, M. and E. Pastén. 2003. "Chile: Enter the Pension Funds" in Charles Oman, ed. *Corporate Governance in Development*. Paris: OECD and CIPE.

Alonso, Guillermo. 2000. *Política y Seguridad Social en la Argentina de los 90*. Buenos Aires: Miño Dávila Editores.

Alvarez, Carlos. 1993. "La Corporación de Fomento de la Producción y la Transformación de la Industria Manufacturera Chilena" in *Transformación de la Producción en Chile*. Santiago: CEPAL.

Amable, Bruno. 2003. *The Diversity of Modern Capitalism*. Oxford: Oxford University Press.

Amsden, Jon. 1972. *Collective Bargaining and Class Conflict in Spain*. London: Weidenfeld and Nicolson.

Anderson, Charles. 1970. *The Political Economy of Modern Spain*. Madison: University of Wisconsin Press.

Andrade, Denise. "Investment in Brazil in the 1990s: Sectoral and Regional Views." BNDES, Unpublished manuscript, 2000.

Anuario El Pais. Various years. Madrid: Ediciones El PAIS.

Arce, Moisés. 2005. *Market Reform in Society*. University Park: Pennsylvania State University Press.

Archanco Fernández, Francisco. 1994. "El Sector de la Construcción Naval en España: Oportunidades y Amenazas." *Economía Industrial* 295: 111–20.

Argentine Association of Automakers (ADEFA). Various years. Annual Reports. Buenos Aires: ADEFA.

Armersto, S., Figueroa, R. and E. Córdoba. 2001. *Crónicas del Centenario*. Comodoro Rivadavia: Ediciones Crónica.

Bibliography

Armijo, Leslie and Philippe Faucher. 2002. "'We Have a Consensus': Explaining Political Support for Market Reforms in Latin America." *Latin American Politics and Society* 44: 1–40.

Astudillo, Javier. 2001. "Without Unions, but Socialist: The Spanish Socialist Party and Its Divorce from Its Union Confederation." *Politics and Society* 29: 273–96.

Azpiazu, D., E. Basualdo, and M. Khavisse. 1986. *El Nuevo Poder Económico*. Buenos Aires: Hyspamérica.

Azpiazu, Daniel. 1994. "La Industria Argentina ante la Privatización, la Desregulación y la Apertura Asimétrica de la Economía: La Creciente Polarización del Poder Económico" in Hugo Notcheff and Daniel Azpiazu, eds. *El Desarrollo Ausente*. Buenos Aires: Flacso.

1989. "La Promoción a la Inversión Industrial en Argentina: Efectos Sobre la Estructura Industrial" in B. Kosacoff and D. Azpiazu, eds. *La Industria Argentina: Desarrollo y Cambios Estructurales*. Buenos Aires: CEAL-CEPAL.

Azpiazu, Daniel and Eduardo Basualdo. 1994. *La Siderurgia Argentina en el Contexto del Ajuste, las Privatizaciones y el MERCOSUR*. Working Paper no. 33. Buenos Aires: Instituto de Estudios sobre Estado y Participación (IDEP).

Azpiazu, Daniel and Bernardo Kosacoff. 1989. "Las Empresas Transnacionales en la Industria Argentina" in B. Kosacoff and D. Azpiazu, eds. *La Industria Argentina: Desarrollo y Cambios Estructurales*. Buenos Aires: CEAL-CEPAL.

Baer, Werner and Annibal Villela. 1980. "The Changing Nature of Development Banking in Brazil." *Journal of Inter-American Studies and World Affairs* 22: 423–40.

Baklanoff, Eric. 1992. "The Political Economy of Portugal's Later 'Estado Novo': A Critique of the Stagnation Thesis." *Luso-Brazilian Review* 29: 1–17.

1986. "The State and Economy in Portugal: Perspectives on Revolution, Corporatism and Incipient Privatisation" in W. Glade, ed. *State Shrinking: A Comparative Enquiry into Privatisation*. Austin, TX: ILAS.

1978. *The Economic Transformation of Spain and Portugal*. New York: Praeger.

Ballestero, Alfonso. 1989. *Buscando Petróleo*. Madrid: Espasa-Calpe.

Banas, Geraldo. 1984. *Os Donos Do Brasil*. Sao Paulo: Editora Banas.

Barnes, Colin. 1995. "Privatization Experience in Portugal" in P. Cook and C. Kirkpatrick, eds. *Privatisation Policy and Performance: International Perspectives*. New York: Prentice Hall/Harvester Wheatsheaf, Hemel Hempstead.

Barrera, Manuel. 1994. "Política de Ajuste y Proceso de Democratización: Sus Efectos sobre los Trabajadores." *Revista Mexicana de Sociología* 1: 105–29.

Barreto, José and Reinhard Naumann. 1998. "Portugal: Industrial Relations under a Democracy" in A. Ferner and R. Hyman, eds. *Changing Industrial Relations in Europe*. Oxford: Blackwell.

Barros, Robert. 2002. *Constitutionalism and Dictatorship*. Cambridge: Cambridge University Press.

Barrutia, Xavier. 1998. "Altzairgintzaren Ibiblera eta Berregituraketa: Altos Hornos de Vizcaya," Ph.D. Dissertation, Department of Economics, Bilbao: Universidad del País Vasco (UPV).

Bates, Robert. 1992. "Macropolitical Economy in the Field of Development" in James Alt and Kenneth A. Shepsle, ed. *Perspectives on Positive Political Economy*. Cambridge: Cambridge University Press.

Bates, Robert and Anne Krueger, eds. 1993. *Political and Economic Interactions in Policy Reforms*. Oxford: Basil Blackwell.

Bibliography

Beccaría, Luis and Aída Quintar. 1995. "Reconversión Productiva y Mercado de Trabajo: Reflexiones a Partir de la Experiencia de SOMISA." *Desarrollo Económico* 35: 401–17.

Becker, David. 1983. *The New Bourgeoisie and the Limits of Dependence*. Princeton, NJ: Princeton University Press.

Belmartino, Susana. 2005. *La Atención Médica Argentina en el Siglo XX*. Buenos Aires: Siglo XXI.

Bennett, D. and K. Sharpe. 1990. "The State as a Banker and Entrepreneur: The Last Resort Character of the Mexican State's Economic Intervention, 1917–1976." *Comparative Politics* 12: 165–89.

Bensusán, Graciela. 2000. *El Modelo Mexicano de Regulación Laboral*. Mexico: Plaza y Valdes-FLACSO.

Bensusán, Graciela and Maria Cook 2003. "Political Transition and Labor Revitalization in Mexico." *Research in Sociology of Work* 11: 229–267.

Berger, Suzanne. 1981. *Organizing Interests in Western Europe*. Cambridge: Cambridge University Press.

Berman, Sheila. 2006. *The Primacy of Politics*. Cambridge: Cambridge University Press.

Bermeo, Nancy. 1994. "Sacrifice, Sequence and Strength in Successful Dual Transitions: Lessons from Spain." *Journal of Politics* 56: 601–27.

  1990. "The Politics of Public Enterprise in Portugal, Spain and Greece" in Ezra Suleiman and John Waterbury, eds. *The Political Economy of Public Sector Reform and Privatization*. Boulder, CO: Westview Press.

Bisang, Roberto. 1998a. "La Estructura y Dinámica de los Conglomerados Económicos en Argentina" in W. Peres, ed. *Grandes Empresas y Grupos Industriales Latinoamericanos*. Mexico: Siglo XXI.

  1998b. "Apertura, Reestructuración Industrial y Conglomerados Económicos." *Desarrollo Económico* 38: 143–76.

  1996. "Perfil Tecno-Productivo de los Grupos Económicos en la Industria Argentina" in J. Katz, ed. *Estabilización Macroeconómica, Reforma Estructural y Comportamiento Industrial*. Buenos Aires: CEPAL-Alianza.

  1989. "Factores de Competitividad en la Siderurgia Argentina." Working Paper no. 32. Buenos Aires: ECLA.

Bisang, Roberto and Martina Chidiak. 1995. "Apertura Económica Reestructuración y Medio Ambiente: La siderurgia Argentina en los 90." Working Paper no. 19. Buenos Aires: CENIT.

Blair, Calvin. 1964. "Nacional Financiera: Entrepreneurship in a Mixed Economy" in R. Vernon, ed. *Public Policy and Private Enterprise in Mexico*. Cambridge, MA: Harvard University Press.

Blanch, Jordi. 1991. "Valoración Bursátil de las Empresas y Participación Industrial de la Banca" in A. Torrero, ed. *Relaciones Banca-Industria: La Experiencia Española*. Madrid: Espasa-Calpe.

Blyth, Mark. 2002. *Great Transformations: Economic Ideas and Institutional Change in the Twentieth Century*. Cambridge: Cambridge University Press.

Boix, Carles. 1998. *Political Parties, Growth and Equality*. Cambridge: Cambridge University Press.

  1997. "Privatizing the Public Business Sector in the Eighties: Economic Performance, Partisan Responses and Divided Governments." *British Journal of Political Science* 27: 473–96.

Bibliography

Bonelli, Regis. 1998. "Las Estrategias de los Grandes Grupos Económicos Brasileños" in W. Peres, ed. *Grandes Empresas y Grupos Industriales Latinoamericanos*. Mexico: Siglo XXI.

Brady, Henry and David Collier. 2004. *Rethinking Social Inquiry*. Lanham, MD: Rowman & Littlefield.

Brooks, Sarah. 2009. *Social Protection and the Market: The Transformation of Social Security Institutions in Latin America*. Cambridge: Cambridge University Press.

Brooks, Sarah and Marcus J. Kurtz. 2007. "Capital, Trade and the Political Economies of Reform." *American Journal of Political Science* 51: 4.

Buesa, Mikel and José Molero. 1988. *Estructura Industrial de España*. Madrid: FCE.

Burachik, Gustavo and Jorge Katz. 1997. "La industrial farmacéutica y farmoquímica en los años 90" in J. Katz, ed. *Apertura y Desregulación en el Mercado de Medicamentos*. Buenos Aires: CEPAL-ALIANZA.

Burawoy, Michael. 1996. "The State and Economic Involution: Russia through a China Lens." *World Development* 24: 1105–17.

Burawoy, Michael et al. 2001. Review Symposium. *American Journal of Sociology* 106, no. 1099: 1137.

Burgess, Katrina. 2004. *Parties and Unions in the New Global Economy*. Pittsburgh: University of Pittsburgh Press.

Burgess, Katrina and Steven Levitsly. 2003. "Explaining Populist Party Adaptation in Latin America: Environmental and Organizational Determinants of Party Change in Argentina, Mexico, Peru, and Venezuela." *Comparative Political Studies* 36: 859–80.

Cabezas, Mabel. 1988. "Revisión Metodológica y Estadística del Gasto Social en Chile: 1970–1986." *Notas Técnicas*, no. 114. Santiago: CIEPLAN.

Cabrera, Mercedes and Fernando Del Rey Reguillo. 2002. *El Poder de los Empresarios*. Madrid: Taurus.

Cáceres Ruiz, Juan. 1997. *La Actividad del Instituto Nacional de la Industria en el Sector Naval: Una Visión Histórica*. Working Paper 9705. Madrid: Fundación Empresa Pública.

Cameron, David. 1978. "The Expansion of the Public Economy: A Comparative Analysis." *American Political Science Review* 72: 1243–61.

Camp, Roderic. 1989. *Entrepreneurs and Politics in 20th Century Mexico*. New York: Oxford University Press.

Campero, Guillermo. 1984. *Los Gremios Empresarios en el Período 1970–83*. Santiago: ILET.

Cappoccia, Giovanni and Daniel Kelman. 2007. "The Study of Critical Junctures: Theory, Narrative, and Counterfactuals in Historic Institutionalism." *World Politics* 59: 341–69.

Carr, Raymond and Juan Pablo Fusi. 1979. *España de la Dictadura a la Democracia*. Barcelona: Planeta.

Carreras, Albert and Xavier Tafunell. 1996. "La gran empresa en la España contemporánea: Entre el Mercado y el Estado" in M. Aceña and F. Comín, eds. *La Empresa en la Historia de España*. Madrid: Civitas.

Carvalho, Ruy and Roberto Bernardes. 1998. "Cambiando con la Economía: La Dinámica de las Empresas Líderes en Brasil" in W. Peres, ed. *Grandes Empresas y Grupos Industriales Latinoamericanos*. Mexico: Siglo XXI.

Castellani, Ana. 2006. "Los ganadores de la 'década perdida': La consolidación de las grandes empresas privilegiadas por el accionar estatal. Argentina 1984–1988" in Alfredo Pucciarelli, ed. *Los Años de Alfonsín*. Buenos Aires: Siglo XXI.

Bibliography

Castiglioni, Rosana. 2001. "The Politics of Retrenchment: The Quandaries of Social Protection under Military Rule in Chile, 1973–1990." *Latin American Politics and Society* 43: 37–66.

Castillo, Mario and Raúl Alvarez. 1998. "El Liderazgo de las Grandes Empresas en Chile" in W. Peres, ed. *Grandes Empresas y Grupos Industriales Latinoamericanos*. Mexico: Siglo XXI.

Casanovas, Federico. 1999. "Desregulación del Sector Salud." M.A. Thesis, Instituto Superior de Economistas de Gobierno, Instituto Torcuato Di Tella, Buenos Aires.

Cassens, Stinj, D. Kingebiel, and M. Lubrano. 2001. "Corporate Reform Issues in Brazilian Equity Markets." IFC Working Paper. Washington, DC: World Bank.

Castañer, Xavier. 1998. "La Política Industrial: Ajustes, Nuevas Políticas Horizontales y Privatización" in Joan Subirats and Javier Goma, eds. *Políticas Públicas en España*. Barcelona: Ariel.

Castellani, Ana. 2006. "Los ganadores de la 'década perdida': La consolidación de las grandes empresas privilegiadas por el accionar estatal. Argentina 1984–1988" in A. Pucciarelli, ed. *Los Años de Alfonsín*. Buenos Aires: Siglo XXI.

Castillo, M. and A. Quispe. 1996. *Reforma estructural y reconversión empresarial: Conflictos y desafíos*. Lima: Consorcio de Investigación Económica.

Cavallo, A., M. Salazar, and O. Sepúlveda. 1989. *La Historia Oculta del Régimen Militar: Chile 1973–88*. Santiago: Antártica.

Cavarozzi, Marcelo. 1975. "The Government and the Industrial Bourgeoisie in Chile: 1938–1964." Ph.D. Dissertation, Department of Political Science, University of California, Berkeley.

Centeno, Miguel. 1997. *Democracy within Reason*. University Park: Pennsylvania State University Press.

Centro de Industriales Siderúrgicos (CIS). 1996. *Estadísticas Siderúrgicas*. Buenos Aires: CIS.

Cerezo, J. L. 2005. "El sector de construcción naval en España. Situación y perspectivas." *Economía Industrial* no. 355–356: 185–196.

Cerezo, José and Antonio Sánchez-Jáuregui. 1996. "Spanish Shipbuilding: Restructuring Process and Technological Updating from 1985 to 1995" in *International Conference on Marine Industry*. Vol. 1. Varna: Bulgarian Society of Naval Architects and Marine Engineers.

Cerutti, Mario. 2002. *Empresariado y Empresas en el Norte de Mexico*. Bogotá: Universidad de los Andes.

——— 2000. *Propietarios, empresarios y empresa en el norte de México*. Mexico: Siglo XXI Editores.

Chandler, Alfred. 1990. *Scale and Scope*. Cambridge, MA: Belknap Press.

Chemical Week. 1996. "Dow Makes a Play in Plastics." November, p. 48–50.

——— 1992. "Argentina Set for Privatization of Petrochemical Industry." December, p. 14.

Chibber, Vivek. 2004. *Locked in Place*. New Delhi: Tulia Books.

Chudnovsky, Daniel. 1979. "The Challenge of Domestic Enterprises to the Transnational Corporation's Domination: A Case-Study of the Argentine Pharmaceutical Industry." *World Development* 7: 45–58.

Cicciari, María Rosa. 1999. "Evolución económica del complejo petrolero de la Cuenca del Golfo San Jorge en un contexto de cambio structural: El mercado laboral de Comodoro Rivadavia, 1985–1997" in A. Salvia, ed. *La Patagonia Privatizada*. Buenos Aires: La Colmena.

Cinco Dias. 2003. "La Política del Ajuste Duro." February.

328   *Bibliography*

Clifton, J., F. Comin, and D. Fuentes. 2003. *Privatisation in the European Union.* London: Kluwer.

Colectivo Autónomo de Trabajadores (CAT). 1985. *La Batalla de Euskalduna.* Bilbao: Editorial Revolución.

Collier, David. 1995. "Trajectory of a Concept: 'Corporatism' in the Study of Latin American Politics" in Peter H. Smith, ed. *Latin America in Comparative Perspective.* Boulder, CO: Westview Press.

  ed. 1979. *The New Authoritarianism in Latin America.* Princeton, NJ: Princeton University Press.

  1976. *Squatters and Oligarchs: Modernization and Public Policy in Peru.* Baltimore: Johns Hopkins University Press.

Collier, David, Jody LaPorte, and Jason Seawright. 2012. "Putting Typologies to Work: Concept Formation, Measurement and Analytic Rigor." *Political Research Quarterly* 65: no. 2.

Collier, David and James Mahoney. 1996. "Insights and Pitfalls: Selection Bias in Qualitative Research." *World Politics* 49: 56–91.

Collier, Ruth Berins. 1999. *Paths toward Democracy.* Cambridge: Cambridge University Press.

  1992. *The Contradictory Alliance.* Berkeley, CA: IAS.

  1982. "Popular Sector Incorporation and Political Supremacy: Regime Evolution in Brazil and Mexico" in S. Hewlett and R. Weinert, eds. *Brazil and Mexico: Patterns in Late Development.* Philadelphia: ISHI.

Collier, Ruth Berins and David Collier. 1991. *Shaping the Political Arena.* Princeton, NJ: Princeton University Press.

  1979. "Inducements versus Constraints: Disaggregating Corporatism." *American Political Science Review* 73: 967–86.

Collier, Ruth and Samuel Handlin, eds. 2009. *Reorganizing Popular Politics: Participation and the New Interest Regime in Latin America.* University Park: Pennsylvania State University Press.

Conceicao, Arminda, Antonio de Sousa, and Adriano Rocha. 1983. *O Sector Empresarial Do Estado em Portugal e nos Paies Da CEE.* Villa Da Maia: CEEPS.

Contín, Ignacio. 1996. "La Desregulación del Sector Petróleo: Consecuencias Empresariales y Efectos sobre la Competencia." Ph.D. Thesis, Universidad Pública de Navarra, Pamplona, Spain.

Contín, Ignacio, Aad Correljé, and Emilio Huerta. 1998. "The Spanish Distribution System of Oil Products: An Economic Analysis." Working Paper 29/98. Navarre: Departamento de Gestión Empresaria, Universidad Pública de Navarra.

Cook, María. 2007. *The Politics of Labor Reform in Latin America.* University Park: Pennsylvania State University Press.

Cornelius, W., A. Craig, and J. Fox. 1994. "México's National Solidarity Program: An Overview" in W. Cornelius, A. Craig, and J. Fox. *Transformation of State-Society Relations in Mexico: The National Solidarity Strategy.* La Jolla, CA: Center of U.S.-Mexican Relations.

Costallat, Karina. 1997. "Efecto de las Privatizaciones y la Relación Estado-Sociedad en la Instancia Provincial y Local: El Caso Cutral Có y Plaza Huincul." Working Paper no. 7. Buenos Aires: CEPAS.

Corkill, David. 1999. *The Development of the Portuguese Economy.* London: Routledge.

  1994. "Privatization in Portugal" in V. Wright, ed. *Privatization in Western Europe: Pressures, Problems and Paradoxes.* London: Pinter.

Bibliography 329

1993. *The Portuguese Economy since 1974*. Edinburgh: Edinburgh University Press.

Corrales, Javier. 2002. *Presidents without Parties: The Politics of Economic Reform in Argentina and Venezuela in the 1990s*. University Park: Pennsylvania State University Press.

1998. "Coalitions and Corporate Choices in Argentina, 1976–1994: The Recent Private Sector Support for Privatization." *Studies in Comparative and International Development* 32: 24–51.

Correljé, Aad. 1994. *The Spanish Oil Industry: Structural Change and Modernization*. Tinbergen Institute Research Series no. 84. Amsterdam: Thesis Publishers.

Cortes, Rosalía and Adriana Marshall. 1999. "Estrategia Económica, Instituciones y Negociación Política de la Reforma Social en Noventa." *Desarrollo Económico* 39: 195–212.

Costas, Antón and Rosa Nonell. 1996. "Organización de los Intereses Económicos, Función Empresarial y Política Económica en España: El Caso de la CEOE" in P. Martín Aceña and F. Comín, eds. *La Empresa en la Historia de España*. Madrid: Civitas.

Cotler, Julio. 1975. "The New Mode of Political Domination in Peru" in A. Lowenthal, ed. *The Peruvian Experiment*. Princeton, NJ: Princeton University Press.

Coutinho, Luciano and Flavio Rabelo. 2003. "Brazil: Keeping It in the Family" in Charles Oman, ed. *Corporate Governance in Development*. Paris: OECD and CIPE.

Cristi, Renato. 2000. *El Pensamiento Político de Jaime Guzmán*. Santiago: LOM.

Cypher, James. 1990. *State and Capital Accumulation in Mexico: Development Policy since 1940*. Boulder, CO: Westview Press.

Dahse, Fernando. 1979. *El mapa de la extrema riqueza*. Santiago: Aconcagua.

Daley, Anthony. 1996. *Steel, State and Labor: Mobilization and Adjustment in France*. Pittsburgh: University of Pittsburgh Press.

Danani, Claudia. 2003. "Condiciones y prácticas sociopolíticas en las políticas sociales: Las obras sociales, mas allá de la afiliación" in J. Lindenboim and C. Danani, eds. *Entre el Trabajo y la Política*. Buenos Aires: Biblios.

Davolos, Patricia. 2001. "Después de la privatización: Trayectorias laborales de trabajadores con retiro voluntario." *Estudios del Trabajo* no 21: 69–94.

Delamata, Gabriela. 2004. *Los Barrios Desbordados*. Buenos Aires: Eudeba.

De Quinto, Javier. 1994. *Política Industrial en España: Un Análisis Multisectorial*. Madrid: Ediciones Pirámide.

Dirección de Estudios del Banco Central de Chile. 1989.

Domínguez, José. 1993. *SOMISA: Reconversión, o muerte*. Buenos Aires: Editorial El Otro Mundo.

Dornelas, Antonio. 2003. "Industrial Relations in Portugal: Continuity or Controlled Change" in F. Monteiro, J. Tavares, M. Glatzer, and A. Cardoso, eds. *Portugal: Strategic Options in European Context*. Lanham, MD: Lexington Books.

Draibe, Sonia. 2002. "Social Policies in the 1990s" in R. Baumann, ed. *Brazil in the 1990s: An Economy in Transition*. Hampshire: Palgrave.

Dresser, Denise. 1994. "Bringing the Poor Back In: National Solidarity as a Strategy of Regime Legitimation" in W. Cornelius, A. Craig, and J. Fox, eds. *Transformation of State-Society Relations in Mexico: The National Solidarity Strategy*. La Jolla, CA: Center of U.S.-Mexican Relations.

Dubin, Kenneth. 2008. "Legacies of Inequality: The Labor Market Consequences of Authoritarian Rule in Spain." Paper submitted to the meeting of the American Political Science Association (APSA), Boston.

Bibliography

2002. "Consolidating Conditionality: The Legacies of Authoritarianism and Triple Incorporation in Contemporary Spanish Labor Relations." Ph.D. Dissertation, Department of Political Science, University of California, Berkeley.

Durand, Francisco. 2002. "Business and the Crisis of Peruvian Democracy." *Business and Politics* 4: 319–41.

1994. *Business and Politics in Peru, the State and the National Bourgeoisie.* Boulder, CO: Westview Press.

Eaton, Kent. 2004a. *Politics beyond the Capital: The Design of Subnational Institutions in South America.* Stanford, CA: Stanford University Press.

2004b. "Designing Subnational Institutions: Regional and Municipal Reforms in Post-Authoritarian Chile." *Comparative Political Studies* 37: 218–44.

2002. *Politicians and Economic Reform in New Democracies: Argentina and the Philippines in the 1990s.* University Park: Pennsylvania State University Press.

Edo Hernández, Valentín and Raquel Paredes. 1992. "Análisis del Gasto Público en Reconversión Industrial en España." *Hacienda Pública* 120: 269–88.

Edwards, Sebastian. 1995. *Crisis and Reform in Latin America: From Despair to Hope.* Washington, DC: World Bank.

Edwards, Sebastian and Alejandra Cox. 1991. *Monetarism and Liberalization.* Chicago: University of Chicago Press.

Ekiert, G. and S. Hanson. 2003. "Time, Space and Institutional Change in Central and Eastern Europe" in G. Ekiert and S. Hanson, eds. *Capitalism and Democracy in Central and Eastern Europe.* Cambridge: Cambridge University Press.

Ekiert, Grzegorz. 2003. "Patterns of Post-Communist Transformations in Central and Eastern Europe" in G. Ekiert and S. Hanson, eds. *Capitalism and Democracy in Central and Eastern Europe.* Cambridge: Cambridge University Press.

Ellison, Christopher and Gary Gereffi. 1990. "Explaining Strategies and Patterns of Industrial Development" in G. Gereffi and D. Wyman, eds. *Manufacturing Miracles: Paths of Industrialization in Latin America and East Asia.* Princeton, NJ: Princeton University Press.

Enciclopedia Nacional del Petróleo, Petroquímica y Gas. Various years. Madrid: Ediciones Oilgas.

Erickson, Kenneth. 1977. *The Brazilian Corporative State and Working Class Politics.* Berkeley: University of California Press.

Erickson, K. and K. Middlebrook. 1982. "The State and Organized Labor in Brazil and Mexico" in S. Hewlett and R. Weinert, eds. *Brazil and Mexico: Patterns in Late Development.* Philadelphia: ISHI.

Escobar, Modesto. 1993. "Works or Union Councils? The Representative System in Medium and Large Sized Spanish Firms." Working Paper 1993/43. Madrid: Centro de Estudios Avanzados.

Espina, Alvaro. 1992. "Diez Años de Política Industrial." *Leviatán* 50: 39–65.

1991. "La Política de Rentas en España" in F. Miguelez and C. Prieto, eds. *Las Relaciones Laborales en España.* Madrid: Siglo XXI.

Esping-Andersen, Gosta. 1990. *The Three Worlds of Welfare Capitalism.* Princeton, NJ: Princeton University Press.

Etchemendy, Sebastián. 2005. "Old Actors in New Markets: The Transformation of the Populist/Industrial Coalition in Argentina, 1989–2001" in María Victoría Murillo and Steven Levitsky, eds. *Argentine Democracy: The Politics of Institutional Weakness.* University Park: Pennsylvania State University Press.

Bibliography

2004a. "Revamping the Weak, Protecting the Strong and Managing Privatization: Governing Globalization in the Spanish Take-Off." *Comparative Political Studies* 37: 623–5

2004b. "Repression, Exclusion and Inclusion: Government-Union Relations and Patterns of Labor Reform in Liberalizing Economies." *Comparative Politics* 36: 273–90.

2001. "Constructing Reform Coalitions: The Politics of Compensations in Argentina's Economic Liberalization." *Latin American Politics and Society* 43: 1–35.

1995. "Límites al Decisionismo? El Poder Ejecutivo y la Formulación de la Legislación Laboral" in R. Sidicaro and J. Mayer, eds. *Política y Sociedad en los Años del Menemismo*. Buenos Aires: Universidad de Buenos Aires.

Etchemendy, Sebastián and Ruth B. Collier. 2007. "Down but Not Out: Union Resurgence and Segmented Neocorporatism in Argentina: 2003–2007." *Politics and Society* 7: 363–401.

Etchemendy, Sebastián and Vicente Palermo. 1998. "Conflicto y Concertación: Gobierno, Congreso y Organizaciones de Interés en la Reforma Laboral del Primer Gobierno de Menem." *Desarrollo Económico* 37: 559–90.

Evans, Peter. 1995. *Embedded Autonomy*. Princeton, NJ: Princeton University Press.

1987. "Class, State and Dependence in East Asia: Lessons for Latin Americanists" in F. Deyo, ed. *The Political Economy of the New Asian Industrialism*. Ithaca, NY: Cornell University Press.

1982. "Reinventing the Bourgeoisie: State Entrepreneurship and Class Formation in Dependent Capitalist Development." *American Journal of Sociology* 88: 211–47.

1979. *Dependent Development*. Princeton, NJ: Princeton University Press.

Evans, Peter and James Rauch. 1999. "Bureaucracy and Growth: A Cross-National Analysis of the Effects of 'Weberian' State Structures on Economic Growth. *American Sociological Review* 64: 748–65.

Evans, Peter, and John Stephens. 1988. "Studying Development Since the Sixties: The Emergence of a New Comparative Political Economy." *Theory and Society* 17: 713–745.

Eyal, Gil, Ivan Szelenyi, and Eleanor Townsley. 1998. *Making Capitalism Without Capitalists*. New York: Verso.

Fajnzylber, Fernando. 1985. *La Industrialización Trunca de América Latina*. Mexico: Centro de Economía Transnacional.

Falcón, Ricardo. 1993. "Políticas neoliberales y respuestas sindicales" in O. Moreno, ed. *Desafíos para el Sindicalismo en Argentina*. Buenos Aires: Legasa.

Falleti, Tulia. 2010. *Decentralization and Subnational Politics*. Cambridge: Cambridge University Press.

2006. "Theory-Guided Process Tracing in Comparative Politics: Something Old, Something New." *APSA-CP* 1: 9–14.

Farinas, J., Jordi Jaumandreu, and Gonzalo Mato. 1989. "La Empresa Pública Industrial Española: 1981–1986." *Papeles de Economía Española* 38: 199–216.

Fayad, Marwan and Homa Motamen. 1986. *The Economics of Petrochemical Industry*. New York: St. Martin's Press.

Fazio, Hugo. 1997. *Mapa Actual de la Extrema Riqueza en Chile*. Santiago: LOM.

Feigenbaum, H., J. Henig, and C. Hamnett. 1998. *Shrinking the State: The Political Underpinnings of Privatization*. Cambridge: Cambridge University Press.

Feldman, Silvio. 1991. "Tendencias a la sindicalización en Argentina." *Estudios del Trabajo* 2: 79–109.

Bibliography

Feldmann, Magnus. 2007. "The Origins of Varieties of Capitalism: Lessons from Post-Socialist Transitions in Estonia and Slovenia" in B. Hancké, M. Rhodes, and M. Thatcher, eds. *Beyond Varieties of Capitalism*. Oxford: Oxford University Press.

FIEL. 1995. *El Sistema de Seguridad Social*. Buenos Aires: FIEL-CEA.

1990. *Protection of Intellectual Property Rights*. Buenos Aires: FIEL.

Finchelstein, Diego. 2010. "Different States, Different Nationalizations: A Comparative Analysis of the Process of Firms' Internationalization in Latin America." Ph.D. dissertation, Department of Political Science, Northwestern University.

2004. "El comportamiento empresario durante la década del 90: El Grupo Macri." *Realidad Económica* 203: 26–49

Fishman, R. and C. Mershon. 1993. "Workplace Leaders and Labor Organization: Limits on the Mobilisation and Representation of Workers." *International Contributions to Labor Studies* 3: 67–90.

Fishman, Robert. 1990. *Working Class Organization and the Return to Democracy in Spain*. Ithaca, NY: Cornell University Press.

Fitzgerald, Edmund. 1979. *The Political Economy of Peru 1956–78*. Cambridge: Cambridge University Press.

Fourcade, Marion. 2009. *Economists and Societies*. Princeton, NJ: Princeton University Press.

Fourcade, Marion and Sarah Babb. 2002. "The Rebirth of the Liberal Creed: Paths to Neoliberalism in Four Countries." *American Journal of Sociology* 108: 533–79.

Foxley, Alejandro. 1983. *Latin American Experiments in Neoconservative Economics*. Berkeley: University of California Press.

Fraile Balbín, Pedro. 1992. *Interés Público y Captura del Estado: La Empresa Pública Siderúrgica en España 1941–1981*. Working Paper no. 9203. Madrid: FIES.

French Davis, Ricardo and Dagmar Raczynski. 1990. "The Impact of Global Recession and National Policies on Living Standards in Chile (1973–89)." Working Paper CIEPLAN, Notas Técnicas no. 97. Santiago.

Freytes Rey, Ada. 1999. "Las relaciones laborales en la actividad sidero-metalúrgica: Informalidad y fragmentación" in Arturo Fernández and Raúl Bisio, eds. *Política y Relaciones Laborales en la Transición Democrática Argentina*. Buenos Aires: Lumen-Humanitas.

Frieden, Jeffrey. 1991. *Debt, Development and Democracy*. Princeton, NJ: Princeton University Press.

Fundación Fondo Para la Investigación Económica y Social (FIES). 1985. "Representatividad y Organización de CCOO y UGT: Una Comparación Europea." *Papeles de Economía Española* 22: 235–41.

Gadano, Nicolás. 2000. "Determinantes de la Inversión en el Sector Petróleo y Gas en la Argentina" in Daniel Heyman and Bernardo Kosacoff, eds. *La Argentina de los Noventa*. Buenos Aires: CEPAL-EUDEBA.

Gadano, Nicolás and Federico Sturzenegger. 1998. "La Privatización de las Reservas en el Sector Hidrocarburífero: El Caso de Argentina." *Revista de Análisis Económico* 13: 75–115.

Gámir, Luis. 1999. *Las Privatizaciones en España*. Madrid: Pirámide.

Garay, Candelaria. 2009. "Associational Linkages to Labor Unions and Political Parties" in R. Collier and S. Handlin, eds. *Reorganizing Popular Politics*. University Park: Pennsylvania State University Press.

2007. "Social Policy and Collective Action: Unemployed Workers, Community Associations, and Protest in Argentina." *Politics and Society* 35: 301–28.

Bibliography

García Becedas, G. 1989. *Reconversiones industriales y ordenamiento laboral*. Madrid: Tecnos.

García de Polavieja, Javier and Andrew Richards. 2001. "Trade Unions, Unemployment and Working-Class Fragmentation in Spain" in N. Bermeo, ed. *Unemployment in the New Europe*. Cambridge: Cambridge University Press.

García Hermoso, José. 1990. "El Presente de la Empresa Pública Industrial. El Grupo INI" in F. Martín Aceña and F. Comín, eds. *Empresa Pública e Industrialización en España*. Madrid: Alianza.

Garret, Geoffrey. 1998. *Partisan Politics in the Global Economy*. Cambridge: Cambridge University Press.

Garrido, Celso. 1998. "El Liderazgo de las Grandes Empresas Industriales Mexicanas" in W. Peres, ed. *Grandes Empresas y Grupos Industriales Latinoamericanos*. Mexico: Siglo XXI.

Gatica Barros, Jaime. 1989. *Deindustrialization in Chile*. Boulder, CO: Westview Press.

Geddes. Barbara. 1995. "How Politicians Decide Who Bears the Costs of Liberalization" in Ivan Berend, ed. *Transition to a Market Economy at the End of the 20th Century*. Munich: Sudosteuropa-Gesellschaft.

1994. *Politician's Dilemma*. Berkeley: University of California Press.

George, Alexander and Andrew Bennett. 2005. *Case Study and Theory Development in the Social Sciences*. Cambridge, MA: MIT Press.

Gerchunoff, Pablo. 1992. "Petróleo" in Pablo Gerchunoff, ed. *Las Privatizaciones en Argentina*. Buenos Aires: Instituto Torcuato Di Tella.

Gerchunoff, P., C. Bozzalla, and J. Sanguinetti. 1994. "Privatización, Apertura y Concentración: El Caso del Sector Siderúrgico Argentino." Series Reforma Política Pública. Santiago: ECLA-Santiago de Chile.

Gerchunoff, Pablo and José Luis Machinea. 1995. "Un Ensayo sobre la Política Económica Después de la Estabilización" in Pablo Bustos, ed. *Mas Allá de la Estabilidad*. Buenos Aires: Fundación Friedrich Ebert.

Gerchunoff, Pablo and Juan Carlos Torre. 1996. "La Política de Liberalización Económica en la Administración de Menem." *Desarrollo Económico* 36: 733–67.

Gereffi, Gary and Donald Wyman, eds. 1990. *Manufacturing Miracles: Paths of Industrialization in Latin America and East Asia*. Princeton, NJ: Princeton University Press.

Gerring, John. 2001. *Social Science Methodology: A Criterial Framework*. Cambridge: Cambridge University Press.

Gibson, Edward. 1997. "The Populist Road to Market Reform: Policy and Electoral Coalitions in Mexico and Argentina." *World Politics* 49: 339–70.

Gibson, Edward and Ernesto Calvo. 2000. "Federalism and Low-Maintenance Constituencies: Territorial Dimensions of Economic Reform in Argentina." *Studies in Comparative International Development* 35: 3.

Gillespie, Richard. 1990. "The Break-Up of the 'Socialist Family': Party-Union Relations in Spain, 1982–1989." *West European Politics* 13: 47–61.

Gobierno de Chile. 2010. Sitio Histórico Eelectoral (http://www.elecciones.gov.cl/). Accessed October 2010.

Goertz, Gary. 2009. "Point of Departure: Intension and Extension" in David Collier and John Gering, eds. *Concepts and Method in the Social Science*. Oxon: Routledge.

Golbert, Laura. 1998. "Los Problemas de Empleo y las Políticas Sociales." *Boletín Informativo Techint* 258: 53–71.

Bibliography

Golden, M., M. Wallerstein, and P. Lange. 1999. "Postwar Trade Union Organization and Industrial Relations in Twelve Countries" in H. Kitschelt, P. Lange, and G. Marks, eds. *Continuity and Change in Contemporary Capitalism*. Cambridge: Cambridge University Press.

Golden, Miriam. 1997. *Heroic Defeats: The Politics of Job Loss*. New York: Cambridge University Press.

Goldstein, Andrea. 2002. "Embraer: From National Champion to Global Player." *CEPAL Review* 77: 97–115.

1999. "Brazilian Privatization in International Perspective: The Rocky Path from State Capitalism to Regulatory Capitalism." *Industrial and Corporate Change* 8: 673–711.

Goldstein, Andrea and Ben Schneider. 2004. "Big Business in Brazil: States and Markets in the Corporate Reorganization of the 1990s" in Edmund Amann and Ha-Joon Chang, eds. *Brazil and South Korea: Economic Crisis and Restructuring*. London: Institute of Latin American Studies.

Gómez, Marcelo. 1997. "Conflictividad Laboral durante el Plan de Convertibilidad (1991–95)." *Estudios Sociológicos* 45: 639–89.

Gómez Mera, Laura. 2007. "Macroeconomic Concerns and Intrastate Bargains: Explaining Illiberal Policies in the Brazilian Automobile Sector." *Latin American Politics & Society* 49: 113–40.

González, Manuel. 1979. *La Economía Política del Franquismo*. Madrid: Tecnos.

Gonzáles Portilla, Manuel. 1994. "Industrilización y Política en la Restauración: La Formación de una Nueva Elite Política" in Pedro Carsa Soto, ed. *Elites. Prosopografía Contemporánea*. Valladolid: Universidad de Valladolid.

Gordillo, Mónica. 1999. "Movimientos Sociales e Identidades Colectivas: Repensando el Ciclo de Protesta Obrera Cordobés de 1969–1971." *Desarrollo Económico* 39: 385–408.

1991. "Los Prolegómenos del Cordobazo: Los Sindicatos Líderes de Córdoba dentro de la Estructura de Poder Sindical." *Desarrollo Económico* 31: 163–87.

Gorenstein, Silvia. 1993. "El Complejo Petroquímico Bahía Blanca: Algunas Reflexiones sobre sus Implicancias Espaciales." *Desarrollo Económico* 32: 575–601.

Graham, Carol. 1994. *Safety Nets, Politics, and the Poor: Transitions to Market Economies*. Washington, DC: Brookings Institution.

1991. "From Emergency Employment to Social Investment." Brookings Occasional Papers. Washington, DC: Brookings Institution.

Graham, Carol and Cheikh Kane. 1998. "Opportunistic Government or Sustaining Reform? Electoral Trends and Public Expenditures Patterns in Peru." *Latin American Research Review* 33: 67–104.

Greskovits, Béla. 1998. *The Political Economy of Protest and Patience*. Budapest: Central European University Press.

Grzymala-Busse, Anna. 2002. *Redeeming the Communist Past: The Regeneration of Communist Successor Parties in East Central Europe after 1989*. Cambridge: Cambridge University Press.

Guillén, Mauro. 2005. *The Rise of Spanish Multinationals*. Cambridge: Cambridge University Press.

2001. *The Limits of Convergence: Globalization and Organizational Change in Argentina, South Korea, and Spain*. Princeton, NJ: Princeton University Press.

Gunther, Richard. 1992. "Spain: The Very Model of Elite Settlement" in J. Higley and R. Gunther, eds. *Elites and Democratic Consolidation*. Cambridge: Cambridge University Press.

Bibliography

Gwartney, J., R. Lawson, and W. Block. 2001. *Economic Freedom of the World*. Vancouver: Fraser Institute.

Hachette, Dominique and Rolf Luders. 1993. *Privatization in Chile*. San Francisco: ICS Press.

Hachette, Dominique, Rolf Luders, and Guillermo Tagle. 1993. "Five Cases of Privatization in Chile" in M. Sánchez and R. Corona, eds. *Privatization in Latin America*. Washington, DC: IDB.

Haggard, S., S. Maxfield, and Ben Schneider. 1997. "Theories of Business and Business-State Relations" in Silvia Maxfield and Ben Schneider, eds. *Business and the State in Developing Countries*. Ithaca, NY: Cornell University Press.

Haggard, Stephen. 1995. *Developing Nations and the Politics of Global Integration*. Washington, DC: Brookings Institution.

    1990. *Pathways from the Periphery*. Ithaca, NY: Cornell University Press.

Haggard, Stephen and Robert Kaufman. 1995. *The Political Economy of Democratic Transitions*. Princeton, NJ: Princeton University Press.

    1992. "Introduction" in S. Haggard and R. Kaufman, eds. *The Politics of Economic Adjustment*. Princeton, NJ: Princeton University Press.

Haggard, Stephen and Sylvia Maxfield. 1996. "The Political Economy of Financial Internationalization." *International Organization* 50: 35–68.

Haggard, Stephen and Steven Webb. 1994. "Introduction" in S. Haggard and S. Webb, eds. *Voting for Reform*. New York: Oxford University Press.

Hagopian, Frances. 1998. "Negotiating Economic Transitions in Liberalizing Polities: Political Representation and Economic Reform in Latin America." Working Paper. Weatherhead Center for International Affairs. Cambridge, MA: Harvard University.

Hall, Peter. 2003. "Aligning Ontology and Methodology in Comparative Politics" in J. Mahoney and D. Rueschemeyer, eds. *Comparative Historical Analysis in the Social Sciences*. Cambridge: Cambridge University Press.

    1999. "The Political Economy of Europe in an Era of Interdependence" in H. Kitschelt et al., eds. *Continuity and Change in Contemporary Capitalism*. Cambridge: Cambridge University Press.

    1997. "The Role of Interests, Institutions, and Ideas in the Comparative Political Economy of Industrialized Nations" in M. Lichbach and A. Zuckerman, eds. *Comparative Politics: Rationality, Culture and Structure*. Cambridge: Cambridge University Press.

    1989. *The Political Power of Economic Ideas*. Princeton, NJ: Princeton University Press.

    1986. *Governing the Economy*. New York: Oxford University Press.

Hall, Peter and David Soskice. 2001. *Varieties of Capitalism*. Oxford: Oxford University Press.

Hamann, Kerstin. 2001. "The Resurgence of National-Level Bargaining: Union Strategies in Spain." *Industrial Relations Journal* 32: 154–72.

    2000. "Linking Policies and Economic Voting: Explaining Reelection in the Case of the Spanish Socialist Party." *Comparative Political Studies* 33: 1018–48.

Hancké, B., M. Rhodes, and M. Thatcher. 2007. "Introduction: Beyond Varieties of Capitalism" in B. Hancké, M. Rhodes, and M. Thatcher, eds. *Beyond Varieties of Capitalism*. Oxford: Oxford University Press.

Hellman, Joel. 1998. "Winners Take All: The Politics of Partial Reform." *World Politics* 50: 203–34.

336 *Bibliography*

Hipsher, Patricia. 1994. "Political Processes and the Demobilization of the Shantytown Dweller's Movement in Redemocratizing Chile." Ph.D. Dissertation, Cornell University.

Hirschman, Albert. 1968. "The Political Economy of Import-Substituting Industrialization in Latin America." *Quarterly Journal of Economics* 82, February, 1–32.

Houseman, Susan. 1991. *Industrial Restructuring with Job Security: The Case of European Steel.* Cambridge, MA: Harvard University Press.

Howell, Chris. 2003. "Varieties of Capitalism: And Then There Was One?" *Comparative Politics* 36: 103–24.

Howell, Thomas, W. Noellert, J. Kreier, and Alan Wolff. 1988. *Steel and the State: Government Intervention and Steel Structural Crises.* Boulder, CO: Westview Press.

Huber, Evelyne. 1983. "The Peruvian Military Government, Labor Mobilization and the Political Strength of the Left." *Latin American Research Review* 43: 57–93.

Huber, Evelyne and John D. Stephens. 2001. *Development and Crises of the Welfare State.* Chicago: University of Chicago Press.

Huneeus, Carlos. 2000. *El Régimen de Pinochet.* Santiago: Sudamericana Chilena.

Huntington, Samuel. 1991. *The Third Wave.* Norman: University of Oklahoma Press.

IAE. 1997. "The Techint Group and Somisa's Privatization (1991–92)." Unpublished report. Buenos Aires: Escuela de Dirección y Negocios, Universidad Austral.

Iankova, Elena. 2002. *Eastern European Capitalism in the Making.* Cambridge: Cambridge University Press.

Indicadores Económicos y Sociales, 1980–1988. Santiago: Banco Central de Chile.

Instituto Nacional de Estadísticas (INE). 1990. *Anuario Estadístico de España.* Madrid: INE.

   1984. *Encuesta Industrial.* Madrid: INE

Instituto Nacional de Estadística, Geografía e Informática (INEGI). 1991. *La Industria Siderúrgica en Mexico.* Mexico: INEGI.

   1986. *La Industria Automotriz en Mexico, 1980–1985.* Mexico: INEGI.

Instituto Nacional de Estadísticas y Censos (INDEC). 1989. *Censo de la Industria Manufacturera.* Buenos Aires: INDEC.

Instituto para el Desarrollo Industrial (IDI). 1997. *La Industrial Argentina 1990–1996.* Nota 61. Buenos Aires: IDI-UIA (Unión Industrial Argentina).

Instituto Petroquímico Argentino (IPA). 1999a. *Información Estadística de la Industria Petroquímica y Química.* Buenos Aires: IPA.

   1999b. *La República Argentina y su Industria Petroquímica.* Buenos Aires: IPA.

International Labor Organization (ILO). Various years. Statistical Yearbook. Geneva: ILO.

Irigoyen, Alberto. 2006. "Hacia una nueva ley de protección de la propiedad intelectual: El Caso de la Industria Farmacéutica Argentina." Ph.D. dissertation, Department of History, Torcuato Di Tella University.

Jabbaz, Marcela. 1996. *Modernización Laboral o Flexibilidad Salarial.* Buenos Aires: CEAL.

James, Daniel. 1988. *Resistance and Integration.* Cambridge: Cambridge University Press.

   1981. "Rationalisation and Working Class Response: The Context and Limits of Factory Floor Activity in Argentina." *Journal of Latin American Studies* 13: 375–402.

Jelin, Elizabeth and Juan Carlos Torre. 1982. "Los nuevos trabajadores en América Latina: Una reflexión sobre la tesis de la aristocracia obrera." *Desarrollo Económico* 22: 3–23.

Bibliography

Jenkins, Rhys. 1984. "The Rise and Fall of the Argentine Motor Vehicle Industry" in Rich Kronish and Kenneth Mericle, eds. *The Political Economy of the Latin American Motor Vehicle Industry*. Cambridge, MA: MIT Press.

Jensen, Michael. 1989. "Eclipse of the Public Corporation." *Harvard Business Review* 67: 61–73.

Johnson, Chalmers. 1987. "Political Institutions and Economic Performance: Government-Business Relations in Japan, South Korea and Taiwan" in F. Deyo, ed. *The Political Economy of the New Asian Industrialism*. Ithaca, NY: Cornell University Press.

Katzenstein, Peter. 1985. *Small States in World Markets*. Ithaca, NY: Cornell University Press.

Katznelson, Ira. 1997. "Structure and Configuration in Comparative Politics" in M. Lichback and Alan Zuckerman, eds. *Comparative Politics: Rationality, Culture and Structure*. Cambridge: Cambridge University Press.

Kaufman, Robert and Alex Segura-Ubriego. 2001. "Globalization, Domestic Politics and Social Spending in Latin America." *World Politics* 53: 553–87.

Kaufman, Robert and Guillermo Trejo. 1997. "Regionalism, Regime Transformation and PRONASOL: The Politics of the National Solidarity Program in Four Mexican States." *Journal of Latin American Politics* 29: 717–45.

Keck, Margaret. 1992. *The Workers Party and Democratization in Brazil*. New Haven, CT: Yale University Press.

Kessler, Timothy. 1998. "Political Capital: Mexican Financial Policy under Salinas." *World Politics* 51: 36–66.

King, Gary, Robert Keohane, and Sideny Verba. 1994. *Designing Social Inquiry*. Princeton, NJ: Princeton University Press.

King, Lawrence. 2007. "Central European Capitalism in Comparative Perspective" in B. Hancké, M. Rhodes, and M. Thatcher, eds. *Beyond Varieties of Capitalism*. Oxford: Oxford University Press.

2002. "Postcommunist Divergence: A Comparative Analysis of the Transition to Capitalism in Poland and Russia." *Studies in Comparative International Development* 37: 3–34.

King, Lawrence and Iván Szelenyi. 2005. "Postcommunist Economic Systems" in N. Smelser and R. Swedberg, eds. *Handbook of Economic Sociology*. Princeton, NJ: Princeton University Press.

Kingstone, Peter. 2001. "Why Free Trade 'Losers' Support Free Trade: Industrialists and the Surprising Politics of Trade Reform in Brazil." *Comparative Political Studies* 34: 986–1010.

1999. *Crafting Coalitions for Reform: Business Preferences, Political Institutions, and Neoliberal Reform in Brazil*. University Park: Pennsylvania State University Press.

Kitschelt, Herbert, Peter Lange, Gary Marks, and John D. Stephens. 1999. "Convergence and Divergence in Advanced Capitalist Democracies" in H. Kitschelt et al., eds. *Continuity and Change in Contemporary Capitalism*. Cambridge: Cambridge University Press.

Kohli, Atul. 2004. *State-Directed Development*. Cambridge: Cambridge University Press.

Korpi, Walter. 2006. "Power Resources and Employer-Centered Approaches in Explanations of Welfare States and Varieties of Capitalism: Protagonists, Consenters, and Antagonists." *World Politics* 58: 167–206.

Kosacoff, Bernardo. 1995. "La Industrial Argentina: Un Proceso de Reestructuración Desarticulada" in Pablo Bustos, ed. *Mas Allá de la Estabilidad*. Buenos Aires: Fundación Friedrich Ebert.

Bibliography

Kozulj, Roberto. 1991. "Política de Precios en los Hidrocarburos: Un Estudio Comparativo de los Casos de Argentina y Brasil 1970–1989." *Desarrollo y Energía* no 2: 127–89.

Kozulj, Roberto and Victor Bravo. 1993. *La Política de Desregulación Petrolera en Argentina: Antecedentes e Impactos*. Buenos Aires: CEAL.

Kronish, Rich. "Latin America and the World Motor Vehicle Industry: The Turn to Exports" in Rich Kronish and Kenneth Mericle, eds. *The Political Economy of the Latin American Motor Vehicle Industry*. Cambridge, MA: MIT Press.

Krueger, Anne. 1993. *Political Economy of Policy Reform in Developing Countries*. Cambridge, MA: MIT Press.

Kurtz, Marcus. 2004. *Free Market Democracy and the Chilean and Mexican Countryside*. Cambridge: Cambridge University Press.

2002. "Understanding Third World Welfare State under Neoliberalism: The Politics of Social Provision in Chile and Mexico." *Comparative Politics* 34: 293–313.

2001. "State Developmentalism without a Developmental State: The Public Foundations of the 'Free Market Miracle' in Chile." *Latin American Politics and Society* 43, no. 2: 1–26.

1999. "Chile's Neoliberal Revolution: Incremental Decisions and Structural Transformations." *Journal of Latin American Studies* 31: 399–427.

Kurtz, Marcus and Sarah Brooks. 2008. "Embedding Neoliberal Reform in Latin America." *World Politics* 60: 231–80.

Larroulet, Cristian. 1984. "Reflexiones en Torno al El Estado Empresario en Chile." *Estudios Públicos* 14: 129–192.

Lavín, Joaquín. 1986. *Miguel Kast: Pasión de Vivir*. Santiago: Zig-Zag.

Leff, Nathaniel. 1978. "Industrial Organization and Entrepreneurship in Developing Countries: The Economic Groups." *Economic Development and Cultural Change* 26: 661–75.

Levi, Margaret. 1997. "A Model, a Method and a Map: Rational Choice in Comparative and Historical Analysis" in M. Lichbach and A. Zuckerman, eds. *Comparative Politics: Rationality, Culture and Structure*. Cambridge: Cambridge University Press.

Levitsky, Steven. 2003. *Transforming Labor-Based Parties in Latin America*. Cambridge: Cambridge University Press.

Levitsky, Steven and Lucan Way. 1998. "Between a Shock and a Hard Place: The Dynamics of Labor-Backed Adjustment in Poland and Argentina." *Comparative Politics*, January, 171–92.

Levy, Jonah D. 1999. *Tocqueville's Revenge: State, Society and Economy in Contemporary France*. Cambridge, MA: Harvard University Press.

Levy, Jonah D., Mari Miura, and Gene Park. 2006. "Exiting *Etatisme?* New Directions of State Policy in France and Japan" in Jonah D. Levy, ed. *The State after Statism*. Cambridge, MA: Harvard University Press.

Lieberman, Sima. 1995. *Growth and Crises in the Spanish Economy: 1940–93*. London: Routledge.

Lijphart, Arend. 1971. "The Comparable-Cases Strategy in Comparative Research." *Comparative Political Studies* 8: 158–77.

Linz, Juan. 1964. "An Authoritarian Regime: Spain" in E. Allardt and Y. Littunen, eds. *Cleavages, Ideologies and Party Systems*. Helsinki: Academic Bookstore.

Linz, Juan and Amando De Miguel. 1966. *Los Empresarios ante el Poder Público*. Madrid: Instituto de Estudios Políticos.

Bibliography

Linz, Juan and Alfred Stepan. 1996. "The Paradigmatic Case of Reforma Pactada–Ruptura Pactada: Spain" in J. Linz and A. Stepan, eds. *Problems of Democratic Transition and Consolidation*. Baltimore: Johns Hopkins University Press.

Lipset, Seymour M. 1960. "The Political Process in Trade Unions: A Theoretical Statement" in W. Galenson and S. M. Lipset, eds. *Labor and Trade Unionism*. New York: John Wiley & Sons.

Llach, J., P. Sierra, and G. Lugones. 1997. *La Industria Automotriz Argentina*. Unpublished manuscript. Buenos Aires.

Llanos, Mariana. 1998. "President-Congress Relationships in Argentina: The Case of Privatization under Alfonsín and Menem." Ph.D. Dissertation, Oxford University.

Lodola, Germán. 2005. "Protesta Popular y Redes Clientelares en Argentina. El Reparto Federal del Plan Trabajar." *Desarrollo Económico* 44: 515–533.

　2004. "Neopopulismo y compensaciones a los perdedores del cambio económico en América Latina." *Dialogo Político* 2: 11–37.

Logan, John. 1983. "Worker Mobilization and Party Politics: Revolutionary Portugal in Perspective" in G. Lawrence and H. Makler, eds. *Contemporary Portugal: The Revolution and Its Antecedents*. Austin: University of Texas Press.

López, Andrés. 1997. "Desarrollo y Reestructuración de la Petroquímica Argentina" in Daniel Chudnovsky and Andrés Lopez, eds. *Auge y Ocaso del Capitalismo Asistido: La Industria Petroquímica Latinoamericana*. Buenos Aires: ECLA-Alianza.

　1994. "Ajuste Estructural y Estrategias Empresarias en la Industria Petroquímica Argentina." *Desarrollo Económico* 33: 515–40.

Lora, Eduardo. 2001. "Structural Reforms in Latin America: What Has Been Reformed and How to Measure it." Research Department Working Paper Series 466. Inter-American Development Bank.

Lozano, Claudio. 1992. "La Privatización de SOMISA." Working Paper 22. Buenos Aires: Instituto de Estado y Participación (IDEP).

Lucita, Eduardo. 1999. *La patria del riel: Un siglo de luchas de los trabajadores ferro-viarios*. Buenos Aires: Pensamiento Nacional.

Luna, Juan Pablo. 2010. "Segmented Party-Voter Linkages in Latin America: The Case of the UDI." *Journal of Latin American Studies* 42: 325–356.

M&S Consulting. 1994. *La Industria Petroquímica*. Sectoral Overviews 7. Buenos Aires.

Madrid, Raúl. 2003. *Retiring the State: The Politics of Pension Privatization in Latin America and Beyond*. Palo Alto, CA: Stanford University Press.

Magaloni, Beatriz. 2008. *Voting for Autocracy*. Cambridge: Cambridge University Press.

Mahoney, James. 2007. "Qualitative Methodology and Comparative Politics." *Comparative Political Studies* 40: 122–44.

　2004. "Comparative Historical Methodology." *Annual Review of Sociology* 30: 81–101.

　2000. "Path Dependence in Historical Sociology." *Theory and Society* 29: 507–48.

　1999. "Nominal, Ordinal, and Narrative Appraisal in Macrocausal Analysis." *American Journal of Sociology* 104: 1154–96.

Mahoney, James and Gary Goertz. 2004. "The Possibility Principle: Choosing Negative Cases in Comparative Research." *American Political Science Review* 98: 653–69.

Mahoney, James and Dietrich Rueschemeyer. 2003. "Comparative Historical Analysis: Achievements and Agendas" in J. Mahoney and D. Ruechemeyer, eds. *Comparative Historical Analysis in the Social Sciences*. Cambridge: Cambridge University Press.

Majluf, N., N. Abarca, and D. Rodríguez. 1997. *Grandes Grupos Económicos en Chile*. Santiago: Dolmen.

Makler, Harry. 1983. "The Consequences of Survival and Revival of the Industrial Bourgeoisie" in L. Graham and D. Wheeler, eds. *In Search of Modern Portugal*. Madison: University of Wisconsin Press.

　1979. "The Portuguese Industrial Elite and Its Corporative Relations: A Comparative Study of Compartmentalization in an Authoritarian Regime" in G. Lawrence and H. Makler, eds. *Contemporary Portugal: The Revolution and Its Antecedents*. Austin: University of Texas Press.

Malloy, James. 1977. "Social Security and the Working Class in Twentieth Century Brazil." *Journal of Interamerican Studies and World Affairs* 19: 35–60.

Mamalakis, Markos. 1996. *Historical Statistics of Chile: Forestry and Related Activities*. Vol. 3. Westport, CT: Greenwood Press.

　1976. *The Growth and Structure of the Chilean Economy*. New Haven, CT: Yale University Press.

Manzetti, Luigi. 1999. *Privatization South America Style*. Oxford: Oxford University Press.

Maravall, Fernando and Oscar Fanjul. 1987. "Política Industrial, Competencia y Crecimiento (1960–1980)" in Fernando Maravall, ed. *Economía y Política Industrial en España*. Madrid: Pirámide.

Maravall, José María. 1993. "Politics and Policy: Economic Reforms in Southern Europe" in L. Bresser Pereira, A. Przeworski, and J. Maravall, eds. *Economic Reforms in New Democracies: A Social Democratic Approach*. Cambridge: Cambridge University Press.

　1978. *Dictatorship and Political Dissent*. London: Tavistock.

Mares, Isabela. 2003. *The Politics of Social Protection*. Cambridge: Cambridge University Press.

Márquez, Daniel. 1999. "Entre la crisis del valor social del trabajo y la fragilidad de la identidad del trabajador: Cuenca del Golfo de San Jorge" in A. Salvia, ed. *La Patagonia Privatizada*. Buenos Aires: La Colmena.

Marshall, Adriana and Laura Perelman. 2004. "Estructura de la negociación colectiva en la Argentina: Avanzó la descentralización en los años noventa?" *Estudios del Trabajo* 23: 3–30.

Martín Aceña, Pablo and Francisco Comín. 1991. *INI 50 años de industrialización en España*. Madrid: Espasa-Calpe.

Martínez, Javier and Alvaro Díaz. 1996. *Chile: The Great Transformation*. Washington, DC: Brookings Institution.

Martínez, Robert. 1993. *Business and Democracy in Spain*. Westport, CT: Praeger.

Martínez Lucio, Miguel. 1998. "Regulating Employment and Social Fragmentation" in A. Ferner and R. Hyman, eds. *Changing Industrial Relations in Europe*. Oxford: Blackwell.

Maxwell, Kenneth. 1995. *The Making of Portuguese Democracy*. Cambridge: Cambridge University Press.

McDermott, Gerald. 2004. "Institutional Change and Firm Creation in East-Central Europe: An Embedded Politics Approach." *Comparative Political Studies* 37: 188–217.

McGillivray, Fiona. 2004. *Privileging Industry*. Princeton, NJ: Princeton University Press.

McGuire, James. 1997. *Peronism without Perón*. Stanford University Press.

　1996. "Strikes in Argentina." *Latin American Research Review* 31: 127–49.

Mercado Review. August 1989. Buenos Aires: Editorial Coyuntura.

Bibliography

Middlebrook, Kevin. 1995. *Paradoxes of Revolution: Labor, the State and Authoritarianism in Post-Revolutionary Mexico.* Baltimore: Johns Hopkins University Press.

Migdal, Joel. 1988. *Strong Societies and Weak States.* Princeton, NJ: Princeton University Press.

Ministry of Economy, Argentina. 1999. *Caracterizcion y Evolucion del Gasto Publico Social, 1980–1997.* Buenos Aires.

Ministry of Industry and Energy, Spain. *Informe Sobre la Industria Española,* various years. Madrid.

  1983. *Libro Blanco de la Re-Industrialización,* Madrid.

Ministry of Labor and Social Security, Argentina. 2003a. *Plan Jefas y Jefes de Hogar Descupados, Un Año de Gestión.* Buenos Aires.

  2003b. *Boletín de Estadísticas Laborales,* Ministry of Labor and Social Security, May.

  2002. "Personal Comprendido en Convenios o Acuerdos de Empresa." Unpublished manuscript. Buenos Aires: Collective Bargaining Management Office.

Mizala, Alejandra. 1985. "Liberalización financiera y quiebra de empresas industriales: Chile, 1977–82." Working Paper CIEPLAN, Notas Técnicas no. 165. Santiago.

Molina, O. and M. Rhodes. 2007. "The Political Economy of Adjustment in Mixed Market Economies: A Study of Spain and Italy" in B. Hancké, M. Rhodes, and M. Thatcher, eds. *Beyond Varieties of Capitalism.* Oxford: Oxford University Press.

Montero, Alfred. 2001. *Shifting States in Global Markets.* University Park: Pennsylvania State University Press.

  1999. "State Interests and the New Industrial Policy in Brazil: The Privatization of Steel, 1990–1994." *Journal of Interamerican Studies and World Affairs* 40: 27–62.

Montero, Cecilia. 1997. *La Revolución Empresarial Chilena.* Santiago: CIEPLAN-Dolmen.

Moore, Barrington Jr. 1966. *Social Origins of Dictatorship and Democracy.* Boston: Beacon Press.

Morales, Eduardo. 1987. "Políticas Públicas y Ambito Local. La Experiencia Chilena" in J. Borja et al., eds. *Descentralización del Estado.* Santiago: FLACSO.

Morales, Mauricio. 2010. *Database on Elections in Chile.* Santiago: Universidad Diego Portales.

Morera, Carlos. 2002. "Trasnacionalización de los grupos de capital financiero en México: Límites y contradicciones" in J. Gambina, ed. *La Globalización Económico Financiera.* Buenos Aires: CLASCO.

Morley, S., R. Machado, and S. Pettinato. 1999. "Indexes of Structural Reform in Latin America." Serie Reformas Económicas no. 12. Santiago: Economic Commission for Latin America and the Caribbean (ECLAC).

Moulián, Tomás and Isabel Dujisin. 1988. "La Reorganización de los partidos de la derecha entre 1983 y 1988." Working Paper 388. Santiago: FLACSO.

Moya, Carlos. 1994. *Señas de Leviatán. Estado Nacional y Sociedad Industrial en España 1936–1980.* Madrid: Alianza.

Munck, Gerardo. 2004. "Tools for Qualitative Research" in Henry Brady and David Collier, eds. *Rethinking Social Inquiry.* Lanham, MD: Rowman & Littlefield.

  1998. *Authoritarianism and Democratization.* University Park: Pennsylvania State University Press.

Muñoz, Oscar. 1989. "Crisis and Industrial Reorganization in Chile." *Journal of Latin American Studies and World Affairs* 31: 169–92.

  1986. *Chile y su Industrialización.* Santiago: CIEPLAN.

342   *Bibliography*

Muñoz, Oscar and Ana María Arraigada. 1977. "Orígenes Políticos y Económicos del Estado Empresario en Chile." Working Paper 16. Santiago: CIEPLAN.

Murillo, Victoria. 2009. *Political Competition, Partisanship and Policy Making in Latin American Public Utilities.* Cambridge: Cambridge University Press.

  2001. *Labor Unions, Partisan Coalitions and Market Reforms in Latin America.* Cambridge: Cambridge University Press.

  1997. "Union Politics, Market-Oriented Reforms and the Re-Shaping of Argentine Corporatism" in D. Chalmers et al., eds. *The New Politics of Inequality in Latin America: Rethinking Participation and Representation.* Oxford: Oxford University Press.

Murillo, Victoria and Andrew Schrank. 2005. "With a Little Help of My Friends: Partisan Politics, Transnational Alliances and Labor Rights in Latin America." *Comparative Political Studies* 38: 971–999.

Nataf, Daniel. 1995. *Democratization and Social Settlements.* Albany: State University of New York Press.

Navarro, Mikel. 2004. "La larga marcha de la siderurgia española hacia la competitividad." *Economía Industrial* 355–56: 167–84.

  1990. *Política de Reconversión: Balance Crítico.* Madrid: EUDEMA.

  1989. *Crisis y Reconversión de la Siderurgia Española 1978–1988.* Madrid: Junta Del Puerto de Pasajes, Ministerio de Obras Públicas y Urbanismo (MOPU).

  1988. "La Política de Reconversión en España: El Caso de la Siderurgia." Ph.D. Dissertation, Economics Department, Universidad de Deusto.

Nelson, Joan. 1990. "Conclusions" in Joan Nelson, ed. *Economic Crisis and Policy Choice: The Politics of Adjustment in the Third World.* Princeton, NJ: Princeton University Press.

  1992. "Poverty, Equity and the Politics of Adjustment" in S. Haggard and R. Kaufman, eds. *The Politics of Economic Adjustment.* Princeton, NJ: Princeton University Press.

  1994. "Labor and Business Roles in Dual Transitions: Building Blocks or Stumbling Blocks?" in Joan Nelson, ed. *Intricate Links: Democratization and Market Reforms in Latin America and Eastern Europe.* Brunswick, NJ: Transaction.

Nofal, Beatriz. 1989. *Absentee Entrepreneurship and the Dynamics of the Motor Vehicle Industry in Argentina.* New York: Praeger.

Novaro, Marcos and Vicente Palermo. 2003. *La Dictadura Militar 1976–83.* Buenos Aires: Paidós.

Novick, Marta and Ana M. Catalano. 1996. "Reconversión Productiva y Relaciones Laborales en la Industria Automotriz Argentina." *Estudios del Trabajo* 11: 63–99.

Nunes, Joao and Luiz Montanheiro. 1997. "Privatisation in Portugal. An Insight into the Effects of a New Political Strategy." *Competitiveness Review* 7: 59–78.

ODEPLAN. 1976. *Chile: Estrategia y Perspectivas de Desarrollo.* Santiago: ODEPLAN.

O'Donnell, Guillermo. 1973. *Modernization and Bureaucratic-Authoritarianism.* Berkeley: Institute of International Studies, University of California.

O'Donnell, Guillermo and Philippe Schmitter. 1986. *Transitions from Authoritarian Rule: Tentative Conclusions about Uncertain Democracies.* Baltimore: Johns Hopkins University Press.

Oil and Gas Journal. 1994. "Spain's Downstream Restructuring Sparking Scramble by Marketers." 92: 31–36.

Olmos, Miguel. 1984. *La Batalla de Sagunto: Breve Historia de la Siderurgia Saguntina.* Valencia: Fernando Torres.

Bibliography

Organization for Economic Cooperation and Development (OECD). 1991. *Employment Outlook*. Geneva: OECD.

Orlanski, Dora and Andrea Makón. 2003. "De la Sindicalización a la Informalidad: El Caso Repsol-YPF." *Revista Argentina de Sociología* 1: 7–23.

Ortega Martínez et al. 1989. *Corporación de Fomento de la Producción: 50 Años de Realizaciones*. Santiago: Universidad de Santiago de Chile.

Ortiz, Luis. 1999. *Convergencia o Permanencia de los Sistemas de Relaciones Laborales*. Serie Tesis Doctorales no. 24. Madrid: Instituto Juan March.

Ostiguy, Pierre. 1998. "Peronism and Anti-Peronism: Class-Cultural Cleavages and Political Identity in Argentina." Ph.D. Dissertation, Department of Political Science, University of California, Berkeley.

1990. *Los Capitanes de la Industria*. Buenos Aires: Legasa.

Oxhorn, Philip. 1995. *Organizing Civil Society*. University Park: Pennsylvania State University Press.

Oxhorn, Philip and Graciela Ducatnzeiler. 1998. "Economic Reform and Democratization in Latin America" in P. Oxhorn and G. Ducatnzeiler, eds. *What Kind of Democracy? What Kind of Market?* University Park: Pennsylvania State University Press.

Palermo, Vicente and Marcos Novaro. 1996. *Política y Poder en el Gobierno de Menem*. Buenos Aires: Grupo Editorial Norma.

Paramio, Ludolfo. 1992. "Los Sindicatos y la Política en España, 1982–1992" in A. Guerra and J. Tezanos, eds. *La Década del Cambio*. Madrid: Sistema.

1990. "Los sindicatos y el sistema político en la España democrática: De la clandestinidad a la huelga general." *Sistema* 94–95: 73–81.

Paura, Vilma. 1995. "Ajuste y Desocupación: El Caso de Comodoro Rivadavia, 1975–1993." *Ciclos* 5: 113–31.

Pérez, Sofía. 2000. "From Decentralization to Reorganization: Explaining the Return to National Bargaining in Italy and Spain." *Comparative Politics* 32: 437–58.

1997. *Banking on Privilege: The Politics of Spanish Financial Reform*. Ithaca, NY: Cornell University Press.

Pérez Companc. Various years. *Memoria y Balance General*. Buenos Aires: Pérez Companc.

Pierson, Paul. 2004. *Politics in Time*. Princeton, NJ: Princeton University Press.

2000. "Increasing Returns, Path Dependence and the Study of Politics." *American Political Science Review* 94: 251–67.

1994. *Dismantling the Welfare State?* Cambridge: Cambridge University Press.

Pierson, Paul and Theda Skocpol. 2002. "Historical Institutionalism in Contemporary Political Science" in I. Katznelson and H. Milner, eds. *Political Science, the State of the Discipline*. New York: Norton.

Pion-Berlin, David. 1989. *The Ideology of State of Terror: Economic Doctrines and Political Repression in Argentina and Peru*. Boulder, CO: L. Rienner.

Pistonesi, H., F. Figueroa de laVega, and M. Torres. 1990. "La Política de Precios del Petróleo y Derivados Aplicada en Argentina en el Período 1970–1986." *Desarrollo y Energía* 1: 71–114.

Pizzorno, Alessandro. 1978. "Political Exchange and Collective Identity in Industrial Conflict" in C. Crouch and A. Pizzorno, eds. *The Resurgence of Class Conflict in Western Europe since 1968*. London: Macmillan Press.

Polanyi, Karl. 2001 [1944]. *The Great Transformation*. Boston: Beacon Press.

Pollack, Marcelo. 1999. *The New Right in Chile 1973–97*. New York: Macmillan Press.

Bibliography

Pop-Eleches, Grigore. 2009. *From Economic Crises to Reform: IMF Programs in Latin America and Eastern Europe*. Princeton, NJ: Princeton University Press.

Posner, Paul W. 2004. "Local Democracy and the Transformation of Popular Participation in Chile." *Latin American Politics and Society* 46: 55–81.

Przeworski, Adam. 1991. *Democracy and the Market*. Cambridge: Cambridge University Press.

Przeworski, Adam and Henry Teune. 1970. *The Logic of Comparative Social Inquiry*. New York: Wiley.

Raczynski, Dagmar. 1994. "Social Policies in Chile: Origins, Transformations and Perspectives." Working Paper no. 4, Democracy and Social Policy Series. Notre Dame, IN: Kellogg Institute for International Studies.

1988. "Social Policy, Poverty, and Vulnerable Groups: Children in Chile" in G. Cornia, R. Jolly, F. Stewart, and G. Andrea, eds. *Adjustment with a Human Face*. Vol. 2. Oxford: Clarendon Press.

Raczynski, Dagmar and Caludia Serrano. 1985. *Vivir la Pobreza*. Santiago: CIEPLAN.

Ramírez, Hernán. 2007. *Corporaciones en el Poder*. San Isidro: Lenguaje Claro.

Rands Barros, Mauricio. 1999. *Labor Relations and the New Unionism in Contemporary Brazil*. New York: St. Martin's Press.

Recio, A. and J. Roca. 1998. "The Spanish Socialists in Power: Thirteen Years of Economic Policy." *Oxford Review of Economic Policy* 14: 139–58.

Remmer, Karen. 1998. "The Politics of Neoliberal Economic Reform in South America, 1980–1994." *Studies in Comparative International Development* 33: 3–29.

1989. "The Politics of Military Rule in Chile, 1973–1987." *Comparative Politics* 21: 149–70.

Remmer, Karen and Erik Wibbels. 2000. "The Subnational Politics of Economic Adjustment." *Comparative Political Studies* 33: 4.

Repetto, Fabián. 2002. *Gestión pública y desarrollo social en los noventa. Las trayectorias de Argentina y Chile*. Buenos Aires: Prometeo.

Revista Oilgas: Petróleo, Petroquímica Y Gas. 1999. No. 379, July–August, Madrid.

1994. No. 318, July–August, Madrid.

Rey Román, Benito. 1987. *La ofensiva empresarial contra la intervención del estado*. Mexico: UNAM.

Reyneri, Emilio. 1989. "The Italian Labor Market: Between State Control and Social Regulation" in P. Lange and M. Regini, eds. *State, Markets and Social Regulation*. Cambridge: Cambridge University Press.

Rhodes, Martin. 2001. "The Political Economy of Social Pacts: 'Competitive Corporatism' and European Welfare Reform" in Paul Pierson, ed. *The New Politics of the Welfare State*. Oxford: Oxford University Press.

Riethof, Marieke. 2002. "Responses of the Brazilian Labor Movement to Privatization" in A. Jilberto and M. Riethof, eds. *Labour Relations in Development*. London: Routledge.

Rigby, M. and M. Aledo. 2001. "The Worst Record of Europe? A Comparative Analysis of Industrial Conflict in Spain." *European Journal of Industrial Relations* 7: 287–305.

Roberts, Kenneth. 2002. "Social Inequalities without Class Cleavages in Latin America's Neoliberal Era." *Studies in Comparative International Development* 36: 3–33.

1998. *Deepening Democracy? The Modern Left and Social Movements in Chile and Peru*. Stanford, CA: Stanford University Press.

1995. "Neoliberalism and the Transformation of Populism in Latin America." *World Politics* 48, no. 82: 116.

Bibliography

Roberts, Kenneth and Moises Arce. 1998. "Neoliberalism and Lower Class Voting Behavior in Peru." *Comparative Political Studies* 31: 217–46.

Robertson, Graeme. 2004. "Unions, Politics and Protest in New Democracies." *Comparative Politics* 36: 253–72.

Rodrigues, Miguel and Alvaro Mendonca. 1989. *Os Novos Grupos Economicos.* Lisbon: Texto Editora.

Rofman, Alejandro and Susana Peñalva. 1995. "La industria siderúrgica estatal en un marco de crisis y reestructuración global." *Revista Mexicana de Sociología* 52: 3–29.

Rofman, Alejandro. 1998. "Reforma o un Nuevo Rol para el Estado: Un Análisis Crítico a Partir de las Recientes Experiencias Privatizadoras." *Aportes* 11: 47–73.

Rogowski, Ronald. 1989. *Commerce and Coalitions.* Princeton, NJ: Princeton University Press.

Rosa Balbi, Carmen. 1997. "Politics and Trade Unions in Perú" in M. Cameron and P. Mauceri, eds. *The Peruvian Labyrinth.* University Park: Pennsylvania State University Press.

Rougier, Marcelo. 2004. *Industria, Finanzas e Instituciones en la Argentina: La experiencia del BANADE.* Buenos Aires: UNQ.

Royo, Sebastián. 2000. *From Social Democracy to Neoliberalism: The Consequences of Party Hegemony in Spain.* New York: St. Martin's Press.

Ruiz, David, ed. 1993. *Historia de Comisiones Obreras.* Madrid: Siglo XXI.

Ruiz Tagle, Jaime. 1985. *El Sindicalismo Chileno después del Plan Laboral.* Santiago: PET.

Ruiz Tagle, Jaime and Roberto Urmeneta. 1984. *Los Trabajadores del PEM.* Santiago: PET.

Saéz, Raul. 1987. "La Privatización de CAP." Working Paper no. 180. Santiago: CED.

San Román, Elena. 1999. *Ejército e Industria: El Nacimiento del INI.* Barcelona: Crítica.

Santamaría, Javier. 1988. *El Petróleo en España: Del Monopolio a la Libertad.* Madrid: Espasa-Calpe.

Saro Jáuregui, Gabriel. 2000. *Convergencia y Redes de Políticas: La Reconversión de la Siderurgia Integral en Gran Bretaña y España.* Serie Tesis Doctorales no. 26. Madrid: Instituto Juan March.

Schady, Norbert. 2000. "The Political Economy of Expenditures by the Peruvian Social Fund (FOCONDES), 1991–1995." *American Political Science Review* 94: 289–304.

Schamis, Héctor. 2002. *Re-Forming the State.* Ann Arbor: University of Michigan Press.
  1999. "Distributional Coalitions and the Politics of Market Reforms in Latin America." *World Politics* 51: 236–68.

Schipani, Andrés. 2008. "Organizando el Descontento. Movilizaciones de Desocupados en Argentina y Chile durante las Reformas de Mercado." *Desarrollo Económico* 48: 85–117.

Schmidt, Vivien. 2009. "Putting the Political Back into Political Economy by Bringing the State Back in Yet Again." *World Politics* 61: 516–46.

Schmitter, Philip. 1982. "Reflections on Where the Theory of Neocorporatism Has Gone and Where the Praxis of Neocorporatism Might Be Going" in G. Lehmbruch and P. Schmitter, eds. *Patterns of Corporatist Policymaking.* London: Sage.
  1979. "The 'Regime d'Exception' That Became the Rule: Forty Years of Authoritarian Domination in Portugal" in G. Lawrence and H. Makler, eds. *Contemporary Portugal: The Revolution and Its Antecedents.* Austin: University of Texas Press.

Schneider, Ben. 2009a. "Hierarchical Market Economies and Varieties of Capitalism in Latin America." *Journal of Latin American Studies* 41: 553–75.

2009b. "Big Business in Brazil" in L. Martinez Diaz and L. Brainard, eds. *Brazil as an Emerging Superpower*. Washington, DC: Brookings Institution.

2004a. *Business Politics and the State in Twentieth Century Latin America*. Cambridge: Cambridge University Press.

2004b. "Organizing Interests and Coalitions in the Politics of Market Reform in Latin America." *World Politics* 56: 456–79.

1991. *Politics within the State: Elite Bureaucrats and Industrial Policy in Authoritarian Brazil*. Pittsburgh: University of Pittsburgh Press.

Schneider, Cathy. 1995. *Shantytown Protest in Pinochet's Chile*. Philadelphia: Temple University Press.

Schrank, Andrew. 2007. "Asian Industrialization in Latin American Perspective: The Limits to Institutional Analysis." *Latin American Politics and Society* 49: 183–200.

2005. "Conquering, Comprador or Competitive: The National Bourgeoisie in the Developing World." Paper submitted to the 100th meeting of the American Sociological Association (ASA), Philadelphia.

Schrank, Andrew and Marcus Kurtz. 2005. "Credit Where Credit Is Due: Open Economy Industrial Policy and Export Diversification in Latin America and the Caribbean." *Politics and Society* 33: 671–702.

Schvarzer, Jorge. 1996. *La Industria que Supimos Conseguir*. Buenos Aires: Planeta.

1993. "Expansión, Maduración y Perspectivas de las Ramas Básicas de Procesos de la Industria Argentina. Una Mirada Ex-Post desde la Economía Política." *Desarrollo Económico* 33: 377–402.

1978. "Estrategia Industrial y Grandes Empresas: El Caso Argentino." *Desarrollo Económico* 18: 307–51.

Schwartz, P. and M. J. González. 1976. *Una Historia del INI, 1941–1946*. Madrid: Tecnos.

Scokpol, Theda and Margaret Somers. 1980. "The Uses of Comparative History in Macrosocial Inquiry." *Comparative Studies in Society and History* 22: 174–97.

Seatrade Review. 1992. "Objectives in Sight." May, 85–87.

1990. "Not of the Hook Yet Despite Level of Orders." July–August, 111–115.

Seawright, Jason and David Collier. 2004. "Glossary" in Henry Brady and David Collier, eds. *Rethinking Social Inquiry*. Lanham, MD: Rowman & Littlefield.

Segura, Julio and Arturo González Romero. 1992. "La Industria Española: Evolución y Perspectivas." *Papeles de Economía Española* 50: 140–72.

Sehnbruch, Kirsten. 2003. "From the Quantity of Employment to the Quality of Employment." Ph.D. Dissertation, Jesus College, University of Cambridge.

Seidman, Gay. 1994. *Manufacturing Militancy*. Berkeley: University of California Press.

Senén González, Santiago and Fabián Bosoer. 1999. *El Sindicalismo en Tiempos de Menem*. Buenos Aires: Corregidor.

Sennes, R. and R. Camargo Mendes. 2007. "Public Policies and Brazilian multinationals." Paper presented to the conference "Seminário Consolidação Regional e Expansão Global das EMN Latino Americanas." Sao Paulo.

Shadlen, Kenneth. 2009. "The Politics of Patents and Drugs in Brazil and Mexico: The Industrial Bases of Health Policies. *Comparative Politics* 42: 41–58.

2006. "The Politics of Property and the New Politics of Intellectual Property in the Developing World: Insights from Latin America." Paper presented at the 47th Annual Meeting of the International Studies Association, San Diego.

2004. *Democratization without Representation*. University Park: Pennsylvania State University Press.

Bibliography

Sheahan, John. 1987. *Patterns of Development in Latin America*. Princeton, NJ: Princeton University Press.

Shleifer, Andrei and Daniel Treisman. 2000. *Without a Map: Political Tactics and Economic Reform in Russia*. Cambridge, MA: MIT Press.

Shonfield, Andrew. 1965. *Modern Capitalism*. New York: Oxford University Press.

Short, R. P. 1984. "The Role of Public Enterpises: An International Comparison" in R. Floyd, C. Grey and R. Short, eds. *Public Enterprise in Mixed Economies*. Washington, DC: IMF.

Sierra Fernández, María del Pilar. 2000. "Reconversión e Internacionalización de la Siderurgia Española." *Economía Industrial* 333: 101–13.

Sikkink, Kathryn. 1991. *Ideas and Institutions*. Ithaca, NY: Cornell University Press.

Silva, Eduardo. 1996. *State and Capital in Chile*. Boulder, CO: Westview Press.

Silva, Patricio. 1995. "Empresarios, Neoliberalismo y Trancision Democrática en Chile." *Revista Mexicana de Sociología* 57: 2–25.

Singh, Ajit. 1995. "Corporate Financial Patterns in Industrializing Economies." IFC Technical Papers, no. 2. Washington, DC: World Bank.

Smith, W. Rand. 1998. *The Left's Dirty Job*. Pittsburgh: Pittsburgh University Press.

Smith, William. 1992. "Hyperinflation, Macroeconomic Instability and Neoliberal Restructuring in Democratic Argentina" in Edward Epstein, ed. *The New Argentine Democracy*. New York: Praeger.

Snyder, Richard. 2001a. "Scaling Down: The Subnational Comparative Method." *Studies in Comparative International Development* 36: 93–111.

2001b. *Politics after Neoliberalism: Re-Regulation in Mexico*. Cambridge: Cambridge University Press.

Spalding, Rose. 1994. "Capitalists and Revolution." Hellen Kellogg Institute Working Paper no. 202. Notre Dame, IN: Kellogg Institute for International Studies.

Stallings, Barbara. 1992. "International Influence on Economic Policy: Debt, Stabilization and Structural Reform" in S. Haggard and R. Kaufman, eds. *The Politics of Economic Adjustment*. Princeton, NJ: Princeton University Press.

Stallings, Barbara and Wilson Peres. 2000. *Growth, Employment, and Equity: The Impact of the Economic Reforms in Latin America and the Caribbean*. Washington, DC: Brookings Institution.

Stark, David. 1995. "Not by Design: The Myth of Designer Capitalism in Eastern Europe" in J. Hausner, B. Jessop, and K. Nielsen, eds. *Strategic Choice and Path Dependency in Post-Socialism*. Aldershot, England: Edward Elgar.

Stark, David and Laszlo Bruszt. 1998. *Postsocialist Pathways*. Cambridge: Cambridge University Press.

Stinchcombe, Arthur. 1968. *Constructing Social Theories*. New York: Harcourt.

Stokes, Susan 2001. *Mandates and Democracy: Neoliberalism by Surprise in Latin America*. Cambridge: Cambridge University Press.

1997. "Democratic Accountability and Policy Change: Economic Policy in Fujimori's Peru." *Comparative Politics* 29: 209–26.

Stoleroff, Alan. 2001. "Unemployment and Trade Union Strength in Portugal" in N. Bermeo, ed. *Unemployment in the New Europe*. Cambridge: Cambridge University Press.

1992. "Between Corporatism and Class Struggle: The Portuguese Labor Movement and the Cavaco Silva Governments." *West European Politics* 15: 118–50.

Story, Dale. 1986. *Industry, the State and Public Policy*. Austin: University of Texas Press.

Strath, Bo. 1987. *The Politics of De-Industrialisation*. London: Croom Helm.

348 *Bibliography*

Stumpo, Giovanni. 1997. "Evolución, Reestructuración y Exito Exportador de la Industria Chilena de Celulosa y Papel" in N. Bercovich and J. Katz, eds. *Reestructuración Industrial y Apertura Económica*. Buenos Aires: Alianza.

Sturzenegger, Federico and Mariano Tommasi, eds. 1998. *The Political Economy of Reform*. Cambridge, MA: MIT Press.

Suleiman, Ezra and John Waterbury. 1990. "Introduction" in E. Suleiman and J. Waterbury, eds. *The Political Economy of Public Sector Reform and Privatization*. Boulder, CO: Westview Press.

Svampa, Maristella and Sebastián Pereyra. 2003. *Entre la Ruta y el Barrio: La Experiencia de las Organizaciones Piqueteras*. Buenos Aires: Biblos.

Tafel, Heather and Dexter Boniface. 2003. "Old Carrots, New Sticks: Explaining Labor Strategies toward Economic Reform in Eastern Europe and Latin America." *Comparative Politics* 35: 313–33.

Tamames, Manuel. 1978. *La Oligarquía Financiera en España*. Barcelona: Planeta.

1966. *La Lucha Contra los Monopolios*. Madrid: Tecnos.

Tanaka, Martín. 2004. "Las Restricciones Políticas en la Reforma de Mercado en Perú" in C. Wise and R. Roett, eds. *La Política Posterior a la Reforma de Mercado en América Latina*. Buenos Aires: GEL.

Teichman, Judith. 2001. *The Politics of Freeing Markets in Latin America*. Chapel Hill: University of North Carolina Press.

1995. *Privatization and Political Change in Mexico*. Pittsburgh: University of Pittsburgh Press.

Tendencias Económicas. Various Years. *Annual Report*. Buenos Aires: Consejo Técnico de Inversiones.

Thacker, Strom. 2004. *Big Business, the State and Free Trade*. Cambridge: Cambridge University Press.

Thelen, Kathleen. 2004. *How Institutions Evolve*. Cambridge: Cambridge University Press.

2003. "How Institutions Evolve. Insights from Comparative Historical Analysis" in J. Mahoney and D. Rueschemeyer, eds. *Comparative Historical Analysis in the Social Sciences*. Cambridge: Cambridge University Press.

1999. "Historical Institutionalism in Comparative Politics." *Annual Review of Political Science* 2: 369–404.

1991. *Union of Parts: Labor Politics in Postwar Germany*. Ithaca, NY: Cornell University Press.

Thorp, Rosemary and Geoffrey Bertram. 1978. *Peru 1880–1977*. London: Macmillan.

Tobar, Federico. 2000. "Dimensiones Económicas de la Reforma del Seguro de Salud en Argentina." Unpublished manuscript. Buenos Aires.

Todesca, Jorge. 1998. *La Oferta de Productos Siderúrgicos Planos en la Argentina: Relaciones con la Industria Automotriz*. Unpublished manuscript. Buenos Aires.

Tomic, Blas and Raul Gonzalez. 1983. "Municipio y Estado: Dimensione de una relación clave." Working Paper, PRELAC. Santiago de Chile.

Torre, Juan Carlos 2004. "El Proceso Político Interno de los Sindicatos en la Argentina" in *El Gigante Invertebrado*. Buenos Aires: Siglo XXI.

1998. *El Proceso Político de las Reformas en América Latina*. Buenos Aires: Paidós.

1990. *La Vieja Guardia Sindical y Perón*. Buenos Aires: Sudamericana.

1989. *Los Sindicatos en el Gobierno (1973–76)*. Buenos Aires: CEAL.

ed. 1988. *La Formación del Sindicalismo Peronista*. Buenos Aires: Legasa.

Bibliography

1974. "The Meaning of Current Workers' Struggles." *Latin American Perspectives* 1: 73–81.

Tortella, Gabriel. 1990. "CAMPSA y el Monopolio de Petróleos" in F. Martín Aceña and F. Comín, eds. *Empresa Pública e Industrialización en España*. Madrid: Alianza.

Trebat, Tomas. 1983. *Brazil's State-Owned Enterprises*. Cambridge: Cambridge University Press.

Treisman, Daniel. 2003. "Cardoso, Menem, and Machiavelli: Political Tactics and Privatization in Latin America." *Studies in Comparative and International Development* 38: 93–109.

United Nations (UN). 1974. International Standard Industrial Classification (ISIC), Second Revision. New York: UN.

United Nations Industrial Development Organization (UNIDO). 1997. *Industrial Development Global Report*. New York: UNIDO.

1990. *Industrial Development Global Report*. New York: UNIDO.

1985. *Industrial Development Global Report*. New York: UNIDO.

1984. *Argentina*. Industrial Development Review Series, 460. Vienna: UNIDO.

1983a. *The Changing Role of the Public Industrial Sector in Development*. Vienna: UNIDO.

1983b. *The Role of Public Industrial Enterprise in Mexico*. Industrial Development Review Series, 428. Vienna: UNIDO.

Universidad Argentina de la Empresa (UADE). 1998. "La Industria Automotriz en Argentina." Sectoral Report Series. Buenos Aires.

Valdés, Francisco. 1994. "From Bank Nationalization to State Reform: Business and the New Mexican Order" in M. Cook, K. Middlebrook, and Molinar Horcasitas, eds. *The Politics of Economic Restructuring: State-Society Relations and Regime Change in Mexico*. La Jolla, CA: Center of U.S.-Mexican Relations.

Valdés, Juan. 1995. *Pinochet's Economists: The Chicago School in Chile*. Cambridge: Cambridge University Press.

Valenzuela, Arturo. 1991. "The Military in Power: The Consolidation of One-Man Rule" in P. Drake and I. Jaksic, eds. *The Struggle for Democracy in Chile*. Lincoln: University of Nebraska Press.

Valsaliso, Jesús. 2003. "Crisis y reconversión de la industria de construcción naval en el País Vasco." *Ekonomiaz* 54: 52–67.

Vladés, Teresa. 1987. "El Movimiento de Pobladores: 1973–1985: La Recomposición de las Solidaridades" in J. Borja et al., eds. *Descentralización del Estado*. Santiago: FLACSO.

Vass, Uisden and Carlos Valiente-Noailles. 1992. "The New Argentine Petroleum Law Regime." Unpublished manuscript.

Vega García, Rubén. 1995. *CCOO de Asturias en la Transición y la Democracia*. Oviedo: Unión Regional CCOO de Asturias.

1991. *La Corriente Sindical de Izquierda: Un Sindicalismo de Movilización*. Gijón: Ediciones de la Torre.

Vergara, Pilar. 1990. *Políticas contra la Extrema Pobreza en Chile, 1973–1988*. Santiago: FLACSO.

1985. *Auge y Caída del Neoliberalismo en Chile*. Santiago: FLACSO.

Viguera, Aníbal. 2000. *La Trama Política de la Apertura Económica en la Argentina (1987–1996)*. La Plata: Ediciones al Margen/UNLP.

Villarreal, Sofía. 1987. "La Unión Industrial Argentina" in J. Nun and J. C. Portantiero, eds. *Ensayos sobre la Transición Democrática en Argentina*. Buenos Aires: Puntosur.

Bibliography

Vispo, Adolfo. 1999. "Reservas de Mercado, Cuasi-Rentas de Privilegio y Deficiencias Regulatorias: el Régimen Automotriz Argentino" in D. Azpiazu, G. Gutman, and A. Vispo, eds. *La Desregulación de los Mercados*. Buenos Aires: Grupo Editorial Norma.

Waterbury, John. 1989. "The Political Management of Economic Adjustment and Reform" in Joan Nelson, ed. *Fragile Coalitions: The Politics of Economic Adjustment*. Washington, DC: Overseas Development Council.

Weir, Margaret. 1992. "Ideas and the Politics of Bounded Innovation" in S. Steinmo, K. Thelen, and F. Longstreth, eds. *The New Institutionalism: State, Society and Economy*. Cambridge: Cambridge University Press.

Weyland, Kurt. 2002. *The Politics of Reform in Fragile Democracies*. Princeton, NJ: Princeton University Press.

2001. "Clarifying a Contested Concept: Populism in the Study of Latin American Politics." *Comparative Politics* 34: 1–23.

1999. "Neoliberal Populism in Latin America and Eastern Europe." *Comparative Politics* 31: 379–401.

Whitehead, Laurance. 1987. "Inflation and Stabilisation in Chile 1970–77" in R. Thorp, and L. Whitehead, eds. *Inflation and Stabilisation in Latin America*. London: Macmillan.

Wibbels, Erik. 2005. *Federalism and the Market*. Cambridge: Cambridge University Press.

Williamson, Peter. 1985. *Varieties of Corporatism*. Cambridge: Cambridge University Press.

Willis, Elisa. 1995. "Explaining Bureaucratic Independence in Brazil: The Experience of the National Economic Development Bank." *Journal of Latin American Studies* 27: 625–61.

Wirth, John. 1970. *The Politics of Brazilian Development*. Stanford, CA: Stanford University Press.

World Bank. 1997. *World Development Report*. Washington, DC: World Bank.

1980. "The Hundred Largest Chilean Non-Financial Enterprises" in *Chile: An Economy in Transition*. Washington, DC: World Bank.

Wozniak, Lynne. 1992. "The Dissolution of Party-Union Relations in Spain." *International Journal of Political Economy* 22: 73: 89

1991. "Industrial Restructuring and Political Protest in Socialist Spain." Ph.D. Dissertation, Department of Political Science, Cornell University.

Wright, Vincent. 1994. "Industrial Privatization in Western Europe: Pressures, Problems and Paradoxes" in V. Wright, ed. *Privatization in Europe*. London: Pinter.

Wright, Vincent and George Pagoulatos. 2001. "The Comparative Politics of Industrial Privatization: Spain, Portugal and Greece" in Heather Gibson, ed. *Economic Transformation, Democratization and Integration into the European Union*. London: Palgrave.

Zufiaur, José María. 1985. "El Sindicalismo Español en la Transición y la Crisis." *Papeles de Economía Española* 22: 202–34.

Zysman, John. 1983. *Governments, Markets and Growth*. Ithaca, NY: Cornell University Press.

Index

ACENOR (steel), 92
ACERINOX-ROLDAN (stainless steel), 92
ACESITA (steel), 306
Acindar (steel), 72, 80, 102, 104
actors
  industrial, 250
  insider, 7, 22, 29, 32, 44, 54, 65, 67–69, 155, 166, 257, 259, 274, 300, 311
    Corporatist, 8
    Statist, 8
  labor, 180–87
  organized, 36, 37, 44, 189, 270, 277
  outsider, 7, 23, 32, 222, 300, 311
  protected, 6, 26, 36, 112, 128, 221
  social, 91
ADEFA (automakers' association), 77, 118, 209
AESA (Astilleros Españoles, shipbuilding), 78, 96, 97–100, 200
Aguero, Fernando, 227
AHM (Altos Hornos del Mediterráneo, steel), 90, 196
AHV (Altos Hornos de Vizcaya, steel), 61, 80, 87, 90–91, 93–95, 96, 196, 198
Alianza Democrática (party), 224
Allende, Salvador, 222, 235, 244, 249, 250, 285, 295
Alsogaray, María Julia, 205
Altos Hornos Zapla (steel), 102, 105
Aluar (aluminum), 64, 65, 80
Aluar-Madanes (aluminum), 123, 124
Alugasa (aluminum), 122
Aluminio Español (aluminum), 122
Amín, Raul, 209
Amoco (oil), 109, 136
Amorim (cork), 267, 279
Andraca, Roberto, 251
Angelini (fishing and forestry), 226, 246, 250
ANSSAL (National Administration of the Health System), 161
antidumping, 9, 34, 66, 89, 103, 104

antipoverty, 12, 272
APRA (party), 268, 290
Arcelor (steel), 199
Arcelor-Mittal (steel), 93, 95
Areas of Urgent Re-Industrialization, 62
Argentina, 47, 48, 62–66, 176, 223, 229, 244, 246, 272, 274, 285, 291, 295, 298, 302, 303, 307, 310, 311, 314
  1989–99, 5, 8
  1990s reforms, 27, 53–57, 75–77, 86–87
  auto industry, 34, 63, 117–20, 209–12
  bourgeoisie, 71–72
  bureaucratic payoffs, 11
  cement industry, 63
  compensation by sector/firm/group, 66
  concertation, 108–12, 161–62
  Corporatist liberalization, 54, 161–67
  currency board, 6
  democracy, 154
  deregulation, 62–66
  Index of Structural Power (1985), 82
  industrial conditions at onset of liberalization, 248
  labor adjustment, 155, 179–87
  market reform, 153, 181
  market-share compensation, 22
  oil industry, 108–17, 206–9
    production, 113
  petrochemical industry, 127, 128–38
  petroleum, 63
    production, 114
  pharmaceutical industry, 64, 120–22
  privatization, 264
  raw steel production, 105
  sectoral concentration of domestic business groups, 247
  steel industry, 34, 102–8, 202–5
  top nonfinancial firms (1988), 80
  top thirty industrial firms (1988), 79
  top thirty industrial firms by sales, 245

351

Index

Argentina (cont.)
  unemployment, 157
  workforce reduction, 192
Aristrain (steel), 92
aromatics, 135
assets
  awarding state, 162
  control over type, 146
Astander (shipbuilding), 100
Astano (shipbuilding), 96, 100
Astilleros de Cádiz (shipbuilding), 100
Astra (oil), 72, 80, 109, 110, 115
Atanor (petrochemicals), 130
Authoritarianism, 4, 36, 44, 198, 221, 223,
  227, 232–34, 236–39, 253, 273–74, 295,
  297, 301
third-wave, 240–42
Autolatina (autos), 80, 117, 118, 120

Bagó (pharmaceuticals), 121, 122, 124
Baklanoff, Eric, 278
Balay-Safel (reconversion society), 61
BANADE (bank), 295
Banco Central, 142
Banco Comercial Portugués, 267
Banco do Brasil, 264
Bancomer, 271
Banesto Bank, 143
Bank of Spain, 12, 142
bargaining
  collective, 7, 16, 41, 48, 162, 167, 170,
    178, 182, 210, 267–68, 273,
    286, 310
  decentralized, 167–69
  neocorporatist, 268
Barreras (shipbuilding), 100
Batasuna (union), 198
Bates, Robert, 26
Bazan (shipbuilding), 96, 97
BBVA (bank), 308
Berger, Suzanne, 8
Bermeo, Nancy, 278
BHC (financial/real estate), 246
BHC/Vial (financial group), 225–26, 250
BNDES (National Developmental Bank), 12,
  17, 33, 257, 262, 281–83, 295, 307,
  309, 314
BNDESPar (BNDES investment arm), 264
Bolivia, 54, 177
  1985, 27
borrowing, 28
bourgeoisie, 307
Bozano (financial group), 263, 264

Brazil, 47, 57, 129, 257, 272, 274, 281–83, 285,
  286, 289–90, 292, 295, 296, 302, 306, 309,
  311, 314
  1990–2002, 5, 7, 261–66
  fixed parity, 6
  market reform, 265
  privatization, 264
    industrial, 264
  state *dirigisme*, 11
  Statist liberalization, 17
  subsidies, 261–66
Bridas (oil), 72, 80, 109, 115, 130
Brooks, Sarah, 29, 309
Brunelli, Naldo, 202
Bruszt, Laszlo, 29, 30, 303
BSCH (bank), 308
Buchi, Hernan, 226
Bunge & Born (economic group), 75, 130
Burawoy, Michael, 29, 30
Burgess, Katrina, 29, 167
business groups, 7, 10, 25, 47, 55, 222, 264,
  266, 273, 282, 294, 295, 301
  defined, 277
  domestic, 3, 40, 258, 269, 270, 273, 298–99,
    304–8
  strong, 15, 45, 54
  weak, 15, 45, 54

Caetano, Marcello, 267, 278, 285, 288
Calvo, Ernesto, 28
Cambio 90 (party), 18, 276
Campo Durán (refinery), 206
CAMPSA (distribution monopoly), 138, 142
Cananea (mining), 271
CAP (steel), 147, 243, 245, 249, 251, 306
Capelástegui, Fernando, 91
capitalism
  Coordinated Market, 313
  Dependent Market, 313
  Hierarchical Market, 313
  Liberal, 313
    Dependent, 313
  Mixed, 313
  state, 285
Cardoso, Fernando Henrique, 7, 11, 257, 262,
  264, 298
Carnation Revolution, 240
Caro Figueroa, Armando, 161, 182
CAS (social stratification measurement)
  survey, 230
CASA (aviation and defense electronics), 61
CAT (union), 200
Cavaco Silva, Aníbal, 8, 11, 258, 266, 298

Index

353

Cavallo, Domingo, 57, 64, 76, 161
Cavarozzi, Marcelo, 243
CCOO (Workers' Commissions), 154, 159–60, 167, 178, 181, 197, 312
  Metals Federation of, 196, 199
CEA (Argentine Businessmen's Council), 138
CELSA (steel), 92
Celulosa Arauco (paper pulp), 147, 243, 249
Celulosa Constitución (chemical pulp), 147, 243, 245, 249
CEMA (neoliberal think tank), 13
Cemex (cement), 270, 280, 310
CENSA (shipbuilding), 199
Centeno, Miguel, 13
Centromin (mining), 284
CEPA (oil producers' association), 77
CEPSA (oil), 138, 142, 308
Cerro Verde (copper), 269
CGT (union), 159, 162, 163, 181, 209, 290, 311
CGTP (workers' confederation), 267, 276, 288, 291, 296
Chacarillas speech, 234
Champalimaud (cement), 266, 278, 308
Chandler, Alfred, 38
Chicago School of Economics, 12, 134, 221, 224, 225, 235, 236, 250, 253
Chile, 4, 37, 47, 48, 54, 155, 176, 272, 274–76, 281, 285, 286, 292, 295, 298, 302, 306, 312, 314
  1973–89, 5, 8
  1975, 27
  1975–82, 221, 225–27
  alternative liberalization, 43–45
  Chicago School of Economics influence, 12
  deregulation, 22
  fixed parity, 6
  industrial conditions at onset of liberalization, 248
  Market liberalization, 17, 268
  market reform, 228, 253
  paper pulp industry, 250
  per capita public social expenditures, 1970, 228
  privatization of state-owned stock, 226
  regime support, 236–39
  sectoral concentration of domestic business groups, 247
  steel industry, 251–52
  top thirty industrial firms by sales, 245
  worker compensation, 227–31
Chilectra (electricity distributor), 252
Chilquinta (electricity), 252
Christian Democrats, 224
Chrysler (autos), 119–20, 210

CIADEA (autos), 72, 117, 118–19
CILFA (chamber of local pharmaceutical producers), 65, 77
CIMPOR (cement), 266
CIS (Center for Local Steel Industrialists), 77
Cities Services/Occidental (oil), 109
Citroen (autos), 119
clientelism, 30, 239, 272
CLT (Consolidation of Labor Laws Framework), 289
CMPC (paper pulp), 243, 250
CNI (National Agency of Intelligence), 233
CNS (Center of National Syndicalism), 178
CNT (labor union), 177
CODELCO (mining), 244, 251
coercion, 17, 36, 155, 177, 234–36, 239, 242, 276
Cofap (motor vehicle parts), 282
COFIDE (Corporation for Financial Development), 284
Collier, David, 47, 179, 286, 291
Collier, Ruth Berins, 47, 179, 286, 287, 291
Collor de Mello, Fernando, 7, 11, 257, 262, 264, 298
comisiones obreras (workers' commissions), 178, 288
Communism, labor-based, 287–89
Communist Party, 288
compensation, 32, 36–43, 236–39, 273, 313
  alternative views, 30–31
  authoritarian, 14, 37
  business, 38–40
  degree, 85
  democratic, 14, 36, 37, 54, 67–69, 87
  market-share, 6, 7, 8, 12, 16, 32, 34–36, 38, 40, 43, 53, 54, 62–66, 86, 89, 109, 120, 126, 138–45, 154, 156, 162, 209, 257, 266–68, 269, 270–72, 273, 285, 300, 310
  neoliberal, 31–36
  policies and models, 9, 223
  political dynamics, 44
  relative, 229
  state-driven, 25
  types, 6–7, 32
  World Bank, 31
  unemployment, 172, 227
  working-class, 40–43, 169–75
Compensatory Index, 147, 148
  dimensions and scoring, 147
concertation, 6, 7, 10, 15, 40, 42, 43, 53, 54, 138–45, 156, 161–67, 189, 258, 266–68, 273, 297, 300
Committee for the Reconversion of the Auto Industry, 118, 209

354 *Index*

concertation (*cont.*)
  formal, 117–18
  informal, 102–4
  tripartite, 285, 298
CONFIEP (association), 268
conflict, industrial, 189
Contreras, Manuel, 233
Convertibility Plan, 57
Cook, María, 269
Corcuera, José, 213
CORFO (Corporation for Development), 47,
  222, 242, 249, 295
Corrales, Javier, 28, 31
CPCS (Committee for Social Dialogue), 224, 267
critical juncture, 4, 22, 302, 303
Croissier, Luis, 85
Cruzat (financial/real estate), 225, 246, 249, 250
CSI (Corporation for Integrated Steel), 95,
  123, 197
CSI (Corriente Sindical de Izquierdas,
  union), 200
CSI-Aceralia (integrated steel), 61, 92–93,
  96, 124
CSN (Companhia Siderúrgica Nacional, steel),
  263, 265, 281
CTA (Congress of Argentine Workers), 159,
  311
CTM (union), 271, 286, 287, 296
CTP (workers' confederation), 290
CUF (Union of Factories Company), 278
CUT (union arm of the leftist party PT), 265,
  290, 312
CVRD (Companhia do Vale Rio Doce, mining),
  264, 281
Cydsa (chemicals), 280
Czech Republic, 29, 313

Davignon Plan, 173
De Castro, Sergio, 224, 225
De la Madrid, Miguel, 18, 261, 270, 298
Decree 593/73, 134
democracy, 273, 304
  compensation, 176–77, 274
  delegative, 276
  liberalization, 3
  protected, 234
deregulation, 4, 6, 12
  biased, 308
  financial, 28, 225
  labor, 27, 53, 229, 302, 311, 312
  partial, 6, 7, 15, 16, 29, 31, 34, 38, 41, 55, 65,
    86, 108, 117–18, 126, 138, 161, 162, 163,
    165, 171, 189, 270, 273, 295, 300

petroleum, 109
protectionist, 66, 111, 140, 149, 209, 301
  sectoral, 124, 207, 270
  tariff, 28, 251
Desc (petrochemicals), 270, 271
DGFM (steel), 103, 134
Díaz, Rodolfo, 161
DINA (National Intelligence Agency), 233
Directives for Shipbuilding Aids, 97
domestic industrial firms, 6, 7
Dow Chemical, 136, 138
downsizing, 6, 8
Ducilo (petrochemicals), 129
Dupont (petrochemicals), 132
Durand, Francisco, 276, 284
Duro Felguera (shipyard), 199

early retirement, 33
East Asia, 3, 4, 260
East Central Europe, 313
Eastern Europe, 3, 260, 313
EC (European Commission), 86
Echeverria, Luis, 280
Economic Emergency Law, 76
economic power, concentrated, 80
economy, semiclosed, 248, 259
Edwards (financial/real estate), 246, 250
Ekiert, Grzegorz, 29–30, 303
ELA-STV (Basque Workers' Solidarity), 159,
  197, 200
Electrolux, 61
ELF (oil), 145, 308
Embraer (planes), 258, 264, 265, 282,
  306, 307
employment programs, 6, 33
ENAMI (mining), 245
ENAP (oil), 243, 245
ENCE (pulp and paper), 61
ENDASA (aluminum), 122
ENDESA (electricity), 61, 75, 243, 252,
  307, 308
ENDIASA (food and agriculture), 61
ENFERSA (fertilizers), 61
Enpetrol (oil), 78
Ensenada (refinery), 206, 208
Ensidesa (steel), 78–79, 90, 94, 96, 196
EOI (Export Oriented Industrialization), 57
EON (electricity), 307
EPF (Employment Promotion Funds), 33, 168,
  169, 172, 197, 213
equity incentives, 31
ERT (Explosivos Río Tinto, chemicals), 61, 80,
  85, 87

Index

355

ESOP (Employee Share Ownership Program), 166, 171, 175, 204
and insiders, 174
Espina, Alvaro, 74, 213
Espíritu Santo, 278
Estado Novo, 278
ethylene, 128, 135
EU (European Union), 86
European Monetary System, 300
Euskalduna (shipbuilding), 100, 153, 199, 200, 201
Evans, Peter, 282
exchange rates, fixed, 6, 53
explosives, 128
Exxon (oil), 109

Falange, 178
FATLyF (Electricity Workers), 166
FDI (Foreign Direct Investment), 57, 144, 271, 280, 294, 306, 308, 313
Federal Work Law, 286
Feliu, Manuel, 248
Ferrosur Pampeano (cargo rail), 65
Fiat (autos), 70, 117, 119, 120, 210
FIEL (neoliberal think tank), 13, 64, 163
Fierro (private group), 143
Finame (finance program), 262
financial credits, 33
Finchelstein, Diego, 262, 310
Fishman, Robert, 215
FOARSA (steel), 92
FOETRA (national union), 185
FONCONDES (antipoverty program), 33, 266, 269, 271
Fonseca, 278
Forca Sindical, 290
Ford (autos), 117
Fortabat (cement), 72, 124
France, 101, 314
Franco, Francisco, 56, 69, 177, 240, 257, 277, 278, 285, 303
Frondizi, Arturo, 71, 112, 119, 179
Fujimori, Alberto, 8, 221, 258, 268, 269–70, 276
Fundidora Monterrey (steel), 271
Futaleufú (electricity), 64
Futura (pension fund), 166, 209

Garovaglio (petrochemicals), 72, 134
Gas Natural, 307
Gener (electricity), 252
General Motors (autos), 119–20, 210

Gerdau (steel), 96, 283
Gerencias (management offices), 59, 74, 91, 92, 96
Germany, 10, 101, 260
Gibson, Edward, 28
Giménez, Tucapel, 276
Goertz, Gary, 260
Golden, Miriam, 159
González, Felipe, 44, 157, 167, 186
Goulart, Joao, 289
Graham, Carol, 33, 37
Gramsci, Antonio, 240
gremialista (movement), 234–38, 240, 252
Greskovits, Béla, 31
Gruvesa (reconversion society), 61
GSB (steel), 92, 95
Guzmán, Jaime, 234, 236, 240, 252

Haggard, Stephen, 26, 30
Hall, Peter, 8, 13, 312, 314
Hamann, Kerstin, 31
Hanson, S., 29, 303
Haya de la Torre, Victor Raul, 290
Hellman, Joel, 34
Hierro-Perú (mining), 269, 284
Huber, Evelyne, 42
Huillca, Pedro, 276
Huneeus, Carlos, 12, 238, 239, 252
Hungary, 29, 313
Hysalmex (steel), 108

Iankova, Elena, 30
IANSA (sugar), 243, 245
Ibáñez, Gonzolo, 252
ICI (Imperial Chemical Industries/Duperial, petrochemicals), 129, 132
IMF (International Monetary Fund), 33
Imperio (insurance), 267
INACESA (cement), 245
Index of State Industrial Strength, 295
INDRA (information technology), 61
INDUPA (petrochemicals), 130, 131, 132–34
industrial and labor adjustment, 5, 6
industrial business associations, 16
Industrial Promotion Regime, 71
industrialization
autarchic, 70
early and late, 277–78
late, 46
industry
strength of state, 293
structure at the outset of adjustment, 246

INESPAL (aluminum), 61, 122–24
INFONAVIT (housing), 271, 287
INFORSA (pulp), 245, 250
INH (National Institute of Hydrocarbons), 139
INI (National Industrial Institute), 13, 17, 33, 47, 61, 69, 85, 90, 142, 222, 295, 307
INSA (tires), 245
institutionalization, 234–36
Instituto de Previdencia Social, 289
INT-CIG (union), 200
International Petroleum, 284
Intersindical (union confederation), 288
INTG (Inter-Union of Galician Workers), 159
IPAKO (petrochemicals), 130, 132–34, 136
IPIC (International Petroleum Investment Company), 145
Iritecnia, 107
Iron March, 197
ISA (Argentine Steel Investment), 204
ISI (Import Substitution Industrialization), 3
   factors in alternative adjustment paths, 5
ISIC (industrial subsector), 245
Italy, 101
Iveco (autos), 117, 119
IZAR (shipbuilding), 61, 97, 122–24
Izquierda Unida (United Left, party), 291

James, Daniel, 179
Japan, 297
Jiménez, Tucapel, 233

Kast, Miguel, 235, 236, 238
Katznelson, Ira, 304
Kessler, Timothy, 28
King, Lawrence, 29, 30, 313
Kirchener, Néstor Carlos, 272, 314
Klabin (paper and forestry), 282
Koppers (petrochemicals), 132
Korea, 4, 96, 101, 260
Kurtz, Marcus, 28, 309

LAB (union), 198, 200
labor
   adjustment, 183, 188, 189–217
      costs, 174
   bureaucratic organization, 285–86
   incorporation, 47
      state-authoritarian, 48
   organized, 296–97, 310–11
      strength, 297
Labor Plan, 227
Larroulet, Cristian, 235
Lavinia (sea trade), 100

Law 27/84, 60, 61
Levitsky, Steven, 29, 167
liberalization
   alternative explanations, 11–13
   alternative models, 43–45
   assessing reform paths, 29–30
   Communist strategy, 288
   components, 6, 53
   Corporatist, 5, 7, 8, 18, 22, 35, 41, 62–66, 103, 154, 156, 160, 216, 257, 295, 298, 300, 301, 305, 311
   cross-national comparison, 20
   Eastern Europe, 29–30
   historical labor and business preferences, 45–49
   industrial
      models, 127
      and the working class, 157–60
   institutionalist, 26
   legacies, 304–12
   Market, 5, 8, 12, 17, 18, 23, 170, 187, 216, 221, 268–69, 298, 300, 301, 304, 311, 312
      partial, 104
   Mixed, 5, 18, 270–72, 298, 300, 301, 305
   models, 8, 11, 46, 258, 275, 303–4
   multidimensional logic, 27
   neoclassical, 24, 26
   political construct, 25
   protectionist, 7, 32
   regime type, 13–19, 274–77
   social-democratic, 31
   Socialist strategy, 61
   Statist, 5, 7, 8, 17, 18, 22, 59–62, 155, 156, 160, 188, 216, 257, 261, 274, 297, 298, 300, 301, 305, 310, 311–12
   tariff, 8, 27, 155, 221
Lingieri, José Luis, 161
Linz, Juan, 178
Lisnave (ships), 267
Lodola, Germán, 230
Loma Negra (cement), 64, 65
López Portillo, José, 287
Lukoil (oil), 307
Luksic (food and others), 226
Lula da Silva, Luiz Inácio, 272, 311

Macri (autos), 124
Madanes (aluminum), 72
Mahoney, James, 260, 302
Manzetti, Luigi, 264, 269
Map of Extreme Poverty in Chile, 230
market reform, 29, 30
   constituencies for neoliberal, 28–29
   in developing countries, 26–28

Index

357

neoliberal, 36–43
partial (protectionist), 34
post-Communist, 30
market reserves, 28
Matarazzo (food), 282
Matte (pulp and paper and others), 226, 246
McGillivray, Fiona, 20, 39
means-tested/poverty alleviation programs, 33, 37
Mello (petrochemicals), 266, 279
Menem, Carlos, 8, 44, 53, 57–58, 63, 103, 120, 130, 157, 161, 163, 166, 171, 202, 264, 269
Mercedez Benz (autos), 117, 120
Mercosur, 209
Mexico, 54, 129, 155, 176, 223, 259, 261, 272, 274, 276, 279–81, 285, 286–87, 291, 295, 296, 298, 308, 310
1982–94, 5, 18, 270–72
market-share compensation, 22
MFA (Movement of the Armed Forces), 288
Miguel, Lorenzo, 203
Minera Mexico (mining), 270–71
Ministry of Industry, 307
Mittal (steel), 93
Molina, O., 314
Monsanto (petrochemicals), 129, 132
Montero, Alfred, 262
Monterrey Economic Groups, 279–81
Moore, Barrington, 8
Morales Bermúdez, Francisco, 284
Mothers' Centers, 236, 238
Motor Vehicle Regime (decree 2667), 117–18, 209
Multibanco Comermex (bank), 271
Murillo, Victoria, 28, 29, 30, 169, 181

NAFINSA (National Financial Company), 280, 281, 295
National Development Plan, 71
natural gas, 128
Navarro, Mikel, 59, 174
neoliberalism, 164, 217
authoritarian, 301
components of orthodox, 226
embedded, 309
paralleling third-wave democratization, 37
pragmatic, 224
radical, 233, 249, 253
state-dominated pre-, 285
Nippon Steel, 263
nonconcertation, 60
Nueva Democracia (group), 238

ODEPLAN (State Planning Office), 230, 236–38
Oil Sector Restructuring Law (Ley Reordenamiento del Sector Petrolero), 139
olefins, 128
Onganía, Juan Carlos, 115, 180
Os Novos Grupos Econômicos, 279
Ouro Preto Agreement, 57

PASA (petrochemicals), 129, 130, 132
Pathfinder (electronics and explosives), 306
Patria y Libertad (Fatherland and Freedom party), 234
patrimonialism, 30
patronage, 239–42
payoffs, bureaucratic, 42, 45, 156, 189, 191, 207, 261, 296
features, 169
PBB (Petroquímica Bahía Blanca, petrochemicals), 130, 131, 134, 135, 136
PBQP (Brazilian Program of Productivity and Quality), 262
PCE (Spanish Communist Party), 178
PCI (Industrial Competitive Program), 262
PDVESA (oil), 116
Pechiney (aluminum), 122, 132
PEM (antipoverty program), 228, 229–30, 237, 266
PEMEX (oil), 116, 271
pension reform, 27, 166–67
Pérez Companc (oil), 68, 72, 76, 80, 109, 110, 112, 115–17, 124, 129–31, 132, 133, 137
Perón, Juan, 71, 119, 179, 212
Peronist Party, 11, 56
personalism, 30
Peru, 47, 54, 155, 176, 272, 274, 276, 283–85, 286, 290–92, 298, 312
1990–2000, 5, 258, 268–69
1990–99, 8
Market liberalization, 17
Petrobras (oil), 116, 258, 264, 281–82, 306–7, 314
Petrogal (petroleum), 267
Petrolera San Jorge (oil), 115
PETROLIBER (construction consortium), 143, 145
Petromar (oil), 269
PETROMED (oil), 138
PETRONOR (oil), 138
Petroperu (petroleum), 284
Petroquímica Cuyo (petrochemicals), 130
Peugeot (autos), 117
PEXSE (drilling), 207, 209

PGM (Petroquímica General Mosconi, petrochemicals), 130, 134, 135
Pierson, Paul, 31
Pinochet, Augusto, 8, 23, 33, 37, 221, 223, 226–27, 232–34, 240–42, 248, 253, 276
Pinto & Soto Mayor (bank), 266
Pizzorno, Alessandro, 40, 170
PJ (Justicialista Party), 56, 179
PND (National Program of Privatization), 264
poblaciones (shantytown dwellers), 238, 241
POJH (Occupational Program for Heads of Households), 228, 229–30, 237
Poland, 29, 313
Polanyia, Karl, 28
political incorporation, patterns, 286
Popular Front, 47, 242–43
Popular Party, 11
Popular Unity coalition, 235
populism, labor-based, 179, 286–87
populist reforming parties, 30
Portucel (holding group), 267
Portugal, 223, 274, 278–79, 285, 287–89, 291, 295, 296, 308, 314
  1985–95, 5, 8, 258, 266–68
  concertational policymaking, 11, 266–68
  employment programs, 11
  European Monetary system, 6
  market-share compensation, 11, 22
possibility principle, 260
Prereform State Industrial Power, 294
PRI (party), 19, 270, 277, 279–80, 286–87, 311
Private Oil Workers, 217
privatization, 6, 11, 27, 28, 34, 53, 55, 65, 89, 258, 261, 266, 269, 270, 283, 298, 302
  Corporatist, 7
  Eastern Europe, 29
  industrial, 100, 124, 131, 269
    compensatory, 145–48
    noncompensatory, 249–52, 261
  methods, 146
  oil-field, 109
  sequential, 60, 258, 306
  state role, 146
  Statist, 7
  targeted, 86, 107, 124, 138
  through open POS, 147
PRONASOL (antipoverty program), 33, 259, 266, 271, 277, 300
property, cross-ownership, 29
Propulsora Siderúrgica (steel), 102, 105
PSA-Peugeot (autos), 120
PSD (party), 11, 266

PSOE (Socialist Worker's Party), 11, 31, 44, 56, 59, 73, 139, 159–60, 182, 312
PT (Worker's Party), 290
Puerta, Manuel, 172, 186
PYMAR (reconversion society), 97

Química Argentina (pharmaceuticals), 121

Radical Party, 242
Rapanelli, Néstor, 75
Reconversion and Reindustrialization Law, 59, 60, 73, 85, 90, 122
reconversion plans, 7, 97
Reconversion Societies (Sociedades de Reconversión), 59
Redondo, Nicolás, 160, 181
regime
  bureaucratic-authoritarian (BA), 285
  Motor Vehicle, 118
  Promotion, 105
  types, 5, 17, 25, 67
    democratic, 67
    importance of identifying, 14, 67
Renault (autos), 117, 119, 120
rent-seekers, 24, 26
Report on Spanish Industry (Informe Sobre la Industria Española), 62
Repsol (oil), 61, 75, 139, 140, 149, 307, 308
Repsol-YPF (oil), 209
Resistance, Argentinian, 180
retirement, early, 169
Richards (petrochemicals), 72, 134
Roda (steel), 96
Rodríguez, Pablo, 234
Roemmers (pharmaceuticals), 121
Roig, Miguel, 75
Royal Dutch Shell (oil), 111
Russia, 30

Sagunto (steel), 196, 198, 201, 216
Salazar, Antonio de Oliveira, 240, 267, 277, 278, 285, 287
Salinas, Carlos, 13, 18, 261, 270–71, 272, 276, 277, 298
San Nicolás (metalworkers), 202, 203, 216
Sánchez Junco, Jose, 91
Santander (bank), 145
Santiago lower chamber election, 241
Scania (autos), 117
Schneider, Ben Ross, 283, 313–14
SEAT (autos), 59, 69, 78
Serfin, 271
SERPLAC (Planning Regional Office), 237

Index

359

Sevel (autos), 80, 117–20, 211
severance packages, 31, 33, 61, 168, 169, 171, 203, 206–7, 213, 214, 229
Shadlen, Kenneth, 29, 36, 65, 121
Shell (oil), 109, 136
Shleifer, Andrei, 31
Shonfield, Andrew, 8
shop-floor councils (jurados de empresa), 178
Sidegasa (steel), 92
SIDENOR (special steels), 61, 92, 95, 123, 124
Siderar (steel), 102, 104, 108, 203
Siderca (steel), 102, 104
Siderperú (steel), 269, 284
Sidor (steel), 108
Sigdo Koppers (food and wood), 306
Silva, Eduardo, 224, 233, 252, 253
sindicatos (syndical associations), 287
Skocpol, Theda, 304
Slovakia, 313
Slovenia, 314
SMATA (autoworkers' union), 118, 120, 209–12, 217
Smith, W. Rand, 73
Soares, Mário Alberto Nobre Lopes, 279
Socialists, Democratic, 224
Sociedad Española de Construcción Naval (shipbuilding), 100
SOCMA (autos), 72, 117, 119
SOFOFA (industrial association), 225, 248
soft credits, 6
SOGRAPE (wines), 267, 279
Solchaga, Carlos, 73, 186
Solvay (petrochemicals), 132, 137
SOMISA (steel), 102, 105, 108, 146, 171, 202, 216
SOMISA/SIDERAR (steel), 251
SONAE (wood and pulp), 267, 279
SOQUIMICH (chemicals), 245, 306
Soskice, David, 312, 314
Southern Europe, 31
Spain, 47, 59–62, 176, 229, 246, 274, 281, 283, 285, 286, 288, 292, 295, 296, 297, 302, 306, 309, 311, 314
  1980s reforms, 53–57, 73–75, 85–86
  1982–96, 5, 7
  alternate liberalization, 43–45
  aluminum industry, 122–23
  auto industry, 59
  bourgeoisie, 69–71
  compensation distribution by sector, 214
  concertation, 138–42
  democracy, 154
  employment programs, 11

European Monetary system, 6
  gasoline industry, 141
  Index of Structural Power (1982), 83
  industrial conditions at onset of liberalization, 248
  industry, 57–58
  labor adjustment, 155, 186–87
  labor evolution, 158
  noncompensatory privatization, 22
  oil industry, 34, 127, 142–45
  privatization, 11
  reconversion plans, 11
  reconversion subsidies, 17
  shipbuilding industry, 98, 100–1, 199–202
  state dirigisme, 11
  Statist liberalization, 17, 54, 167–69
  steel industry, 59, 90–96
  subsidies, 11, 59–62
  top nonfinancial firms (1982), 80
  top thirty industrial firms (1984), 79
  top thirty industrial firms by sales, 245
  unemployment, 157
  workforce reduction, 192
stabilization, 6, 28
  classic, 76
  exchange-rate, 224, 300
  macroeconomics, 300
  price, 259
Stark, David, 29, 30, 303
state, 308–10
state dirigisme, 6, 7, 9, 45, 53, 59–62, 73, 89, 90–93, 189, 261–66, 301
State Reform Law, 63, 76, 110, 162, 166
structural power, 79
Suanzes, Juan Carlos, 69, 85, 94
subsidies, 6, 7, 15, 16, 30, 32–33, 43, 53, 55, 59–62, 89, 126, 128–38, 156, 161, 168, 189, 257, 261, 273, 283, 295, 296, 300, 313
  compensatory, 32
  defined, 32
  direct, 33, 61
  financial, 61
  Market, 12
  Statist, 8, 12
SUPE (state oil workers union), 111, 164, 166, 206
suspension, 167, 186, 199, 200, 211
Sweden, 10, 260, 297

Tabacalera (food and agriculture), 61
Tabaqueria (tobacco), 267
Taiwan, 260

Index

Tamet (steel), 107
targeted spending, 28
tariff liberalization, 6
tax exemptions, 6, 33, 62
Techint (steel), 63, 72, 80, 102–8, 124, 137, 146, 203, 205, 310
Tec-Petrol (oil), 110
Teichman, Judith, 28, 30, 276
Telebras, 264
Telefónica, 307, 308
Third Republic's Popular Front, 180
Thyssen (steel), 107, 136
Tinto (chemicals), 61
Total (oil), 110
Toyota (autos), 120, 210
Transener (electricity transport), 77
Treisman, Daniel, 29, 31
Triaca, Jorge, 202
TRIPS (Trade Related Aspects of Intellectual Property Rights), 64, 121
typology, 9

UCIN (steel), 92
UDI (political party), 18, 44, 222, 239, 241–42, 251, 276, 312
UGT (General Union of Workers), 154, 159, 167, 177, 181, 182, 197, 200, 267, 312
  Metals Federation of, 196
UIA (Argentine Industrial Union), 77
ultractividad, 162, 170
Ultramarino, 278
unemployment, 6, 33
UNESID (private association of steelmakers), 78, 90
Unicer (beers), 267
Unidad Popular, 48
unilateral state imposition, 6, 268
UNINSA (steel), 94
Unión Naval del Levante (shipbuilding), 97
unions, 25, 274, 298, 310–11
  Basque, 200
  collective rights, 167
  compensation, 176
  Corporatist, 8
  deregulation, 227
  dimensions, 189
  EPFs (Employment Protection Funds), 168
  Federation, 192, 206, 208
  First Grade, 206
  First Grade Federations, 192
  First Grade Industry, 192
  horizontal, 180, 181–83, 189
  independent, 289–90

influence on policy, 161
  local, 168, 185, 198
  national, 11, 41, 261
    and compensation, 300
  organizational power, 16, 46
    index, 296
  reconversion, 168
  regional, 154
  sectoral, 212
  shop-floor, 156, 179, 184, 190, 210, 213, 217, 229
  state-controlled, 48, 287
  state-independent, 3
  strong, 15, 41, 43, 156, 189, 273
  syndical, 287
  trade, 41, 180, 212
    and bureaucratization, 41
    organization, 202
  Vertical Syndicate, 48, 177, 178, 180, 183–87, 189–90, 192, 214, 216
  weak, 16, 41, 43, 156, 189, 273, 313
United Kingdom, 101
United States, 10, 260
UOM (metalworkers' union), 118, 202, 210
UPCN (national administration state employees), 217
Urquijo (bank), 70
Uruguay, 57
Usiminas (steel), 263, 306
Usinor (steel), 93, 199

Vale (mining, aluminum and forestry), 258, 306, 307
Vargas, Getúlio, 281, 282, 289
Varieties of Capitalism (Hall and Soskice), 299, 312
Velasco Alvarado, Juan, 284, 291
Velazco, 285
Venezuela, 304
Vicente, Oscar, 111
Vicunha (textiles), 282
Vicunnha (financial group), 263
Villegas, José Blanco, 77
Visa (beer and food products), 270–71, 280
Vitro (glass), 280
Vitro-Cydsa (glass and synthetic fibers), 270–71
Vliegenthart, Arjan, 313
Volkswagen (autos), 117
Votorantim (cement and metals), 282, 283

Weber, Max, 240
White Book on Reconversion and Re-Industrialization, 73

Index

Worker's Bank, 287
Worker's Statute, 178, 194, 212
working class, 6, 40–43, 311
works councils, 48, 162, 178, 184, 187, 191, 194, 198, 201, 211, 213, 216, 289, 292, 303, 314
World Bank, 31, 33

YPF (Yacimientos Petrolíferos Fiscales, oil), 109, 131, 133, 134, 171, 206, 308
Yuraszeck, Carlos, 251

Zorraquín (group), 132, 134
Zorraquin, Federico, 138
Zysman, John, 8